OPERATION EXODUS

Also by Gordon Thomas

Non-Fiction

Descent Into Danger
Bed of Nails
Physician Extraordinary
Heroes of the R.A.F.
They Got Back
Miracle of Surgery
The National Health Service and You
Thames Number One
Midnight Traders
The Parent's Home Doctor (With Ian D Hudson, Vincent Pippet)
Turn By the Window (With Ronald Hutchinson)
Issels: the Biography of a Doctor
The Day the World Ended (With Max Morgan-Witts)
Earthquake (With Max Morgan-Witts)
Shipwreck (With Max Morgan-Witts)
Voyage of the Damned (With Max Morgan-Witts)
The Day Guernica Died (With Max Morgan-Witts)
Enola Gay / Ruin from the Air (With Max Morgan-Witts)
The Day the Bubble Burst (With Max Morgan-Witts)
Trauma (With Max Morgan-Witts)
Pontiff (With Max Morgan-Witts)
The Year of Armageddon (With Max Morgan-Witts)
The Operation
Desire and Denial
Trial: the Jesus Conspiracy
Journey Into Madness
Enslaved
Chaos Under Heaven
Trespass Into Temptation

Gideon's Spies
Magdalene: Woman Of The Cross / The 13th Disciple
Seeds of Fire
The Assassination of Robert Maxwell: Israel's Super Spy (With Martin Dillon)
The Secret Armies of the Cia
Secrets and Lies
The Black Book of the Cia (With Yvonnick Denoel)
Inside British Intelligence: 100 Years of MI5 and MI6

Fiction

The Camp on Blood Island
Torpedo Run
Deadly Perfume
Godless Icon
Voices In the Silence
Organ Hunters
Poisoned Sky

Screenplays

Emmett (With Gordon Parry)
Enslaved
Organ Hunters
The Jesus Conspiracy
Chaos Under Heaven
Mambo
Underpass
Desire and Denial
Doctor of Hope
Citizen Maxwell
The Hostage
Tiananmen
Connections (With Declan White)

OPERATION EXODUS

EXODUS

The perilous journey from the Nazi camps
to the Promised Land . . . and back

GORDON THOMAS

JR
BOOKS

First published in Great Britain in 2010 by
JR Books, 10 Greenland Street, London NW1 0ND
www.jrbooks.com

A catalogue record for this book is available from the British Library.

Picture credits (b=bottom, m=middle, t=top)

Eity Deutch/Jill Samuels Productions Ltd: pages 9 (t), 13 (b), 15 (t), 19 (b), 25
(b), 29 (t)
Louise Nathanson: pages 4, 13 (b), 23
Jill Samuels Productions Ltd: pages 11 (b)
United States Holocaust Memorial Museum: pages 5 (t), 8 (t), 10, 12, 16 (b),
20 (b), 21, 32
Yad Vashem Archive: pages 16 (t), 17, 18 (t), 27 (t), 28,
With thanks to Harold Gardner: pages 14 (b), 20 (t), 22 (t), 24, 25 (b)
With thanks to Yossi Cohen: page 19 (t)
With thanks to Noah Klieger: page 25 (t)
With thanks to Yosef Reich: page 29 (b)
Rex Pictures: page 9 (b)
Corbis: pages pages 1 (m), 26, 30
PA Photos: pages 2, (t), 5 (b), 22 (b)
Getty Images: page 3

ISBN 978-1-906779-26-9

1 3 5 7 9 10 8 6 4 2

Printed in the UK by MPG Books, Bodmin, Cornwall

Initiated and original research by
Jill Samuels

CONTENTS

Gordon Thomas would like to thank:

Edith Maria Thomas
Emer Lenehan
Madeleine Morel
Barbara Lowenstein
Norman Kurz
Catherine Bailey
Jessica Feehan
Joanna Macnamara
Lesley Wilson

Jill Samuels dedicates this work to the memory of her late sister, Susan Jayne Samuels/Inverne and to the enormous courage of her parents, Daphne and Roy Samuels.

Remembering . . . Rene Kenny and Elaine Samuels, Lorraine Benson, Barbara Harris and Peter Bloom, Bluma Feld, Edith Gould, Dina Rabinovitch, Angela Spector, Reg and Pearl Robinson, Walter and Richard Swindon, and Joan Wayne.

Acknowledging . . . Anthony Julius, Louise Nathanson, Mick Davis, Marilyn Ofer, Omri Bezalel, Lord Levy, Lilly Goodkind, Hezi Bezalel, Roy Escapa, and Menachem Golan.

The Characters

The Crew of Exodus

Because of the secrecy of their voyage, there is no existing official record of the crew and the positions they held on *Exodus*. However, its members included the following:

Aronoff, Murray	*Cook*
Ahronowitz, Yitzhak 'Ike'	*Captain*
Barak, Enava	*Radioman*
Baruch, Kurt	*Deck Hand*
Beeri, Schmuel	*Deck Hand*
Bernstein, Bill	*First Mate*
Crabson, John	*Engineer*
Foreman, Ben	*Cook*
Goldstein, Myron	*Deck Hand*
Grauel, Reverend John	*Galley Chef*
Harel, Yossi	*Commander*
Kalm (Kalmanowitz), Eli	*Deck Hand*
Kolomeitzev, Arye	*Deck Hand*
Levine, Frank	*Deck Hand*
Leidner, Harold	*Radioman*
Lester, Sol	*Deck Hand*
Lippschitz, Abe	*Pharmacist*
Livney (Lifshitz), Avi	*Deck Hand*
Lowenthal, David	*Deck Hand*
Lutz, Abbot	*Deck Hand*
Malovsky, Danny	*Deck Hand*
Margolis, Reuven	*Deck Hand*
Marks, Bernard	*2nd Mate (later Captain)*

Millman, Dave	*Deck Hand*
Millman, William 'Big Bill'	*Helmsman*
Mills, Dov	*Cook*
Nadler, Nat	*Electrician*
Ritzer, Arthur 'Stanley'	*Cook*
Rofe, Roger	*Engineer*
Schiller, Samuel	*Engineer*
Schulman, Paul	*Deck Hand*
Segal, Zeev	*Deck Hand*
Selove, Lou	*Deck Hand*
Siegel, Abe	*Deck Hand*
Sklar, Lennie	*Deck Hand*
Smeckler, Simone	*Nurse*
Stanczak, Frank	*Chief Engineer*
Starek (Kochavi), David	*Deck Hand*
Sygal, Avraham	*Deck Hand*
Verdi, Terry	*Cook*
Weinsaft, Harry	*Cook*
Weinstein, Cyril	*Helmsman*
Weiss, Mike	*Deck Hand*

The Passengers

There were 4,515 passengers on board *Exodus* who were caught up in events over which they had no control. Those who survived are today spread throughout the world. The names of those whose stories made this book possible are listed below.

Baumstein, Mordechai
Bergman, Miriam
Biber, Rachel (not her real name)
Cohen, Yossi
Feinstein, Daniel
Goldman, Johann
Klieger, Noah
Kronenberg, Freddie
Landau, Gerald
Levi, Helena

Memakov, Efraim
Neimark, Fira
Pevvetz, Mike
Pevvetz, Hannah
Pevvetz, Pessia
Porat, Aviva
Reich, Yosef
Rosemont, Mordechai
Stolowitzky, Michael and Gertruda
Tiroche, Zvi
Yakubovich, Zvi

The Palestine Patrol

(Ranks held at the time of Operation Exodus)

Austin, D.W., Lieutenant Commander, Captain HMS *Charity*
Bailey, E.A.S., Lieutenant Commander, Captain HMS *Childers*
Barwell, Geoffrey, Able Seaman, HMS *Cardigan Bay*
Carey, Lawrence, Able Seaman, HMS *Ajax*
Conway-Ireland, C.B., Captain, Captain HMS *Ajax*
Cunningham, Sir John, First Sea Lord, Royal Navy
Fardell, G.E., Commander, Captain HMS *Chequers*
Glover, Geoffrey, Able Seaman, HMS *Ajax*
Pearce, Roger, Lieutenant, later Admiral of the Fleet, *HMS Childers*
Watson, R.D., Captain, Captain HMS *Chieftain*
Wickin, J.V., Captain, Captain HMS *Cardigan Bay*
Wilkinson, J.V., Commander, Captain HMS *Cheviot*
Wyld, R.H.C., Commander, Captain HMS *Rowena*

Other Interviewees

Leo Bernstein
Harold Gardner
Ralph Goldman
Denis Healey

'When it comes to the end of World War Two, it will not be the end of our war. With the defeat of the Nazis, it becomes our bounden duty to go to any extreme necessary to rescue what the Germans have left of the various Jewish communities. We will have to lead those survivors openly or by stealth through war-torn lands and across borders to the sea and thence to the shores of their homeland, to bring home on our shoulders those of our people who have been left alive.'

David Ben-Gurion
First Prime Minister of the State of Israel

Prologue

The rise to power of Adolf Hitler from 1933 spread unease throughout Germany's Jewish community, though many believed they could still coexist alongside the Nazis. However, the Jews increasingly found their religion marked them out for persecution, and by the time war came and the Wehrmacht raced across Europe, they began to find themselves herded on to trains to places that would soon become infamous worldwide: Auschwitz-Birkenau, Buchenwald, Dachau, Mauthausen . . . In all there would be 32 camps where over six million Jews died. This was the Holocaust.

In the summer of 1947, a ship designed for 400 passengers was carrying 4,500 refugees and a crew of young American volunteers, US war veterans and battle-hardened men of the Haganah, the Jewish underground army. All were caught up in an event unparalleled in history: a precursor for the foundation of a nation and its people. This is the previously untold story of the passengers and crew of the *Exodus*, who fought a sea battle like no other to get to Palestine, their Promised Land, *Eretz Yisrael*.

Painful and raw, displaying the extraordinary courage, passion, faith and determination necessary to rise above impossible odds, the story they tell is of a people pursuing a dream 2,000 years old and it stands as a judgement on the inhumane treatment of the Jews.

David Ben-Gurion, Israel's first prime minister, said of the Haganah, 'You were largely responsible for bringing our new nation to life. The very word "Haganah" – "Defence" – imposed heavy duties on those who served with incredible strength to overcome all dangers by ingenious devices to accomplish deeds that have become almost legendary.'

In 1922 the League of Nations had given Great Britain the role of preparing Palestine for 'self-rule and remedying the short-comings and after effects of Ottoman rule'. A British High Commissioner was appointed to rule, supported by British military forces and civil servants. The Mandate government controlled a land where 589,000 Muslims, 71,000 Christians and 83,000 Jews lived in uneasy peace. A year later Winston Churchill, then the Colonial Secretary, decided to limit legal Jewish immigration to 16,500 people a year. His decision was based 'on the absorptive capacity of the area'.

There was no limit on Christians or Arabs settling in Palestine. Despite the restriction, however, boats continued to land Jewish refugees from Hitler's Germany on the beaches between Haifa and Tel Aviv. Arab anger grew to a full-scale revolt against the Mandate over the mounting numbers of illegal Jewish immigrants being smuggled in. To maintain the peace the Mandate government had two battalions and two warships based in Haifa. Their orders were unequivocal: to stop the illegal immigration and pacify the Arabs.

These orders remained in force while Hitler's persecution intensified and Jews became even more desperate to emigrate to Palestine. The Jewish Agency set up a secret organisation known as Aliyah Bet with groups in London, Paris, Vienna and the United States to assist them. By the outbreak of the Second World War they had landed almost 7,000 refugees on the shores of Palestine. For the British, these were 'illegal immigrants'.

When the war ended in 1945, Jews expected that Palestine would become freely accessible to survivors of the Holocaust. The Mandate's attitude was summed up in a confidential Foreign Office note sent to the British Control Office for Germany and Austria on 5 July 1946: 'We must have a clear definition of the term "German Jew" and must prevent German Jews automatically immigrating to Palestine.' The document had been approved by Ernest Bevin,

Britain's Foreign Secretary, considered by many to be anti-Semitic, and a vocal opponent of Aliyah Bet.

This exchange marked the increasing bitterness on both sides as Britain's post-war Labour government became even more determined to halt Aliyah Bet's clandestine attempts to bring out of Europe the dispossessed who wanted nothing more than to go to their spiritual homeland. To do so the Jews set up a secret fleet. Their crews were members of the Haganah's Palyam naval unit.

A total of 64 ships sailed from ports in France, Italy, Yugoslavia, Greece, Bulgaria and Romania carrying almost 70,000 men, women and children. Some 15,000 went to Latin America, nearly 13,000 to the United States, 6,000 to Australia and a smaller number to South Africa. But the majority went to Palestine. In doing so, they created the grounds for Jewish statehood. What happened on *Exodus* was a turning point in illegal immigration.

The *Exodus* crew and passengers were united by a moral certainty that what they were doing was something almost mystical: the right of return to *Eretz Yisrael* became the reason their fathers and elder brothers had fought Nazi oppression. For Paul Shulman, later the first commander of the Israeli navy, 'They gave their time and their will, their strength and determination. They worked without pay, without fanfare, without reward or promise, and well understood the risks to their lives. They were men whose sense of justice transcended all else.'

In writing this book I was able to draw upon the recollections not only of *Exodus* passengers and crew but also of members of the Palestine Patrol of the Royal Navy, who sent a fleet of destroyers led by cruiser HMS *Ajax* to overpower *Exodus*. The Naval Staff History records their action as 'successfully using the minimum amount of force under very trying circumstances'.

Understandably, those on board *Exodus* took a very different view in their accounts of the battle at sea that took place. Their vivid and priceless recollections have been complemented here by official records and a wide range of published and private material, including diaries and an unpublished manuscript, which have enabled them to be placed in context. Describing their traumatic experiences was clearly not easy for those on board, especially those whose first language was not English. But coming through their words is the clarity of truth.

Over 60 years have passed since the events described here and no one knows how many of *Exodus*'s passengers are still alive. Indeed, two of the key players in the drama, the ship's commander, Yossi Harel, and its captain, Ike Ahronowitz, died during the writing of this book. Fortunately, they had already been interviewed and their memories form part of its mosaic of voices.

Many people have spoken about the voyage for the first time outside the circle of families and friends and they display here a sense of pride which lightens their recollections. Despite the brutality and degradation they endured during and after the Holocaust, they provide remarkable demonstrations of how survivors can hold on to their deep-rooted values. No one has expressed for them those values better than the late Rabbi Albert Friedlander. In 1987 I sat in his synagogue office in London – coincidentally on the 40th anniversary of the voyage of *Exodus* – and the scholarly rabbi offered me this thought: 'We are still maimed sufferers with injuries that will not heal. We have lost members of our families. We have lost the great community of Eastern Jewry. We have lost the most special warmth and gaiety of Sephardic Jewry along the Mediterranean. We have lost our scholars and our simple people. All wiped out by the evil in the Nazi camps. We mourn the millions of children and we wonder what the world would have been like if their lives had been permitted to flower.'

Operation Exodus evolved out of a meeting between the documentary film-maker Jill Samuels and my publisher, Jeremy Robson. I thank them both, Jeremy for his extensive knowledge of the subject and Jill for the unique interviews and research that made this book possible.

Gordon Thomas
Bath, England

Chapter 1

The House of Secrets

In November 1946 a stocky man with a high-domed forehead, bushy eyebrows and piercing eyes arrived in New York, his fourth visit since the end of the Second World War. He had first come to the city in 1915, then a slim youth with bushy black hair and a knife scar on his arm from an unprovoked attack by an Arab while he was walking along the shore of the Sea of Galilee. Each time he had come to America it was to visit, not to stay: his spiritual home was Palestine. His ambition then had been, as it was now, to help build a home for the Jewish people, one where they could hold their heads up high and be proud, and hopefully live in peace after all they had suffered. Each time he came to New York he sensed his hopes were coming that much nearer than they were when – in a rooming house with a view of the Statue of Liberty – he wrote to his wife, Paula: 'Out of sorrow and pain, the national consciousness is taking form; the thought of resurgence in Israel captivates all hearts and is bringing them closer.'

Along with other immigrants, he had toiled in Palestine from dawn to dusk in the fields, building roads, turning arid, malaria-infested land into collective cooperative settlements. They would form the foundation for a thriving, working nation.

Born in the small industrial town of Plonsk, northwest of Warsaw, and named David Gruen by his father, a lawyer, this young man had been 19 years old when he arrived in Jerusalem. Since his childhood, he had been committed to his father's Zionism. But as he later said,

'It was not enough to listen to my father. I wanted to live Zionism, not just talk about it.'

He had also set up a newspaper in Palestine to revive the Hebrew language as the prime tongue for his fellow immigrants. Only then would the Jews scattered across the world have a home they could call their own, he had written in his first editorial and proudly signed it, 'David Gruen – Editor'. As he was about to take it to the print shop, he looked at the document and, reaching for a pen, crossed out his name. He felt it would be more appropriate to use a Hebrew one. He was 24 years old when he made the decision to be known as David Ben-Gurion, naming himself – appropriately – after one of the leaders of the Jewish revolt against the Romans.

Now, on his latest visit to New York as chairman of the Jewish Agency, he was the most powerful Jew in Palestine. Soon he would be its first prime minister. People would wait in line to pledge him their support for the Agency, for Israel. He would accept their money gratefully, with a quick nod of thanks. It was his way.

Hostesses would compete to hold dinner parties in his honour and guests listened in awe to his endless fund of stories. He was a man who spoke knowledgeably about two world wars, the sun of imperial Britain beginning to set, the people of Asia starting to awake to independence and how America had assumed world leadership. He had anecdotes to illustrate the vicissitudes and upheavals around the globe. But always he came back to one theme: how within less than half a century there had descended upon the Jewish people a storm of savage blows more fearsome than any they had endured since the Roman legions laid waste to their land and, in AD 70, destroyed the sacred Temple they had built on Jerusalem's Mount Moriah.

On that November Sunday morning, Ben-Gurion had come to a duplex overlooking New York's Central Park to use his oratory to persuade the men gathered around the table to dig deep into their pockets, even deeper than some of them had done before on similar occasions. But for the moment he continued to stare out of the suite's dining-room window high above the park.

Fresh snow had fallen overnight and children were throwing snowballs at each other. Behind him in the room, Ben-Gurion sensed the men around the breakfast table were waiting for him to speak. They all knew why he was there; he always wore his dark blue bespoke suit when fund-raising. As usual, he would give them a homily to lead into what he wanted. He had already whetted their appetites while they ate breakfast – something he never did on these occasions except for taking a cup of coffee – by telling them of his visit to the Displaced Persons camps in Europe.

Still staring down at the playing children, finally he began to speak: 'Three hundred years ago, the *Mayflower* left Plymouth, England, to bring the pilgrims to the New World. How many Englishmen and Americans know the precise date and the food they ate on the day of departure?'

He turned and looked at each of the silent men. Some he had met before: Rudolf G. Sonneborn, leader of New York's Jewish community, who had regularly hosted fund-raising breakfasts and dinners for Jewish causes in his well-appointed apartment.

Next to him sat Dewey Stone, a Boston philanthropist. He was a regular guest at the table, not only for his significant financial contributions, but for the contacts he brought, three of whom were seated around him. Others included a senior Wall Street broker and Morris Ginsberg, a shipping magnate. Some were strangers to Ben-Gurion, but he knew each was a powerful and wealthy man. Sonneborn never invited anyone else to partake of lox and bagels on such occasions. For the newcomers, Ben-Gurion had an extra-warm smile.

'We are here today because our people are still not free. They can never be free until we bring them home to their land. I have been looking out of the window at children playing in the snow. A month ago I was in Europe, talking to Jewish survivors who had seen children shot in Auschwitz for doing that. Or had been forced to march through the snow until they dropped dead from starvation. It is to make sure that will never happen again that you are here. It is as simple as that. Money to help our Aliyah Bet find the boats to bring home children like those I watched in the park. Children like you have. To bring their parents home. And their grandparents. Their cousins. To bring every Jew home to our homeland.'

Even before he had reached his seat at the table, there was thunderous applause. Within minutes five million dollars had been pledged.

Two men had arrived in New York with Ben-Gurion, both travelling on British passports. Ya'akov Dori, chief of staff of the Haganah, and Theodore (Teddy) Kollek, Ben-Gurion's executive secretary. They would advise on how the donations should be distributed by Rudolf Sonneborn.

For the past year Sonneborn had controlled a fund-raising operation across the Jewish community in America, running it with the same quiet efficiency he did his chemical factories. In New York, Philadelphia, Boston, Baltimore, Washington, DC and on the West Coast, Jews had met to raise funds.

Leo Macey Bernstein, an energetic 31-year-old who ran a successful real estate business in Washington, DC, was a fund-raiser for the United Jewish Appeal and was used to 'not being told how the money would be spent. Maybe it was to buy a ship to bring Holocaust survivors out of Europe. Perhaps guns to defend our people against Arabs in Palestine. We were never told, just asked to give. And we did. Anything from a dollar to a thousand bucks. All we knew it was urgently needed.'

On 13 November 1945, a year before Ben-Gurion had addressed the fund-raising breakfast, Britain's Foreign Secretary, Ernest Bevin, had bluntly rejected President Truman's demand that Britain should immediately admit 100,000 Holocaust survivors to Palestine. Bevin had said only 1,500 a month could enter.

Now Ya'akov Dori had come to America with Ben-Gurion to buy ships to challenge Bevin's decision. Beside him at that breakfast table was Morris Ginsberg, president of the American Steamship Corporation in New York. Turning to Dori, he said he would provide two Canadian corvettes and have them converted into cargo vessels in the city's Brewster Dry Dock and registered under the Panamanian flag.

Ben-Gurion asked how long before that could happen. Morris Ginsberg made a quick mental calculation, then replied, 'Six months, David, maybe a little sooner.'

Ben-Gurion grunted. 'That's too long, we need ships now. Big ships. Fast ships that can outrun the British Navy.'

Ginsberg promised to check what was available.

Late one afternoon in December 1946 force of habit made a number of men each walk a distance apart down Hayarkon Street on Tel Aviv's seafront. One was a lecturer at the Hebrew University, set in a pine grove on the heights of Mount Scopus in Jerusalem. Another was a soft-spoken tailor who had escaped from Germany the year Hitler came to power. A third was a pale, scholarly faced lawyer. The fourth man coming down the street was a bank teller. The fifth worked in the Water Supply Bureau. The last was a trade union leader. Nobody who worked with them knew what they did after leaving their workplaces. Even their families did not know why they came or what they did in the pink-painted house they entered, number 45, halfway down the street. They were in fact members of the Haganah High Command.

After days of rain which had whipped spray off the Mediterranean with stinging force, the weather had cleared and the Mandate police patrols were back on the streets. Britain's High Commissioner, Sir Alan Cunningham, had ordered the patrols to be reinforced. The decision was seen by the Jewish population as a further sign the administration was becoming increasingly pro-Arab at the political level. From the Negev Desert to the border with Lebanon, Arabs were being urged by the Mufti of Jerusalem to mobilise and drive out the Jews.

The Haganah's own spies had learned that weapons hidden during the years of war in Europe were being brought out from behind false panels and from under floorboards in the Arab Quarter of Jerusalem, or removed from crates of cheap souvenirs waiting to be sold to the first post-war tourists the Mufti had promised would return once the Jews were expelled. But it was not only the threat posed by the Arabs which troubled the men walking down Hayarkon Street. What increasingly concerned them was the anti-Jewish attitude of Britain's Labour government and the Mandate. Only recently, when Rabbi Mordechai Weingarten, Jerusalem's most respected religious leader, had protested about the number of armed Arabs moving through the Jewish Quarter in the Old City, his protest had been dismissed by the Mandate police chief.

While a ban remained on the import of arms into Palestine, Foreign Secretary Ernest Bevin had authorised yet another weapons contract with Iraq. A secret codicil added, 'The use of the arms is to discharge Iraq's responsibility to the Arab League.'

What concerned the Haganah most of all was the Royal Navy's rigorous patrolling of Palestine's coastal waters. Not only were illegal immigrant ships being intercepted, but at the same time the Mandate virtually ignored the hundreds of Arab guerrillas coming from Syria, Jordan and Egypt.

When Ben-Gurion had raised the matter, the Mandate spokesman blandly denied that there was any infiltration. But copies of intelligence reports leaked to the Haganah show that the Mandate not only knew the dates and times guerrillas were entering the country, but opted to do nothing, as each report was marked, 'No action needed'.

The documents had been copied from the office of Brigadier C.K. Clayton, Britain's senior intelligence officer in Palestine, by his secretary, a middle-aged English woman who had been seduced by a handsome officer in the Haganah. The latest report revealed the Royal Navy's Palestine Patrol would, in January 1947, begin to extend its range to incorporate Cyprus. In a concluding paragraph Clayton wrote:

It is my considered opinion, formed from my monitoring of recent Arab meetings in Damascus and Cairo, that we must deal with the illegal immigration as firmly as possible if a war is to be avoided. If hostilities do break out then the blame must rest with the Jews. They remain not open to reason as is evidenced by the number of illegals they have managed to bring ashore. Many have turned out to be of military age (16–35) and have been trained in their DP camps. I am treating it as a priority to discover what arms Jews have brought into the country. It may also only be a matter of time before the Jews make use of larger ships than at present.

Outside the house on Hayarkon Street a young man greeted each arrival with a formal '*shalom*' and the code names he knew them by – Ammon, Amos, Ari, Efraim, Jacob, Reuben, Rudy, Svi. All were bound by the oath of secrecy they had sworn on their first day in the Haganah, just as all recruits to the clandestine army were. Then, after being taught how to carry messages or track the movements of important Arabs and Mandate officers, recruits would be taken for training in the remote wadis of the Negev Desert, where the sand muffled the crack of a rifle. In the cool of the evening they used potatoes and oranges to practise grenade throwing. So limited was ammunition that a defining moment for each recruit came when an instructor handed him a single live round of fire. It marked his full induction into the Haganah.

The High Command had been summoned to their headquarters in Hayarkon Street after an envelope had arrived at the house from Ben-Gurion in New York. It contained copies of advertisements placed by the Maritime Commission in Washington, DC, offering ships for sale. Each boat had its price tag. Like a croupier dealing cards, the senior Haganah man around the table, Reuben, dealt out the adverts. The others studied each one, shrugged or shook their heads. Finally Reuben handed over the last advertisement. It was a photo of *President Warfield*, a Chesapeake steamer, with a price tag of $50,000. The ship was described as 'salvageable but requires some work to become seaworthy'.

When Efraim asked where anyone would find that kind of money, Reuben replied that this was why Ben-Gurion had gone to New York.

*

Days after Ben-Gurion's fund-raiser breakfast, Ze'ev Shind arrived
in New York on the overnight train from Montreal. He carried a
perfectly forged Canadian passport to match the address he had
given as his home in the city.

In 1938 he had been one of three Polish Jews living in the cramped
top floor of an apartment near the Eiffel Tower in Paris, organising
throughout Europe illegal immigration to Palestine. When France
fell, Shind was sent to the Mediterranean to continue to find ships to
sail to Palestine's beaches. Since then he had travelled to South
America, North Africa, Turkey and the United States – anywhere he
heard there was a boat for sale.

His orders had continued to come from Room 17 in the
Histadrut Executive Building, the headquarters of the Jewish Trade
Union, on Tel Aviv's Allenby Street. No one paid any attention to
the young men who took turns to stare out of the room's window;
they were the Haganah lookouts ready to signal the approach of a
British patrol.

Then desks would immediately be cleared of paperwork and the
short-wave radio transmitter hidden in a cupboard. To any
unwelcome visitor, the dozen men and women in the room would
appear to be industrious clerks dealing with union affairs.

Room 17 was the centre of the illegal immigration network, code-
named Apparat. In charge was a dynamic young Haganah officer,
Eliyahu Golomb. Upon his narrow shoulders rested the responsibility
of ultimately ensuring Jews in the Reich could immigrate to Palestine.
Pinned on the wall behind his desk was a sheet of paper on which was
written in Hebrew: 'The key to immigration is our people, not the
land, not the lifeless crust of earth, but the dynamism and creation of
farmers and factory hands.'

That excerpt from a Ben-Gurion speech had driven Golomb to
work long days and even longer nights, catnapping on the floor in the
early hours, grabbing a sandwich when he could. From the cramped
room, its air full of cigarette smoke and the aroma of strong coffee,
he sent orders to Ze'ev Shind and other Aliyah Bet operatives
scattered around the Mediterranean ports to find boats: 'I need ships.

I need them now. And I need safe landing sites to avoid the Mandate coastal patrols. I want everything now!'

Golomb's words would echo around Room 17 as darkness fell or a new sun rose. He reminded everyone they must not haggle over exorbitant prices for boats, just as they must be ready to offer substantial bribes for passports and visas.

Over the years Shind had bought documents from the diplomats of Mexico, Colombia, Honduras and Peru. Finally he had been handpicked for his latest mission. The tall, red-haired and bespectacled Aliyah Bet agent was to set up a company for one specific purpose: to establish the true market value and seaworthiness of *President Warfield*. His Haganah code name was 'Danny', chosen because his hair gave him the look of an Irishman, along with his pale blue eyes which had the steely look of someone who lived by his wits.

Using his Haganah contacts in the city, Shind had opened an office on the fifth floor of an old building on 24th Street in New York. It had one desk, two chairs and a filing cabinet. He had a signwriter stencil on the door 'Weston Trading Company – Marine Surveyors'. He had chosen the name from an obituary he saw in the *New York Times*. He rarely used the office telephone, preferring to use street pay phones: he wanted to be sure no one tapped his conversations.

Danny discovered that three marine surveyors had inspected *President Warfield*. One represented the Patapsco Scrap Corporation, the second represented the Boston Metal Corporation and the third had been commissioned by the Potomac Shipwrecking Company, who had said *President Warfield* was worth no more than $6,500 as scrap. The lowest bid had been Patapsco's at $1,500. Boston Metal's surveyor had placed the ship's worth at $5,000.

The Maritime Commission, responsible for selling off all wartime ships with no further use, rejected the offers. Shind had called the agency in Washington, DC, and asked what offer would be acceptable. When told to make one, he said he would call back.

Next day he took a train to Baltimore. Waiting for him was Captain William Ash. The burly, beret-wearing sailor had been recommended by Morris Ginsberg as someone to guide Shind through the world of American ship-brokering. Ash, a Polish Jew who had emigrated from Russia in the 1920s, had a colourful background. He had been a deep-water seaman who rose to become a captain and enlisted in the US Maritime Service during the war, before setting himself up as a marine surveyor. Eventually he became the vice-president of the labour union for merchant seamen. Ginsberg had told Ben-Gurion that if he wanted someone to buy a ship or find a crew, Ash was the man.

Ze'ev Shind would never forget Ash's words after they shook hands at the Baltimore railway station: 'He peered at me and said I looked like the man he'd been told to expect, "tall and skinny with a fireball for hair". Then he was galloping along with his words: "I know roughly what you want. A ship to bring home Jews. But I want to impress upon you that if there's anything illegal done, then you've got the wrong man." I began to wonder how this was going to play out. Then he was off again: "I know how to legally procure ships and send them anywhere you want. What you do with a ship outside this country, I don't care. I will do my end legally. Okay?" I nodded and he was off again. He gave me a lecture on how to do this. I had to form a Panamanian company. Then we would go out and buy whatever ship was on the market at a fair price. He suggested we call our company Arias and Arias. I asked why. He stared at me. "Because it has a ring to it, okay?"'

The new company would operate out of Weston's office. Letterheads and envelopes were to be printed. Captain Ash would be listed as the company's president. Ash asked one more time: 'Okay?'

It had been snowing the day Shind and Captain Ash clambered on board *President Warfield*, one of a long line of derelicts anchored on the James River on the Bay of Baltimore, and spent the morning tramping through the boat. With the wind off the Chesapeake whistling in the rigging, they barely exchanged a word while Ash scribbled in a small notebook. Back on shore he had given the hulk a final stare in the fading daylight. Shind recalled: 'Finally he asked me how much I wanted to pay. I said as little as possible, though I recognised it would need a deal of fixing. "Sure will. How much money you got?" I said enough. He just stood in silence looking at his notebook, as he was deciding on a figure. "Okay, so make your phone call."'

Shind telephoned the Marine Commission to be told that *President Warfield* had been sold as scrap to the Potomac Shipwrecking Company for $8,000.

Next day, back in New York, he was summoned to the office of Dewey Stone's attorney on Park Avenue. Ben-Gurion had already told Shind that Herman Goldman handled all of the Haganah's legal business in the United States, especially the purchasing of ships that could be used to bring immigrants to Palestine. He had his own network of shipping agents who told him what was coming on the market.

Goldman was a rotund man with silvery hair and a surprisingly strong handshake for someone Shind estimated to be in his seventies. He produced an envelope and handed it to Shind, explaining it contained a certified cheque for $50,000. Shind was to lodge it in an account with the Chemical Bank. The money was to be used to buy *President Warfield*, refurbish it for sea, and hire a captain and crew.

'He was all business and said the less people knew why I was in New York the better for everyone. He gave me the name of a director at Potomac Shipwrecking I should contact to buy the ship. The guy would probably try and haggle a little. My top price would be ten thousand dollars. But nothing above that. After I had concluded the deal, Goldman said he would take over the legal side of things. There was a style about him; no wonder he moved in the same circles as Ben-Gurion.'

The entire deal, from depositing the cheque to the phone call to Potomac Shipwrecking, took under an hour. There had been no negotiation. Shind had simply offered his top price and Weston Trading became the owner of *President Warfield*.

It was second nature for Shind to now begin his own checks into the background of his purchase. It was his way of anticipating any surprises. But even he was unprepared for the history of the ship.

*

Like a thief in the night waiting for the moon to sink and leave the sky black and without stars, another nightmare tore apart Miriam Bergman's sleep. In her 80th year, every moment still remained so vivid, so heartbreaking, so shocking, so momentous, from those unforgettable days of fear that were to climax at sea in July 1947.

Miriam's fifth birthday, 25 February 1932, was the day Adolf Hitler became a German citizen, enabling him to take his seat in the Brunswick State Parliament and give his fledgling National Socialist Party a political voice. Miriam now knew that had been the starting point for her nightmare.

Miriam's father, Leon, was a tailor in the Grunewald suburb of Berlin. Jews had lived there from around 1880 after fleeing the pogroms of Russia and Poland. Among their neighbours the Bergmans were regarded as a middle-class family. Close to their home were the *mikveh* where, along with their neighbours, they took their weekly ritual bath; a bakery which supplied unleavened bread for Passover; the *cheder*, which Leon helped to fund and where, when the time came, she would go for religious instruction.

Every Friday morning since she was old enough to walk, Miriam had accompanied Else, her mother, carrying some *cholent* – a dish of goose breast, beans and potatoes, that would be placed in one of the baker's ovens to cook.

The bakery was a centre for neighbourhood discussion: who was pregnant, whose husband had pulled off a deal, which of the Gentile farmers was selling the fattest chickens. The world beyond the close-knit Jewish community hardly ever intruded, but that morning the bakery was filled with voices, uneasy and angry voices reading the newspaper the baker had produced. It reported a tirade by Hitler in the Brunswick State Parliament against the Jews.

The air filled with the aroma of fresh bread and raised voices. Her hand gripping her mother's, her eyes going from one agitated woman to another, it was Miriam's first conscious encounter with anti-Semitism.

Freddie Kronenberg's terror included his time raising and lowering the barrier at Auschwitz under the arch bearing the words

Arbeit Macht Frei, work makes free. In every dream there was Dr Josef Mengele waiting on the ramp for the prisoners to emerge from the cattle trucks, using his cigarette to decide their fate. A flick to the right with the butt in his gloved hand and a prisoner lived, at least for the moment; a flick to the left led immediately to the crematoria. In his nightmare Freddie saw his mother consigned to the gas chambers. But always at the last moment he was pulled aside by Mengele. The claw-like grasp on his arm, the cold eyes, were as vivid now in Freddie's old age as the first time. So was the way Mengele had fingered the crucifix around Freddie's neck, nodding, coming to a decision. A guard had thrown black breeches and a cap at Freddie, together with a pair of boots, and escorted him to the barrier. Freddie had become the gatekeeper to hell.

Helena Levi was the same age as Freddie, born in April 1928. Her father, Hermann, had been a respected obstetrician in a Hamburg teaching hospital. In her nightmare a newly born baby always suddenly appeared. She cradled him against her thin dress, wrapped in the shawl she had removed from the body of the woman who had begged Helena to take her child. The infant had died shortly after the start of the death march in the depths of a Prussian winter. It was so cold, Helena's urine had frozen to her legs. The SS guards used their whips to drive them on as, in the distance, the sound of advancing Russian guns could be heard. Helena cradled the baby, which she could not, *would not* give up, until an SS guard had torn the infant from her grasp and hurled it into the snow, shouting she would walk faster without her burden. Then, in her nightmare, there was no longer snow but energy-sapping sun to drain Helena as she tried to protect another newborn baby while all around her the battle on board the ship *Exodus* raged. Suddenly the infant was no longer in her arms. Had it been snatched and thrown over the side? The question always jerked her awake. Soaked in sweat, Helena would lie still, trying to calm herself, knowing the terrible dream would return again. It always did.

*

The outbreak of the First World War between Britain and Germany found Turkey an ally of Kaiser Wilhelm's forces. The political wing of Zionism, which Theodor Herzl had founded, moved to London, where the leadership passed to the charismatic Dr Chaim Weizmann.

Herzl was the son of a comfortable middle-class Viennese Jewish family, a newspaperman and a Jew with little concern for his race and religion until that day in January 1895 when he had been sent to Paris to report the trial of another Jew, Captain Alfred Dreyfus, found guilty of treason. Herzl had stood among a screaming crowd outside the court on the Champ de Mars.

'Kill the traitor! Kill the Jews!'

He had returned to Vienna a changed man, knowing it was not the blood of Dreyfus that the mob had demanded; it was the blood of all Jews. A year later he published a book that was to become famous, Der Judenstaat, in which he advocated the foundation of a Jewish state by international agreement. 'If you wish it,' he wrote, 'it is no dream.' From then on he devoted his life and energies to the Zionist cause, convening the first Zionist Congress at Basel in 1897.

After Herzl's death, Chaim Weizmann would eventually inherit his mantle. As he wrote to his future wife, Vera, 'I feel that a heavy burden has fallen on my shoulders.' Born in Russia in 1874, Weizmann had already started to make his academic mark as a research chemist at German and Swiss universities before taking up a post at Manchester University in 1904. He became a naturalised British citizen in 1910. Any lingering barrier to his religious background was swept away when the First World War started. By then Weizmann, now Professor of Chemistry at Manchester, had displayed his scientific skills by discovering a process to synthetically manufacture acetone for explosives. The War Office was in urgent need of Weizmann's discovery to supply shells for its armies in France.

Within a year Weizmann had become a figure of real influence, respected in the inner circles of the English Establishment. His contribution to the war effort opened more doors within government and he used his connections to lead the discussions in London for Palestine to become a Jewish homeland. On 31 October 1917, he helped to draft a letter for Lord Rothschild – head of the English branch of the powerful Jewish banking family – to send to Arthur James Balfour, the Foreign Secretary. Two days later a reply came from Balfour. For Weizmann, as for every Jew, the reply seemed to contain a momentous promise:

> His Majesty's government view with favour the establishment in Palestine of a national home for the Jewish people, and will use their best endeavours to facilitate the achievement of this object, it being clearly understood that nothing will be done which may prejudice the civil and religious rights of existing non-Jewish communities in Palestine, or the rights and political status enjoyed by Jews in any other country. I should be grateful if you would bring this declaration to the knowledge of the Zionist Federation.

For the Jews, the ratification in 1920 of what became known as the Balfour Declaration and the appointment of Britain to administer Palestine began promisingly. The first High Commissioner would be Herbert Samuel, who was 50 years old and the first Jew elected to Parliament. As Home Secretary, he had played a key role in the drafting of the Declaration. In Jerusalem, Jewish leaders formed a National Council to work with him. Then, in 1921, Winston Churchill, Britain's Colonial Secretary, visited Palestine and reaffirmed his support for Zionism: 'When I get back to London I have no doubt I shall be told that but for the Zionist Movement there would be no need to keep such a large British garrison, at so great an expense, in this country. The Jewish Community all over the world must provide me with the means of answering all adverse criticism. I must be able to say that a great event is taking place here, a great event in the world's history. It is taking place without injury or injustice to anyone. It is transforming waste places into fertile; it is planting trees and developing agriculture in desert lands. The pioneers of this work are picked men, worthy in every way of the greatness of the ideal and the cause for which they are striving, and in that way you will give me the means to answer effectively those who wish to prevent this experiment.'

For Jewish leaders like David Ben-Gurion and Chaim Weizmann, Churchill's words were the encouragement their people needed to believe that Herzl's call for the dream to become reality was well on the way to being realised.

However, the Arabs responded with armed attacks, rampaging through the narrow streets of Jerusalem's Jewish Quarter, marking all Christian shops and homes with a chalked cross, meaning they were not to be touched. Those belonging to Jews were to be attacked: Jewish shops and synagogues were set alight, Jewish women were raped, six Jews died and over 200 were injured. One pogrom lasted three terrifying days and nights.

In the following six years, the steady flow of immigrants from Europe continued. New roads were built and more settlements established. Land that had once been swamps infested with malaria-bearing mosquitoes was drained and made fertile, after it had been bought from absentee Arab landlords glad to be rid of it. Tel Aviv and Haifa doubled in size. But the Arab onslaughts persisted. In Jaffa 43 Jews were murdered and 143 seriously injured. Samuel's administration did nothing. He had told the Mandate Commission that 'the basic principle of my administration policy is to deal with the Arabs as if there has been no Balfour Declaration'.

Samuel suspended Jewish immigration and distributed to the Arabs land which the Mandate controlled. Samuel departed from Palestine in 1925, leaving behind a bewildered and angry Jewish population. The Arab attacks continued.

Chapter 2

Stirrings

On 24 October 1927, the American shipping millionaire Solomon Davies Warfield died in his sleep. A few days before, he had made his last visit to the shipyard on the banks of the Christina River at Wilmington, Delaware, where riveters were laying down the hull of the ship which would bear his name.

News of Warfield's death reached Winston Churchill by letter at Blenheim Palace, the family home of generations of Dukes of Marlborough, his ancestors. Warfield's death reminded Churchill of his forgotten promise to the shipowner to help resolve the 'Jewish problem'. He promptly wrote a strongly worded article for the New York *Zionist Record* on his interpretation of the Balfour Declaration.

At the British Embassy in Washington, DC, Ambassador Sir Ronald Lindsey drafted a furious telegram to the Foreign Office, couched in language far from normal in diplomatic circles: 'The article makes my blood boil. It can only induce Jews in America, who might otherwise wish to take a moderate view, to refrain from doing so. They will expect the government to take a pure Zionist policy and then the chicken will come home to roost with Mr Winston Churchill.'

On Monday 29 February 1928, an icy-cold day, many of the 400 mourners who had attended Solomon Warfield's funeral assembled in the Baltimore shipyard of Pusey and Jones to witness the completion of the first stages in the construction of *President Warfield*.

Throughout the long winter, welders and riveters had worked to create the hull on the slipway. It glistened under its coating of white paint as the sun suddenly burst through the overcast sky a few minutes before noon. Guests sipping scalding coffee as they waited for the launch agreed the break in the clouds was a good omen.

The elegant hull was a reminder of the golden years of steam boating when life had been more leisurely and smacked of the Old South of plantations and servants. Though the main deck was yet without its decking and the elaborate superstructure had still to be fitted, there was little doubt in the shipyard crew's seasoned eyes that the end result would be a superb vessel.

At noon precisely, Warfield's niece climbed on to the launch platform. She was handed a bottle and, this being the eighth year of Prohibition, a local newspaper reporter noted that the master of ceremonies told the onlookers it contained only spring water. However, as she hurled the bottle it exploded in a cascade of foam that bubbled like champagne against the prow to a rousing cheer.

On New Year's Day 1929, in the arid scrubland of up-country Sudan, a dark-haired, aquiline-faced man dressed in the khaki of the Sudan Defence Force sat in his pup tent. On the floor beside his truckle bed were the remains of a bottle of Scotch whisky, a Christmas gift from a friend in London. Subaltern Orde Charles Wingate had drunk it sparingly, with the same deliberation that went with everything he did. Beside him on the bed were an Arab-language dictionary and a Hebrew tutorial; he had borrowed both books from the library of the School of Oriental Studies in London, from where he had graduated before being posted to Sudan.

He was 26 years old and responsible for administering an area larger than the Scottish Highlands. Under his command were 300 Sudanese soldiers whom he led against the elephant poachers and hostile tribesmen who threatened villagers in the area.

But Wingate's mind had begun to turn to a life beyond the arid land over which he was judge and jury, and where his only entertainment was playing the gramophone with the few scratched records he had brought with him. In a trunk beneath his bed were newspaper accounts of what was happening in Palestine, reports of Arab attacks and the desperate attempts of Jews to organise their defences. On his occasional visits to Khartoum, he had picked up copies of *The Times* that described what was happening. Slowly but surely Wingate, at first pro-Arab, had begun to change his mind. In his letters home, he began to espouse the Jewish cause, a decision that suited his combative nature, always ready to champion the underdog. He saw Jewish settlers as 'People who have been treated like this through scores of generations and yet at the end of it all remain undefeated. I feel I belong to such people.'

If there was a moment it was then, in the parched atmosphere of his outpost, that Orde Wingate became a Zionist. He asked his sister to send him books about Zionism and the latest newspaper reports about the struggle of settlers. The more he read the more Wingate realised the present tactics of the Jews would not work. They must move out of their stockades to meet the Arab terror at its source. That would need better training and more weapons. Mobile units should be formed. An attack must penetrate the centres of Arab population. Special-operations teams had to be formed. The newspaper reports said that the Jews were heavily outnumbered. Well, thought Wingate, he had faced the same problem here in Sudan against rapacious tribesmen. But he had confronted and beaten them with his tactics. These could be applied to helping the Jews.

Throughout the harsh winter months of 1928, workers swarmed over *President Warfield*. Carpenters worked in the saloons, creating ivory-panelled walls for polishers to add the final gloss. Glaziers positioned storm-proof glass to provide a safe and uninterrupted view around the stern deck. The smoking room was panelled in mahogany. The dance floor of the social hall was off limits to all builders who did not remove their work boots. The gallery deck was enclosed with specially reinforced glass to protect tropical plants in ceramic tubs. Fitters positioned the hand-carved double staircase in the main saloon so it rose through two decks. Electricians fitted magnificent chandeliers, while plumbers installed baths in the staterooms, each with a constant supply of hot water, a luxury never before offered by any Chesapeake ship. An art dealer had been sent to Solomon Warfield's mansion to select oil paintings for hanging in the ship's public rooms. Engineers fitted and tested the four-cylinder engine that was capable of producing a cruising speed of 18 knots. Workmen hoisted the 30-foot-tall smoke stack, already painted with its black and red band. Masts fore and aft were erected and the white burgee house flag flew.

Finally the pilothouse equipment was installed: the four-foot mahogany steering wheel, the brass binnacle to its right, the engine-room telegraph on the left. On the hurricane deck was a wooden platform on which the officer of the watch would pace in front of the 11 sealed windows on the bridge. *President Warfield*'s overall length was 330 feet, with a draft of 15 feet 6 inches, and she was licensed to carry 400 passengers in comfort to rival transatlantic liners. The shipyard had delivered on time with no overrun.

On 13 July 1929 *President Warfield* began three days' trial, entering Chesapeake Bay, flags flying at full dress, smoke streaming from her stack and water curling along her sleek hull.

Among the crew were some who might well have followed the tradition of superstitious sailors by feeling uneasy that she had begun her trials on Friday the 13th.

Baron Edmond James Rothschild, scion of the most powerful banking dynasty in Europe, stood at one of the windows of his chateau deep in the lush French countryside. In a few days he would celebrate his 84th birthday. In appearance he looked and dressed as he had done for 50 years. His hair had turned white in middle age and he kept it carefully trimmed so that it matched his full beard and bushy eyebrows. He always wore a bow tie from his collection, along with a silk shirt and morning dress. He spoke French and English in a cultured, mellifluous voice. It was his eyes people noticed; they had a steady gaze, which came from a lifetime of appraising paintings, rare manuscripts and furniture in salerooms throughout the world. Pride of place in the chateau went to the framed red shield that had once hung on the parlour wall of the small house in the ghetto in Frankfurt's Judengasse, where Meyer Amschel Rothschild had founded the dynasty. It was a reminder for Edmond of how, penniless and with often only the clothes they wore, other Jews had made their way across Europe, through the mountains and ravines of Albania, Romania, Turkey and Syria to Palestine, impoverished.

Edmond Rothschild was in Damascus buying antiquities when he first heard about their plight. He provided each family with a monthly allowance until they were self-sufficient. Moshavim, collective settlements, sprang up all over Galilee and the hills of Judea, and as they expanded, so did the Zionist Movement. Rothschild contributed money and aid for the development of the settlements and became known as 'the Father of the Yishuv' (the Jewish community in Palestine).

This was the reason that had brought Chaim Weizmann to see him.

Rothschild had listened carefully as his guest expressed his fear that the Arabs would rise, forcing the Jews to defend themselves to avoid a bloodbath as bad as the pogroms from which they had escaped. He had interposed, 'And the British?'

Weizmann had been blunt: 'They will continue to do little.'

His host had responded, 'We both know it is the birthright of every Jew to come home. The next wave of immigrants will need to come by ship. It will be safer. Safer and quicker. But everything must be done to encourage Arab and Jew to live together and for the British to ensure they do. One thing is certain, I will continue to help.'

In his home in Rehovot, southeast of Tel Aviv, Chaim Weizmann listened as his impassioned dinner guest, David Ben-Gurion, warned that the Grand Mufti of Jerusalem, the spiritual leader of the Muslims, was bent on terror, with his firebrand speeches calling for Holy War against the Jews. During the Second World War the Mufti had sided with the Germans, eventually fleeing to Berlin.

Weizmann gently reminded his guest that the very heart of Zionism was a policy of rapprochement and mutual understanding towards the Palestinian Arabs. While the British Army and police had done little to deal with Arab attacks, for the Haganah to launch a massive counteroffensive would almost certainly bring the full might of the Mandate down on them.

Two weeks later, Ben-Gurion returned to Weizmann with one of the most prominent Jews in Haifa, David Hacohen, head of the country's largest construction company. His contacts had made him a popular figure among the staff of the Mandate. No one suspected that Hacohen, with his sleek hair, boisterous laugh and risqué stories, was a high-value source of information for the Haganah.

He had recently expanded his business into Sudan, building new barracks for the army and comfortable housing for senior officers. After the three men settled in their host's book-lined study, Hacohen explained he had met a young British officer, Orde Wingate, in the Sudanese capital.

'He seems able to use no more than a platoon of his men to defeat three times that number of Arabs.'

What's more, Hacohen told them, Wingate had become a Zionist and planned to come to Palestine. Weizmann had looked quizzically at Ben-Gurion, and Hacohen vividly remembered the lively discussion that followed, which ended with Weizmann saying he had one request.

'If he comes here I want to see him.'

On 30 January 1933, in Berlin, Miriam's father, Leon Bergman, listened as another roar of '*Sieg heil!*' came over the wireless broadcast from the stadium a few streets from the family home. From a window he had seen hundreds of swastika flags fluttering over the huge amphitheatre where, since dawn, crowds had been converging, led by marshals in their brown shirts and armbands. The tramp of boots and raucous voices singing Party songs as they passed his house had continued for hours. Trains from all over Germany had brought Party members to listen to Hitler.

Over the wireless came another cheer. Despite the *Kachelofen*, the large stove in the kitchen, Leon shivered again. The new Chancellor had just promised that, now he was in power, he would deal with the Jews 'the way they should be dealt with'.

Jacob Kronenberg had followed his daily routine, leaving home in a suburb of Nuremberg and travelling to the city centre, where he worked as a clerk in an accounting firm. In his late thirties, he had been married for six years. His wife, Christabel, was unable to bear children and they had adopted the son of her cousin when she died. The boy was called Freddie and was a chubby, cheerful child. The Kronenbergs were not religious and Jacob liked to appear no different from his German neighbours: he sent them Christmas cards, displayed a Yuletide tree in the living room and took the family to the city's traditional market to buy gifts for Freddie to mark the birth of Christ. Hebrew was hardly spoken at home, except when cousins came visiting from the country.

Though his parents were Hungarian Jews who had settled in Bavaria in the last century, Jacob believed he had become completely absorbed into the German way of life, even to the point where he wondered whether he should leave his Jewish employer and seek work with one of the city's Catholic firms. Christabel had urged him to stay where he was, reminding him that his salary was good and work was hard to find. All Jacob had to do was continue to take care to say or do nothing which would include him in the diatribes against the Jews Hitler continued to deliver over the wireless and in the Party newspapers.

As the tram came closer to the city centre, Jacob noticed there were storm troopers everywhere. Some were posting slogans calling for a boycott of Jewish businesses. For the first time, he felt uneasy. He folded his newspaper and placed it in his briefcase, covering the skullcap which his employer insisted he should wear at work. Walking towards his office, Jacob saw that several shops in the Jewish quarter had their windows smashed and contents thrown into the streets. His unease grew.

Waiting outside the doorway of the building where he worked were several more troopers holding clubs. One beckoned Jacob forward. Another moved to block his retreat. A third grabbed his briefcase and tossed its contents on to the cobbles. The skullcap was held up for the others to see. A blow from a club smashed Jacob's teeth. He collapsed on to the ground, only to be hauled to his feet. A trooper produced a knife and cut away the legs of Jacob's trousers and pulled off his underpants to paint his genitals with a dye. Finally a placard was attached around his neck announcing: 'I am a dirty Jew.'

With a final kick, Jacob was sent staggering into the building, where he found the office had been vandalised. Lying on the floor were his employer and other members of staff. Each had been severely beaten. Daubed on the walls were swastikas. Similar attacks were happening all over Germany.

Jacob Kronenberg's long and painful recovery had been helped by neighbours, many of whom were Catholics or Lutherans. He had telephoned one from the wreckage of his office and the man, seeing the state of Jacob's injuries, had called another neighbour, a nurse. She had arrived with a first-aid kit. While she began to tend Jacob's wounds and those of his colleagues, the man went out and returned with clothes for Jacob and drove him home.

In the weeks that followed, a dentist who lived in the same street as the Kronenbergs made him a set of dentures. Meanwhile, the nurse had arranged for Jacob to see a neurologist, who assured him there had been no serious damage to his skull. When Jacob wanted to pay, the doctor shook his head and said, 'We are not all Nazis.'

That evening the nurse had brought crucifixes for each of the family and arranged for Freddie to be admitted to a Catholic school. Like the other children, he wore his cross with pride and learned for the first time to recite the words of the Lord's Prayer. Other neighbours brought the Kronenbergs teacakes and toys for Freddie, to show the family was still welcome in their midst.

But elsewhere Jews were increasingly subjected to hostility. Shopkeepers refused to serve them and they were reviled when they left their homes. Thousands were hurt, many seriously, some fatally. Anti-Semitism progressively became a campaign of hatred and by 1935 the first of 35,000 German Jews had sold up their homes at well below market value. All they asked for was sufficient money to leave Germany to go to the only place they felt they would be safe: Palestine.

Yet hundreds of thousands of other Jews chose to remain: doctors, teachers, scientists, businessmen – the backbone of any society. They believed that eventually Hitler would come to see their value in his plans to create a new Germany.

Dr Hermann Levi, Helena's father, proudly told her that, with her curly brown hair and pale skin, she looked like Shirley Temple, the child movie star. At the Catholic school where she was a pupil, she was one of two Jewish girls in her class. When there was religious instruction, they were both ordered to wait outside in the corridor. But otherwise Helena's life was little different from that of her classmates. In the summer she ran for the school's junior athletic team and during the winter she skated on the city ice rink with some of her schoolfriends, while at weekends she went walking with her parents in the countryside.

One day Helena's friend did not show up at school. That night her father said her friend's family had gone to Palestine.

That was the evening metal grilles were placed over the windows of the synagogue where the Levis worshipped; the rabbi said it was a necessary precaution after other synagogues in the city had had their windows broken. He had asked his congregation to be vigilant, but to do nothing to antagonise the Nazis. Similar requests were being made by other rabbis around the country.

At school Helena continued to stand every morning with her classmates and raise her arm in the Hitler salute before repeating the teacher's words of thanks to the Führer for making Germany once more strong. His framed portrait hung on the wall, as it did in every classroom in the school, just as in all other schools, hospitals and public offices across the country. Hitler's photograph was also on every cover of Helena's class books, depicting him in lederhosen and surrounded by a group of smiling children in the Bavarian countryside.

One morning her teacher abruptly ordered Helena to the front of her class and announced that she could no longer be allowed to give thanks to Hitler and marched her to the door, shouting, 'Get out, you dirty little Jew!'

About to begin a ward round, Dr Hermann Levi was summoned to the hospital administrator's office and told his employment was being immediately terminated. Shocked, he asked why.

'Because you are a Jew!'

In every German city, town and village, the same words were being repeated.

Juden sind hier unerwünscht. Jews are not wanted here.

Judenrein – ethnic cleansing of Jews – had started. They were no longer only branded as 'undesirables' to be imprisoned in concentration camps. They were enemies of the state, to be punished by death.

In September 1936, Orde Wingate arrived in Palestine, promoted to captain and intelligence officer in the Mandate. Years of exposure to sand and swirling winds in Sudan had given him a permanent tan and his own special relationship with the world, marked by a detachment from the frivolities of life. He awoke an hour before dawn and brushed his body with a bundle of sticks instead of bathing. In every way he did not fit the conventional profile of a garrison officer: mess dinners and Saturday night dances were events he ignored; his uniforms were often unpressed and his shoes scuffed.

The evening Orde Wingate settled into the Savoy Hotel in Haifa, his first visitor was David Hacohen. Since their first meeting in Khartoum, they had remained regular correspondents and Wingate's letters had shown increasing fluency in Hebrew. From time to time Hacohen had sent him books and newspaper accounts in Hebrew of the attacks on the settlers. Now, as he sat in Wingate's hotel room, Hacohen saw a burning passion about him: 'No wasted words, no formal politeness. His first words were, "Tell me what your Zionists are doing."'

Wingate pulled off a shoe and sock, produced a pencil out of his pocket and began to use it to massage his foot in between taking notes. After a moment's silence, he tore out a page and handed it to Hacohen, who, close to tears, read these words:

> I count it as my privilege to help you fight your battle. To that purpose I want to devote my life. I believe that the very existence of mankind is justified when it is based on the moral foundation of the Bible. Whoever dares raise a hand against you or your enterprise here should be fought against. Whether it is jealousy, ignorance or perverted doctrine which has made your neighbours rise against you, or 'politics' which makes some of my countrymen support them, I shall fight with you against any of these influences. But remember, this is your battle. My part, which I say I feel to be a privilege, is only to help you. Please will you open for me the hearts of the Jews in this country?

Hacohen carefully folded the paper and placed it in his pocket. Then, impulsively, he gave Wingate a bear-like hug and kissed him on both cheeks, the tears flowing freely down his face.

Now, weeks later, Hacohen had done what Wingate had asked. He would introduce the intelligence officer to the most powerful Jews in Palestine.

The men gathered around the dining table in Chaim Weizmann's house were responsible for the defence of the settlements. Daily the battles to save them from attack became more unequal; in the last six months a further 86 settlers had been killed.

Seated opposite Weizmann was David Ben-Gurion. Around him were Itzhak Cohen, the head of the Haganah, and his area commanders, Levi Abrahami, Eliyahu Cohen and Eliyahu Golomb. On either side of Weizmann sat David Hacohen and Orde Wingate.

Over dinner Wingate insisted on speaking Hebrew and bemused the others with his fervour for Zionism.

As dinner progressed, he told them that in the past month he had visited every Arab town and village in Palestine and had discovered how arms were being smuggled across the border from Jordan and Lebanon. He produced a map on which he had marked the smuggling routes. The others looked at each other, a new respect in their eyes. Wingate passed the paper to Itzhak Cohen, who studied it and then handed it around the table. When Cohen was about to hand the paper back, Wingate stopped him, saying, 'Keep it. You will need to remember the coordinates if we are going to work together.'

For an hour he held his listeners in thrall. For Cohen, 'There was a marked difference between him and all the other Englishmen I had met before. An honesty and a determination that spoke of the truth.'

Pausing only to sip water, Wingate looked at each man in turn, hunching his slightly rounded shoulders and fixing his penetrating gaze on each of his listeners. In his insistent, growling voice, he continued, 'The Administration, to a man, is anti-Jew and pro-Arab. Unless you fully recognise what that means, then I am wasting my time. And that includes you, Dr Weizmann. Your present hopes are a waste of time.'

Ben-Gurion was no longer frowning. The others looked at each other in astonishment. No one had spoken to Chaim Weizmann in such a blunt manner. He nodded for Wingate to continue.

When he spoke there was a deep certainty in his words: 'You must carry the fight to the Arabs. Do what they do. Strike in small numbers in the dead of night. You have to be unorthodox. You have to lay ambushes along the Arab supply lines. You must be ready to penetrate the centres of the Arab populations. For all this you will need to be trained. A new force will have to be created.'

Once more he paused. In the silence men looked at each other. David Hacohen recalled it was David Ben-Gurion who broke the silence, asking who would train this new force.

For the first time Orde Wingate smiled. He would, of course.

The questions continued. How would he do that? Why would he be allowed to do so by his own commanders? How would he find the time? What would be the benefit to the Mandate?

Wingate raised his hand: 'I have already discussed the matter with my superior and told him it is imperative that night patrols be organised to stop the arms smuggling. My superior has agreed that I will be responsible for organising your patrols and training your men in the art of night attacks. Your own units will be reinforced by a stiffening of British officers and men. I will select them myself.'

Itzhak Cohen spoke: 'I want to believe you. We all want to believe you, to be sure, but to select and train such a force will take time.'

Wingate told them about his training methods in Sudan, how raw Sudanese peasants had been transformed in a few weeks into a formidable fighting unit. He was confident that here, in Palestine, he would be dealing with men who already had a grasp of military tactics. Once he had shown them how to adapt to the special operations he had in mind, others could be selected from the settlements and trained. Each recruit would be chosen for his capacity to carry out dangerous missions and to keep them secret – even from his own family.

Chapter 3

Mounting Opposition

In the autumn of 1937, Chaim Weizmann and David Ben-Gurion travelled to Paris with members of Aliyah Bet. Weizmann had been assured by Edmond Rothschild that bank accounts would be opened in Paris, Brussels, Vienna and Berlin to obtain foreign passports and visas for immigrants. For Weizmann the documents had become increasingly urgent: 'Almost six million Jews are doomed to be pent up in places where they are not wanted and for whom the world is divided into places where they cannot live and places where they cannot freely enter.'

The immigration policies of the United States made hope of going there beyond the reach of most Jews; increasingly isolationism and growing anti-Semitism stalked the nation. The historian William Manchester observed: 'For the majority there were no foreign affairs at all. Hitler's talk that Lebensraum, living space, could only be acquired by military action was a word that many Americans could not easily pronounce.'

America slumbered on.

On 8 July 1938, on a hot summer's evening in Vienna, the largest synagogue in the city's Jewish quarter was packed to hear its rabbi report on his visit to the Conference of Refugees, which he had attended in Evian, France, to discuss the possibility of accepting emigrants. Jewish leaders from across Europe had spoken of the fears of their people. Finally, the heads of the foreign delegations had stepped up to the podium to announce their decision.

The United States' spokesman said his country would admit no more than 23,370 Jews from Germany and Austria in the coming year. Britain's delegate repeated a familiar argument that 'reluctantly we possess no territory suitable for the resettlement of large groups'.

Australia's delegate declared, 'As we have no real racial problems, we are not desirous of importing one.'

New Zealand concurred. Canada, Colombia, Uruguay and Venezuela agreed to accept only farmers. Nicaragua, Honduras, Costa Rica and Panama jointly announced they could not accept 'traders or intellectuals'.

Peru's spokesman devoted his minute on the podium to praising the United States for 'its caution and wisdom in strictly limiting the number of Jews'.

Only Denmark and Holland agreed to open their borders without qualification.

A few days after the synagogue meeting a prematurely bald man with protruding eyes arrived in Vienna's Jewish quarter. His name was Moshe Bar-Gilad and he had come in response to a call for help from the city's Jewish elders after the Evian conference. From all the ghettos of Europe, similar pleas came. Bar-Gilad had been assigned to handle the plight of Austrian Jews.

At his first meeting with Vienna's Jewish community, its leaders made no secret they had expected someone more worldly, not this slow-speaking farmer who had rented a room in a cheap hotel and answered their questions about what he would do, what he could achieve, with the polite request to be patient. He had his own question: could someone recommend a tailor where he could buy a new suit, nothing too expensive?

Three days later Bar-Gilad, dressed in a dark business suit, walked into Vienna's Prinz-Eugen-Strasse. Until three months ago the imposing mansion halfway along the tree-lined avenue had been the home of Leopold Rothschild, another member of the banking family. The Anschluss – Hitler's takeover of the country – had added over nine million Austrians to the Reich, as well as incorporating vast industrial and material resources.

Hanging over the mansion's entrance was a huge swastika and fixed to the door was a polished brass plate bearing the words: 'Central Bureau for Jewish Emigration'. When Bar-Gilad started to walk up the mansion's steps, an SS guard barred his way.

Bar-Gilad handed over a document. It was typed on the headed notepaper of the headquarters in Berlin of the Supreme Reich Agency that combined the SS and the Gestapo. It confirmed the bearer had a permit to travel around the Reich as the representative of the Union of Communal Settlements in Palestine for the sole purpose of arranging the departure from the Reich of Jews approved by the agency. The document bore the stamp of Reichsführer of the SS Heinrich Himmler.

The astonished sentry politely motioned Bar-Gilad to follow him into the building.

His arrival at the centre of where the fate of hundreds of thousands of Jews continued to be decided had been planned with meticulous care by the three members of Aliyah Bet in Paris, Yehudi Ragin, Ze'ev Shind and Zvi Yeheli. Each had taken turns to brief him, and warned that if he was not believed he risked almost certain death. He had calmly said that he was ready to do what they asked.

Bar-Gilad travelled to Berlin and walked into Gestapo headquarters, where he was thrown into a basement cell and brutally interrogated. He had stoically stuck to his story that he wanted to discuss a proposal of benefit to the Reich: allowing an unlimited number of Jews to go to Palestine would not only seriously disrupt the Mandate, but also provide Germany with a powerful propaganda victory, one that Dr Goebbels would know how to maximise.

For 24 hours Bar-Gilad had been closely questioned by a number of increasingly senior members of the Gestapo. How could he guarantee what he promised? What would it all cost? If his fellow Jews were allowed to leave, how would they get to Palestine? Supposing they remained in Europe, in Denmark and Holland, the two countries which had welcomed them at the Evian Conference? Where was the value to

Germany in having hordes of Jews promoting trouble close to the Reich borders? The questions had been endlessly repeated. Each time Bar-Gilad had answered in his slow, measured voice: only Jews willing to go to Palestine would be allowed to travel. Finally, he was given his document bearing Himmler's stamp and told to go to Vienna to discuss his plans with the Central Bureau for Jewish Emigration. Moshe Bar-Gilad had cleared the first hurdle in his extraordinary mission.

Standing in the entrance hall of the Rothschild mansion, its silk wallpaper hung with framed paintings the family had been ordered not to remove when they were evicted, he waited to meet Adolf Eichmann, the bureau's director.

Eichmann's office had once been Leopold Rothschild's library and contained hundreds of leather-bound books. A furled swastika on a stand was placed to one side of the desk behind which Eichmann sat in his immaculate SS uniform. At another desk sat a woman in SS uniform, a note taker.

It took two weeks to complete the arrangements. Two million Reich marks were transferred from the Rothschild Bank in Paris to the Reich Central Bank in Berlin. The money was described as a 'facility fee'. Farms confiscated by the bureau would become training camps for Jews to learn agricultural skills. Bar-Gilad had been given a letter signed by Eichmann, and a senior SS officer accompanied him to the concentration camps to select those he wanted. For Bar-Gilad, 'It was the most difficult part of my mission, refusing all the other prisoners' families and the elderly, who deserved to go. But the deal I had made with Eichmann did not allow them to be included. To break his terms would be the end of everything.'

Eichmann insisted that every Jew who went to the farms would have their spartan accommodation, food and farming equipment paid for by the Rothschild Fund, as well as covering the cost of the SS guards who would 'protect' the camps. Finally each exit visa would be a 'special one' and double the already hefty price charged.

Substantial further sums of money were transferred into the Reich Central Bank. Eichmann demanded a minimum of 400 Jews should be ready to sail to Palestine every week on ships that the Aliyah

Bet must provide. Shind led the search for boats around the Mediterranean ports.

News of the training camps had reached the Jewish communities across the Reich and applications to go there poured into the Zionist office in Vienna. Meanwhile, those selected by Bar-Gilad had to report to their local Gestapo headquarters three times a week to provide progress reports on their departure.

In August 1938, Bar-Gilad was summoned to Eichmann's office and told that the number of emigrants had to be increased to at least 1,000 a week, otherwise twice that number of Jews would be sent to the concentration camps.

Sacked from his hospital post, Dr Hermann Levi had found employment as an office cleaner, then as a gravedigger in a Christian cemetery. Both times he was dismissed because of his religion. Helena had found a job as a laundry delivery girl. One day the door to a house on her round had been answered by a former classmate. The girl shouted for her mother and said, 'There's a dirty Jew here.' Helena lost her job.

Shortly afterwards, her mother had contracted pneumonia and Dr Levi had gone to his old hospital to ask if they would admit her. The administrator refused. A former colleague had given Dr Levi medicine to treat his wife at home, in the room they now rented in the area of Hamburg designated by the city authorities for Jews. When Helena's mother died, she was buried in the Jewish cemetery near the synagogue where the family still worshipped. Dr Levi found another job, this time with the city's refuse-collecting department. Once more he was sacked after one of his former patients had informed the authorities. A new law forbade any public body to employ Jews.

All over the Grossdeutsche Reich, Greater Germany, Jews were facing increasing discrimination, humiliation and often violence. As Helena later recalled: 'A Jew had no rights. The average German didn't care: the more Jews they could drive out, the more of our assets they could take from us. Long ago our home had been sold and we were now living off anything we could sell.'

For weeks she and her father had searched for work, knocking on doors of houses in the wealthiest area of the city only to be turned away with a familiar refrain: 'We don't employ dirty Jews.'

One Sunday in the autumn of 1938, when they cycled into the countryside, they came across an old farmer struggling to replace a wheel on his hay cart. After they helped push the cart into the farmyard, he invited them to tea and by the end of the afternoon they learned he was a childless widower. Now in his late seventies, it was all he could do to manage his small herd of cows. He asked them no questions about themselves. Helena would remember how he finally stood up from his armchair by the fireplace and looked at them.

'He said he knew we were Jews but our religion did not concern him. All he wanted to know was could we work hard. My father then told him our story. When he had finished, the old man shook his head. "*Mein Gott,*" he said.'

He offered to employ Helena as a housekeeper and her father as his herdsman. They could live in the loft above the cowshed and in return they would have their meals and a small wage. That night, their belongings piled on the cart and pulled by the farmer's horse, Dr Levi and Helena left Hamburg.

On 9 November 1938, Kristallnacht exploded into Jacob Kronenberg's life with a crash as the roof of the nearby synagogue where he and his family had once worshipped collapsed. Christabel, his wife and Freddie still wore their crosses, but Jacob felt such a display of faith was too ostentatious.

He told them to remain indoors while he went to investigate. Firemen were hosing the adjoining buildings to protect them, but making no attempt to save the synagogue despite the pleas of the onlookers. Leather-coated Gestapo men armed with clubs were herding members of the congregation on to trucks. Those who protested were hit. An elderly rabbi emerged from the flames carrying a bundle of documents. An SS officer grabbed the documents and, when the old man protested, he was clubbed senseless. Jacob turned and ran, shocked by what he had seen, terrified of what it could mean for his family.

In Vienna, Moshe Bar-Gilad had gone to bed early in his rented room. The past weeks had left him exhausted from dealing with Eichmann's office and travelling across the Reich to organise the emigration. He was jerked from sleep by the sound of screams. From his window he saw a group of SS soldiers smashing the door of an apartment block. Minutes later they emerged into the street, dragging a man, a woman and a teenage girl. The soldiers were laughing as they pulled at the nightclothes of the women and began to sexually assault them. Finally all three were thrown on to a truck already half-filled with other Jews. In the distance the sky was reddening from another burning synagogue.

Throughout the Reich, the horror continued.

In all, more than 7,000 Jewish shops were plundered and then set on fire, and 267 synagogues were ransacked. Jewish graveyards were desecrated, including the one where Helena's mother was buried. Some 30,000 Jews were rounded up in Germany and 20,000 in Austria to be sent to concentration camps.

By dawn on 10 November, 171 Jewish apartment houses were still smouldering in Hamburg, Munich and Berlin after orders from the Gestapo to let them burn to the ground. At noon an order signed by Heinrich Müller, Gestapo Chief, Berlin Headquarters, announced that all those who looted Jewish shops were not to be prosecuted and were entitled to keep their spoils. During the night 36 Jews had been killed and 38 wounded for 'resisting arrest' across the Reich.

On 12 November, Reichsmarshall Hermann Goering announced that the Jewish population would have to pay a collective billion Reich marks for 'the damage done by the riots they are responsible for'.

In Room 17 in Tel Aviv Eliyahu Golomb sent an urgent coded message in Hebrew by radio to Aliyah Bet's Paris office that Bar-Gilad was to organise the immediate transport of all those in the Austrian training camps to the nearest port: 'Even if the boats are intercepted by British patrols once they reach Palestine waters and are brought into Haifa, they will only be held in detention camps far better than the Nazi concentration camps. Hitler intends to exterminate our race.'

On a spring day in 1939, Chaim Weizmann walked down Whitehall and turned into Downing Street, the narrow road he had come to call his Via Dolorosa, the street in Jerusalem along which Christ had finally made his way to his execution on Golgotha. Weizmann said he felt much the same sense of inevitability as he entered No. 10 to make one final plea to Prime Minister Chamberlain to help the Jews.

Weizmann intended to hand him a document that had been sent to him from the mayor of Leipzig, Carl Goerdeler, containing a detailed exposé of conditions of Jews in the concentration camps.

When Weizmann was shown into the Cabinet Room, Chamberlain was waiting with the head of the Civil Service, Sir Warren Fisher, who motioned him to sit opposite them at the long table. According to Weizmann, after he handed over Goerdeler's document to Fisher, 'The Prime Minister sat before me like a marble statue; his expressionless eyes were fixed on me and he never said a word.'

Five minutes after Weizmann had entered, Fisher rose and escorted him out of the room; Chamberlain had still not said a word. At the door of No. 10, Fisher shook hands with Weizmann and handed back Goerdeler's document, explaining that there was no chance of the Prime Minister ever reading it.

For Chaim Weizmann the shadow over the fate of the Jews in Europe was growing darker by the day.

While the number of Jewish emigrants had increased to some 34,000 a year, there were many thousands more still in Germany whose freedom Moshe Bar-Gilad could now buy, not only through Eichmann's bureau, but through the Gestapo Visa Office in Berlin.

The newly formed department was run by Angelo Metossiani, an Italian-born former policeman who was having an affair with a

Berlin Jewess. He told Bar-Gilad, 'In a "Greater Germany", my conscience is also affected by the anti-Jewish policy of our leader.'

Over dinner in a Berlin restaurant, Metossiani introduced a member of his staff, Stefan Karthaus, an Austrian, who said, 'If it is a matter of providing your Jews with visas we will gladly so do.'

It was an astonishing offer, not least because they asked for no money.

Since early morning on a fine June day in 1939, Bar-Gilad had stood on a platform at the Nordbahnhof, Vienna's railway station, watching tearful Jewish children whose families were trying to reassure them through their own tears.

David Ben-Gurion and Chaim Weizmann had successfully used their political skills to bring out children from Nazi Germany. It was the birth of what became known as the *Kindertransport*.

In London, Churchill had led the public campaign to help bring this about and his call had echoed in Washington, DC and European capitals. In Berlin, Foreign minister Joachim von Ribbentrop found himself daily lobbied by foreign diplomats. The turning point came when Magda Goebbels, the wife of propaganda minister Joseph Goebbels and mother of their six children, convinced her husband to persuade the Führer that letting the children go would show the 'caring side' of the Reich. Hitler finally agreed and 10,000 children would be allowed to travel to Britain.

On that June morning, the older boys wore their best suits and the younger ones were in shorts and sweaters; the girls wore dresses and knee-high socks and many held their favourite doll. Each child carried a small suitcase or a travel bag containing all the clothes and toiletries they were allowed to take, together with 20 Reich marks. Pinned to their clothes was one of the visas which had been signed by Karthaus and stamped over Metossiani's signature. Each document bore a bold red 'J'.

Bar-Gilad had collected the permits from Gestapo headquarters on Berlinerstrasse. Back in Vienna he had begun the difficult task of selecting the names of the children who would board the train waiting in the station. Goebbels had sent a film crew to record its departure and cameramen moved among the milling crowd, handing out candy bars to the children and urging the families to smile. As the platform clock drew closer to the departure hour, the children clung to their parents and the sound of the engine building up steam created further tension.

To Monika Levenson's embarrassment, 'My mother insisted on checking my new suitcase to make sure she had packed all my best clothes, because she had read that people in England liked foreigners to look tidy.'

Another mother held her daughter in her arms until an SS trooper standing guard at a carriage door grabbed the child and dumped her on board. The little girl burst into tears and an older one led her to a compartment. The mother screamed she wanted to say goodbye. The trooper pushed her back into the crowd.

Johann Goldman, 15 years old, would remember his moment of separation: 'My father kissed me, tears in his eyes, and kept saying how proud he was to have a son like me, and my mother clung to me and repeated she would love me more for every day until we met again. Then my elder brother, Henri, who was 24 and did not qualify to go, put his arms around me and said it was not too late for me to change my mind. One of the troopers separated us and shoved me on the train. Above the calls of "*Einsteigen,* all aboard", I heard my father shouting he would see me soon.'

Johann would never see his parents and brother again. It was years before he learned they had died in Auschwitz-Birkenau.

As the train pulled out of the station, Monika Levenson saw her mother trying to press her face against the compartment window, tears streaming from her eyes and mouthing, '*Ich liebe Dich,*' over and over. Monika was another child who would never see her mother again.

Most of the children were going to foster parents in Britain in Jewish homes, others went to children's homes and non-Jewish families. But for those waiting on the European side of the Channel for a ship to take them to America, it was often more difficult. Long-settled Jewish families in Holland and France were fearful of what could happen to them as they saw the spread of *Judenrein*, ethnic cleansing. They became increasingly concerned for their own futures and they did not find it easy to absorb children from the *Kindertransport* into their families.

Johann Goldman had a visa allowing him to enter the United States. Ever since he had seen photographs of the Empire State Building, he had dreamed of little else except going to New York. A few months earlier a distant relative of his mother had agreed to take him. She lived in a suburb of Brooklyn called Brownsville. He had found nothing in his school atlas about Brownsville, but Brooklyn was a name that conjured up for the romantic-minded boy images he had seen only on the cinema screen: its famous bridge, the Dodgers' stadium, the huge billboards lining the streets, the latest cars, the palace-like movie theatres. All this had made the separation from his family a little easier to bear, along with his father's parting words on the platform that they would all meet in 'beautiful Brooklyn'. For Johann it was a reunion he eagerly anticipated.

Chapter 4

War on All Fronts

Nat Nadler prepared for another day as an electrician in Brownsville. He had graduated from Brooklyn's High School as a fully fledged electrician, the first in his family to achieve any kind of certificate since his parents had emigrated in 1923 from Germany, driven to do so by the increasing political and financial instability of the country. Many of the immigrants who had held good positions in Europe – teachers, lawyers, nurses and doctors – found work hard to get once they passed the scrutiny of New York's immigration officers. Their lack of English drove them to take jobs as draymen, hod carriers and laundrywomen.

Nat's father spoke four languages, but he could find employment only as a waiter for a dollar a week and whatever leftovers the cook let the staff take home, which otherwise would be thrown into the bins that other migrants scavenged through.

Many migrants learned their English from the comics which chronicled the adventures of Dick Tracy and Secret Agent X-9, and spent a dime to go to the Saturday morning movies to see an appealing young actor, James Cagney, pay homage to the FBI. Brownsville children, like kids across America, collected Quaker Oats box tops for G-Men badges.

Nat had one of the badges stuck inside his toolbox, as many young tradesmen did. He had become a sought-after electrician, not only for his skills and speed in wiring a fuse box, but because he did it for as little as he needed to charge. He had seen what the Depression had done to his parents and neighbours. Wedding rings would be sold, furniture pawned, life insurances cashed in. Increasingly a husband would sell vegetables on the pavement outside his home; a wife would offer a wash, set and manicure in her kitchen for a few cents. Newspapers were full of reports of unemployed textile workers setting up looms in their living rooms. A doctor placed an advert in a local newspaper saying that 'any woman expecting a stork to visit your home must have cash ready to pay before delivery'.

Nat's family slowly became aware of the fate of their loved ones when their rabbi read out letters at the synagogue received from Jewish organisations in Europe. He also urged the congregation to listen to the radio networks, which had started to transmit Hitler's broadcasts, each ending with the warning that Germany was ready to 'defend itself against the global Jewish threat'.

Hitler frequently identified President Roosevelt as one of the architects of this threat. For many American Jews, the world had suddenly shrunk as the sound of hatred coming from Germany filled their living rooms.

Leon Goldberg, who had lived in the shadow of Grunewald Stadium, would no longer be able to hear the thunderous chants of '*Heil Hitler! Sieg heil!*' On a sunny afternoon in early August, he had sent Else, his wife, and Miriam, their daughter, to a relative living near the border with France, promising he would join them once he had sold off the last of their house furnishings. Among the belongings Else packed was her *cholent* pot; she was hopeful in the countryside there would be fresh vegetables and meat to fill it once more. Two days later Leon was arrested in a round-up by SS storm troopers and sent to Dachau. He would die there.

After Kristallnacht, Jacob Kronenberg finally wore the cross his neighbour had given him as well as a swastika badge on his lapel, which all his Catholic work colleagues displayed. On the bus to work Jacob made a show of reading the Party morning newspaper, which carried the usual approving reports of Hitler's latest speech. Jacob had asked his wife, Christabel, to avoid shopping in the few Jewish shops that remained open and, like him, to avoid going near the burnt-out synagogue that stood like a stark reminder of Kristallnacht. Freddie, their son, was growing into a strong healthy child and had been enrolled into the Hitler Youth Movement.

In the countryside outside Hamburg, Dr Hermann Levi and his daughter, Helena, had settled into their life on the farm. They never read the newspapers or listened to the wireless – except for the occasional concert. They were tanned from their outdoor life and well fed from the meals Helena cooked for her father and the old farmer. The farmhouse was spotless under her care and she had come to regard the old man as her *Opa* (grandfather). Nevertheless, the reality of approaching war regularly passed the farm, as military convoys headed for Hamburg and Luftwaffe aircraft flew overhead.

To the north of Hamburg, on an isolated stretch of the Baltic coast near Usedom, Werner von Braun, dressed in the immaculate black uniform and boots of an SS Untersturmbannführer, led Heinrich Himmler and a small group of his senior officers on a tour of Peenemünde's laboratories and workshops, where over a hundred scientists and engineers worked. Here, von Braun was in charge of Germany's secret guided-missile programme.

Himmler said that if von Braun needed more space, it could be arranged. When von Braun replied that he would like a site buried underground, Himmler said that would not be a problem as 'our concentration camps are full of strong young Jews'.

From the dockside of Yugoslavia's dilapidated port at Kator, Moshe Bar-Gilad watched the last of the 427 young Jews he had brought out of the training camps in Austria filing through the control point the harbour police had set up to inspect their Mexican visas.

On his last visit to Berlin, Bar-Gilad had obtained several hundred more visas from his two Gestapo contacts allowing entry into a number of South American countries. But they warned him the supply must end. After Kristallnacht, Reinhard Heydrich, Deputy Fürher of the SS, claimed that, in the ransacking of synagogues, documents had been found revealing 'a Jewish plot to overthrow the government'. The SS had begun a huge round-up to take Jews to concentration camps.

As the last of the young Jews cleared the final security check, Bar-Gilad relaxed. Officially their ship, *Colombo*, was destined for Puerto Judrez in Mexico's Yucatan area. The voyage was estimated to take 20 days. Only Bar-Gilad knew its real destination was a sandy beach in Palestine.

On 19 August 1939, Chaim and Vera Weizmann were driving across France, on their way to Geneva to attend the 21st Zionist Conference, over which Weizmann was to preside. That morning the wireless announced Moscow had broken off talks with delegations from Paris and London seeking non-aggression pacts.

By the time they reached Geneva, his sense of foreboding increased as he took his place on the platform in the Geneva Theatre. Beside him sat David Ben-Gurion, a brooding figure constantly checking his speech. Backstage there had been tension between them when Weizmann suggested that the conference should be shortened, given the prevailing threat of war.

Ben-Gurion objected. When he stepped up to the podium his deep growl echoed around the auditorium: 'Arab murder and savagery has gone on for three years and there is no sign of an end. The Yishuv is confused and feels now more helpless, more despairing. The murder and atrocities we witness so often are not simply the doings of bandits, rioters or robbers. It is political terrorism, with a definite aim with widespread political Arab support.'

Only at the end did his 90-minute speech deal with Hitler: 'He may occupy Austria by brute force, destroy Jews and threaten France. We are a small people with no army, no state, no power to compete. We cannot over-awe the world. Our strength lies in one great asset: the moral purity of our lives and works, our aspirations and our philosophy.'

He was given a standing ovation. Ben-Gurion had caught the mood of the audience.

To Weizmann it seemed they 'were escaping from the realities. In the coming world struggle, we stand committed more than any other people to the defence of democracy.'

That evening Weizmann walked, tears in his eyes, among the delegates to say he hoped they would meet again next year in Jerusalem. He spent extra time with the Polish delegation, embracing each member and murmuring the prayer, 'God grant that your fate be not that of the Jews in your neighbouring land.'

The Polish delegates were among the three million of their countrymen who would perish in the concentration camps and the gas chambers.

On the morning of 24 August 1939, Orde Wingate stood on a rocky outcrop on the side of Mount Carmel, watching through his powerful binoculars the Royal Navy destroyer HMS *Ivanhoe* escorting *Colombo* towards the port of Haifa. The rusty-hulled steamer had been intercepted during the night as it steamed slowly towards Palestine waters southwest of the Carmel lighthouse. Moshe Bar-Gilad's hope to bring his pioneers from Austria had failed.

Wingate had been recalled to Mandate headquarters to train more commandos to deal with the increasing Arab violence: rail derailments, bank robberies, telegraph sabotage, murderous hold-ups of Jews on the roads and even more frequent killings of Arabs who worked for the Mandate. His lectures to the new recruits were wide-ranging and each talk offered revealing glimpses of his own character: 'Great soldiers are serious and diligent', 'a coarse and savage man makes a very bad soldier', 'learn discipline and calmness from the professional soldier, but don't imitate his brutality, stupidity and drunkenness'. His lecture on 'Soldiers' Commandments' concluded with Oliver Cromwell's exhortation to his men: 'Know what you fight for and love what you know.'

Standing beside Wingate was a young Jewish commando who had become one of Wingate's most trusted strategists. Yossi Harel had been born Yossef Hamburger, the son of a grocer in the Old City of Jerusalem and a hauntingly beautiful but tragically mentally disturbed mother. How much her illness had played its part in his decision to leave home at 14 he kept to himself.

Yossi's language skills – English, French and Arabic – had been developed in his teens while studying after working long hours in a quarry to boost the family income. His physical strength was matched by his moral code and lively intelligence, and when he was only 15 he had been invited to join the Haganah, which needed young people who could spy on the British Army without raising suspicion. When his father, sister and twin brother moved from Jerusalem to run a café by the Dead Sea, Yossi remained behind. His mother, whom he loved dearly, was increasingly caught up in her own illness and Yossi did not know how best to deal with her. He stayed away from home and made the Haganah a substitute for his family. After work he trained with them and debated ideology, and he regularly climbed Mount Scopus to improve his physique and fitness.

He tested himself spiritually as well, once walking alone with only a bottle of water across the parched landscape to Masada. There, 2,000 years earlier, his ancestors had taken their own lives rather than surrender to the Roman legions surrounding them. Their heroic story was never far from Yossi's mind as he grew up under the Mandate occupation.

It was a time when Palestine was filled with funeral processions, victims of Arab attacks. Yossi had lost count of the times he had helped carry the blood-soaked shrouds to a grave. New immigrants had barely set foot on *Eretz Yisrael* before they were buried in graves often inscribed with 'Unknown' or 'Anonymous'. Yossi knew the Haganah needed help. That help came on a Sabbath evening when a man in a rumpled suit drove into the settlement in Hanita, where Yossi had a room to sleep. All around him were the youths and men of the Haganah.

As Yossi recalled to his biographer, Yoram Kaniuk: 'The man, slumped a bit in his appearance, evoked the image of an ascetic priest. His blue eyes, thinness and gait gave him an aura of mystery. In one hand was a Bible, with an attached note from Chaim

Weizmann and Ben-Gurion that introduced him as Captain Wingate, a great friend.'

In Wingate Yossi had found a mentor. The two men became firm friends, mutually attracted by a common reticence, a deep sense of responsibility and an abiding integrity.

They fought side by side in endless battles against often superior Arab forces. Afterwards they would sit together, Yossi listening while Wingate planned the next attack.

On that baking August day, he was a wiry, deeply tanned youth who looked older than his years. When he joined Wingate's commandos, he showed his skills as an interpreter. Wingate had a reputation for being impatient with translators and several had been fired after a tongue-lashing. Wingate had cast around for someone who could keep up with his growled commands; though he spoke good Hebrew and Arabic, he insisted on speaking only English when issuing orders. Yossi performed admirably.

Walking back down Mount Carmel, Wingate had given one of his dry chuckles: 'As long as you remember there is a time and a place for everything, anything is possible if God wants that of you. Moses knew that.'

Yossi was now 22 years old and would play a vital role in the ensuing story of *Exodus*.

On the balmy evening of 1 September 1939, her engine pistons drove *President Warfield*'s propeller shaft at a hundred revolutions a minute on her voyage from Baltimore to Norfolk. In a month's time the hurricane season would arrive in the Caribbean and once more Captain Foster's hard-won knowledge would be critical.

On 4 September 1939, a different threat faced everyone on board after the radioman emerged from his shack at the back of the bridge and handed Captain Foster a message. Having read it, he went down to the dining room, walked on to the podium where the ship's orchestra was playing and motioned them to stop. In the sudden silence he announced, 'Ladies and gentlemen. I have received a copy of the wire service message confirming England has declared war on Germany.'

Captain Foster stilled the gasps and asked the passengers to stand and sing the National Anthem.

At 300 miles an hour, the rising sun behind him, Wolfram Freiherr von Richthofen, scion of the distinguished Prussian family, swept across the Polish border in his fighter plane. Below, rumbling out of Silesia and Germany, were the tanks and troop carriers of the Wehrmacht. Von Richthofen had been chosen by Hermann Goering to lead the first air attack of the Second World War, flying the Messerschmitt BF-10 he had piloted in the Spanish Civil War when his Condor Legion had destroyed the historic Basque capital of Guernica on 27 April 1937.

His Messerschmitt led similar air attacks on towns and villages inside the Polish border. The highly mobile panzers' thrusts and the howling Stuka dive-bombers worked together with the infantry as they launched a succession of pincer movements through and around the Polish defences. In all there were 52 German divisions, a total of one and a half million well-trained soldiers against a Polish army a third of that size.

By dusk, the Polish air force had ceased to exist. On 3 September, Britain and France honoured their guarantee to protect Poland and declared war on Germany. In London, Winston Churchill accepted Chamberlain's offer of a post in the government as First Sea Lord. It was the same appointment he had held at the outbreak of the First World War in 1914. From the Admiralty a signal was flashed to all Royal Navy ships and land installations: 'Winston is back.'

Nat Nadler's family in Brownsville, like Jewish families everywhere, stayed glued to their radios, listening to the short-wave transmissions from Warsaw, repeating every 30 seconds the 11 stirring notes of the opening of a Chopin polonaise, the signal that although the rest of Poland was being overrun, the country's capital was still free.

On 4 September, a sunny morning with the sea lapping below him, Johann Goldman stood on top of a dyke, part of a network of defences holding back the North Sea to prevent the fishing port of Den Helder being flooded at high tide. All around him stood fishermen, farmers and their wives, members of a close-knit community on the edge of the Waddensee north of Amsterdam. Like him, they too had paused to stare at the sight in the sky. Beside stood his aunt, Sara-Marta, his mother's widowed sister.

A tall, grey-haired woman in a severe dress and a bonnet, Sara-Marta had met Johann off the train when it arrived from Vienna at Amsterdam railway station. She explained that there was no ship yet to take him to America, but once a week they would go to the Jewish Agency Office in the city to enquire when a berth would be available. In the meantime, he would live with her. Every Monday they made the journey, only to be told to return the following week. Finally, one of the agency workers said there would be no more sailings. Johann had held back his tears and suggested he should return to Vienna to his parents. The worker had gently explained that was not possible. No Jews were being readmitted to Austria.

The following day they had gone back to Amsterdam, this time to the Jodenbuurt, the Jewish quarter close to the city centre, where a friend of Sara-Marta lived. Hannah Cohen was another widow with one son, Jacob. The boy was a year older than Johann and the two teenagers struck up an immediate friendship as Jacob set off to show him the city. Johann, a child from Vienna, had never really taken to the small-town life of Den Helder. Here in the streets of Amsterdam he found all he wanted. Johann became a regular visitor to Amsterdam.

He had just returned from the city on that September morning when he stood with his aunt on the dyke counting the specks in the sky. There were 29. Earlier, the radio in Sara-Marta's kitchen had reported that the Royal Air Force had landed fighter squadrons behind the French port of Calais and advance units of the British Expeditionary Force had come ashore at Ostend to stop any German incursion. Johann decided the specks were too large for fighters and there was agreement among the older men that they had never seen such a sight as the formation, spread over several miles of sky. They concluded that such an impressive display of power meant the war would soon be over and life could return to normal. When that happened, Sara-Marta reminded Johann, he would be able to join his family in Brownsville.

Next day in Washington, DC, President Roosevelt declared that the United States would remain neutral. For many Americans, the fact that he felt it necessary to do so increased awareness that war could still cross the Atlantic. New York's Transportation Board announced that subways would make perfect bomb shelters and Standard Oil said it would replace any German sailors on its tankers with American-born seamen. A manufacturer changed the name of its best-selling range, Dictator Carpets, to Liberty Carpets. The nation's armchair strategists stuck pins with coloured heads into large maps of Europe: black pins for Germany, blue for Britain and red for France. So great was the demand for pins that stores ran out. Grocers found customers were ordering sugar in 100-pound sacks, canned meat by the case and flour in 50-pound bags in the event war brought food shortages. There were none, and never would be, in the United States.

At sea, the battle of the Atlantic was starting. U-boat 39 was sunk by Royal Navy destroyers, the first German naval loss of the war. Next day the Royal Navy's aircraft carrier *Courageous* was torpedoed in the western approach off the southwest coast of Ireland while on anti-submarine patrol. Over 500 men drowned. It was the first Royal Navy ship lost in battle.

On 19 September 1939, Hitler told Britain and France that peace would be declared if Germany's territorial gain was accepted. The two allies refused. In a joint statement both governments said, 'We will not permit a Nazi victory to condemn the world to slavery and to end all moral values and destroy liberty.'

Three days later, Hitler travelled to the front line to watch the final destruction of Warsaw as wave after wave of Luftwaffe bombers attacked the now defenceless city. On 27 September, Warsaw finally surrendered. More than 140,000 Polish troops laid down their arms. The notes of the Chopin polonaise stopped as Warsaw radio fell silent.

The BBC began to use as a prelude to all its programmes beamed into Europe the dots and dash of the Morse code symbol for V, for victory. In unoccupied countries the sound was used for knocks on doors, blown on train whistles and honked on car horns. People waved to each other with two stretched fingers in the V sign; in cafés cutlery was arranged in the symbol. Goebbels announced it stood for *Viktoria*, the complete triumph of Hitler.

Days before the outbreak of war, Chaim and Vera Weizmann arrived back in London from Geneva. Uppermost in his thoughts was the fate of Jews waiting in Mediterranean ports with visas that would almost certainly now be useless to gain them entry into the United States and other countries. Meanwhile, Jews in Bohemia, Moldovia, Slovakia and Romania were being rounded up in their thousands, victims of the swiftest and most brutal operation in modern times. In Poland extra trains were needed to carry Jews to the concentration camps.

The Chamberlain government continued to deny entry to Palestine. Weizmann noted: 'Turned back by Royal Navy patrols, the boats are unable to discharge their cargoes and returned into the hands of the advancing Nazis. A Hitler victory will mean the obliteration of the Jewish people. Yet there are no people more frantically eager to contribute to the common cause against Nazism than the Jews.'

Already his sons, Michael and Benjamin, had enlisted. Michael had joined the RAF to train as a fighter pilot; his brother was an anti-aircraft gunner on the south coast.

A few days after he arrived in London, Weizmann received a telephone call from Winston Churchill's secretary, asking him to come to lunch the following day. He asked who else would be there, as he always liked to know in advance whom he would meet. There was a moment's pause before the reply. There would be another guest, Stewart Menzies. Replacing the telephone, Weizmann slowly exhaled and turned to Vera, saying, 'Now that *is* a surprise.'

Stewart Menzies was the new head of MI6, Britain's Secret

Intelligence Service. Shortly after noon, Weizmann walked past the sandbagged entrance into the Admiralty, where Churchill's secretary escorted him upstairs. His host was standing before a coal fire in his private dining room and Menzies was already with him. A naval officer tended a bar and in the centre of the room the table was already laid with silver reputed to have come from Lord Nelson's *Victory*.

Sipping his whisky, Churchill was full of optimism about the war, having greeted Weizmann with the words, 'We'll have the better of Hitler. Then the Jews will live in peace again.'

Weizmann pointed out Chamberlain's Colonial Secretary, Malcolm MacDonald, long an opponent of immigration to Palestine, had refused visas for 25,000 Jewish children in Poland to enter the country because it would 'offend the Arabs'.

Weizmann asked Churchill what would happen in Palestine after the war was over. 'My host had sipped his drink before asking: what did I wish to happen? I said that Zionists would have a state of some three or four million Jews in Palestine. Churchill puffed steadily on his cigar. "Yes. Yes, I quite agree with that."'

Menzies told Weizmann there was a way he could help make that happen. Chaim Weizmann was about to be enrolled into the dark world of intelligence gathering.

Until this book, the only clue to his role would be a small paragraph buried in the depth of his autobiography: 'About a month after the declaration of war, I went on a special mission to Switzerland to try and find what substance there was in the rumours that the Germans had prepared new methods of chemical warfare.'

Else and Miriam Goldberg had been sent by Leon to safety in the small town of Pirmasens, on the border between France and Germany. Else had written several times to her husband, but there had been no reply. Meanwhile, she wondered whether she and her daughter should cross over into France, where they might be safer. French broadcasts reported that more RAF planes and British soldiers had landed along the Channel coast to defend the country against German attack. Else thought that with Britain's help Hitler would not attack France and decided to remain in Pirmasens.

One morning when she came out of a grocery store with Miriam, she saw that both ends of the street were blocked with army trucks and that SS troopers, accompanied by Gestapo officers, were conducting a round-up. People whose papers were not in order were put on the trucks. When a trooper saw the name Goldberg on Else's document, he called to a Gestapo agent that two more Jews had been located.

That night Else and Miriam arrived at a *Frauenlager*, a detention camp for women and children on windswept Lüneburg Heath between the small towns of Bergen and Belsen. Soon the *Frauenlager* would become part of the concentration camp network.

Dr Levi and Helena, helped by the old farmer, were taking hay for winter storage from the horse-drawn cart when an army truck entered the yard. At its wheel was an army veterinarian and beside him sat a Gestapo officer. The vet emerged and explained he had come to examine the animal to assess its suitability for military service. The old farmer protested that without his horse he could not run the farm. The vet began his examination, listening to the horse's heart and checking its hooves, while the Gestapo officer turned to Dr Levi and Helena and said they did not look like farm workers and demanded to see their papers. He studied them carefully and then looked at Dr Levi: '*Sie sind Juden.*'

That evening Dr Levi and Helena were put on separate trains of cattle trucks. Helena's train was destined for the *Frauenlager* on Lüneburg Heath. Dr Levi's train would end up in Neuengamme, a concentration camp. All the trucks carried a notice: 40 persons or eight horses.

On 14 October 1939, Werner von Braun accompanied Albert Speer, minister of supplies, and a small team of engineers to the Harz Mountains in central Germany. At the entrance to a cave there, the group changed into protective overalls, donned miners' helmets and made their way below ground past rock faces icy cold to the touch and oozing putrid water. Von Braun regularly paused to give orders. *Here we will have a research laboratory. Over there we will have a rocket fuel store. Here we will need a ramp. Powerful ventilators. A rail system.* Notes were made and photographs taken.

Speer smiled with satisfaction. He had found the young scientist his underground facility needed to manufacture the weapons von Braun had promised would satisfy Hitler's rocket fever.

When Chaim Weizmann arrived in Basel, Switzerland, the hills behind the town had already received their first dusting of winter snow, softening the huge complex of the world headquarters of the Sandoz Drug and Chemical Corporation.

Over the years he had built up a network of scientists who kept him abreast of advances in chemical weapons. One was the director of research at Sandoz. Over dinner, he told Weizmann that a new chemical factory was being built at Dyhernfurth in the forests of Silesia in western Poland. It would be one of the largest and most secret plants in the Third Reich; a mile and a half long and half a mile wide, it was intended to produce 3,000 tons of tabun nerve gas every month. It would not just manufacture the gas, but would fill tens of thousands of bomb casings and artillery shells with the agent. Another 20 factories were planned to be built in the next three years which, between them, would produce a further 12,000 tons of poison gas every month. These would include two types of mustard gas – Sommer-10 and Winter-Lost – and a terrifying incendiary gas which would be produced exclusively for the SS and cause clothes and hair to burst into flames. All the gases would be tested on concentration camp prisoners.

Upon Weizmann's return to London Churchill arranged for him to be appointed honorary chemical adviser to the Ministry of Supply. Weizmann gathered a small group of chemists and between them they set to work devising the aromatisation of heavy oil into high-octane fuels for fighter planes. The research was slow and dangerous – and hampered by Weizmann's efforts to go into mass production:

'We ran up against vested interests in the chemical field, which were strongly opposed to the entry of outsiders.'

For Chaim Weizmann, it was a salutary reminder of how matters were conducted even during war in the upper echelons of industry.

Early in December 1939, Johann had once more returned to Amsterdam, this time to see the Christmas lights with Jacob. They wandered past the window displays and the potted fir trees with their lights. But the mood was sombre with talk of war: how long before the Nazis swept into the country?

That evening, instead of going home, Jacob had brought Johann to an office building overlooking Wertheim Park in the Jewish quarter. The building was in darkness, but standing in the doorway was a man. He recognised Jacob and inspected Johann's now useless visa to go to America before allowing him to pass. In a crowded back room, the air was hazy with tobacco smoke, and Jacob explained the people here were labourers from the city's shipyards and factories. In their work clothes, tool bags at their feet, they looked formidable. On the platform an older man was explaining they were there to form patrols to defend Jewish shops and their quarter's synagogues against the Dutch Nazi Party, the NSB. All those who were prepared to do this should raise a hand. Johann and Jacob were among the first to do so.

They had become members of *knokploeg*, the first of the resistance groups in the city.

Chapter 5

Action Stations

Thousands of Poles had continued to flee from Warsaw after the Luftwaffe air attacks had destroyed their homes and businesses. A pall of smoke still hung over the once beautiful city, where the bodies of men, women and children now lay buried beneath the ruins and the stench of death was carried on the swirling snowflakes that enveloped the refugees, covering their wagons, carts and barrows and the frozen carcasses of dead animals, their stomachs burst open by putrefaction.

Wedged among the retreating multitude was a magnificent motor car, the only Cadillac in Poland. The repeated hooting of the klaxon horn and the purr of its powerful engine marked its progress. Not even the dirt caking its huge headlamps or the snowflakes dissolving on its long bonnet could hide the limousine's majestic appearance.

The custom-built vehicle had been made for Jacob Stolowitzky, the wealthiest Jewish industrialist in the country. His fortune was founded on supplying metal and wood for all the train rails and sleepers in Poland and Russia. It had brought him a palace for a home, a beautiful wife, Lydia, and a son, Michael, a happy and contented child being raised in the security only wealth can bring. Attending to his every need was Gertruda, his nanny. She was a tall, statuesque, 30-year-old blonde with a winning smile and a quiet determination to succeed in all she did. A devout Catholic, Gertruda came from a poor family in Danzig where every zloty was counted and a portion of income was given to the Catholic Church at its weekly collection.

From early on, Gertruda and Lydia were united by a shared love for Michael. Lydia's hauntingly beautiful face would light up with a smile each time she watched Gertruda bathe and feed her son, and more than once she had said what a wonderful mother Gertruda would make. For the nanny no praise could be higher. When Jacob was away on his trips to Europe, the two women would sit and talk about their religions and their very different upbringings which had brought them together. The barrier between mistress and servant had never arisen; there was respect on both sides.

Shortly before war started Jacob had gone to Paris to settle yet another deal. When news came that Warsaw was under attack, he mobilised his contacts and offered payment of 10 million zlotys to have his family brought out of the country. But the offer never reached the man who could have authorised the deal, Adolf Eichmann.

Jacob's attempts to contact Lydia had failed because the telephone lines between Paris and Warsaw had been cut when a German bomb struck the main Warsaw telephone exchange. With no news from her husband, Lydia decided to travel with Michael and Gertruda to Vilnius, the Lithuanian capital, where the family had friends among the Jewish community who would shelter them. They left Warsaw at dusk in the Cadillac, and for two days the chauffeur had brought them past the carnage of war and around the bomb craters on the road before they finally reached the border crossing. It was unmanned. They did not know Lithuania's government was in discussion to join the Soviet Union.

Under a sunset which turned the Egyptian desert beyond the Suez Canal a glowing reddish-gold, Yossi Harel sat beside a British Army truck of the 32nd Airborne Division at Abu Sueir in the Canal Zone. Parked nearby were some of the RAF transport planes he knew he would never be trained to fly. Full of hope, he had joined the queues of young Jews at the Mandate recruiting office in Haifa the day after war broke out. He had been told that his Palestinian passport precluded him from joining the RAF as a pilot, but he would be enlisted as a truck driver in the British Army. Two days later he was flown to Egypt and had spent his time driving out into the desert to pick up paratroopers after their practice jumps.

The day before Yossi left Palestine, he had found time to say farewell to Orde Wingate, who had been recalled to England. As they parted, Wingate, in an unusual sign of affection, had embraced Yossi and reminded him they were both 'instruments of fate. All you must do is to remember all you have learned from our conversations and one day your dreams will come true.'

Those words had lodged in young Harel's mind, exciting his imagination of what it would be like to be standing on the bridge of a ship and giving orders, his childhood dream.

One night in December 1939, Jacob Kronenberg crashed his car on the way home in Nuremberg. He was cut free from the wreckage and rushed to hospital. It may have been while being prepared for emergency surgery that someone – perhaps a nurse or a doctor – noticed he was circumcised. The hospital security officer was called. His decision was absolute.

A Jew. You do not need to save a Jew.

Within an hour a police car had collected Christabel and Freddie Kronenberg and brought them to Nuremberg's central police station. It was the start of the journey that would see Freddie become the gatekeeper at Auschwitz, saved by a whim of Dr Mengele. Christabel died in Auschwitz. The fate of Jacob Kronenberg would remain unresolved.

During a March night in 1940, Johann Goldman and Jacob Cohen stood on a corner of one of the streets leading into Amsterdam's Jewish quarter, watching a Talmudic scholar in his black robe and side curls under his black hat disappear into a building.

Further up the street were members of *knokploegen*, dockers and factory labourers, smelling of cigar smoke and coal dust, faces hidden by their black hoods. Johann knew each was carrying an iron bar and a length of chain and wore handmade knuckledusters. Among them were a couple of muscular students from the city's technical college who had enrolled in the *knokploegen* to fight the Dutch Nazis, the NSB.

But with every success, the attacks by the NSB on Jewish shops and buildings in Amsterdam increased. While Jewish community leaders urged their people to show restraint, the Nazis continued their attacks. That night Johann and Jacob were among those called to a meeting of the *knokploegen* and had been assigned the role of lookouts for the attack on an NSB gathering.

For the past hour they had watched thugs go into a house at the corner of the street. When the last man went into the building, Johann flashed a signal with his torch.

A factory worker smashed open the door with a sledgehammer. From inside the house came startled shouts and the crunch of iron and steel on bone. In minutes it was all over. The battle group was out of the building, leaving behind them seriously injured NSB members. One would die in hospital within days.

Two months later, on 10 May 1940, Germany invaded the Low Countries: Holland, Belgium and Luxembourg. That day in London, Neville Chamberlain resigned and Winston Churchill became Britain's new prime minister. For four days Holland held out against the blitzkrieg. Six days later, it fell, and over the following weekend the British Army began to conduct its heroic evacuation from the beaches of Dunkirk. On 22 June, France surrendered and a new fascist government was established in the city of Vichy. Soon Amsterdam, like all the towns and cities of the Low Countries, was filled with the tramp of jackboots and the sound of German trucks stopping outside houses to arrest Jews.

Moshe Bar-Gilad was waiting in a café on the waterfront of the small port of Sulina at the mouth of the Danube in Romania. Waiting was something to which he had become used. Only his face showed that stress was taking its toll, flecking his hair with grey and introducing lines around his eyes and mouth. It would surely be just a matter of time, he had told himself, before he was caught by the Nazis. So many of his colleagues in the Aliyah Bet had suffered that fate. But until that happened, Moshe Bar-Gilad had a mission to fulfil.

It had preoccupied him ever since he had come over the border from the safety of Switzerland into the increasingly dangerous Italy of Benito Mussolini. In March, the Duce had met Hitler in the Brenner Pass to settle the date for Italy's entry into the war. Already the persecution of Italian Jews had intensified. Thousands had been rounded up and those who had avoided arrest had gratefully accepted Switzerland's offer of sanctuary.

From Milan, Bar-Gilad had made his way to Trieste, where he had hoped to find one of the few remaining ships he had bought for Aliyah Bet. But *Hilda* was no longer in the harbour and no one seemed to know where she had gone. The ship's passengers, among the first for whom he had obtained exit permits from Austria, were not traceable either. Sensing that further probing might arouse the interest of the port authorities, he had moved on to Sulina, where he hoped the other ship, *Maria*, on which Aliyah Bet had paid a substantial deposit, would still be. It had taken him a week to reach the harbour, after a journey across Yugoslavia, dogged by bad news. Germany had invaded Denmark and Norway. Finland had finally fallen to the Russians. All around Europe frontiers were fast closing.

At the far end of the harbour was *Maria*. For Bar-Gilad: 'There was still £10,000 left to pay before the owner would release the boat and I was in a predicament; the total sum of money I had was 87 US dollars.' More worryingly, his enquiries revealed there were no Jews in Sulina, let alone the 700 young pioneers from training camps in Austria he had arranged would sail on *Maria*.

Standing on the dockside was a man in a hat and belted trench coat. Bar-Gilad had seen other men dressed like that: Gestapo officers. Was he one of them – or perhaps from a Romanian security organisation?

The man was neither. He was an MI6 officer, one of a number of agents of the Secret Intelligence Service based around the Mediterranean coast to disrupt Germany's war effort. The officer made a proposition. He would pay the balance to buy *Maria*, locate the refugees and provide them with genuine travel documents to Palestine, where the Mandate would admit them. Afterwards, *Maria* would be brought back to Sulina and sunk in the mouth of the Danube to block all German sea traffic using the river.

He had left Bar-Gilad to ponder the startling offer. For two long hours Bar-Gilad had sat in the café deliberating what to do. Was this a trap? A cruel plan to exploit the fate of the Jews by having him round them up on to the boat, only for them to be arrested and shipped off to a concentration camp? The officer had returned – this time with one of the Jews. He and Bar-Gilad had spoken in Hebrew and the refugee explained that the other pioneers had been hiding in the countryside around Sulina. The officer told Bar-Gilad the ship had been paid for and a crew would arrive at nightfall, when the emigrants would set sail for Palestine.

Three days later, the *Maria* arrived in Haifa.

Over a number of days the Old Bay Line on Baltimore's Pier 10 had been transformed. Gigantic cardboard cutouts of the company's paddle steamers hung from the fronts of buildings. Enlargements of newspaper stories recalled the history of the line's fleet, flags adorned shop fronts and portraits of the company's past presidents hung from office windows. At the centre of the celebrations, *President Warfield* proudly flew the line's pennant, a red flag with a white 'B'. A procession of ancient victorias, broughams and horse-drawn cars clattered along the pier, bringing the official party – the state governor, the mayor of Baltimore and the city managers of towns along the Chesapeake. A red carpet had been laid for the invited guests to board the ship. By noon on 23 May 1940, everything was ready to mark the centenary of the line.

At 6.30 in the evening, as she had done every departure day, *President Warfield* set off down the Chesapeake. On board in the smoking room a fountain bubbled with champagne cocktails and the ship's band played a reprise of melodies. Dinner included terrapin and pheasant and toasts were made with 1870 Madeira and the finest wines.

Among the passengers was David Brierly. The genial Royal Navy captain's invitation to join the celebration had been arranged by the Department of the Navy; its secretary was one of the few who knew why Brierly was there. He was on attachment to the department from the Admiralty. After becoming prime minister, Winston Churchill had persuaded President Roosevelt to provide 50 US destroyers that Britain needed to try and stem the losses at sea the U-boats continued to cause. Sensing his request had come at the right moment, Churchill had added, 'I will gladly take any other ships available to help us.' Brierly had been given the task of scouting the East Coast ports to prepare a secret report for the president on their suitability.

While the celebrations on board continued, Brierly had inspected *President Warfield* from stern to prow, noting, among much else, that above the rudder was a second steering wheel operated by cables in the pilothouse, which could steer the ship in an emergency. Forward was a large freight deck capable of carrying a number of automobiles and cargo. The 170 staterooms could be easily converted to hold many more than the elegantly dressed couples who now occupied them. In his notebook, he added, 'All steel work tight. Lumber sound.'

At midnight the ship's band struck up 'Auld Lang Syne'. David Brierly joined in the singing, knowing how prescient the words were.

Gertruda stood at the foot of Lydia's bed, cradling little Michael as she continued to watch his mother. The only sounds in the bedroom were the whirring of the ceiling fan and Lydia's shallow breathing. Other women might have been eager to have the death watch over, but Gertruda had, from childhood, helped relatives prepare to die: her grandmother, an aunt, a distant cousin. It was part of her Catholic upbringing. Lydia had suffered a cerebral haemorrhage that the hospital doctors said was terminal and they had sent her home.

Since then Gertruda's world beyond the room's drawn curtains was no longer of concern: her world was *here*, where she bathed Lydia and attended to her other needs. When Lydia wanted to talk in her slurred speech, Gertruda responded, and when she wanted to rest,

Gertruda made sure she was not disturbed by visitors; some of them held Lydia's hand, fingers barely touching her skin, as if such contact might cause her pain, while others stood at the bedside, staring silently at Lydia, as if no words could communicate their sorrow. Gertruda knew better. Lydia needed to feel she was still part of life and that was why Gertruda had created a timetable for when she would not only feed Lydia, bathe and change her nightdress, but bring Michael to the bedside and encourage him to tell his mother what he had been doing. Once a week the rabbi came. He asked few questions and left. Gertruda's strong Catholic faith reassured her that no one, including Lydia, wholly died, that earthly death should be seen as a return to a better world.

Now, on that summer afternoon, Gertruda knew that Lydia wanted to say something and she came forward with Michael still in her arms. Unlike others she had helped to die, Gertruda sensed with Lydia there was no unwillingness to surrender to her own inevitable fate. As Lydia's lips began to move, Gertruda bent closer, still holding Michael. That moment would remain in Michael's memory: 'Gertruda later told me my mother said she knew her time had come and she had one last request to make. That Gertruda would save me and take me to Palestine.'

Until then Gertruda had been a devoted nanny. Now she had been asked to take the place of Michael's birth mother. Gertruda looked down at Lydia's still face. She stepped back from the bed. There was no more she could do for Lydia. Her responsibility was now Michael. She would become his new mother.

On a muggy morning in mid-June 1942, David Brierly and two other men stood around a conference table in the Commerce Building in Washington, DC. John McLay was a descendant of one of England's aristocratic families and David Boyd a shrewd London businessman. From New Zealand and Australia to the ports of South American and India, shipping companies had sold them seaworthy vessels to convoy war supplies to Britain. When last in Washington they had been on their way to the Caribbean and the United States had been at peace. Before the Japanese attack on Pearl Harbor, there had been several secret meetings between Churchill and President Roosevelt. After the last one, Churchill had returned to London to brief the War Cabinet that Roosevelt shared his view that the day would come when the war must be carried to the shores of Nazi-occupied Europe and 'the very evil heart of Hitler's Berlin lair'. To succeed would require shallow-draught boats suitable for crossing the English Channel.

McLay and Boyd had come to acquire them. David Brierly laid out on the table a selection of photographs and blueprints of 25 ships immediately available on the East Coast. Brierly's experienced visitors quickly rejected a dozen. The rest they began to study more carefully. Another six were turned down as not being seaworthy enough to cross the Atlantic. The remainder passed muster. The last three were Chesapeake steamers. Pointing to a photograph and a builder's set of blueprints, Brierly had smiled: 'I like to leave the best until last. She looks ideal.'

The two Englishmen agreed. A set of signatures on a document cemented the deal. Requisition Order 227753 formalised the transfer to the British Ministry of War Transport of *President Warfield*.

At 4pm on Sunday 11 July 1942, a single resounding blast came from the smoke stack of *President Warfield*. People paused and, like mourners at a passing funeral cortège, some lowered their heads when she began her last journey as the Bay Line flagship. Just 10 minutes later she reached its mooring at the Maryland Dry Dock Company. The air was filled with the sound of hammering as cranes moved back and forth on their tracks. The demands of war called for a 24 hours a day, seven days a week schedule.

Waiting on the dockside was the team assigned to refit the ship: welders with their blowtorches, riveters and drillers with their equipment, electricians carrying their toolboxes. Each was a specialist in what they had to do. Since Pearl Harbor they had done it many times. Led by their crew chief, they went below deck. Shortly afterwards came the first sound of a drill.

*

In Berlin, Werner von Braun was once more shown into Hitler's spacious study by the Führer's frumpish senior secretary, Christa Schroeder, to discuss the blueprint for his latest rocket, the V-2.

Hitler's enthusiasm, von Braun later recalled, was infectious. Could 2,000 rockets be launched every month? Von Braun nodded. Would each one contain 2,000 kilos of explosives? Another nod. Von Braun had one request. The war effort had placed a serious strain on labour supply. A new site would be needed to weaponise the V-2 and that would require more slave workers.

Hitler picked up a telephone on his desk and gave orders to Albert Speer. The concentration camps were to be emptied of every able-bodied man, woman and child if needs be, to meet the requirements of the rocket programme. Failure would not be tolerated.

Von Braun left Hitler's office as the Reich's latest slave master.

The urgency to meet the timetable of war enveloped *President Warfield*. Gilt-framed mirrors and paintings from Solomon Warfield's mansion were taken down, wrapped in dustsheets and carried to removal vans. With them went cabin bathroom fittings, handcut glass and chandeliers, fine linen tablecloths and bedding. Carpets were ripped up. Flowerpots which had graced the upper deck were lowered over the side on to a flat-back truck. It was like the ransacking of a medieval palace.

In place of the artefacts came the armaments. A crane positioned mounts for four 20mm guns and the steel plating for a heavier gun, a 12-pounder, before it was bolted to its platform. Drillers fitted steel plating to protect the gunners and additional oil tanks to increase the ship's sailing range. Around the pilothouse labourers positioned a six-inch coating of asphalt for protection. Other workmen used steel plating to protect cargo doors and hawse pipes.

The overhang at main deck level, which characterised all Chesapeake steamers, momentarily caused a problem. A naval architect from the Admiralty assigned to the New York headquarters of the British Ministry of War Transport ordered the overhang be boxed in with heavy timbers. The sleek hull, which had attracted so many admiring glances since it had slid down the slipway on that Monday in February 1928, disappeared behind a planked casing.

On the day of her final inspection, David Brierly felt as if 'the make-up on a Hollywood star has been torn away to reveal she is an old hag'. For two hours he clambered over the ship with the Admiralty architect, ready to answer any questions. There were none. *President Warfield* was ready for war.

In the Third Reich 15-year old Helena Levi, like all the other prisoners, went to work before dawn and returned to the conce-ntration camp at Mittelbau-Dora 12 hours later. The same harsh lights which encircled the camp lit her workplace far below ground. In her striped blue-and-white stained prison dress, her feet encased in the boots of an older woman who had died of exhaustion, Helena's life was governed by the shouts of the guards – '*Schnell! Schnell!*' – and the crack of their whips on someone's back as she carried the next piece of rock to a dumper truck and, when it was full, pushed it along the rail track to the surface. They were building von Braun's under-ground site for his V-2 rocket.

Helena had been among the first batch of prisoners. Within weeks, 12,000 slave workers toiled below ground. Conditions were appalling and soon the death rate was so high that a crematorium had to be built near the entrance. Beside it was a multiple gallows on which prisoners suspected of sabotage, up to a dozen at a time, were hanged; they were left for a whole day for all to see before being cut down. With little ventilation and no sanitation or running water, malnutrition and disease were rife. Prisoners licked the putrid water oozing from the rock walls and the ground was slippery with faeces. The work was back-breaking and there was the constant threat of a tunnel collapsing. Several did cave in, but being buried alive could only have been a welcome relief to escape this Dante's Inferno.

At daybreak on 20 August 1942, a military bus stopped beside *President Warfield*'s mooring on Pier 3 on Baltimore's Pratt Street. As the passengers emerged, the air was filled with unfamiliar accents:

Scottish, Welsh, cockney and the broader voices of the English shires. This was the Merchant Navy crew who had come to sail *President Warfield* to England.

As was the case in every sea port on the East Coast of America, the fate of the ships which sailed from these ports was an abiding concern to their citizens. In cathedrals, churches and synagogues they offered up prayers for the safety of their crews.

In Washington, DC, Leo Bernstein murmured his own Jewish devotion as he watched worshippers enter St Mary's Catholic Church across the road from his expanding real-estate business. His family were descendants of those who had settled around Washington's 5th Street, survivors of the pogroms in Eastern Europe in the last century who had come to the United States. Leo had other relatives who were now in the hands of the Nazis. Everything he said and did was motivated by trying to save them. He was among the best fund-raisers in Washington for the United Jewish Appeal to help the war drive. After Pearl Harbor, he had given generously and knew how much he could expect from every person he approached, reminding them that each dollar would be used to help all the Jews in Europe. It was not only their fate that filled his prayers but the hope that God would answer his wish that the ships which left the East Coast would be spared to go and bring those Jews to the safety of *Eretz Yisrael*.

So strong was his belief that, in the third year of the war, he had started to put aside a portion of his income and encouraged others to do the same to help those desperate Jews in Europe. The more Leo prayed for their freedom the stronger grew his feeling they would be saved.

Johann Goldman and Jacob Cohen, each wrapped in a fisherman's anorak against the chill wind blowing off the North Sea, stood on the dyke at Den Helder watching the Kriegsmarine E-boat speeding by. For the past three days they had timed when it passed on its coastal patrol: 2pm and 7pm on its return to the naval base further up the coast. It was the hour when local fishing boats set out for a night's fishing. The youths had discovered that the German sentry in his hut on the quayside never counted the fishing boats as they left or returned to the harbour. Their plan had developed from there.

There was a boat laid up in the harbour on which Johann's uncle had worked before he was among the Jews deported to work in the Reich's war factories. Johann had not told his aunt what he and Jacob planned to do. For the past two days they had checked the engine and filled its fuel tank. After watching the E-boat speeding past, they had once more gone to the harbour, two more fishermen going to prepare their boat for an evening's fishing. Once at the fishing grounds, they intended to sail to England.

As they passed the hut, the sentry emerged, rifle in hand, and asked for their papers. Inside the hut was a man in the familiar topcoat and fedora of the secret police. The sentry handed the papers over to the Gestapo officer. He read them and emerged from the hut before waving to a closed truck parked further up the road to come forward. Johann and Jacob's plan to escape to England was over.

On board *President Warfield* Captain Williamson saw the dark shadow of the coastline long before he felt the easing of the swell that told him land was not far away. Within an hour, they were in the lee of the Western Isles, passing South Uist and heading towards the Inner Hebrides off the west coast of Scotland. Ahead rose the hills of Argyll and Bute. Beyond lay their destination, Belfast.

Chapter 6

Westward Bound

For Gertruda, Easter 1943 would be a further opportunity to see how much Michael had absorbed in her determination to pass him off not only as her child, but as one who, like her, behaved as a devout Catholic. Every day, as he grew into a strong, sturdy boy, she taught him the Ten Commandments, the Catechism and the significance of the figure of Jesus on the cross she had bought for him in a shop selling Catholic artefacts in Cathedral Square in the Old Town. She encouraged him to call her *Mutti*, mother; she called him her little Mickey. Every Sunday she took him with her to Vilnius's archdiocesan cathedral, having shown Michael how to bow his head towards the giant statue of Christ towering over the cathedral altar and make the sign of the cross. Among the congregation sat the German occupiers and their families. The officers in their Wehrmacht grey uniforms often nodded at her and patted Michael on the head, sometimes asking if, when he grew up, he would like to be a soldier. Gertruda always smiled non-committally.

In contrast to the officers were the Lithuanian and Ukrainian soldiers who had been enlisted to round up Jewish children. There were now thousands in the ghetto: babies, little toddlers, all snatched from their parents on a day Gertruda would never forget. Truckloads of Ukrainians had jumped from the lorries and grabbed the children of doctors, dentists, shopkeepers and lawyers in the Jewish community. One young mother, Marsha Segal, recalled: 'The guards looked everywhere; they opened every cellar and pulled out the children, like catching rabbits, and from attics, from gardens, from *everywhere*. Mothers tried to give them wedding rings, everything they had. To describe how the children were herded on to those lorries is impossible. And in our house we had a small family; the little boy was a beautiful child with huge grey-blue eyes and I always used to tell him stories in the evening. I loved him. He was found hiding in the garden behind bushes and he was taken. He jumped from the lorry; then we knew the children were beyond rescue because the little boy was shot.'

It was to avoid such a fate that Gertruda had schooled Michael to become a Catholic. Because she spoke fluent German, word had spread among the local farmers that she would write letters to the occupying authority to obtain the permissions which controlled their lives. In return, Gertruda was paid with fresh-laid eggs and occasionally a chicken.

After morning Mass when the weather was fine, she chose to walk with Mickey through Vingis Park, the city's largest, or along the banks of the Vilna or Neris rivers. Sitting on the grass, Gertruda would explain to him the meaning of what the priest had been saying during his sermon. When the rivers froze in winter, they watched fishermen drill holes in the ice and fish with baited hooks. To the German patrols, they looked like any other mother and son.

It would be years before Michael learned that Vilnius was known throughout the Jewish Diaspora as Yerushalayim de Lita – the Jerusalem of Lithuania – comparable only to Jerusalem itself as a world centre for the study of the Torah. The city's large Jewish population had once worshipped in a hundred different synagogues; only the Choral Synagogue would survive once the Nazis set about destroying the last vestiges of Judaism in the city.

A year had now passed since Michael's mother had been buried in the Vilna Gaon Cemetery, one of the Jewish graveyards in Vilnius. Gertruda had made the decision that neither she nor Michael would visit the grave, because it would be dangerous to arouse the curiosity of one of the German patrols that, day and night, were on the look-out for any Jew who had managed to avoid being sent to the ghetto in the Old Town.

The Vilnius ghetto was typical of many in the Reich. Its population was cut off from the rest of the city and only those with permits to work for the Germans could come and go through the guarded entrances. Yet when they were first sent to its ghetto, many Vilnius Jews felt a sense of relief, as they could walk without being afraid of being abused or severely beaten. The ghetto was an enclave of narrow, curved streets and alleys, a mixture of elegant Gothic and Renaissance architectural styles that masked the reality of life in its confines.

Sanitary conditions were inadequate, food and clean drinking water limited and medicine virtually non-existent. People shivered to death through the absence of fuel. Like all the others in the Reich, the ghetto was run by a Nazi-appointed Jewish committee, the *Judenrat*, and discipline was in the hands of the *Ordnungsdienst*, a Jewish police auxiliary. Both were despised for cooperating with the Nazis.

It was this world of tension and fear that Gertruda had started to enter. She had learned that one of the doctors who had attended Michael's mother while she was in hospital was himself now in the ghetto, one of a handful of physicians there. Gertruda's first hurdle had been to see if she could help him. This problem had been overcome when she managed to find an old building which had doors opening into the ghetto from the street outside.

With Michael safely tucked up in bed after saying the prayers she had taught him, Gertruda would gather up food and a bottle of clean water and make her way into the ghetto to visit the doctor.

Her repeated acts of kindness were repaid a few months later when Michael was taken ill. Knowing she could not risk calling for another doctor in case he saw that Michael was circumcised and reported the fact he was a Jew, Gertruda had once more gone into the ghetto. The physician had immediately agreed to risk both their lives by making a house call. After examining Michael, he prescribed bed rest and bowls of chicken soup and soft-boiled eggs.

On her next visit, Gertruda had brought the doctor a chicken and a dozen eggs. But the risk for anyone helping a Jew was escalating. Outside her apartment block was a large notice warning that any

Gentile hiding a Jew faced summary execution. There were hundreds of similar posters all around Vilnius.

On Easter Sunday in 1943, Gertruda had dressed Michael in the new topcoat, trousers and boots she had bought him. He would look as smart as any of the children at morning Mass. The bells were ringing out across the city and they were about to enter Cathedral Square when a German patrol stopped them. What happened next remained in Michael's memory a lifetime later. When asked how he could remember so vividly, he would simply reply: 'How could I forget? There were four soldiers. They surrounded us, pointing their rifles. One of them said to me, "Take down your pants." I shook my head. Gertruda had said that when I played with some of the local boys and I had to go to the bathroom, I must never pee in front of the other boys because they would see I was circumcised and tell the Germans I was a Jew. We lived in that sort of climate. Betrayal was common. People did it to gain favours or, in the case of turning in a Jew, often enjoying what they had done. Gertruda had pulled me to her and asked the soldier what gave him the right to order her son to take down his trousers. The soldier repeated the order, "Take down your pants, boy!" The moment I did, I knew Gertruda and I would be dead. One of the soldiers grabbed me before she could move and pulled at my pants. Suddenly a voice shouted, "Halt! Leave him alone! The boy is not Jewish!"'

The startled soldiers stepped back, lowering their rifles. Facing them was an SS officer who had smiled at Gertruda in church.

'*Raus!*' he shouted at the soldiers.

They saluted and hurried away.

When Gertruda thanked him, the officer shrugged: 'It is getting to be dangerous here. We are not all savages. But you must take care.'

He touched the peak of his hat and marched away.

From the steps of the cathedral, Gertruda turned and looked back across the square. The officer was gone. But in her mind a plan was forming of how she could further protect Michael.

Daniel Feinstein was among hundreds of children in the ghetto. He was 10 years old when he had been brought there by Ukrainian soldiers in an *Action*, a round-up, in which his parents had been murdered by them. Daniel now knew that such killings were a regular event.

Other boys already there had told him he was lucky to be alive; Ukrainians liked to kill children. He had learned much else in the ghetto. Boys found that their hair stopped growing and girls that their menstruation ceased. An older boy said it was a symptom of confinement.

Religious customs were forbidden. Sickness was rife. People wore hand-me-down clothes. Begging for food was routine, as was stealing.

One day an SS officer strolling through the ghetto smiled at a little girl and asked if she would like a sweet. The child nodded and he told her to open her mouth. When she did he shot her in the mouth.

It had taught Daniel not to take anything from the soldiers who regularly came to the ghetto to snatch people to be sent to the concentration camps. It was also a reminder that he must survive so that one day he could help others.

Chaim Weizmann planned to work yet another long day. As usual, he awoke before dawn in the suite he and Vera occupied in the Dorchester Hotel, overlooking London's Hyde Park. After a breakfast of coffee and toast, he walked across the park, his briefcase filled with scientific papers that he had read into the small hours and would hand to his chemists in their cramped laboratory in a small house in Knightsbridge.

Weizmann was now 69 years old and his lifestyle remained exhausting: long transatlantic flights followed by late-night meetings with senior military officers in his capacity as the Ministry of Supply's senior adviser on chemical warfare; demands made in his role as president of the Zionist Federation; lectures to scientific institutes; fund-raising dinners for Jewish organisations. In between, he wrote briefing papers for Churchill's Cabinet. At every opportunity, he raised the question of the fate of the millions of Jews in the concentration camps.

In his office was a filing cabinet filled with evidence of Nazi atrocities and stories of Jewish resistance. The information had been passed on by journalists of neutral countries, who were still able to report from inside the Reich, and members of the foreign governments-in-exile in London. From time to time, he also received reports from MI6. Since his successful mission to Basel to discover the extent of Nazi plans for chemical warfare, his relationship with Stewart Menzies, its chief, had developed and he received copies of reports dealing with Jewish underground groups in several ghettos.

But Weizmann increasingly found the fate of Europe's Jews was not a priority in either London or Washington, DC. When he had tried to raise the matter with President Roosevelt, 'I found his response was cordial but non-committal.'

Weizmann had urged Churchill to order the BBC to publicise information gathered by MI6 on conditions in the concentration camps. But the BBC prevaricated. An internal memo argued: 'To stress the racial aspects of the killings would be to identify them as Jews and this would have some negative impact on the propaganda value of showing the Nazis were carrying out mass murder.'

But within the Cabinet the issue of what Deputy Prime Minister Clement Attlee called 'the Jewish Question' continued to command Churchill's attention. His demand for Jews to emigrate en masse to Palestine after the war 'irrespective of the quota' had been discussed at a War Cabinet meeting on 5 March 1942. Instead the Cabinet approved a resolution that 'all practical steps should be taken to discourage illegal immigration to Palestine at the end of the war'.

The obdurate attitude of some Cabinet members was not just anti-Semitism, but an ignorance of what was happening in Europe; there were many people who claimed 'psychological barriers' made it hard for them to comprehend what they were hearing. When the BBC finally began to broadcast warnings to the Germans promising retribution for their crimes against the Jews, the policy-makers of the Foreign Office argued that 'too much publicity will inevitably generate pressure by the Jewish lobbyists to force us to mount special rescue operations which would be detrimental to the war effort'.

Arthur Randall, the head of the Foreign Office Refugee Department, minuted on 22 February 1943: 'The Jewish disaster is only part of the vast human problem of Europe under Nazi control. Other parts are starving children, the deliberate extinction of the Polish and Czech intelligentsia, forced labour and spiritual perversion of youth.'

The Ministry of Information refused to publicise what it called 'any special mention of the Jews as it would be believed that a people singled out for such treatment were probably a bad lot. Therefore to make special mention of their plight would increase domestic anti-Semitism by making the home public more conscious of their own animosities towards their Jewish neighbours.'

Richard Law, Under-Secretary of the State at the Foreign Office, had answered an appeal by Weizmann to establish a separate relief organisation for Jews: 'The Jews have without doubt suffered enormously by Hitler's deliberate policy. But other people have suffered as well, and to separate the Jews as a racial problem would surely play into the hands of anti-Semitism.'

It was against this attitude that Chaim Weizmann continued to fight for the lives of the millions of Jews in the Nazi death camps.

Freddie Kronenberg began another year in Auschwitz. He was 15 years old and, apart from his duty to raise and lower the barrier at the camp gate, he had been made a *Laufer*, one of the messengers assigned to Joseph Kramer, the camp's SS *Kommandant*.

Throughout the day, he carried messages in envelopes from Kramer to the SS commanders of various sub-camps and to Dr Mengele in his medical facility. Freddie learned to ignore the barking guard dogs and the pleading from prisoners for him to help them. There was nothing he could do, would dare do.

Freddie had taken messages to the industrial area of Auschwitz where Zyklon-B, the poison used in the gas chambers, was manufactured by Degesch, a subsidiary of the I.G. Farben chemical conglomerate. Every day covered trucks containing fresh quantities of the poison were driven along what Kramer called *der Himmelstrasse*, the gateway to heaven.

One day Kramer gave Freddie an envelope to take to the SS

commander of the 'sorting hut'. Prisoners were sifting through women's corsets and dresses and filling buckets with jewellery: wedding rings in one, earrings in another, necklaces and brooches in a third. The buckets were sealed with sacking. The piles of clothes were neatly folded and packed into boxes. All were marked for transportation to Germany.

Every morning the camp orchestra, prisoners who had been selected by Alma Rose, its conductor, who was a niece of the celebrated composer Gustav Mahler, played marches at the camp gate as workers were escorted to the industrial area. In the evening when they returned, the orchestra played Strauss waltzes and often SS guards came and stood to listen.

For Freddie, another horror marked the onset of Passover in 1943. Three young boys who worked in an ammunition factory had been caught trying to sabotage the shells. All the prisoners were marched to the gallows in the middle of the camp. Standing at the foot of the platform were the three boys, hands bound behind their backs. One by one they walked to the gallows. Each shouted defiance before the trapdoor dropped. The youths were left to hang for two days before Kramer, on one of his walkabouts, said he found the stench too upsetting and ordered the bodies cut down for cremation.

Day and night trains filled with Jews poured into Auschwitz from all over Eastern Europe to replace the hundreds of thousands of prisoners who had been gassed and cremated. Their ashes were disposed of by the *Sonderkommando*, the special Jewish unit selected to work in the gas chambers and crematoria. One of them had burned the bodies of his wife and children and, when Kramer learned of this, he sent Freddie with an order to have the *Sonderkommando* executed in case he went mad and attacked the *Kommandant* on his walks.

On 4 January 1944, Werner von Braun, wrapped in a heavy fur-collared coat against the sub-zero temperatures, arrived at the Mittelbau-Dora facility to watch the first of the rockets being loaded on to trucks for their journey west to be launched against England.

Helping to load the trucks was Helena Levi and hundreds of slave labourers working under von Braun's watchful eyes. By nightfall the last of the trucks were loaded and driven away. Werner von Braun in his chauffeur-driven Mercedes followed. Trudging behind came the surviving slave labourers. Helena did not know where they were going. No one did. Lightly clad and ill-shod, they marched on. Those who fell behind were shot by the SS guards and left lying on the frozen ground. In between there were brief halts for food. The guards had ration packs, while the slaves dug up roots from frozen fields.

By February 1944, Miriam Bergman had been inside Bergen-Belsen concentration camp for five years. She knew no other life. She was a pretty teenager and ignored the looks she attracted from guards by dressing as shabbily as possible in the clothes of an old woman.

Early on she had learned that survival depended on understanding the language of the camp. Part German, part Yiddish, it had its own key word: *organise*. It stood for barter: to buy, to sell, to get food to survive. To *organise* her life meant getting into the right work party, inside the camp. Those outside the fences were dangerous, because she could be raped. In one of the kitchens, preferably cooking for the guards, she had an opportunity to steal food. If she couldn't get a job in the kitchen, *organise* meant joining a work party in the guards' hospital compound, where she could get drugs to sell for food. Food kept her alive. Drugs kept her healthy. *Organise* meant when to take her place in the food line so that by the time it came for a cook to serve her, the soup was near the bottom of a barrel, making it thicker and more nourishing. If it contained pieces of meat, there may even be enough to use for bartering: a chunk for a slice of bread. *Organise* was everything.

By 1944, Bergen-Belsen, which had once been considered a 'good' camp – one where extermination was not routine – had become a place where those who survived the death marches were brought; a place no longer with running water or sanitation, where dysentery and typhus vied to kill people; a place where the dead lay on the ground, adding to the stench from the living with their shaven heads and their obscene striped pyjama suits.

It was here that Miriam was determined to continue to *organise* her life so she could wait for the day when liberation would come.

On 6 June 1944, within hours of the start, the home-made wirelesss concealed in the concentration camps told inmates that the great drive into Hitler's Europe had begun. In their huts, among the dead and dying, hope was rekindled. They prayed and continued saying *Kaddish*, the prayer for the dead.

In Auschwitz, Freddie Kronenberg learned the invasion had started when he was given a message to deliver by Kommandant Kramer to an SS officer in his quarters. The man was already half drunk, waving his pistol in the air and cursing the radio for reporting that the Allies had landed in France. He had torn up the message and yelled at Freddie to get out as he closed the door behind him. There was a shot. The officer had killed himself.

In Bergen-Belsen, Miriam Bergman was asleep under her bunk – something she did to protect the tablets she had stolen from the camp hospital – when the woman in the bunk above awoke her to say that soon they would be free. A cook in the hut had heard the news of the invasion on the camp's kitchen wireless.

In Westerbork, Johann and Jacob had sat outside their hut trying to decide how long it would take the first Allied troops to reach the camp. It was now dark and the wireless hidden in the hut had said the invasion had started at dawn. They agreed the Allies must come soon as Holland was close to Britain.

On the march from von Braun's rocket facility, Helena Levi never learned the invasion had started. The guard who carried a wireless had thrown it away after its batteries expired.

On a blustery Saturday evening, 20 May 1944, rain spattering on his hat and raincoat, Lieutenant George Boyer stood on a dockside at Barry Port in South Wales, staring up at his first command, *President Warfield*. In Boyer's briefcase were the documents confirming *President Warfield* had been discharged from the Royal Navy and transferred to the United States Navy, with himself as the ship's commanding officer. There was one matter to be completed. Before he and his officers and the crew standing behind him could step on board, the British flag had to be lowered for the last time. That done, Boyer ordered his crew to board. After he had conducted his ship inspection, he had sat in the wardroom with his officers and addressed them for the first time: 'The sooner we get her looking like a ship in the United States Navy, the better for everyone.' Outside the rain lashed the decks.

President Warfield's short crossing from Barry Port to Plymouth – flying for the first time from her masthead the Stars and Stripes – was accompanied by the continuous roar of aircraft passing overhead to bomb the French coast in support of the Allied troops struggling to advance off the beaches into Normandy.

A team of carpenters was waiting when she arrived in Plymouth harbour to remove the planking. For the first time since Baltimore, her sleek hull was fully revealed. The work done, she slipped her mooring and steamed out of the harbour to join a convoy heading for Normandy. It was daybreak when she anchored in Sector 23 off Omaha Beach. In the distance, smoke rose from the rubble of villages beyond the headlands.

Among the first survivors of the carnage who were brought aboard *President Warfield* to rest were men with harrowing stories. The soldier impaled on barbed wire, his body shredded with machine-gun fire. The RAF Typhoon fighter-bomber laying waste an entire platoon of German soldiers waving pieces of white cloth in one of the ravines which led to the cliff tops. The two old women in nightdresses running across the headlands before a burst of gunfire had sent them tumbling on to the beach. One soldier described a little girl sitting beside a headless pony. There were so many stories.

At night, when Lieutenant Boyer made his last round, he could hear the restless murmuring of the men in their bunks. All too soon they would be ferried back to the shore to rejoin the push deeper into Normandy.

David Ben-Gurion's book-lined office in the Jewish Agency Building in Jerusalem was on the second floor of the fortress-like structure, where for many years its stone walls had enclosed Jewish hopes for fulfilment of their yearning for a homeland. Five years of war in Europe had deepened the lines around his eyes and lips and left his hair whiter and thinner. But well into middle age, Ben-Gurion's voice had lost none of its orator's power.

Since early morning he had sat in the high-backed leather chair behind his desk beneath two framed images on the wall. One was a copy of the Balfour Declaration. The other was a map of Europe on which was superimposed the names and locations of every concentration camp in the Third Reich: names stretching from Westerbork in the west to Treblinka and Sobibor in East Prussia and south to Natzweiler. Clustered in the middle were even more infamous names: Bergen-Belsen, Ravensbrück, Sachsenhausen, Dachau, Mauthausen and Auschwitz. In all there were now 32 places of unspeakable evil where millions of his people had already died and a million more, he feared, waited to be sent to their deaths. Ben-Gurion would include that possibility in the speech he was drafting in his bold handwriting:

> We must be aware of the fallacy that the smashing of Hitlerism alone will free the world of its ills and the Jewish people of its misery. There is something fundamentally wrong in civilisation, if a Hitler can bring the whole of mankind to such a pass, and something fundamentally wrong in the Jewish set-up if, whenever there is any trouble, Jews are singled out as its first and most catastrophic victims. Victory over Hitler will not be an end, but the beginning of a new set-up for the world and ourselves. To build it will need a maximum effort by the entire Jewish people, in the Diaspora and in Palestine. As part of the great human cause, America, England and other nations that champion humanity may be expected to help us. But we must also expect to do the job ourselves. Palestine will be as Jewish as the Jews will make it.

Ben-Gurion's theme for his speech had been on his mind since that June morning when the Palestine Radio Company had interrupted its programme with news of the launch of D-Day. Since then he had listened to every bulletin on the radio in his office and regularly telephoned his old friend Shimshon Lifshitz at the *Jerusalem Post*, the foremost English-language newspaper north of Cairo and Zionism's most articulate public voice in the Middle East.

From the paper's first issue in 1932, Lifshitz had been its head printer and in the composing room were copies of some of the front pages he had set: Hitler coming to power, Kristallnacht, the invasion of Poland, the Battle of Britain, Pearl Harbor and now D-Day. For each event he had chosen a typeface he felt would suit the story and picked out the inverted type with a speed that other compositors envied. After D-Day he had also kept wire service reports from Reuters and the Associated Press of America, and marked them up with a printer's pencil gripped between his stubby fingers for Ben-Gurion to read. On 25 August, hardly able to contain his excitement, he called Ben-Gurion with the news that Paris had been liberated.

He shouted into the phone, 'We are winning. Everywhere we are winning!'

Ben-Gurion had looked at the map delineating the concentration camps and spoke quietly, 'My friend, I am glad for Paris. But will the Allies save our people in time?'

After the call Ben-Gurion added a final paragraph to the speech he would deliver to the meeting of the Jewish Agency:

When it comes to the end of the Second World War, it will not be the end of our war. With the defeat of the Nazis, it becomes our bounden duty to go to any extreme necessary to rescue what the Germans have left of the various Jewish communities. We will have to lead those survivors openly or by stealth through war-torn lands and across borders to the sea and thence to the shores of their homeland, to bring home on our shoulders those of our people who have been left alive.

Chapter 7

The Rabbi's Mission

In their suite in London's Dorchester Hotel, Chaim and Vera Weizmann had become devoted to the BBC Home Service bulletins. For the past three months, since 13 June 1944, the newscasts had led with the devastation caused by Werner von Braun's V-1 rockets, which continued to fall on the capital. The missiles, Vergeltungswaffe-1, or Reprisal-1, had introduced a new horror into warfare, each unmanned weapon flying at 155 miles an hour to deliver a one-ton payload of high explosives. It was identified by its distinctive buzz, followed by the brief silence as its rockets cut out, then the devastating crash as it struck the ground. There were scores of missiles, each 25 feet long, which had been assembled in the underground caves where Helena Levi and her fellow prisoners had then loaded them on to trucks for transportation to launch pads within striking distance of London. The toll from the rockets would eventually leave over 5,000 dead or injured and a million homes, schools, churches and hospitals destroyed or damaged.

For the Weizmanns, there was the option to escape by going to America. Churchill had hinted that no one would think the worse of them for doing that, reminding Weizmann that he had already made an invaluable contribution to the war effort. Invitations to start a new life were accompanied by offers not only to resettle them in a suitable home in the United States, but to supply them with substantial guarantees of funds for any research institute Chaim Weizmann wished to found.

Each offer had been politely declined. The Weizmanns agreed that if they did leave London, there was only one place they would go to: Palestine, and the home in Rehovot that they had planned so carefully but where they had spent little time enjoying its comforts. They also agreed it would be the perfect place to celebrate Chaim's 70th birthday.

He would take with him the assurance from Winston Churchill of a 'plan that would create a Jewish National Home'. The Prime Minister had first hinted at it when he invited Weizmann to lunch at Chequers in November 1944. That night in his diary, Weizmann wrote: 'He spoke of partition and declared himself in favour of including the Negev in the Jewish territory. And while he made it clear there would be no active steps taken until the war was over, he was in touch with Roosevelt on the matter.'

Two days later the Weizmanns set off for Palestine. They arrived in Rehovot to a warm welcome. While Vera began refurbishing their home, her husband set about testing the viability of a new homeland. There was much to encourage him: productivity had leapt since he was last in Palestine, with over 600,000 Jews working to create a powerful democracy, ready to welcome Europe's Jewry once Germany was defeated.

Days after his return, Chaim Weizmann called on David Ben-Gurion in his home on Keren Kayemet Street in Tel Aviv. The two men embraced cordially, then Ben-Gurion led his guest into his study. Like his office in the Jewish Agency, it overflowed with books on philosophy and history. For a while, sipping coffee, they spoke about the war and the fate of the surviving Jews in the camps. Beyond the open study window came the sound of waves crashing on a nearby beach.

Ben-Gurion said it must have been the first sound refugees had heard all those years ago when they stumbled ashore from a blockade-runner. Sitting back in his chair, Weizmann spoke with a new certainty: 'Soon our people will be able to come home without having to do that.'

Ben-Gurion had looked at him intently, then asked, 'How do you know?'

'Mr Churchill has a plan. I do not know the details. But he will make it public when the war is over. Pray it will be soon.'

His host stared, nodding his head, saying nothing.

As autumn 1944 turned to winter, the ocean once more became capricious off Omaha Beach. It tugged fiercely at *President Warfield*'s anchor chain or suddenly shrouded the ship in cloying, acrid fog that reminded Lieutenant Boyer of San Francisco Bay. He had ordered the ship's distinctive whistle to blow every 30 seconds to warn off any other boat in the vicinity. Then, as quickly as it had dropped away, the wind would return with renewed fury to disperse the fog and once more send *President Warfield* bucking like a wild animal as she tried to break from her moorings.

While she remained tethered off Omaha Beach the full horror of the concentration camps began to unfold. British and American interrogation officers pieced together accounts from German prisoners of war. They told the same gruesome stories of summary executions, torture, gassings and piles of cremated bodies. The interrogation reports made their way through the chain of command to General Eisenhower and General Montgomery, who sent them to the War Office in London, where a selection were delivered to Churchill and Stewart Menzies. The MI6 chief took them to the meeting of the Joint Chiefs of Staff, who gathered regularly to discuss progress in the war. The question of what would happen to those who survived the death camps and wanted to go to Palestine was raised. Menzies recommended the matter should be held over until hostilities ended.

Inside Westerbork shortage of food had become critical in the unusually bitter weather that winter. Prisoners slowly wasted away; even the physical effort of scavenging through the waste bins from the camp kitchen left inmates exhausted. The cold turned their huts into ice boxes. Prisoners huddled together and chewed on strips of wood, shoes from one of the newly dead, anything that could be found.

At morning roll call, those who dropped with fatigue were shot where they lay. Those who had died in their sleep overnight were robbed of their clothing and taken away by barrow to the nearest lime pit. Some of the women sold their bodies for a slice of bread or a cup of mushy sugar beet, the fibrous roots used to feed cattle. Steadily starvation did its work. The only flicker of hope came from those huts where there was a smuggled wireless. The Allies were coming slowly, but they were on their way.

Johann Goldman shared the duty of protecting the wireless in their hut from discovery and took turns with Jacob Cohen to go and search for food. One afternoon, when it was Johann's turn, he made his way to the kitchen area; the guards would have eaten their midday meal and the slops would have ended up in the waste bins. Sometimes the guards stood and watched the scavenging. Johann had walked a little distance from the hut when he heard shouting from inside. Jacob appeared, gripped by two guards, followed by an SS officer carrying the wireless in one hand and a pistol in the other. The officer crushed the wireless under his boot and told the guards to release Jacob. Smilingly, the officer ordered Jacob to pick up the pieces of the wireless. As he did so, the officer shot him through the skull and walked away.

Lieutenant Commander Edward Anthony Savile Bailey stood on the dockside in William Denny & Brothers shipyard in Dumbarton, Scotland. He was an imposing figure in his uniform and topcoat with its epaulettes displaying his rank, and passing workmen nodded towards him as they hurried about their business.

Bailey was a veteran of the Atlantic war, with four commendations and a Distinguished Service Cross, awarded for sinking a U-boat. Standing on the dockside, he viewed the ship that soon would be his responsibility: HMS *Childers*. A C-class destroyer, scheduled to be launched in February 1945, with her all-welded structure and a top speed of 31 knots, generated by two three-drum boilers and two-shaft turbines, she would be the first of a generation.

From the dockside Bailey continued to study the destroyer. Its decks were filled with workmen who came and went and from somewhere below their hammers and drills gave life to the ship.

From her square-cut hull to the bows that sheered outwards, she radiated power: the guns were in place, the radar and communications mast aerials had been fitted and her first coat of naval grey applied. In places it was sploshed with dabs of red lead to indicate particular parts of the hull that needed to be checked, as if a woman had applied her lipstick too quickly to match her drab wartime dress. But everything about HMS *Childers*, Bailey decided, was male: from quarterdeck to fo'c's'le and bridge, she was a warship. He could not wait to take her into battle.

On the evening of 12 January 1945, the men made their separate ways through the Old City of Jerusalem, timing their journeys for when the British Army patrols would not be in the area. Each was a senior officer in the Haganah and knew he would be arrested for belonging to an organisation the Mandate had outlawed.

Reaching the narrow, cobbled Street of the Jews, a man stopped before a heavy wooden door in a recessed archway and knocked. The door immediately opened and another man led the way across a stone-slabbed courtyard laid 200 years before into the home of Rabbi Mordechai Weingarten. At the rear of the house was a large study, the rabbi's inner sanctum. On the right-hand doorpost was a *mezuzah*, holding the parchment scroll containing the words of the Shema prayer.

Visitors could only have been awed by the contents of the hand-carved shelves which lined the walls from the marbled floor to the high ceiling, painted a restful shade of green. Crammed on to the shelves were many hundreds of leather-bound books, some well over a century old, and documents in unmarked folders so only Rabbi Weingarten knew what was inside.

There was a volume of the *Shulchan Aruch*, the main codification of Jewish Law and ritual derived from the Talmud. Rabbi Weingarten, himself a Talmudist, was the community's expert on the whole body of Jewish tradition. Copies of documents occupied many shelves. Other shelves held records of the dead, each including details of when *shivah*, the seven-day period of mourning, had started and finished, and when *shloshim*, the second, less intensive ritual of mourning, had ended after 30 days.

One wall of shelving was given over to the speeches and writings of Theodor Herzl, the founder of Zionism, and authors who had written about such diverse subjects as the foundation of the principal ghettos in Europe and the religious holidays of Judaism. The Pentateuch, the first five books of the Old Testament, had a shelf for themselves. On other shelves were political books dealing with not only the history of Judaism, but its impact on other nations. Some were written in Russian, German and Arabic, languages the rabbi spoke. In a corner of that shelf was a copy of the Balfour Declaration.

The contents of the study represented a lifetime of learning by Rabbi Weingarten, now in his 80th year and the oldest member of a family who had lived in the Old City for two centuries. As he received his visitors on that cool January evening, the rabbi embraced each man in turn and motioned for them to be seated on one of the semicircle of chairs already set out.

The rabbi was the chairman of the Old City's Jewish Council, but his influence extended across the Diaspora. A respected figure in British and America Jewry, his contacts extended into the Third Reich. There were Germans – opposed to Hitler and Nazism – who hoped he would speak for them when the war ended in return for providing information. Through his network of contacts, Rabbi Weingarten had developed a clear picture of what was happening to the Jews in the concentration camps.

A committed pacifist, the rabbi nevertheless shared with his visitors the same vision of a free nation. Over the years it had made him a trusted ally, able to obtain information that could be acted upon.

The first person to arrive was Moshe Bar-Gilad, who had travelled from Istanbul. Thinner since the time he had gone to Vienna to negotiate with Eichmann, he still wore the suit he had bought for that occasion. In turn, Eliyahu Golomb, Ze'ev Shind and Yehuda Arazi were greeted by their host. Golomb still bore the signs of a recent illness that had left his face pale and pinched. The other two men had the tired look that came from sharing the burden of the

Haganah leadership; inner conflicts had marked their faces from those times they had been compelled to send one of their subordinates on some dangerous mission that could lead to arrest, imprisonment or even death by hanging after a Mandate court trial. Munya Mardor, who had served with the men in the study, recalled: 'In an illegal military group known intimately to each other in their normal domestic roles, hard decisions were not less painful because we knew our leaders would themselves do what we were asked to carry out. But they often sent us into action without us knowing what it was all about. That required a great deal of trust on both sides.'

Shind spoke English with an American accent, from his visits during the war to the United States with Ben-Gurion on fund-raising missions for the Jewish Agency. Shind's duties included acting as a bodyguard for the Zionist leader and ensuring the transfer of pledged funds.

In the Haganah it was said no novelist would have dared invent Yehuda Arazi. Stocky, with a firm grip, he had dealt with many a criminal during his years as an inspector in the Palestine Police Force, but no one in the Mandate suspected Arazi was a high-value Haganah spy. He had photographed sensitive documents – sometimes entire police files – and carried them to a building near Jerusalem's General Post Office. When a Haganah officer had once asked for specific information, Arazi had replied, 'You get what you get.'

The issue was never raised again. From then on Arazi was regarded as his own man, a maverick like no other. In 1940, he had resigned from the police to join the British Army. On the day he went to the recruiting office, Yossi Harel was in the queue before him. While Harel had ended up as a British Army truck driver in the Libyan Desert, Yehuda Arazi's police experience had attracted Britain's Special Operations Executive (SOE), which had been ordered by Churchill to set Nazi-occupied Europe alight.

Trained in the latest techniques of sabotage, Arazi had been sent to the Balkans with a small team of fellow saboteurs. The unit had remarkable success in blowing up trains and railway trucks with explosives shaped as coal. A price had been put on the group by the Gestapo, which at one time had over a hundred agents trying to capture Arazi and his men. In London, Arazi was regarded as a key operative. No one suspected he had also remained a Haganah spy. As well as relaying the details to London on the radio set SOE had given him, Arazi copied them to Room 17 in the Histadrut Building on Allenby Street in Tel Aviv, where Golomb still kept concealed in his desk the radio receiver/transmitter.

The last to arrive was David Shaltiel, the son of an old Sephardic family from Hamburg, who was younger than the others, with horn-rimmed glasses and a prominent nose. In his early teens he had shrugged off the constraints of religious life and scandalised his devout mother by eating pork on the fast day of Yom Kippur, the holiest day in the Jewish calendar. He had emigrated to Palestine, arriving with a kitbag on his shoulder. The wiry youth with a charming manner had landed a job as a bellboy in a Tel Aviv hotel. A wealthy guest offered him a post as his butler. Shaltiel lasted a month after reading a magazine article about the gambling tables of Monte Carlo. He worked his passage on a steamer to the South of France and played the tables; within days he had lost all his money and joined the Foreign Legion. He was 23 years old. He fought in North Africa and later became a sergeant with the Medaille de la Mérite pinned to his chest. Afterwards he settled in Paris and worked as a salesman for Shell Oil.

The rise of anti-Semitism in Europe rekindled his faith. He joined the Zionist Movement and began to recruit Jewish youths to go to Palestine. Soon his talent came to the attention of the Haganah and he was summoned to Tel Aviv. They liked his style and sent him back to Europe to act as the organisation's arms buyer. In 1936 he was arrested by the German border police trying to smuggle 100,000 Reich marks into the country. He said he was a gambler on his way to a casino in Berlin. He was tortured by the Gestapo, sent to Dachau shortly after it opened and put in charge of the burial squads. He would recall: 'The gravediggers had the best job as they could divide up the corpses' clothes among themselves. I reorganised them so that the fittest dug the graves and the neediest got the clothes.'

In 1939 he was inexplicably released and made his way back to Palestine, welcomed as one of the first authentic heroes of the Haganah.

In the same scholarly voice, which for over half a century had captivated his synagogue congregation, Rabbi Weingarten reminded the men sitting before him that, despite support in London for a Jewish homeland, there still remained a gulf between promises and results. The rabbi walked over to the shelf, picked out a book and identified it as the reports of Britain's Labour Party at their annual conference.

He began to read: '1943. Conference continues to support its traditional policy in favour of building Palestine as the Jewish National Home.' He turned to another page: '1944. Conference accepts there is neither hope nor meaning in a Jewish National Home unless we are prepared to let Jews, if they wish to, enter this tiny land in such numbers as to become a majority. There was a strong case for this before the war. There is an irresistible case now after the unspeakable atrocities of the cold and calculated Nazi plan to kill all the Jews of Europe.'

Rabbi Weingarten closed the book and addressed the Haganah men, as recalled by David Shaltiel: '"But will that be Labour's position after the war?" he asked, and answered the question himself. Nobody could be sure. He said that the reason he had asked us to meet him was to urge us once more to be ready to bring home the survivors of the death camps to their Homeland. He had paused and added, that is Homeland with a capital "H".'

In Auschwitz, the fate of those prisoners in Hitler's largest concentration camp – 20 square miles – who had not been gassed and cremated was being settled by early 1945. Out of the several million who had passed under the barrier Freddie Kronenberg had raised, there were only 125,000 prisoners left. Sitting in Kommandant Joseph Kramer's outer office, waiting for further orders, Freddie could hear Kramer shouting down the phone that the executions would be finished on time.

That night the sound of heavy artillery and gunfire was joined by the bombing of Buna Monowitz – a sub-camp at the end of the Auschwitz complex where chemists had been trying to create synthetic oil. Though the bombs never fell near the gas chambers or crematoria, the air strikes had triggered Kramer's order for the SS guards to complete their demolition as fast as possible and leave no evidence of mass murder.

By 18 January, Kramer and the SS guards had driven away in trucks, leaving behind 7,652 prisoners still alive. One was Freddie. During the long night he had discarded the messenger-boy black uniform he had been forced to wear and hidden himself near one of the mass graves in the compound. Around the camp, the dying bonfires of incriminating documents flickered in the dawn of another day.

Freddie knew then that not only had he survived, but he could focus on escaping from the blood-soaked soil of Auschwitz and plan how to fulfil a dream he had until that moment not dared to admit – going to *Eretz Yisrael*.

On 19 February 1945, with her flat-bottomed hull making her able to negotiate shallow waters, *President Warfield* had been moved from Omaha Beach to the port of Le Havre, further down the coast. From there she began to ferry fresh troops miles up the Seine to the front line.

By April she had brought over 12,000 troops up the river. On each trip the crew yelled out a song they had composed to the tune of the popular Irish ditty 'MacNamara's Band':

> Ooh – we call our ship the *Warfield*;
> She's the finest in the fleet.
> And when it comes to making time,
> She simply can't be beat.
>
> Her boilers are old and rusty,
> But they're full of dynamite.
> One puff of smoke – one splash of brine,
> And then she's out of sight.
>
> Ooh – her pistons clang and her engines bang,
> And the whistle toots away.

The captain cries, 'Full speed ahead,'
And then there's hell to pay.

Her top three decks are made of wood,
And her hull is made of tin.
A credit to our navy is
This Grand Old Hulk we're in!

Miriam Bergman huddled on the filthy floor beneath her bunk. The last of the rats in the hut had been caught, skinned, cooked and eaten by prisoners. She had avoided doing so, fearing the risk of diarrhoea, which had struck so many down. Prisoners lay in their filth. To try and avoid the faeces coming through gaps in the wooden slats of the bunk overhead, she had stuffed them with pieces of cloth and swallowed the last of the tablets she had stolen from the camp pharmacy. Its shelves were now empty of all medicine.

Miriam was sure the diarrhoea had also been carried into the camp by the continuous arrival of prisoners from other camps to the east. There was little food and no water, no sanitation, no medical help. The mortality rate had escalated; 20 more had died in Miriam's hut overnight. There were no more pits in which to bury them, no lime to pour over the bodies. Instead the corpses were left in piles, producing a permanent stench which no piece of cloth wrapped around her face could keep out. But it was not the overpowering smell which filled her with fear that spring morning in mid-April 1945. It was the sound of heavy trucks once more approaching. Each time so far it had preceded the arrival of still more prisoners to be packed into the camp's confines. Yet a few days ago the majority of the guards had left. What could the trucks mean? New guards? Or were the prisoners being moved?

The engine noise was close. Overcoming her fear, Miriam crawled out from under the bunk and staggered to the hut door. Leaning against the frame, she stared in wonder. At the camp's main entrance was parked a vehicle displaying a flag she had never seen before and a soldier in khaki uniform. He was Lieutenant Derek Sington, an intelligence officer with the British Second Army. He sat behind the wheel of his Jeep that was flying the Union flag. Behind him were parked the trucks Miriam had heard, their drivers staring in horror and disbelief at the figures staggering towards them.

A tall figure wearing a skullcap and with a Star of David around his neck stepped forward to the gate, spreading his arms in compassion. To Rabbi Leslie Hardman: 'It seemed as though they had emerged from the shadows of dark, dark corners, no more than wraith-like creatures tottering towards us. As they came closer, they made frantic efforts to quicken their feeble pace. Their skeleton arms and legs made jerky grotesque movements as they forced themselves forward. Their bodies from their heads to their feet looked like matchsticks.'

Gathering himself, trying not to reveal how stunned he felt, Rabbi Hardman cried out, 'You are free. *Ihr seid frei.*'

To Lieutenant Sington the response sounded 'like voices from a supernatural world, inarticulate voices as thin as the skeletal figures before me. Cardboard figures, scarecrows. How could humanity have done this?' He would remember lowering his head to hide not just his tears, but the shame he felt.

Miriam watched, not yet understanding. Tears were something she had not seen for a long time. All she could do was to look around her at the other prisoners and repeat they were free.

For them freedom was often difficult to adjust to. In the words of Helena Levi: 'It took time to be able to wake up knowing you were going to live that day. It was the most wonderful feeling of all. Freedom.'

On that day, 9 May 1945, *President Warfield* was moored at the Quai d'Escole in Le Havre, immobilised after two blades of her propeller had been bent when they struck a submerged object in the River Seine. Late in the afternoon a car drove on to the quay and a thin-faced man in the uniform of the United States Navy stepped out, walking the length of the ship before climbing the gangway. Lieutenant Alfred Sanford Harer had one final mission in his 30-year career: to take *President Warfield* back to the United States.

Chapter 8

'Kibbutz Fourteen' and the Dancing Girls

While welcome-home celebrations were being organised across America for returning servicemen from Europe, in a building on New York's East 60th Street a different kind of activity was being planned. The basement was one of the most famous addresses in the city, the home of the Copacabana nightclub, where Lena Horne, Ella Fitzgerald, Dean Martin, Jerry Lewis and the stunningly beautiful Copa chorus girls performed to packed houses. The 13 floors above were the homes of rich widows and Wall Street brokers. No one suspected that the landlords of the club and Hotel Fourteen's 300 apartments were members of the Haganah. Fanny Barnett and her husband, Rudy, had bought the building in 1944. She called it her 'Kibbutz Fourteen'. It became the New York headquarters for men like Ben-Gurion, Chaim Weizmann and members of the Haganah High Command. Fanny had made sure that suites for 'my specials' were always available for the future leaders of Israel. Golda Meir (then Golda Meyerson) was her favourite 'special'.

The daughter of a carpenter from Kiev, Russia, Golda would become one of the foremost women in modern history and Israel's fourth prime minister (1969–74). To her dying day she never forgot the pogroms which had forced her family to flee to the United States in 1906. In 1921 she came to Palestine to teach on a kibbutz and became a leading figure in the Zionist Movement. In 1948 she was appointed Israel's first ambassador to Russia, changing her name to Meir in 1956, when she became Israel's Foreign Minister.

The most urgent task then facing Jewish leaders was the buying of ships, refitting and registering them under foreign flags and settling the many details involved in maritime commerce. Crews would have to agree to serve without pay – except for pocket money and cigarettes – and sail under Haganah discipline. Finally, secrecy was paramount; not even a wife or mother must know why a crew member had signed on.

Every port from Boston to Baltimore had its Haganah recruiters. In addition to that role, they were to act as fund-raisers, though they were told as little as possible about how the money would be spent.

In Washington, DC, the United Jewish Appeal had set up an office at 1720 16th Street NW, another of the anonymous-looking buildings which Leo Bernstein had located. Within the Jewish Agency people now spoke of him with affection. His sense of humour and relentless determination meant that nothing would stand in the way of his finding money. This had made him an important figure in Washington's Jewish community and a welcome visitor to Kibbutz Fourteen.

Some 6,000 miles from where Leo Bernstein drew up his latest list of potential donors, as night fell across the bleak Baltic landscape of the steppes, Daniel Feinstein helped other prisoners drag bodies of those who had died that day into a pile. Exhaustion, diphtheria and other diseases had claimed their lives on the death march from the concentration camp at Stutthof, one of the sub-camps of Auschwitz. Daniel would remember: 'When we had piled sufficient bodies into what we called human ovens, we burrowed among the bodies to get as far inside as possible for warmth. Those who couldn't get in and had to huddle outside against the bodies would often be dead in the morning. When we crawled out at dawn the SS guards were waiting and beat us before making us dismantle the human oven. But as we marched on until it was dark we built a new oven from the bodies who had died that day.'

Daniel was thin to the bone, but had learned the only way to stay alive was to march all day and help build a 'human oven'. In some ways he felt he was better off. Many of the marchers did not have shoes, only clogs. It was impossible to walk in them in the frost and snow. Daniel had a pair of shoes, but the left and right were not the same, salvaged from corpses during the march. He knew that as long as he could walk he had a chance of living. When the march started, Daniel had calculated there were 29,000 prisoners in the column. Three months later there were only 3,000.

Finally, in April 1945, 60 miles from Berlin, they were liberated by the Red Army. After he had eaten his first warm meal for months Daniel began to wonder how to get to Palestine.

After their meeting with Rabbi Weingarten, the five Haganah officers had been summoned to David Ben-Gurion's office at the Jewish Agency. They found him sombre, even though Radio Palestine was broadcasting endless accounts of the VE celebrations in London and elsewhere. Scattered on his desk were copies of the wire service stories which Shimson Lifshitz had torn off the teleprinter at his newspaper.

Ben-Gurion had circled one report: in London the Labour Party had ended its wartime coalition with the Conservatives, which had forced Winston Churchill to call a general election. Ben-Gurion had spent a frustrating day trying to decide what the implications were, but everyone he tried to reach in London was out celebrating the end of the war. He believed the Prime Minister had deceived Chaim Weizmann with his talk about 'a plan for the creation of a Jewish homeland'.

Concerned himself, and despite his failing health – he had glaucoma – Weizmann had flown back to London to try to get Churchill to confirm the details. After waiting for some days for a meeting with the Prime Minister, he had written to Churchill from his suite in the Dorchester: 'The mere fact of an interview with you would give hope to the Jews. My failure to be granted one will be taken by Jewry as a sign, even though your sympathies are known, you have nothing to say which would relieve and assure us.'

They were the pleas of an ailing man, perhaps already sensing his world was changing. Throughout the war he had been a close supporter of Churchill, accepting his often eccentric outbursts and his messianic predictions about a glorious future for the British Empire. Now, waiting for a telephone call from Downing Street, Chaim Weizmann, the son of a ghetto family from a White Russian hamlet, began to feel less the anglicised Jew able to open almost any door in the kingdom and more a supplicant waiting to be received by an imperious ruler.

He received no reply from the Prime Minister and became convinced Churchill's silence was directly linked to the assassination, in November 1944, of Lord Walter Moyne, Britain's Minister of State in Cairo. The diplomat had been a close personal friend of the Prime Minister.

When he learned of the assassination, Weizmann wrote immediately to Churchill:

> I can hardly find words adequate to express the deep moral indignation and horror which I feel at the murder of Lord Moyne. I know these feelings are shared by Jewry throughout the world. Whether or not the criminals prove to be Palestine Jews, their act illumines the abyss to which terrorism leads. Political crimes of this kind are an especial abomination in that they make it possible to implicate whole communities in the guilt of a few. I can assure you that Palestine Jewry will, its representative bodies have declared, go to the utmost limit of its power to cut out, root and branch, this evil from its midst.

There is no record of whether Churchill replied.

In another attempt to meet Churchill, Weizmann called on Stewart Menzies. The usually affable head of MI6 was cold, telling Weizmann that the assassination had been the work of the breakaway Irgun Zvai Leumi. Weizmann reminded him of his personal opposition to the aims of the extremists, but Menzies gave one of his little shrugs, refused a drink in the Dorchester bar and left. Weizmann knew then that the time he had spent risking his own life for MI6 now meant very little. On the flight home he noted: 'Churchill had made promises of a plan he never intended to keep.

No people have been fooled as the Jewish people had been fooled by the British government.'

On his return to Palestine Weizmann detected that his failure to have seen Churchill would inevitably jeopardise his position as president of the World Zionist Organisation. Rather than face being asked to resign, he decided to send another letter to Churchill, requesting 'a clear statement by the Allies that they do intend to establish a Jewish state in Palestine as an independent member of the British Commonwealth'.

Ben-Gurion was dismayed. Did Weizmann really want the Mandate to rule under another name, giving Jews no real say in an 'independent' nation? It was full statehood he wanted. Nothing less.

But still Weizmann would not give up. He wrote to Churchill's personal secretary, J.M. Martin, making no secret of his personal predicament: 'It would be of immense help to my position if Mr Churchill would indicate that after he has settled the election, he will see his way clear to regard as a priority the formation of a Jewish homeland.'

Again there was no response.

It was already dark when the five Haganah officers who had met with Rabbi Weingarten slipped in through a side door of the Jewish Agency, where Ben-Gurion waited in his office. He wasted no time in telling them that Chaim Weizmann had been betrayed by Churchill, saying it was another example of how Britain had deceived the Jews: 'My greatest regret is that I cannot tell the Jewish people what I really think of Churchill. That could lead to violence here and let our enemies accuse us of having deliberately provoked disorder. But our people were living in a fool's paradise if they thought Dr Weizmann had an offer of a Jewish state in his pocket. There is nobody who felt more deceived, after placing so much trust in Churchill, than Weizmann.'

Ben-Gurion stared at the men before his desk and turned to point at the map with its place names of concentration camps. When he spoke, there was a cold anger in his voice: 'We don't know how many of our people have survived the Nazi charnel-houses. Auschwitz,

Belsen, Dachau. So many of them. Each with their chambers where hundreds, thousands, of our people were gassed every day, every hour of every day. They were brought to their deaths naked, as if to bathe, and the Nazis would peer through peepholes and watch them writhing in their death agonies. Crematoria in which we now know millions of Jews were burned alive. Gallows on which Jews were hanged each holy day for no reason than they were Jews. Ferocious dogs trained on Jews to kill yet more Jews. Jews were used as target practice. Yet some have survived. That is the wonder of it.'

Ben-Gurion had stopped, his emotion and anger for the moment spent. When he continued, that anger was reinforced by determination: 'The miracle is that they have survived where so many were butchered before the gaze of a world, rigid, aloof and indifferent to the state of the people, our people, who have been hounded and tormented for two thousand years. These are the reasons you are here tonight.'

He told them they would have the full support of the Jewish Agency to bring home the survivors to *Eretz Yisrael*. 'You must create new secret roads across Europe. Boats will have to be found around the Mediterranean from anywhere for an unprecedented operation, which will bring home Holocaust survivors.'

In early 1945 a new abbreviation entered the English language: DP. The initials stood for Displaced Person. There were almost 12 million of them, not only survivors of the concentration camps, but the millions who had been left destitute, their homes demolished and workplaces flattened.

For self-protection, Jewish survivors came together, clutching little more than snapshots of their families to remind themselves of their loved ones and their hope of reaching the Promised Land. Every night before going to sleep, voices uttered the same wish: *Next year in Jerusalem*.

The liberators found themselves all too often baffled by the attitude of the DPs. Yet in freeing them from the camps, understandably the Allies had made few plans about how to cope with the great multitude of nomads.

Doctors, nurses and relief workers arriving in the DP camps had little or no experience of dealing with the catastrophe that confronted them and a number returned home. Those who stayed found a lack of coordination. No one seemed to know what to prioritise when at every turn clear-cut decision-making was obviously called for.

Days before the Red Army had liberated Auschwitz, on 27 January 1945, Freddie Kronenberg decided he would leave the camp. He feared the Russians would shoot anyone they discovered had worked for the Nazis. He had hidden in woods, living on roots and leaves, chewing bark and drinking pond water. When the first of the refugee columns passed he tagged along. No one had any clear idea where they were going, except west, away from the camps and the Russians, in the hope of reaching the British or, even better, the Americans. For Freddie, it would be a step closer to Palestine.

To survive until he made that contact, Freddie had joined one of the gangs who hunted like wolf packs, stealing food: mouldy potatoes, turnips and beets, anything to provide the energy to continue moving westwards. Those who became too ill to continue were left to die. Like figures from Orpheus's underworld, the others trudged on.

Freddie had burned the pass signed by Kommandant Kramer that had allowed him to carry messages to all parts of the camp. In the cities and towns he passed through, he saw looters picking over the ruins. In late May, Freddie met his first Americans near Landsberg in Bavaria. Their Jeeps were parked beside a sign stuck in an oil barrel: *American Sector*. The patrol leader was a young lieutenant; his Jeep was loaded with equipment and soldiers stood around smoking and staring curiously at the marchers.

Freddie would recall: 'A number of the soldiers were blacks. Big guys and armed with enough guns to start a war. I hadn't seen anyone like them before. When we tried to smile, they didn't smile back. I had a feeling as if it was horror and disgust at the way we must have looked. Then the officer said he was a Jew from Brooklyn and asked were there any Jews among us? No one moved. I guess we knew too well what that admission had led to under the Nazis. But what the hell? These guys were our liberators so I stuck up my hand. The officer said, "OK, you get to ride with me." You others will have to walk. The DP camp's down the road.'

In a DP camp near Munich, Gertruda had found shelter for herself and Michael Stolowitzky – her Mickey. Since that Easter Sunday in Vilnius, when an SS officer had saved Mickey from certain death at the hands of a German patrol, Gertruda had lived in fear he would be killed before she could fulfil her promise to his mother and bring the child to Palestine. After the encounter with the patrol, she had taken Mickey to her confessor priest and told him what had happened. The priest had said he would immediately baptise Mickey into the Church and make him an altar boy. As the Red Army drew closer, Gertruda had taken him to her family home near Danzig. They had urged her to stay with them; they had enough food and Mickey could be brought up there. Gertruda had told them of her promise to take him to Palestine, where he could live again as a Jew.

She had set off towards the west, walking for weeks, until she was directed by an American patrol to a DP camp.

Churchill's closest ally, Roosevelt, had died in April 1945 from a massive stroke at his home in Warm Springs, Georgia. Within hours, Harry S. Truman had become the 33rd President of the United States. He hardly knew Churchill and the little he did know had not fitted into his up-with-the-sun Missouri farm-boy mentality. He had told his team that Britain's prime minister was 'altogether too grand for me'.

On 25 July, Churchill had stayed up even later than usual to hear the election results. By breakfast he knew that the Conservatives had lost in a Labour landslide and he was going to be driven out of office. The new prime minister was Clement Attlee. His Foreign Secretary would be Ernest Bevin, a member of the wartime coalition government. Within the Zionist Political Committee in London, both men were seen as anti-Semites. At the next Labour Party Conference, Bevin confirmed their view when he said, 'The American campaign for 100,000 Jews to be admitted to Palestine was proposed with the purest of motives. They didn't want too many Jews in New York.' Weizmann's contacts with Bevin had continued to show the Foreign Secretary as 'gratuitously brutal, even coarse, but I cannot say it surprised me. His tone was hectoring. There was not the slightest effort to understand our point of view; there was only an overbearing, quarrelsome approach.'

In Tel Aviv, David Ben-Gurion had already anticipated the attitude of the new Labour government. Bevin left no doubt he would do nothing to antagonise the Arabs. Once more, summoning the last of his strength, Chaim Weizmann had written what would be his final request to Churchill:

> I hope you will realise that I am appealing to you *in extremis* as an old friend with whom it has been my privilege to work for nearly thirty years. I believe that just as you took the helm in the hours of darkness and storm that followed Chamberlain's policy of appeasement, and brought the British ship of state safely to port, you will lend your powerful aid to another people – old and proud as your own, but today decimated, weak, defenceless in the hour of its supreme need. Now is the time our friends can help us, and I know you will be most generous, as you are the most truly understanding among them.

In a brief response Churchill informed Weizmann that his letter had been sent to the new prime minister. Clement Attlee never replied.

The differences between Ben-Gurion and Weizmann became more pronounced. At the first post-war World Zionist Congress in Geneva, as Weizmann would recall: 'It was a dreadful experience to stand before that assembly and to run one's eyes along row after row of delegates, finding among them hardly one of the friendly faces which had adorned my past conferences. I became the scapegoat for the sins of the British government and the "activists", or whatever they would call themselves, turned on me. The Palestinian delegation, led by Mr Ben-Gurion, had made up their minds I was to go.'

No longer president of the Federation, Chaim Weizmann returned to his home in Rehovot with Vera. There he began to create the scientific institute that would bear his name and for which he hoped to be remembered, rather than as the man who had been misled by a person he once trusted: Winston Churchill.

In her private office in Kibbutz Fourteen, Fanny Barnett had locked the door before doing the bookwork she did every Sunday morning. Since those first days when Chaim Weizmann arrived from London and checked into his hotel suite, she had never been busier or happier. She had been his secretary, setting up meetings with important Jews and members of the Roosevelt administration.

Now Fanny had a different role. She was the bookkeeper for the Haganah. Her prime task was to track the ships that had ended their war service and were up for sale or destined for the scrapyard. Many could be bought as scrap for a few dollars a ton, but could they still be made seaworthy? Her other interest was logging the donations coming from fund-raisers all along the East Coast and, increasingly, from Jewish organisations across America. Some of the money came in dollar bills, in certified cheques, many for six figures. A prolific fund-raiser continued to be Leo Bernstein in Washington, DC.

Volunteers also started to come forward to crew boats. Many were Jewish ex-servicemen, but increasingly members of Jewish youth organisations offered to help too. They were all checked by staff at the Jewish Agency at 342 Madison Avenue, who also devoted their time to establishing the seaworthiness of ships as far away as the Pacific and South America. In the utmost secrecy, the Haganah continued to lay the foundations of a fleet to take refugees from Europe to Palestine. But Ben-Gurion constantly reminded Fanny that larger boats were needed.

One Sunday morning, her ledger work completed, she started to go through her records of ships that had sailed off to war from East Coast ports. One name caught her attention. It had sailed from Baltimore after a headline-making life of luxury on the Chesapeake. Fanny made a note to ask Leo Bernstein if he could find out when the ship might be returning from Europe – and in what state the war had left *President Warfield*.

*

On a cool autumn Friday evening in 1945, Stewart Menzies strolled into the Foreign Office. He was dressed in his favourite tweeds, a sure sign he was going to spend the weekend hunting with the Beaufort and Quorn. Riding was his favourite pastime, equalled only by his eye for a shapely pair of legs. MI6 was said to have the curviest secretaries in Whitehall.

His appointment was with the Foreign Secretary, Ernest Bevin. No two men could be more different. Menzies was an Old Etonian, spoke fluent German and French, knew his whiskies, had served in the Life Guards in the First World War, had won a DSC and MC at Ypres, and with his polished accent and impeccable manners he was a regular guest at society dinner tables. He ran MI6 with the same languid style he rode a horse.

With his countryman's bluntness, Ernest Bevin – who had been born and raised in the small village of Winsford in Somerset – maintained a West Country voice that his Foreign Office staff often found difficult to follow. Then he would laugh and say they hadn't been educated like him 'at the University of Life, not some fancy public school'.

Despite his limited education, leaving school at 11 to become a farm labourer and then a truck driver at Bristol docks, Bevin soon decided that the working man was being exploited and joined the local branch of the newborn Dockers' Union. His readiness to argue a member's case with employers made him a popular figure. Soon he climbed the ranks of the trade union movement and in 1922 became general secretary of the Transport and General Workers' Union and a leading figure in the Labour Party.

While not agreeing with Bevin's politics, Churchill had admired his determination and, when he became Britain's wartime prime minister, appointed Bevin as the government's Minister of Labour. It was a shrewd choice: Bevin's working-class background gave him popularity around the docks and factory floors, and turned the country on to a total war-footing focused towards defeating Hitler.

When he became Foreign Secretary, one of his first requests had been for weekly meetings with Menzies to discuss the latest situation over emigration to Palestine. The intelligence chief had become used to the way Bevin responded to a piece of news. If it satisfied him, he would steeple his fingers and slowly nod his massive head. But if what he was told alarmed him, he would whip off his horn-rimmed glasses and give them a vigorous cleaning with a cloth he kept for the purpose on his desk. Without his glasses, the Foreign Secretary would stare owlishly at Menzies before putting them on again and leaning forward in his chair like a bull about to charge.

Bevin had used these mannerisms several times during their last meeting once Menzies told him about the five men Ben-Gurion had sent from Palestine to Austria. That country was in the Russian zone and was regarded by MI6 as a key area from which to collect intelligence on the Soviet Union. Had the five men come on a mission to get information for the Haganah?

Menzies knew several of its members had worked for the SOE and had created their own underground networks in Eastern Europe. But according to MI5 registry records, the Jewish saboteurs had been sent home to Palestine at the end of the war. Was it also possible that the five men had come to establish links with the Russian security service to help it gain a foothold in Palestine – a move that could be a serious problem for the Mandate?

Menzies's station commander in Vienna, George Young, had established that each man had a United Nations Relief and Rehabilitation Administration (UNRRA) pass and carried a letter signed by David Ben-Gurion saying that he had been instructed to visit DP camps in Germany and Austria, as well as the barracks housing the Jewish Brigade Group, which had served with the British Army. Young had checked the register at the hotel where the men had stayed. The names were those on their documents: David Shaltiel, Yehuda Arazi, Ze'ev Shind, Eliyahu Golomb and Moshe Bar-Gilad. Menzies circulated their details to his agents in Europe.

Menzies was careful what information he shared with the Foreign Secretary; at their first meeting, Bevin had challenged MI6's claim to have had 'a good war'. Nevertheless, Menzies knew he shared common ground with the Foreign Secretary in worrying about the threat that Jewish expansion in Palestine posed to Britain's relationship with the Arabs.

At their last meeting, Menzies had been cautiously reassuring. His agent in Munich had reported that the five men spent some of their time working in the two DP camps reserved for Jews in the American zone as physical fitness instructors. Bevin had once again whipped off his glasses to begin polishing while rumbling in his West Country brogue, 'Something is going on.'

Menzies soon found out what. Moshe Bar-Gilad had opened an office in Vienna, operating from a building in the city's Jewish quarter. David Shaltiel had persuaded the French government not only to allow him to set up an office in Paris, but even to let him establish a short-wave wireless link with Tel Aviv. Ze'ev Shind had opened offices in Milan, Prague and Budapest under the name of the Jewish Agency and Yehuda Arazi was going around ports along the Mediterranean coast.

That Friday evening, Menzies was not looking forward to delivering yet another piece of news he would need to give Bevin. In the morning, the director of Naval Intelligence had sent over a copy of a letter the Admiralty's Military Branch, which was responsible for selling off ships no longer required, had received. The letter had been written on company headed paper by a Colonel Frank Bustard, senior partner in Bustard and Sons, Shipping Company. After signing his name, the colonel had added, no doubt proudly, the letters OBE, the Order of the British Empire. The letter explained he had recently been demobilised from active war service and planned to develop his business. Menzies had heard of many officers with ambitious plans now the war was over. One or two he had recruited himself. But Bustard was not looking for employment. He wanted to buy ships and he had the funds available. However, it was the type of ship he wanted that had aroused Military Branch's suspicions. Bustard wanted tank landing craft of all types 'for commercial use and in due course sloops, frigates and corvettes. My client is the Palestine Maritime League.'

Menzies knew the league was linked to Haganah. He told Bevin an order had been given that no sales would be made to the league when serious trouble in Palestine was imminent.

For once the Foreign Secretary had not removed his spectacles. Instead he congratulated his intelligence chief. After Menzies had left to go hunting, Bevin had called the First Sea Lord, Admiral of the Fleet Sir John Cunningham, to prepare the Mediterranean Fleet to be ready to resist any attempt to resume pre-war smuggling of illegal immigrants into Palestine.

On a warm August day in 1945, dressed in his immaculate pressed khaki uniform, his cap squarely on his head, private first class Nat Nadler wore his lowly rank on his sleeve as proudly as any general in the United States Army. Nat had been called up a year ago, expecting to be posted from boot camp to the Pacific to fight the Japanese. Instead he had been sent to Munich in the American zone.

Munich, like other towns in Bavaria, had been heavily bombed, yet the people around him as he walked through Ludwigsvorstadt in the city centre smiled and nodded politely in his direction. How, Nat wondered, could they have forgotten the depth of Hitler's hatred, his Teutonic language, their language, promising death to Nat and all other Jews? Several of the girls walked arm in arm with GIs in giggling intimacy. Nat had been in Germany two months and decided he would never really understand its people.

Earlier that morning Nat had another insight into the mentality of the Germans. He had been posted to an army clothing depot as its chief electrician. It had recently suffered a number of thefts from its stores and, to stop this, a squad of prisoners of war had been ordered to build stronger security fences around the huts. Nat had been in charge of them. When he had returned from a toilet break, he found the prisoners sunbathing. Nat would recall: 'I told them to get back to work. They ignored me. I put my hand on my .45 and told them I wasn't kidding. My German wasn't bad and I knew enough to make them understand. One of them finally stood up, a brute of a guy, and he asked me if I was a fucking Jew. For good measure, he added, "You understand what I'm saying, *Juden?*" I drew my gun and I was pretty close to shooting him. Instead I had him do double-time around the camp, yelling at him to go faster. He finally collapsed and I dragged him back to digging a hole for a pole fence. But it was the way he looked at me which made me realise that his hatred of Jews hadn't been cured by Hitler's death.'

From the bridge of HMS *Childers*, Lieutenant Commander Bailey watched the Rock of Gibraltar drawing closer. In this first week of September 1945, the Atlantic had been as gentle as a mill pond, from the time he had given the order to cast off and HMS *Childers* had moved away from its mooring at Portsmouth into the English Channel, and on down through the Bay of Biscay and past Lisbon.

Now, as Gibraltar drew closer, Bailey was still delighted with the amount of space on the bridge and the sheer extent of equipment available to him: batteries of telephones and voice-pipes, radar screens and an illuminated plotting table keeping track of the ship's movement through the water. There were gunnery-control instruments and an Asdic set. Around him were the two officers of the watch, two signalmen, two lookouts, two Asdic operators and a bridge-messenger. Further forward of the bridge were the guns, which had never been fired in anger – Bailey doubted if they ever would be. Designed for war, HMS *Childers* was going to be, as he had told his first officer, 'a glorified peacetime policeman'.

The destroyer was joining the Royal Navy Palestine Patrol.

Led by the veteran HMS *Ajax*, whose role in the Battle of the River Plate against the *Graf Spee* had become legendary, the patrol formed part of the Royal Navy's powerful Mediterranean Fleet, which was ready to meet any threat to the Suez Canal and deal with attempts to smuggle immigrants into Palestine. The patrol was a much-sought-after posting. Based in Haifa, it made regular visits to Alexandria and Cyprus, where each port had its colourful nightlife. The other attraction was that the patrol could maintain its own routine rather than being under the watchful eye of the Fleet Admiral. And, in the event of trouble, the patrol could call on the main fleet for support, as it was never more than a few hours' sailing time.

With its five light cruisers, nine M- and Hunt-class destroyers, 28 minesweepers, eight sloops and frigates, supported by a Royal Air Force squadron to watch over the Mediterranean, the fleet provided formidable back-up. The arrival of HMS *Childers* would increase that. The Fleet Admiral, Sir John Cunningham, knew it was there because of what Menzies had discovered about the activities of the Haganah men in Europe.

Not only was the Foreign Secretary increasingly opposed to all 'illegal immigration', but Bevin had developed a paranoia that the Soviet Union was determined to create a Jewish state in which Communism would predominate. He had told the Chiefs of Staff Committee: 'The day may soon come when we will have tens of thousands of Jews educated in Communist beliefs that will cause the Arabs to rise and we will face a new war.'

Menzies had continued to feed Bevin with secret reports: 'Our officers have established that the Soviet authorities in Bulgaria and Romania will permit Jews to move through their countries. Only Moscow could have approved this and done so with the connivance of the Jewish Agency over which Ben-Gurion had total control. He would wish nothing better than to embarrass the UK over our determination to maintain our limitation on immigration. He has used our position to arouse considerable sympathy in the United States to our detriment.'

It was against that background HMS *Childers* had been added to the Royal Navy Palestine Patrol. Passing through the Straits of Gibraltar, Lieutenant Commander Bailey had received an encoded signal from Supreme Allied Command Mediterranean: 'It is expected that illegal Jewish immigration will undoubtedly be by sea. Take all steps to prevent ships engaged in this trade from leaving ports. Based on intelligence, large numbers of small craft are likely to be used, including landing craft.'

Accompanying the signal was another, marked HAGANAH: 'The Jewish military organisation comprises strike companies, Haganah and Palmach. Of equal interest to HM Navy is Palyam, the naval arm of Haganah. Some of its members were involved in illegal immigration operations pre-war. Others were trained in underwater sabotage by the SOE. Haganah also has an intelligence/counterintelligence department also trained by the SOE. A best estimate by the Secret Intelligence Service places the total strength of Haganah at around 20,000 personnel.'

Far to the west of Haifa, where HMS *Childers* was heading towards her new base, a 40-foot-long pennant flew from *President Warfield*'s mast bearing the words 'Homeward Bound'. As the East Coast of the United States drew closer, the ship's crew led her passengers in a final chorus of the song they had repeated every day on the voyage across the Atlantic, sung to the tune of 'MacNamara's Band'.

A white light flashed in the dawn, signalling the entrance to Chesapeake Bay. The pennant was pulled down and cut into pieces, a snippet for each of the crew members. Hours later Lieutenant Harer's pinched face broke into a smile as he watched the helmsman ring down for 'stop engine'. It was almost three years to the day since *President Warfield* had set off from an adjoining Baltimore pier.

By nightfall, the crew and passengers – soldiers who had fought from Normandy into the heart of the Third Reich and aircrews freed from camps – had all left. Only Lieutenant Harer and a handful of sailors remained on board to welcome the decommissioning team. They came early next morning, men who knew exactly what they wanted. The guns had already been taken out before *President Warfield* left Europe. Now it was their turn to remove the navigation equipment, the signalling gear, the evaporators, all of the paraphernalia which, three years previously, had changed the Queen of the Chesapeake into a fighting ship.

At 1.20pm on 13 September, Lieutenant Commander Boykin of the Fifth Naval District assembled the remaining crew on deck and read out *President Warfield*'s decommissioning orders. He handed the paper to Lieutenant Harer, who saluted, went to the mast and slowly lowered the Stars and Stripes for the last time. The two officers saluted each other and walked slowly down the gangplank.

Ernest Bevin, Britain's Foreign Minister in the post-war Labour Government. His restrictive immigration policy and determination to stop the *Exodus* reaching Palestine at all costs brought worldwide condemnation.

On 2 November 1917, Authur James Balfour, Britain's Foreign Secretary, wrote to Lord Rothschild the momentous letter that became known as the Balfour Declaration. Balfour (middle) is seen here in Jerusalem with Weizmann (right) laying a corner stone at the Einstein Institiute of Mathematics in 1925.

David Ben-Gurion rests his bowed head on his hands while Chaim Weizmann cups his hand over his eyes. It is as if both men wanted to blot out the looming war. It marked the end of the 21st Zionist Congress in Geneva in 1939. On Ben-Gurion's right is Moshe Shertok (Sharett), who would become Israel's first Foreign Minister.

Menachem Begin, a veteran Polish soldier and a guerrilla fighter in Palestine, presented the British Mandate forces with a serious challenge as he led his men in armed struggle against them. He commanded the infamous terror group, the Irgun.

Golda Meir (Meyerson): her fund-raising skills in the United States played a crucial role in the story of *Exodus*.

Yossi Harel, seen here in later life, was born in Jerusalem. He was 28 years old and a seasoned Haganah intelligence officer who had fought under Orde Wingate when he was appointed commander of *Exodus*. Serving under Captain Ike Ahronowitz inflamed the two men's relationship.

Ike (Yitzhak) Ahronowitz was born in Lodz, Poland, but his family moved to Tel Aviv the year he was born. A fiery young ideologue, he joined the Haganah naval unit and, after studying for eight months in London, he qualified as third, second and finally first officer. It was but a step to becoming captain of *Exodus*, which would make him Israel's most daring and celebrated sailor.

Second left in the front is Ike Ahroniwitz. The 22-year-old looks like a teenager with the face of a streetwise youngster. He had started his life sailing at sea on cargo ships and went on to study at a maritime college in London. There he met Saul Avigur, the Aliyah Bet veteran. After spending an afternoon together in a Lion's Corner House, Avigur recommended Ike to captain *Exodus*.

Exodus, formerly the most luxurious Chesapeake Bay steamer *President Warfield*, docked at Portovenere, Italy. In the top left is a splendid white villa from where the MI6 officer, Count Frederick Vanden Heuvel, kept watch on the ship.

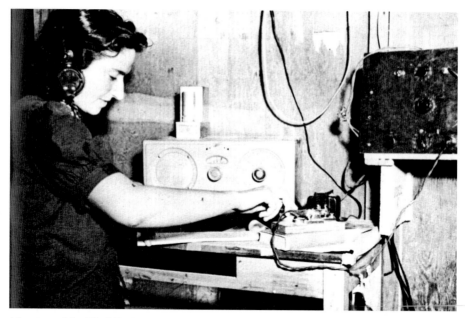

A key part of the Aliyah Bet immigration organisation were the secret radio stations the Haganah had set up around the Mediterranean. This one was hidden in the Italian base Ada Sereni had set up.

The Haganah's most brilliant operative in the South of France, Ada Sereni, a gentle, petite, black-haired woman in her forties. Her contacts were invaluable for providing documents for Jewish refugees. She was the widow of Enzo Sereni (right), the son of the physician to the King of Italy, who had been captured and tortured to death by the Gestapo after parachuting behind German lines. Ada took his place in operations in Italy.

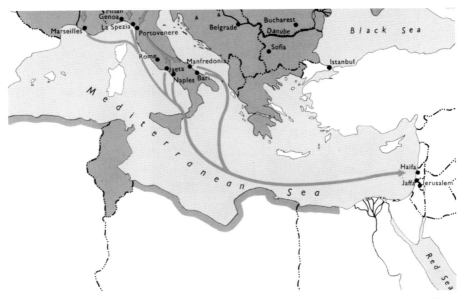

The map shows the jump-off points of the displaced person boats along the Italian coast. These were organised by Ada Sereni and Azar. The first boat set sail in 1946 after the end of the war while *Exodus* was being prepared for its momentous journey. The refugees came down from the camps in Germany through Italy, often by their own volition.

Orde Wingate whom Winston Churchill called 'a man of a genius who might well have become a man of destiny'. He was exceptional in his support for the Jews and his commitment to Zionism even before he came as a British Army intelligence officer to Palestine. There he taught the Haganah the tactics of waging guerrilla warfare against Arab terrorists. Yossi Harel became his aide and the tactics they developed were later adapted to protect *Exodus* as it fought off the Royal Navy.

Yehuda Arazi's code name was *alon*, or oak, an apt name. The British called him the fox. His courage and skills as a former detective in the Palestine Police Force, before he left to join the Haganah, made him an expert in creating escape routes for Jewish refugees – and put a price on his head.

Eli Kalm and Bill Bernstein, First Mate of the *Exodus*, in a jovial mood before the departure of the *President Warfield*. Bill would become the victim of the later battle – clubbed on the head by a boarder he had told his shipmates his premonition that he would die in the battle. He is buried in Martys Row in Haifa cemetery, and is one of many heroes of the voyage.

David Ben-Gurion, the fiery Jewish leader, found in Truman (left) a ready listener over the grim conditions in the DP camps in Germany. Ben-Gurion urged Truman to ask Britain's Foreign Secretary, Ernest Bevin to allow 100,000 Jews to enter Palestine.

At the tender age of 19 Fira Neimark (now Memakov) had escorted 52 small children, survivors of the Holocaust, on board *Exodus*. She and Efraim Memakov, whom Fira met and fell in love with on the ship, were married in the detention camp in Poppendorf then remarried later, in Israel.

A woman on a bunkbed aboard the *Exodus*. The bed was made from planks carried on board from Baltimore and finally assembled at Portovenere.

Sol Lester was one of the 35 American Jews who had volunteered to crew *Exodus*. Many, like Lester, had originally signed on as deck hands. But when his skills as a mechanic became known to Ike Ahronowitz, he was transferred to the engine room and learned to maintain the great flailing piston rods driving the propeller shaft at over a hundred revolutions a minute.

Crushed together against each other in the heat, the passengers reminded each other that all that mattered was they had survived and all they wanted was to reach their homeland.

Born in a remote village near Pinsk in the Russian Empire, Chaim Weizmann became the first President of Israel, the climax of one of the most remarkable careers, one that shaped the history of the Jewish race. His vital role in the creation of the Jewish state brought him into conflict with Winston Churchill, Ernest Bevin and President Roosevelt. He confronted them all with candour and occasionally anger, but above all with the informed wisdom of a lifetime fighting for the creation of Israel.

Lieutenant Roger Pearce of HMS *Childers* was the leader of the naval boarding parties who stormed the *Exodus*. He narrowly escaped falling into the sea when, landing on the ship's deck, he was greeted with a fusillade of tins and potatoes. A battle like no other started. Before he retired from the navy Pearce had become Admiral of the Fleet.

The leader of the Palestine Patrol attack force, HMS *Childers*. The tactics to capture *Exodus* had been devised by its captain, Lieutenant E.A.S. Bailey, a veteran of World War Two. He decided the boarding platform would enable his specially trained sailors to overcome the high super-structure of *Exodus*. But Bailey had not counted on the unexpected resistance of its passengers.

Brooklyn-born and bred, Cyril Weinstein was *Exodus'* third mate and looked like a man whose mind was set only on getting the passengers to Palestine. Physically powerful, he walked with a limp from childhood infantile paralysis. He was an artist and off-duty sketched for children on board. During the battle at sea he worked with Ike to use the steering gear at the stern to time after time outwit the ramming tactics of the Royal Navy destroyers.

Ralph Goldman was a senior Haganah officer in New York who organised fund-raising lunches where the guest speakers included Golda Meir and David Ben-Gurion. There were times when $50 million would be pledged in minutes to finance the purchase of ships like *Exodus*.

Gerald Landau had been put in charge of many of the older children on *Exodus*. One had been Zvi Yakubovich, a survivor of Buchenwald, who would be shot dead by a naval boarder. He was almost 15 years old. Two others would be killed: his friend, 23-year-old Mordechai Baumstein, and Bill Bernstein.

Harold Gardner was a young soldier in the British Army in Palestine before being assigned as a guard on the *Runnymede Park*. His duty was to patrol outside the wire cage containing refugees. He established a friendship with several, including a young Ukrainian woman who spoke near-perfect English. By the time the ship reached Hamburg he was one of the few guards who concluded the refugees should not have been sent back to Germany.

One of the destroyers in the task force which attacked *Exodus*, taken by a young soldier at the time, Harold Gardner.

The flag and name board were raised after the funeral of the mother of the new-born baby on board. The Royal Navy boarders, scattered around the deck, were ordered by their officers to make no attempt to remove the emblems. As the ship came closer to the Palestine coast the passengers united in singing.

Exodus, stopped at sea by the navy task force. The toll was three refugees killed, two hundred wounded and the ship's superstructure ripped to pieces. The boarding teams gathered up the potatoes and tins of food hurled at them to take back to their warships where food was short. Mementos of the fighting were stolen from the refugees' belongings.

Sir John Cunningham, the future First Sea Lord and Commander of the Eastern Mediterranean Fleet including the Palestine Patrol. By the outbreak of the Second World War he was a vice-admiral. After an adventurous war, he was appointed First Sea Lord in 1946.

Exodus approaching Haifa under the guard of the Palestine boarders. The refugees were allowed to fly their flag and display their new name for the ship once known as *President Warfield*. Later, sailing from Port-de-Bouc in France to internment in Hamburg, the refugees on board *Runnymede Park* had displayed their continued defiance by emblazing a swastika on the British Union Jack.

Chapter 9

Preparations

Aliyah Bet had placed Captain William Ash and Ze'ev Shind in charge of locating ships in the United States, outfitting them and finding crews to become blockade-runners. Very different personalities, the two men soon became a close team. No ship was bought until they had mutually settled on the price to be offered and the work required to make it seaworthy for the voyage to Palestine. They agreed that each ship would have a joint crew of Palestinian and American Jews.

Ash's wartime record and connections as the vice-president of the powerful Masters, Mates & Pilots union enabled him to identify captains and crews. US maritime laws required that only an American could skipper a foreign-registered ship out of a US port. Ash solved the problem by appointing to sail with a captain a Jewish mate who would assume command on his final run across the Mediterranean to Palestine.

Nevertheless, the tall, flame-haired Shind had not always found it easy to handle recruiting. The Palestinian Jews had been raised in the strict discipline of Socialist youth movements and had become battle-hardened after serving in the Haganah. To Shind, the easy-going American Jews often appeared naive and undisciplined, and in interviews he found the fact that they were members of the most powerful nation on earth gave them a self-assurance that could verge on arrogance.

Those who passed his interrogation were told to await his call. He warned that if he discovered they had spoken to anybody about Aliyah Bet they would never hear from him again.

Total secrecy applied to everyone involved in the clandestine work of acquiring ships. It had been introduced by Rudolf Sonneborn, the industrialist who had hosted Ben-Gurion's fund-raising breakfast and had created the Sonneborn Institute to secretly buy military equipment to be shipped to Palestine.

The McAlpine Hotel in New York's midtown was where the Haganah's wealthiest and most powerful supporters in the United States met promptly at noon every Thursday. They would come by train from the Midwest and by plane from the West Coast. Others would be chauffeured from Boston, Washington, DC and Baltimore. By the time lunch was served there were generally 50 bankers, philanthropists, shipping magnates, department store and hotel owners and entertainment moguls in the dining room. Two hours later they would have eaten some of the finest food in the city, having pledged to buy a ship or build a hospital or college in Palestine.

For Ralph Goldman, a senior Haganah officer serving in New York, there was always a need to find money to send to the faraway spiritual home of the lunch guests. While few had made the long journey to Palestine to accept gratitude for their generosity, Jewish leaders came to them, led by David Ben-Gurion and Chaim Weizmann. When they could not appear at the top table in the McAlpine dining room due to other commitments, they sent someone many of the diners regarded as the most mesmeric Zionist leader ever to have addressed them: Golda Meyerson.

From the day word went out that she was once more coming to New York as the key speaker, the Jewish Agency on Madison Avenue and Fanny Barnett's office in Hotel Fourteen was besieged with telephone calls for seats. According to Fanny, 'It would have been easier to get into a presidential inauguration banquet.'

No matter how many times Golda Meyerson made the long journey from Jerusalem to New York, she had never failed to enthral her audience. Men who had been guests of President Roosevelt and

President Truman or who had heard Winston Churchill address the Senate and Congress said there was no one who could match her resonant voice.

Movingly, she would remind her audience of the day she had confronted Henry Gurney, the Mandate's Chief Secretary, in his office in Jerusalem to tell him that she and other Zionist leaders planned to go on hunger strike in support of the refugees in Europe. From behind his desk Gurney had stared at her. In an imitation of his 'clipped voice', she mimicked, 'Do you think for a moment that His Majesty's Government will change its policy because *you* are not going to eat?'

She would pause and wait for the silence to last a moment longer. Then her voice would sweep around the room. 'I said, "No, I have no such illusions. If the death of six millions doesn't change government policy, I don't expect my not eating to do so. But at least it will be a mark of solidarity."'

Thunderous applause would then sweep the room. It became one of her most-quoted sentences.

She analysed events taking place in Palestine and articulated their impact on the world beyond: the emergence of anti-Semitism so soon after the war; the persecution of Jews in the Soviet Union; the impoverishment of Iraqi Jews. Golda had a view on everything, what she called 'my Jewish angle'.

In the spring of 1946, Golda Meyerson as back in the city to raise yet more money. On that Thursday she told them she had come to ask for more than ever before: $50 million. Even for the millionaires in the dining room, it was an eye-blinking figure. But as always she knew how to reach her audience.

When Aliyah Bet resumed after the Nazi defeat, two unequal antagonists faced each other in Europe and the Mediterranean. On one side a battered Britain and her empire. On the other side Jews. Many of our people are still homeless refugees. Much to the surprise of the British government we have continued to challenge them with our

brave blockade-runners. Aliyah Bet could not have done what
it has without the power and generosity of people like you. But
we need more money. The British are determined to maintain
the blockade. It has more warships, better intelligence and is
quite prepared to open fire on our little ships. As never before
we need more equipment to fit out more ships. We also need
money to prepare for the coming war with the Arab nations all
around our homeland.

Those $50 million were pledged in minutes.

For Ralph Goldman, it was not only further proof of Golda
Meyerson's powerful oratory but evidence of the privilege it was for
him to be allowed to work in the inner sanctum of the Haganah. His
qualifications – he was a skilled linguist and had a distinguished war
record, serving on the beaches of Normandy and deep in Nazi
Germany – had been stepping stones to his role in helping to make
the ships seaworthy with the money Golda Meyerson collected. To
sail again, to do battle not with the Nazis but with the Royal Navy.

On that late September day in 1946, the sun was still warm on
Yehuda Arazi's back as he drove towards the ancient port of Sète, to
the west of Marseilles. A year had passed since he had last driven this
road. His body was thinner now, fatigue ringed his brown eyes and
his hair was cropped; he thought it made him look no different from
any other Allied soldier out of uniform. In the previous 12 months,
he had visited DP camps outside the American sector and arranged
to have any Jews there transferred to DP camps in it. His letter of
authorisation signed by Ben-Gurion was sufficient to overcome any
objections.

As well as relocating Jews, he was looking for boats to buy to carry
them and the other 70,000 Jewish refugees he estimated were waiting
to be shipped to Palestine.

He had spent the night in a *gasthaus* in the small Bavarian town of
Feldafing, where Hitler had written *Mein Kampf*. The town had
become a designated centre for Jewish survivors of nearby Dachau.

The following day they had gone with him to the nearby DP camp in Landsberg to hear Ben-Gurion speaking. The Zionist leader was on a tour of all the DP camps and spoke powerfully and passionately wherever he went:

> As survivors you will get help to bring you home not only because of what you have survived, but because of who you are – Jews with a long history of surviving. When you reach your homeland, you will play an important role in developing our country. There is a desperate need to do that and we need skilled people of all kinds. We will train others to acquire those skills. That is my promise to each one of you. I have to tell you that we also have to overcome British opposition. My hope that the new Labour government in London would cancel the limitation on immigrants has not been fulfilled. But we will overcome that.

Among the 5,000 who cheered was Gertruda, holding Michael's hand firmly in her own, Freddie Kronenberg, Miriam Bergman and Helena Levi, and 18-year-old Johann Goldman. A British Army truck had brought him from Westerbork, along with other freed prisoners, to Amsterdam railway station. There he had been given papers by a Jewish Agency relief worker confirming he had been a *Kindertransport* child destined for the United States. A British officer who checked his papers before allowing him on to the train told Johann he was being sent to the American zone for 'processing'.

Two rail journeys later, he arrived in Landsberg. He had been there a month before Ben-Gurion came to the camp.

The orphaned Daniel Feinstein, barely 15 years old, had also recently arrived. He had returned to Vilnius, in the hope he would learn news of his sister, Dana, perhaps even find her. It was, he knew, a slim possibility. So many Jews had returned to the ruins of the Old Town on similar searches, only to see their hopes dashed as they saw the ruins of the ghetto. Nobody could live there now. The Nazis, retreating before the Red Army, had committed another act of mass murder in its confines.

Daniel had realised he could not remain in Vilnius. Its streets were filled with the ghosts of yesterday and the roar of Russian trucks and the crunch of marching boots, the sounds of its new occupiers. So he had begun the long journey west, hoping to reach the American or British zones. Like those he trudged with, he had lived off the land and slept rough. But every dawn he hoped the trek would bring him closer to Palestine and that along his journey he would find out what had happened to Dana.

The further west he travelled, the more he met other groups of Jews with similar hopes of finding relatives. To Daniel, 'What they said sounded like a miracle. The Haganah had come to Europe to help us. I kept asking when we would meet them. I was told to be patient. No one knew how to find the Haganah or how we would recognise them. They would find us. Until then we must be patient. But the words of David Ben-Gurion made it all that more possible.'

After Ben-Gurion had finished speaking outside the DP camp sports hall, he had moved among his huge audience, ignoring his American military escort, to hug and kiss the DPs. His words had given them hope, they told him through their tears. He had made Palestine, the homeland, seem much closer. Near to tears himself, Ben-Gurion had met Arazi in an office in the camp. For a long moment he had looked out from a window at the milling crowds outside, smiling and waving at him. He had turned to look at Arazi, no longer trying to blink back the tears: 'My friend, I want to say something to you. I see the hope on their faces, in their voices. They depend on me. I depend on you and all the others working with you. But we must get our people out of here as quickly as possible. We owe them that much and more. I know you will do your very best. So will all of you. But speed is of the utmost importance. To get the boats to take them home is of the utmost urgency.'

Now, almost a year later, Arazi was heading back to Sète with Ben-Gurion's words still fresh in his mind. But before he bought any ships, he needed to settle on a port of embarkation. Unlike the other crowded ports he had visited, Sète was closer to the operational base he had established in Marseilles. It had good road facilities from northern Europe and he had developed contacts with the city's officials. They had introduced him to the local officer for the French intelligence service, DST, who had immediately offered to help when Arazi told him of the warrant for his arrest issued by the Mandate for alleged arms smuggling. The officer had no liking for the British and offered Arazi the protection of the service. He said, 'Anything to upset the British.'

At times evasion had been a close-run matter. In Bordeaux, after checking if the port was suitable to be used by immigrants – he decided it was not – he had gone to the local DST headquarters. Inside he found the senior officer talking to two MI6 agents. The officer had motioned Arazi to take a seat in the corner of the office and continued his discussion with the Englishmen. With a final smile of regret he told them he had no knowledge of a theft from a British Army arms depot in the city. Perhaps they should try the local gendarmerie? Quick handshakes and the MI6 pair were sent on their way. From his desk the Frenchman produced a bottle of Calvados and poured two drinks and nodded for Arazi to join him.

Arazi continued to evade capture with the same cool skills he had demonstrated in avoiding the Gestapo. In every country he visited, the economy had collapsed and the only market which flourished was the black market. Angered that after serving as an SOE saboteur he was now at risk of being arrested and possibly even executed, he decided he would exploit the situation. Everyone seemed to be operating on the black market, so why shouldn't he?

He knew British and American army units routinely circulated requests for missing supplies that were somehow never found. Clothing, trucks and Jeeps were high on the list of stolen goods. He would need transport to bring the immigrants to the boats. How ironic if they could be brought there by British transport. Arazi knew that the person who could make that possible was Eliyahu Cohen, the sergeant-major of 432 Company of the General Transport Corps of the Jewish Brigade. The Brigade was made up of Palestine Jews, volunteers who had become part of the British Army. Many of them had served in the Haganah and Cohen had himself worked with Orde Wingate's commandos. Arazi went to see him in the Brigade's barracks outside Milan. That evening Cohen had taken him to their motor pool; there were over a hundred trucks parked. Arazi needed 50, which Cohen said was no problem.

They shook hands. Yehuda Arazi had solved another problem. He hoped Sète would provide further resolution.

As he drove along Sète's Canal Royale, he could see Ada Sereni, dressed in widow's black from beret to shoes, waiting by the fountain in the middle of the square. In the six months Arazi had known Ada, she had never lost her way of surprising him. But their meeting by the fountain was not a lover's tryst. She wore black because she was a widow still mourning her husband, Enzo, an Italian Jew and the son of the personal physician to the King of Italy. He had also been a Haganah officer who had parachuted behind enemy lines in an attempt to rescue Jews and had been captured and tortured by the Nazis before being executed. He would become a heroic figure across the Diaspora. Ada had taken his place and had become invaluable to Yehuda Arazi. Watching her waving and walking towards him, her long, jet-black hair blowing in the breeze, her pale face smiling, he still found it hard to believe she was already 40.

Before he left Italy he had asked Ada to set up a network to help to bring out Jews from the DP camps. She had used her family connections to do so. One uncle, an admiral in the Italian navy, had jeopardised his own career by obtaining a radio transmitter, which she had installed in her Rome apartment near the Vatican. It enabled her to be in contact with Aliyah Bet's Paris office. But she had wanted another more powerful transmitter, capable of reaching Tel Aviv. Once more Uncle Mario obliged. But still the persuasive Ada had not finished. She asked Uncle Roberto to help locate Jews serving in the British Army's Royal Engineers.

Within a week three of them had turned up on Ada's doorstep. Over coffee she explained that their help was needed to check coves and beaches along the coast between Naples and Salerno to make sure they were not mined. Each cove had to be suitable to bring a boat close to its beach. A week later they returned with information about six suitable landing sites.

Once more Ada called Admiral Mario and asked if he could find her a fishing boat for sale. Two days later he visited her apartment with news of one at a shipyard in Naples. It had been laid up since the start of the war, but it had still taken Ada a day to barter with the owner; in return for making the boat seaworthy, she would pay his price in American dollars, then the most sought-after currency in Italy. The money had been transferred from a bank account set up by Fanny Barnett in New York.

Just 24 hours after the boat was declared seaworthy, 35 refugees had boarded the vessel. They had been hidden in a religious house in Naples run by a Catholic order. The crew of the boat were five members of the Palyam, Haganah's fledgling navy. Ada's request for them was the first occasion she used the radio link to Tel Aviv. Seven days later the crew had landed the immigrants at Caesarea in Palestine, on the same beach where Roman legions had come ashore 2,000 years before.

Over the past six months, Ada had sent over 600 Jews to Palestine in other boats, each given a Hebrew name. But for Yehuda Arazi, her success also contained a danger: 'What was happening was both wonderful and fraught with risk for the entire escape organisation. It may be one thing for the British to just allow a few hundred to get through. But if there was a steady movement of refugees they were bound to retaliate with force. Without sufficient boats the immigrants would be returned to the DP camps and left there to rot.'

He had suggested Ada should meet him in Sète. Over dinner that night she confirmed that his concern had been justified. Three weeks earlier the motor vessel she had renamed *Arba*, which was carrying 997 immigrants, had been intercepted off the coast of Cyprus and escorted into Haifa by the destroyer HMS *Childers*. Arazi said that her network should be suspended for the moment, and they agreed that Sète would be an ideal port for embarking future refugees.

*

In a building on 76th Street in New York, Ralph Goldman was settling down in his new post as director of the Palestine Vocational Service. The name had been created by David Ben-Gurion as the Haganah front organisation to recruit crews for Aliyah Bet. In many ways Goldman was a good choice for the job: he had an affinity with youngsters and was a gifted Hebrew-language teacher. He was also a skilled interviewer and a shrewd judge of character. Most important of all, he had a good understanding of what Aliyah Bet wanted in a volunteer.

Captain Ash and Ze'ev Shind were quick to note and appreciate the way Goldman tapped into Zionist youth movements to find likely candidates. At weekends he travelled to farms the Haganah had bought in New Jersey to teach men agricultural skills and show them how they could create future settlements once they reached Palestine. Those who passed Ralph Goldman's probing interviews were told that signing on as a crew member was not only a quicker way to get to Palestine but also a way to serve their country by working their passage. For Goldman security was all-important.

'I never interviewed anybody in my office. I would choose a coffee shop where we could meet and I would identify myself with a copy of a Jewish newspaper and I made sure we sat in the back of the shop so I could keep an eye on everyone who came in. All the time I was making judgements of an interviewee. How he spoke, the questions he asked, whether he hesitated or talked too much.'

But that initial interview, provided a candidate passed Goldman's patient questioning, was only the beginning. His recommendation was sent to Haganah headquarters on Madison Avenue. There one of the team of checkers took over: usually they were lawyers, detectives, doctors, courthouse clerks, prison officers, social workers – people trained to find records that would confirm whether a volunteer was speaking the truth. It took a couple of weeks to check each one out. Even then there was a final hurdle to clear. The volunteer was sent to Ze'ev Shind or Captain Ash for a final grilling. Those who passed were the best Aliyah Bet got.

But there was still more for Ralph Goldman to do. His talents as a team leader had singled him out to spend time with a specialist Haganah unit responsible for buying guns and ammunition to be shipped to Palestine in one of the Aliyah Bet ships. It was dangerous work and, with the FBI and police tracking the team, there were close calls. Goldman received a telephone message at home one Saturday morning to say that a barrel had broken open on a freeway to reveal it contained gun parts. The story made the front page of the *New York Times*. But the authorities never traced where the barrel was going. From then on it became a rule that a Haganah employee must only use a pay phone to convey a sensitive message.

By the autumn of 1946, the volume of Displaced Persons leaving their camps had declined. They had each received a final shower in the communal bathrooms and were deloused before being trucked to the nearest railway station. Each one clutching an UNRRA-stamped one-way rail pass, they returned to the town from where they had been taken to toil for the Third Reich.

By early winter 1946, the camps became virtually empty except for those holding the Jews. They called themselves the *Shelrit Hapleitah*, Hebrew for the surviving remnant. Jewish relief organisations placed the figure at between 50,000 and 70,000. After roll calls, some left the camps of their own accord, unable to tolerate living in a land where so many of their people had died. They headed west to France and Holland.

One morning a relief agency worker walked into the DP camp hut where Gertruda and Michael lived. Michael was growing into a healthy boy from the extra food Gertruda managed to find for him, along with warm clothes. She still wore the coat she had worn that Easter Sunday when the SS officer had saved Mickey. The worker was making a routine check on the number of DPs in the camp. Michael would recall: 'First she asked us routine questions. Where had we come from? What had we experienced on the way before arriving in the camp? She looked at Gertruda. Was she my mother? Or another relative? Gertruda told her our story. The woman had written it all down then looked at Gertruda. "You are Catholic?"

Gertruda had nodded, adding she had also baptised me into the Church. The woman was astonished. "So you are not a Jew! You should be in a camp for Christians. I can arrange that." Gertruda shook her head. We would stay where we were. I was a Jewish boy and when we arrived in Palestine the first thing she would do was to have a rabbi reaffirm my Jewish faith. The woman had smiled and said, "My God now I have heard everything."'

Throughout the mild Mediterranean winter, Yehuda Arazi and Ada Sereni had been house-hunting along the coast between Marseilles and the French border with Spain and inland to the villages behind Sète where there were boarded-up villas and mansions which had once belonged to the supporters of the Vichy pro-German government led by Marshall Henri-Philippe Pétain. Arazi's French, intelligence contacts in the DST had pointed out the villas and mansions formerly owned by collaborators with the Vichy government who had fled across the border to Spain at the end of the war. Within months the couple had acquired over 30 houses; set in spacious grounds with servants' quarters, stables, barns and storage outhouses, they would make ideal refuges until the boats arrived to take the Jewish DPs to Palestine.

The matter of finding those boats had become more urgent with an unexpected influx of Jews from Poland. Having returned home after the war, they had found anti-Semitism was as rife as ever among their neighbours and they had fled west, back to the camps in the American zone. Their arrival had triggered a further outburst from Ernest Bevin's Foreign Office: 'We are strongly against the idea fostered by many Jewish organisations that Jewry enjoys a supernatural status, but it would indeed be disastrous for the Jews if they were accorded special treatment.'

Denis Healey, who worked closely with Bevin and was then the Labour Party's international secretary, believed the Labour government was very worried that illegal immigrants would ruin Britain's and the West's influence in the Arab world: 'The question was whether we could have found homes for Jews when they would have been unwelcome. The tragedy was the fact they wanted to go to their spiritual home. Ernest had once said the reason the Americans supported the State of Israel is that they didn't want any more Jews in New York, and there was an element of truth in that.'

That attitude confirmed the Foreign Secretary's deepening conviction that Britain must oppose a Jewish homeland. At times he came perilously close to demanding the Jews should be left to exist in those camps in a country where they had already suffered so much. The Jews were caught between recent slavery and fading hopes for the future.

No one could tell Arazi when boats would be available. David Shaltiel and Eliyahu Golomb had visited ports as far apart as the Balearic Islands and Turkey and not found any. Matters had not been helped by the refugees' desperate decision to leave their DP camps, where at least they were fed and kept warm, to make their own way to the Mediterranean. There they had pooled the last of their precious belongings – a piece of jewellery, an ounce of gold, coins and wedding rings – which they had managed to keep safe from thieves in the camps and used them to try and barter with the Greeks, Turks and Romanians offering boats for sale. However ramshackle, the Jews paid the asking price. Then, under cover of darkness which hid the defects – filthy accommodation, mouldy food and engines with little power – they would set sail. All too often, by dawn they were stopped by the vigilant warships of the Palestine Patrol.

The first to be caught was *La Negev*, a 70-year-old barge. HMS *Chieftain*, a destroyer, sent over a boarding party, food and a doctor before escorting the boat into Haifa. One by one, what Chaim Weizmann called 'floating coffins' were caught by the patrol. A seaman on HMS *Ajax* said it was 'like catching fish in a barrel'.

Over a thousand refugees, mostly women and children and old men, were brought into Haifa port and sent to detention camps.

In 1947, Lieutenant Roger Pearce was a deck officer on HMS *Charity*, a destroyer in the Palestine Patrol, based in Haifa. The port had a history going back to the days of King Herod and the town itself rested below Mount Carmel. Twice already the well-liked

Pearce had led boarding parties on blockade-runners. On the first occasion HMS *Charity* took off 586 immigrants, including 49 pregnant women, 18 children, a doctor and two nurses. In the second boarding, off a beach at Tel Aviv, 265 immigrants, including 65 pregnant passengers and four children, were taken on board HMS *Charity* and brought into Haifa. The illegal immigrants received medical attention and were fed. Both interceptions were carried out with almost no violence between immigrants and the ship's crew, but that would change. As Pearce recalled: 'Soon our job was to try to carry out the Foreign Office policy of not having any illegal immigrants arriving in Palestine. We would come alongside one of the illegal ships and try and spot who was the ringleader and we would go aboard and collar him. After that it was reasonably easy. To do it effectively we had special training with the Royal Marines. Sailors are not very good at doing that sort of thing so it was quite interesting.'

Meanwhile, Moshe Bar-Gilad, a fluent Farsi speaker, had extended his search into Persia (now Iran), basing himself in the holy city of Mashad, hoping to bring overland some of the Polish Jews who had fled their homeland as the Germans advanced. Many had been conscripted by the Russians into the Red Army or put to work in factories and collective farms in the Soviet Republics of Turkistan and Uzbekistan. Bar-Gilad had heard that as many as 40,000 Poles were now trying to get home. He created an escape route for them and guided the first group of Jews to the border city of Merv in Turkmenistan. But when he had to travel ahead to check the next stage of the route, the refugees were caught and thrown into prison. Not wishing to see the others suffer a similar fate, he had abandoned attempts to rescue them.

Eliyahu Golomb and David Shaltiel had gone to Cairo to seek help from the long-established Jewish community along the Nile. But the Egyptian Jews looked upon the Zionist aspirations in Palestine, so close to their borders, with mounting apprehension. For them, loyalty to the throne of King Farouk was paramount. It was only when Ruth Klieger, a multilingual German Jewess, arrived in Cairo to help that the community's attitude changed. Within weeks a cheque for £80,000 to buy boats was handed over.

While the money was gratefully accepted, there were still insufficient boats to replace those that the Palestine Patrol was systematically catching.

On a Friday evening in January 1947, Stewart Menzies cancelled his plans to attend a hunt ball and instead entertained a guest at the Travellers Club in Pall Mall, long the haunt of senior politicians and the elite of the intelligence services. The head of MI6 had chosen his favourite table at the rear of the club. From there he could observe everyone arriving, but ensure no one would overhear the booming voice of Reginald Manningham-Buller. He was an outstanding King's Counsel at the Inner Temple and his voice had brought many an admission from a witness. He had been Lord Chancellor and Attorney-General in Churchill's wartime Cabinet. As a Member of Parliament, he had served on a number of government inquiries. The latest had been as legal adviser to the Committee of Inquiry on Palestine.

The committee had been established after President Truman had proposed to Prime Minister Attlee that 100,000 Holocaust survivors should be admitted as soon as possible to Palestine. Bevin had rejected the proposal, making it clear to Menzies: 'Legal or historical arguments must not be allowed to sway Britain's opposition. To do so would have the most serious consequences.'

It was the first time Menzies had heard the Foreign Secretary mention the legal issue and he had invited Manningham-Buller, an expert on the International Law of the Sea, to brief him on how far the Royal Navy could legally intercept and arrest blockade-runners.

Manningham-Buller had reduced the question to three elements: 'To intercept a ship on the high seas which flew no recognised flag, a ship which carried a crew that was not registered, a ship which flew the flag of a former enemy, such as Italy, Romania or Bulgaria. Any of those violations of the law made it permissible for the vessel to be seized with all reasonable force and taken under arrest to the nearest British port.'

Menzies had shown Manningham-Buller a letter written to him on Admiralty notepaper by Admiral Sir Algernon Usborne Willis, commander-in-chief of the Mediterranean Fleet: 'Commanding officers experienced in boarding operations must consider a mile per knot is necessary to give boarding parties a reasonable chance of gaining control. That will include the distance covered by "quarry" during the operation of forming up, ranging alongside, a zigzagging ship, to put on boarders, including a feint or two, to draw the empty bottles and other missiles.'

Manningham-Buller had handed back the document: 'In plain English, our ships can attack an illegal before it gets into the three-mile territorial limit of Palestine waters.'

That night Menzies went back to his office and wrote, in the green ink he used for all important letters, to Admiral Willis: 'The precise legal definition I have been given by Mr Manningham-Buller of the three-mile limit for the purpose of dealing with a ship carrying illegal immigrants can be extended to cover the distance well beyond the Palestine coast so that pursuit of an illegal vessel can be concluded in a seamanlike operation. If a boarding takes place beyond the three-mile limit, the exact position should not be mentioned in signals or in the reports of proceedings by ships taking part in interceptions.'

Menzies had given the fully armed warships of the Palestine Patrol a clearance to act as it wished against ships which Admiral Willis had said possessed 'empty bottles and other missiles' to resist an attack.

Firmly believing that boats would eventually be found, Arazi and Ada had travelled to Milan to see Eliyahu Cohen. He said that not only would he still be able to provide trucks, but he would also help plan the best route to the Mediterranean: for the refugees it would be a long and often uncomfortable trip through Austria, across the northern mountains of Italy and down through France to Sète. Cohen used military maps, ringing points along the route with the letter 'R', explaining they were mansions and farms which had been requisitioned by the advancing Allies but were now deserted.

A delighted Arazi said they would make perfect staging stops on the way south. It was Ada who reminded them the travellers from the DP camps would include a number of elderly men, women and children. Cohen explained that the trucks would have blankets on board and each rest stop would have mattresses as well as food and hot drinks.

As the questions arose, Cohen had ready answers. What if thieves tried to rob the refugees? There would be an armed soldier on every truck, with orders of shoot to kill. Supposing a truck broke down? Or ran out of fuel? Refuelling dumps would be set up along the route. Each truck would carry a radio transmitter to call for help and Jeeps with mechanics would be stationed at regular points. Ada said that she would have a number of nurses she had used in her own network before it was suspended at every staging post. Cohen concluded by explaining that the truck drivers would be carrying military documents that they were taking the DP refugees to another repatriation centre.

Yehuda Arazi, whose own skills in the art of deception were renowned, marvelled at Cohen's detailed planning. That night he and Ada sat in the company mess and toasted him well into the night.

It had been another long day for Leo Bernstein in his Washington, DC office. With the war over, the property market had picked up and the phone had been busy. He was about to close up when it rang again. This time it wasn't an enquiry about a house. It was Abe Kay, the city's biggest builder.

Kay was a leading figure of the United Jewish Appeal. He told Leo that Aliyah Bet was preparing another ship to bring Jews from Europe to Palestine. He was to phone all the United Jewish Appeal donors on his list and ask them to come to his office the following evening. He concluded, 'If you have it, bring gold. But also as many dollars as you can lay your hands on. You'll find out why when you come, but you have to be there.'

By early evening the next day over 300 men had crammed into Leo's office. Shortly afterwards a car arrived filled with young bearded men who were escorted to a corner of the room. One of them carried a large leather suitcase. Leo placed it on one of the desks, behind which his salesmen worked, opened it and explained its purpose. He told them that by the end of the evening he hoped there would be $500,000 in cash deposited. 'More would be good. Gold is fine. But no cheques. They can be traced back to you and you could be arrested.'

Leo looked into the faces around him. When he spoke his voice was harder: 'I have heard the British are trying to get our Treasury to stop any funds going to support what the British call "illegal immigrants". What's illegal about wanting to live in the homeland God gave us? We all know that's why Jews in Europe want to go there. To live like we are allowed to live here in the freedoms all Americans have. That's why we have "*Bricha*", the freedom to go to Palestine by sea. So far the ships have been small, only able to carry a few hundred. But now we need bigger ships to bring them home. That is why the British want to stop those refugees. Britain wants to keep Palestine as it wants it. That is why you are here tonight. To show the British we will not be beaten.'

Once more Leo paused and pointed to the group of young men. 'None of these you know. None will give you their names. But they are sailors. Members of Aliyah Bet. When they leave here tonight your money will ensure that another ship will be bought to sail to Europe to collect maybe 800 Jews, maybe more, and bring them to *Eretz Yisrael*. Isn't that the best possible use you can make of your money?'

The sailors moved to stand beside the suitcase. Each donor dropped his donation into the suitcase. There were hundred-dollar bills and bundles of notes along with bars of gold, gold rings and lockets. Finally the last donation was placed in the suitcase and the lid was closed and strapped. The sailors carried the suitcase to the car and drove off.

Leo never knew how much had been raised but he later learned that the money was used to help the outfitting of *President Warfield*.

In 2009, at the age of 93, Leo Bernstein made an intriguing claim about the drama of that fund-raising gathering. He said that among the sailors who had taken away the suitcase was a mysterious figure: 'He was the captain of the boat that the money was needed for. I don't know his name and I don't think we were introduced. We didn't get names and nobody was telling names. They didn't count the money and tell us what they raised.'

Leo was satisfied that the money was needed to outfit *President Warfield*. So who was the mysterious figure? Was it Ike Ahronowitz, the slim, temperamental Pole and the designated captain of the ship? Or was it Yossi Harel? There is no record of either having being in Washington, DC, at that time. Could it possibly have been a mistake in Bernstein's recollection?

Yet his description of his own role has a ring of clarity that matches reports of other fund-raising gatherings. Could Ike and Yossi have been smuggled into the United States to avoid being questioned by the FBI over their work for the Haganah? Had Teddy Kollek, an energetic Palestinian Jew, deeply engaged by 1947 in breaking the British blockade, made the arrangements for them? Kollek was Ben-Gurion's executive secretary and eventually mayor of Jerusalem in the new State of Israel – a creation that Leo Bernstein had contributed to.

In 1947, MI6 persuaded the FBI to track Kollek's activities, especially in smuggling into the US key personnel of the Haganah, who often came into the country on either Canadian or British passports down through Montreal.

In February 1947, Sir William Stephenson, the head of MI6 in the United States, had written a memo to Stewart Menzies:

> Since the end of WW2 there continues to be a significant increase of Haganah activity out of Canada into New York and Washington. A number of senior operatives of the Jewish Agency are known to be active in both cities whose intention is to attack our government policy to oppose illegal immigration.

There is no doubt that U.S. support for Aliyah Bet in Congress is reflected in political attitudes but also in supporting fund raising to buy ships of an increased tonnage and to warn that organisation of impending danger.

Just who those senior operatives were remains a mystery – which is hardly surprising, given the clandestine nature of the operation and the secret nature of Leo Bernstein's vital fund-raising activities.

Chapter 10

Plans and Proposals

In the spacious office assigned to him on HMS *Moreta*, the Royal Navy shore base at Haifa, the newly appointed First Sea Lord, Admiral Sir John Henry Dacres Cunningham, considered the message he had received on that February morning in 1947 from his namesake, Sir Alan Cunningham, Britain's High Commissioner in Palestine. It read: 'MOST IMMEDIATE. TOP SECRET. We are unable at this moment to guard any more illegal immigrants in this country. I would urge that every other ship on the sea is diverted otherwise the situation may become impossible.'

With his tanned face and pale blue eyes, 61-year-old Sir John had always kept himself wonderfully fit. He still played competition-level tennis and swam for an hour every day. As the highest-ranking sailor in the Mediterranean Fleet, his authority ran from the Rock of Gibraltar to the Suez Canal and Haifa, where he based himself.

On his orders, the Haifa port area was constantly patrolled by two motor launches carrying Mandate policemen armed with sub-machine guns. At night, every warship was lit with arc lamps suspended over the side and its propellers turned every two minutes to drive away swimmers who could be planning to plant limpet mines on ships' hulls. In addition, one-kilo explosive charges were dropped in the water to further deter swimmers. At first light a navy swimmer dived under each warship to search for explosives.

From his office window on that February morning Sir John could see four blockade-runners riding at anchor in the bay after being successfully intercepted by the Palestine Patrol. Even from that distance they looked grubby in the morning sun; their names hurriedly painted on their prows in Hebrew that was already starting to fade. It gave Sir John satisfaction to know it would have needed more than a name change to outwit his captains. There was the *Chaim*, an old Coast Guard cutter registered in Havana, Cuba. A short distance away was *Ben Hecht*, a steamer that had once sailed between Morocco and Málaga in Spain carrying coal and had been renamed by the Haganah after the waspish novelist and playwright. *Shabtai* and *Ha'almoni* were both auxiliary schooners and Sir John guessed they had been renamed after either Old Testament prophets or biblical warriors. A devout Christian, he reminded himself he must find out what the names meant.

On that sunny morning all Sir John knew was that between them the old boats had tried to smuggle ashore another 3,000 illegals who, upon arrest, had defiantly refused to say where they had sailed from in Europe. Their crews had been equally unresponsive, giving only their surnames and refusing to admit they were members of the Palyam. Sir John had come to know the name for the Jewish secret navy; it gained headlines in the *Jerusalem Post* each time a blockade-runner avoided interception. Further out in the bay beyond the breakwater were three other boats holding several hundred more would-be immigrants waiting to be brought ashore, questioned and sent to Mandate detention camps.

Despite their refusal to answer questions, during their search of the boats intelligence officers found a list of bank transfers from the Bank of America for $245,000 to an account run by Dr Joseph Schwartz, the director of the American Jewish Joint Distribution Committee, the Jewish relief organisation known as the 'Joint'. Ralph Goldman later became its executive director. The claim about the transfers is in an MI6 file in the archives, one of several files that deal with the activities of the Secret Intelligence Service between 1944 and 1948.

Gordon Lett, a senior MI6 officer, had set up what he called 'anti-immigration units' staffed by former SOE operatives in Genoa to track the Joint's activities in Europe. Lett's orders were set out in a memo to Menzies he wrote in 1946: 'To penetrate the Haganah and capture the leaders in Europe of its far-flung underground organisation; to intercept clothing and medical aid for the use of refugees; to obtain the names of Haganah diplomatic contacts, especially American; to disrupt those contacts; to deal with border guards the Zionists have bribed; to confiscate all forged travel documents and have the forgers arrested.'

Several of Lett's agents had worked with Yehuda Arazi during the war and sympathised with the immigrants. One was Cathal O'Connor, who felt it was 'very harrowing to be asked to deal with Jews from the Holocaust'.

Others showed less sympathy. Harold Perkins, the MI6 station commander in Rome, proposed to Menzies, 'The way to disrupt the flow of immigrants is to attach limpet mines to refugee ships.'

To carry out such an operation required Menzies to seek the approval of Prime Minister Attlee. If he received any response, it has remained to this day in the 'Y File' category, the most restricted of all in the Secret Intelligence Service's files.

Lett had requisitioned a villa in Portovenere, at the tip of the bay of La Spezia, and from its compound he supervised two interrogation centres for Jews who 'appear more interesting'. One was the Combined Services Detailed Interrogation Centre (CSDIC) in Haifa, which was responsible for questioning captured members of the terrorist Stern and Irgun gangs. The other was a high-security complex at Fayid on the Suez Canal to interrogate the planners of Jewish immigration.

One of its feared interrogators was Maurice Oldfield, a portly homosexual with a taste for Arab youths, who would be a future head of MI6. He described his tactics at Fayid as 'beating and pushing people's heads into buckets of water'.

Back in January, standing watch over the three blockade-runners anchored beyond the breakwater, HMS *Childers*'s captain, Lieutenant Commander Bailey, had requested in writing an interview with the

First Sea Lord to discuss a plan he had devised to board an illegal ship more efficiently.

A document also requiring Sir John's attention on that Monday morning was a letter from Sir William Stephenson, by now coordinator of MI5 and MI6 in North America. Sir John had met Stephenson before coming to Haifa and was impressed with his understanding of the situation that would confront the First Sea Lord in Palestine. Over lunch, Sir John had delivered a forensic analysis of why there would be no solution to the looming conflict until there was an acceptable solution to the immigration situation and the Zionist-Arab impasse which would satisfy the Truman administration. The President's personal support for Zionist aspirations was less strident and he had handed over the question of immigration to his new Secretary of State, General George C. Marshall.

Marshall had been a soldier all his adult life and saw problems through a military prism. Loy Henderson, director of the Office of Far Eastern and African Affairs, recalled the Secretary of State saying, 'There has to be an accommodation with the Jews to get them back on side so as to avoid the Soviets exploiting the situation and then we could all lose the Middle East. Britain should allow a reasonable number of immigrants to travel openly through their Zone in Germany, as the United States and France have done, so they can go to the Mediterranean and use their legal visas to Mexico and other countries.'

Stephenson told Sir John that the majority of those visas had been purchased from corrupt Mexican and other Latin American diplomats by the Haganah, who had paid for them with funds provided by its wealthy American supporters. Stephenson concluded that it was becoming ever more clear that Britain would soon have to cast off the burden of Palestine. Stephenson had now written: 'The Haganah intend to buy ships large enough to send thousands of immigrants at one time to Palestine that will cause an international outcry if they are intercepted and turned away. These ships will be purchased by Jews with powerful connections in Washington. The Jewish vote remains a very significant factor in the calculations of all

US politicians and many will continue to press the Zionist cause with considerable energy.'

On Sir John's desk were also the latest costs to Britain for maintaining its thankless role as peacekeeper. In 1946, over £200 million had been spent on running the Mandate. In that period 69 more British soldiers had been killed, mostly victims of Jewish terrorism. Sir John feared by the end of the year the number would be higher. Yet if the flow of immigrants increased, so would the anger of the Arabs. Caught between two intransigent forces, the situation for Britain was becoming progressively more dangerous.

By the end of 1946, Aliyah Bet had become a highly professional and smoothly run operation to select ships and their crews. Guests at the Thursday luncheons at the McAlpine Hotel would return to Jewish groups in Chicago, Los Angeles, San Francisco and a score of other cities. Demobilised servicemen, hungry for new challenges after serving in Europe, bought tickets for the next train to New York. For Ze'ev Shind: 'The process of checking backgrounds became even more thorough and we became choosy on who we took. Those we suspected wouldn't stay out of bars were turned away. Young Jewish boys are usually not good at holding their liquor. The last thing we wanted was a drunk spilling the beans. The same with volunteers who hadn't much Jewish background and no Jewish education. We wanted only the very best. But Navy veterans were waved through.'

The first boat purchased by Captain Ash was an old Coast Guard cutter. Refitted and sailing under a Honduran flag, she was renamed the *Chaim Arlosoroff*. Soon other ships had been purchased. Each one was bought through a dummy company to conceal any link with Aliyah Bet. One was called FB Company, the initials of Fanny Barnett's name.

Ralph Goldman, along with all his other duties, had the responsibility for obtaining foreign registry for each boat and became a regular visitor to Latin American consulates to hand over an envelope containing a certified cheque and, in return, receive the appropriate documents for the ship to sail under its foreign flag.

Panama registered the first two ships, Honduras the next three. The sixth one was to be *President Warfield*, after she was certified as seaworthy by the Baltimore agent of Lloyd's of London. In the meantime, Captain Ash had arranged for a tug to tow the ship from the James River to Baltimore's waterfront to make it more accessible to work on.

The rotting timbers of Pier Eight at the end of Baltimore's Lancaster Street continued to be coated with the city's sewage and the discharge from a nearby chemical plant, further staining the once pristine white of the hull of the *President Warfield*. The stench hung over the hulk. Every morning at dawn the warren of narrow streets echoed with the roar of trucks and the tramp of workmen making their way to the steamer. Late into the evening the sound of riveting machines, hammering, sawing and the rumble of equipment being rolled along the ice-covered decks filled the air. Refrigeration units, pumps and replacement boilers were each manhandled into position. Men worked from platforms slung over the side to tap the hull for signs of structural weakness. But the ship was ready for many more years at sea. The engine was good for another 100,000 miles. Less could be said for the electrical wiring. When the *President Warfield* had been fitted out for war, the power voltage Britain required had been wired in a hurry and had to be replaced.

From time to time, Ze'ev Shind had come to inspect progress, climbing the gangplank, adjusting his footing to the rocking of the steamer as she responded to the stirring of the dark, poisonous water. He had been impressed how men could work 12 hours a day in such a stench. But there was still a way to go to meet the deadline Captain Ash had set for completion, 25 February 1947. In a dockside café, he and Shind conferred and agreed more workmen were needed to meet the deadline. It added to the already mounting costs: bills from chandlers, engineering firms and electrical suppliers. Each bill was promptly paid out of the Chemical Bank account. The receipts were kept in the Haganah's headquarters in the house on the seafront in Tel Aviv.

*

Nat Nadler had returned from Germany on a troop ship which docked in a very different New York from the one he had left. Then he had just been out of college. Now he was a veteran who had seen more of life than he had expected. It had been one thing to watch a movie newsreel of a bombed Germany, quite another to have actually walked through the ruins; one thing to see a DP camp on screen, another to have smelled its odour. Nat was one of the million men a month the army was discharging and had joined the American Veterans of Israel: 'After I signed on a kid put a piece of paper in my hand with a telephone number. He said, "If you are really interested call this number." I did and was immediately invited for an interview. The address was across the street from the Metropolitan Museum. I rang the bell and the doors opened by themselves. I thought, "*Oy, oy, oy!*" Suddenly there were floodlights shining in my eyes. I couldn't see who was asking the questions as I gave my background. At the end I was told I would get a call. Next day I got one. A voice asked if I was still interested in helping. I said yes. The guy said, "Go to Pier 32 in Philadelphia. Take a bag with you. When you get there ask for Captain Ash."'

Nat Nadler was about to join other young Jews from all over the United States who were receiving similar orders: soldiers who had been in the Normandy landings; marines who had stormed their way across the Rhine; deckhands who had served in the wartime Mercantile Navy. Others were office clerks and college students who had never been to sea before, but were driven by the prospect of adventure and the plight of Jews waiting in Europe to go to *Eretz Yisrael.*

On a moonless night, a fishing boat puttered through the darkness out of the port of Caesarea, south of Haifa. Squatting on the deck among the nets was Yossi Harel. He was close to his 29th birthday, the lines around his mouth giving him the look of an older man. Those who worked with him in the Haganah said his dark brown eyes warned that if someone didn't have an answer he wanted, that someone would have a problem.

There were many stories about Harel: how he taught himself to swim and at night had taken out a rowing boat to learn the basics of steering. Now he was among the Palyam's best navigators. He was a teenager when he joined other young men in Jerusalem to help defend the Yishuv against the Arabs. Even then Harel had had the look of a man 'born to command and take risks', noted the group's leader, Yitzhak Sadeh, who would become a member of the Haganah High Command. Yossi's knowledge and military skills deepened when he joined up with Orde Wingate.

Soon he had become a member of Aliyah Bet, of whom Ben-Gurion later wrote: 'They took their lives in their hands for so-called illegal immigration and the mass escape of Jews from Europe; indeed, who by their courage and steadfastness prepared the way for that near-miracle: the restoration of our sovereign independence.'

Since November 1946, when Harel had first commanded an Aliyah Bet boat bringing immigrants from a Yugoslav port to Palestine, he had carried out many similar missions. Now he was on his way to take part in the biggest of all.

Yossi sensed the crew, young Palestine Jews, eyed him with respect not only because he had fought alongside and been close to the legendary Orde Wingate, but for his own reputation within the organisation.

Watching the shore fade into the night and feeling the swell increase, Yossi could remember that day he had taken Wingate to Caesarea to see its magnificent viaduct, as intact as the day water first ran along the stone culvert built over 2,000 years ago. Wingate had talked about the engineering feat required to build the viaduct, but soon he had returned to discuss the tactics of the Romans, a subject of endless fascination for the Englishman. Yossi asked how Wingate had acquired such knowledge and was told it was from the Bible, that everything worth knowing was in its two testaments.

Beyond the harbour the fishing boat turned southwards, heading out to sea for its rendezvous off the coastal village of Michmoret. Yossi had made such trips several times since he had left the British Army and returned to the Haganah. The skills Wingate had taught him to help the Mandate were now being used against it.

His last mission had been to Athens, his money belt filled with gold coins for a Greek forwarding shipping agent to pay for the consignment of arms to fight the Arabs. Considerable quantities of weapons bought on the black market had been stockpiled in Greece and Italy, and the agent had found a way to send them to Palestine, labelling them as industrial equipment, the sealed cases displaying their export/import licences. They were shipped to Haifa as consignments for companies like the Palestine Electric Corporation. Yossi had been at the port to watch them being unloaded on to waiting trucks, which were driven to one of the Haganah depots hidden across the country. So far 200 Bren guns and spare parts, 1,000 British Army rifles, 500 German Army rifles, 400 machine guns of various types, 500 revolvers and one and a half million rounds of ammunition had been smuggled into the hideouts.

In the early hours the fishing boat came alongside a small freighter flying the Greek flag and Yossi clambered aboard. Three days later the ship reached Italian territorial waters and Yossi climbed down into another fishing smack and came ashore at the port of Taranto in southern Italy. Waiting for him was Ada Sereni. In her open roadster, she drove him north to Cremona, south of Milan, where Eliyahu Cohen had set up a staging post. There 40 of his trucks, which had brought 500 men, women and children out of a DP camp, were being refuelled for the next stage of the journey to Sète.

Sun blinds drawn against the midday sun and a tray of cold drinks on the table between them in his office, Sir John Cunningham listened intently as Lieutenant Commander Bailey described his proposal on how to board a blockade-runner more effectively. The operation should take place at night and initially called for continuous noise and light: light from a destroyer's searchlight focused on the immigrant ship; noise from its 20mm Oerlikons fired across its bow and 40mm Bofors fired over its rigging. All the time the piercing destroyer's siren would punctuate the night and its loudspeakers would repeatedly order the blockade-runner to stop. Drawing closer to it, the destroyer would use a depth-charge-thrower to fire an anchor attached to a steel wire over the blockade-runner's bulwarks and secure it to the patrol ship.

Each destroyer would carry a specially trained boarding party, equipped with tear-gas dispensers used in riots, Lee Enfield rifles and 9mm Lanchester sub-machine guns. Each marine would also carry a two-foot-long baton to fend off opponents or deliver body blows, and wear a white jumper and a white-painted steel helmet along with a leather arm shield similar to those used by Zulus. The boarding team would have two sailors equipped with high-pressure hosepipes to clear the immigrants from the area where the boarders would land.

Bailey concluded his detailed briefing with a warning: 'The threat posed by female immigrants using hat pins must be taken into account. Each boarder should be equipped with a cricket-style box to protect private parts. Equally important is that every boarding member showed pride in his appearance. The immigrants must realise they are dealing with efficient and effective professionals. The important thing is not to deliberately harm or kill anyone. The methods proposed would ensure the illegal ship would be quickly captured.'

The First Sea Lord showed Bailey Stephenson's report that larger immigrant ships could be on the way and told him he would be in charge of stopping them.

The transit camp outside Cremona was a German barracks which had been hurriedly abandoned as its troops withdrew into the Third Reich. Money and workers from the Joint had cleaned and fitted out the huts with bedding, showers, toilets, a kosher kitchen and dining hall. The larder had been restocked with tinned food and fresh vegetables bought locally. A bakery in Cremona provided bagels every day.

Ada and Yossi carefully checked the names of refugees against lists giving their place and country of birth and the concentration camps where they were interned. It was a slow and laborious process, as many refugees had experienced horrors that had left them with memory gaps. Their papers included passes to cross the Italian border into France which had been obtained by Yehuda Arazi. The most important document was a Mexican visa given to each man, woman and child identifying them as a citizen of that country. The visas had been bought by Moshe Bar-Gilad from Mexican diplomats in Madrid. A number of refugees were Jews from Eastern Europe and the camp's welfare workers had bathed, disinfected and clothed them for the next stage of their journey south. Among them was Yosef Reich.

Reich came from Radom, a 14th-century city south of Warsaw that had produced textiles and glassware. The first Jewish families had arrived there in 1798, forming a community in one of the suburbs. They had come from the distant east of Europe: a place of folklore, of pagan forest people, of girls being casually impregnated and their babies left out to die in the winter landscape. Superstition was rife and scores were often settled by husbands or fathers with a knife or axe. Another bloodstain on the land was anti-Semitism, an unabated and all-consuming tidal wave that crossed mountains and rivers, driven on by a terrible lust to seek out and destroy any Jew. In Radom the Jews had found refuge, were allowed to sell their goods to their Christian neighbours and permitted to wear their traditional dress and speak their own language. They lived quiet lives within the sanctity of their faith; the Sabbath was the high point of the week, when, together with religious holidays, there were a few brief hours to relax. By 1939, 24,475 Jews lived in Radom. They included Yosef Reich, his parents and his two brothers and one sister. Hard-working, like their fellow Jews, they were at peace with their mostly Catholic neighbours.

Within their community the family were regarded as industrious and generous, always ready to help. Yosef and his two brothers and sister were well clothed and educated and there were the usual signposts marking the life of the boys: circumcision, bar mitzvah, the first community wedding to attend with their parents as guests. Rosh Hashanah and Yom Kippur (the Jewish High Holidays), Succoth, Hanukkah and Pesach, marked the progress of the Jews of Radom into another year.

But war was coming, and coming closer by the day. Hitler's Germany was exerting pressure, a huge dark and ever-expanding blot. The Sudetenland, the German-speaking part of Czechoslovakia, was already in Nazi hands. Since 1938 the Third Reich had been reaching out for Austria and Poland.

By 1939 Radom's population was 90,039, of which around a third were Jews. Their fate would be given a place in the records of the Nuremberg International War Crimes Tribunal in 1946.

The city was occupied on 8 September 1939 and its Jews fell into German hands. Between March and April 1941 the Germans established two ghettos. As well as Radom's Jews, thousands more from surrounding towns were held there. Although the Jews suffered from starvation, bad hygienic conditions and persecution by the SS and the Gestapo, compared to most other ghettos overall living conditions were relatively bearable. Smuggling food into the ghettos, however, could have deadly consequences and many paid with their lives for attempting to do so.

For the Jews, Zeromski Street in the city centre became an especially terrifying place. It was where the SS set up its headquarters. An excerpt from the testimony given at Nuremberg by one of the city's doctors, David Wajnapel, provides a harrowing picture: 'The house on Zeromski Street became a menace to the entire Jewish population. People walking in the street were dragged into the gateway and ill treated by merciless beatings and by the staging of sadistic games.'

Then the deportations began.

In August 1942 the first round-up took place. About 600 old people and children were shot by the Germans during the course of assembling those to be sent to Treblinka. From then on deportations to the death camps became routine. However, Yosef Reich and his two brothers were assigned to forced labour in an arms factory, where they toiled until they were sent to Auschwitz in 1944. Waiting there was Dr Josef Mengele, his pointing fingers holding a cigarette. Yosef would never forget how 'Mengele took out my younger brother from the line'.

The abiding trauma for many incarcerated in Auschwitz was that part of each of them had died there, choked by the horrific stench from the ovens and chimneys. Day and night it clung to them, impregnated their clothes and skin with the smell of the gassing and burning of the elderly, the women and the children; then there were the pits of burnt bodies and the heaps of clothing, footwear and spectacles which filled warehouses.

Inmates from other death camps who had reached Cremona confirmed it was the same in all the camps: two buckets for the toilet needs of every hundred prisoners; drinking water which left lips cracked; the pieces of bread that prisoners could not swallow; the prisoners who went mad and ran at the guards, screaming they wanted to be shot – and were.

For Ada the recollections of survivors had a powerful and cumulative effect on her. Typical was Yosef's testimony, which evoked the chilling tone of a courtroom murder trial as he described the forced march he and thousands of others endured on their way from Auschwitz as the Red Army closed in and the camp inmates were needed for work elsewhere. He was destined for Buchenwald, once more a slave labourer in the German war machine. Part of the journey involved marching in the depths of winter in January 1945: 'We had no clothes. The weather was very cold and it was snowing. There were about 12,000 of us when we set out. There were about 2,000 when we arrived at Buchenwald. People died from starvation in open fields. We had nothing to eat, only the snow. It is all we had to eat. People died from diphtheria or exhaustion. Any prisoner lagging behind was shot.'

A total of 65,000 prisoners were evacuated from Auschwitz in the beginning of January 1945; 15,000 died on those death marches. By the end of the war in Europe a quarter of a million prisoners had been sent on death marches. Some of their testimonies, like Yosef's account, provide the shocking and unforgettable reality behind the cold statistics of extermination in camps like Buchenwald.

Yosef Reich was sure that what had sustained him before he reached Cremona was the belief that one day he would get to

Palestine. Liberation was a wonderful feeling. But to see *Eretz Yisrael* would be beyond words.

There were others around Yosef in Cremona who had nightmares that kept them awake at night. Miriam Bergman found she could not sleep in a hut where perhaps the soldiers who had killed her parents had slept. Freddie Kronenberg was filled with a sense of remorse that he had been allowed to live while so many had died. Listening to Ben-Gurion's words in the DP camp at Landsberg had both moved him deeply and fed his guilt; he asked himself why he had done so little to help so many people who had died at Auschwitz? *His people.* Why had he sheltered behind a Christian cross?

After Ben-Gurion had moved on from Landsberg, Freddie had gone to a rabbi in the camp and explained why he wore the emblem. The rabbi had said it was no more than that – an emblem. What mattered was that wearing it had saved Freddie's life in the evil of Auschwitz. It did not mean he had to reject his own faith; he could still be a Jew. The rabbi had suggested if it would help he could give Freddie a Magen David – a Star of David – to wear; he could, of course, keep the crucifix as a reminder, but the star might help him understand who he was. Freddie believed that since wearing the six-pointed Magen David, he had begun to come to terms with his guilt. On the day he had left Landsberg, chosen to be among the next group of refugees to go to Palestine, the rabbi had assured Freddie his guilt would fade once he reached that destination and he was able to do what Ben-Gurion had asked of everybody else: help.

When Gertruda arrived in the transit camp in Cremona with Michael Stolowitzky, Mickey, she believed they were only 'a prover-bial step away from reaching Palestine'. Ada had confirmed their papers were in order and that the sea journey would take only a few days. While the boat had not yet arrived, they would wait in a house near the embarkation harbour. A similar promise had been given to all the refugees. The mood in the transit camp was relaxed and even upbeat when Yossi Harel had announced an American inspection team would be arriving in a day or so.

The team worked under the umbrella of the American Jewish

Joint Distribution Committee, the most powerful of all the Jewish relief agencies in Germany. Its staff regularly made inspections of Jewish DP camps and transit centres set up by the Haganah. The Joint had raised over $17 million in the United States since the end of the war. The organisation knew the value of publicity and the visit to Cremona would, as usual, be covered by a team of photographers and reporters. After the formal inspection had ended, the team would select one or two refugees to meet the press. Gertruda regarded such matters as part of the process for getting herself and Mickey to Palestine.

Towards the end of the tour the Joint delegation approached where Gertruda and Mickey stood outside their barracks. The group had smiled and asked their usual questions about living conditions and had started to move on when its leader stared at Gertruda. Michael recalled: 'The woman said Gertruda could not come to Palestine with me because she was Christian and every space on the ship was only for a Jewish person. The woman said she would take care of me and bring me to Palestine. Gertruda said, "No! I am not leaving Mickey with you or anybody. I am taking him to his homeland." The woman said that was impossible. Gertruda said that unless she was allowed to take me she would tell the press. I had never seen her so determined and so angry. "I will tell them what I had promised his mother. How I was with this little boy for the whole war and I had risked my own life. I want to take him and continue living with your people, with him, in your country. But if you don't let me and discriminate against me, I'm going to tell it to the press." They looked at Gertruda in astonishment. Then they whispered among themselves. The delegation's leader looked at Gertruda and said, "You and your little boy will go. That I promise."'

Fira Neimark had the dark eyes and open smile of a child of steppes. It was when she moved that her fine looks could be fully appreciated, or when she cocked her head while listening, or smiled when replying to a familiar question: how had she come to be going to Palestine? When she explained, peopled had looked at her with astonishment and respect. She was barely 19 years old, with the responsibility for bringing with her 52 small children, each a survivor of the Holocaust, to Palestine. For someone so young to have done this single-handedly was extraordinary.

Once more Fira would modestly explain: 'My story is for my parents. They come from a very religious background and all their lives they knew that one day we would all go to *Eretz Yisrael*. But at the end of the war they didn't have the money to buy the papers for us all. But they could manage to find enough money for me to go. I said I would never leave without them. But my father went down on his knees and begged me to go, saying he and my mother would follow. I will never forget that day, 31 December 1945.'

Fira would summarise the next stage of her story succinctly. How she had set off for Cracow in Poland to stay with friends of her parents. She would wait there while they still tried to find the money to buy their exit visas. But soon the border between Russia and Poland had closed. Months later the family in Cracow had sent her on to Lodz, where they had learned the first members of Aliyah Bet had arrived to search for Jews wanting to go to Palestine. The contact was soon made. Fira still spoke only Russian, the men from Aliyah Bet Yiddish, Hebrew and a little English. But they told her she would go to Palestine – along with the children she would care for. Fira's life was about to change.

'I went with the Aliyah Bet people to the Lodz rail station to look around for Jewish children who were lost. We could see right away this is a Jewish child, there is a Jewish child. They didn't know where their parents were, they were gone. We would take them to the place we had prepared for them. They were orphans. Their parents had been taken into the camps never to be seen again. They were lost. Lost to life. Seeing them I felt something inside me. I can't explain the feeling. It was something in my heart. I knew I had to help them and take them away from their past. I had to bring them home to *Eretz Yisrael*. I was put in charge of 52 of them.'

Once she had gathered all the children together, she led them out of Poland to Czechoslovakia, across one border after another into

Austria. They walked only at night to avoid drawing attention to themselves. By day they hid in fields and forests, drank water from mountain streams and ate what food Fira could beg from farmers. Soon her trek through snow-capped mountains, ravines, across rivers and centuries-old paths had come to the attention of welfare workers. At each border they waited to escort the group to safe places where they could sleep in beds and eat hot food. One stopover was at a monastery high in the mountains. Another was a seminary: 'These were Catholic houses, places of God, and we were received with warmth and kindness. At each stage we waited to move to the next stage. Finally we were in Germany.'

They entered through the foothills of the Alps to reach Rosenheim, where Hermann Goering was born and one of the first Nazi banners had been draped across its entrance: *Juden sind hier nicht erwünscht*, Jews are not wanted here. On the outskirts of the town was a camp, one of the 120 sub-camps of Dachau, which had housed slave labourers for the nearby BMW plant. When Fira arrived with her children, there were already over a thousand children in the camp brought there from all over Europe. Some had been there for over a year: stateless persons waiting for papers, waiting for a country to admit them, hoping to go to Palestine.

Fira and her children were housed together in a hut: 'I was a little mother for them. I gave them all my love, everything I had to give. When they were old enough, they helped me with the small ones. I never met children so wonderful. They didn't talk about the war. They were just happy to be safe with me.'

One day a stranger came to their hut. He was tall and suntanned and spoke Yiddish as well as Hebrew. He asked each child to come forward in turn with his or her UNRRA document. He attached to it a pass to enter France and a Mexican visa on which he wrote the name of each child. Finally he gave Fira her travel documents, urging her to make sure every child took care of theirs. She looked at the visa in surprise. Moshe Bar-Gilad had smiled and said they would be going to Palestine.

In Cremona Fira and the other refugees began to board the British army trucks, their doors stencilled in Hebrew with the emblem of the Palestine General Transport Corps.

Bag on his shoulder, Nat Nadler walked along Lancaster Street on Baltimore's waterfront, the smell of sewage and the noxious fumes from a chemical plant increasing at every step. It must have been like this, Nat imagined, when the first steamboats plied their trade from here, with passengers making their way through the narrow streets, the crews sleeping in slum boarding houses on either side of alleys. Now among the boarded-up warehouse windows and cracked paving, only the scuttling rats remained of those days. Nat had kicked several out of his path, sending them squealing into the shadows. Even on this sunny February day the sun never reached street level.

Captain Ash had given Nat precise instructions: when he reached the end of the street he would see *President Warfield*. He made her sound like a passenger liner and Nat had wondered if she was part of the American President Lines, which ran cruises down to South America. It would be a pleasant life as an electrician on a cruise ship: good food, a comfortable bunk, pretty women and constant sun. The reality came when he reached the end of Lancaster Street. He stood there, staring in disbelief and dismay. '*Oy vey!*' He said it once and several more times as he walked along the pier, stepping around gaps in the rotting timbers. The stench was overpowering as he stared up. There was no doubt: the faded name on the stern and bow identified *President Warfield*.

As he began to retrace his steps, a voice boomed down from an upper deck. Nat looked up. A figure in clerical garb, his white collar gleaming and a large silver crucifix on his chest, peered down.

Nat was startled and said to himself in Yiddish, 'What was a priest doing here on a Jewish ship?'

The Reverend John Stanley Grauel was an ordained minister in the Methodist Church who had become a Zionist. The 28-year-old clergyman was an active member of the American Christian Committee for Palestine. The committee had agreed to pay his salary for the time he was abroad so that he could gather information to

promote their work in the United States. He was one of the first of
Captain Ash's recruits because of his seamanship, which had earned
the admiration of veteran yachtsmen along the coast around Boston,
where Grauel sailed his own boat at weekends. There was also his
ability to run a galley and produce hot food in the roughest of seas.
With those skills came his fund-raising role for the committee, for he
displayed a sense of humour and self-confidence in finding people
ready to subscribe to the organisation. Someone with those qualities,
Captain Ash had decided, would be indispensable on *President Warfield*
and Reverend Grauel had agreed to run the ship's galley.

The priest called for Nat to come on board. After confirming
Captain Ash had recruited him, followed by a firm handshake, the
Reverend Grauel took Nat on a tour of the ship to introduce him to
the crew. For the moment they were only names, but they smiled in
welcome and sometimes gave a brief description of their work. Kurt
Baruch, Ben Foreman and Myron Goldstein, in their old US Navy
vests and underpants, were cooks. Roger Rofe and Samuel Schiller
were muscular men, busy at work in the engine room when Nat
arrived, apologising for not shaking hands as theirs were stained with
oil. On various decks Nat was introduced to still more crew. David
Starek spoke fluent Spanish. Reuven Margolis spoke English in a
hesitant voice. Avraham Sygal spoke English with a strong Lithuanian
accent. Frank Levine was the son of Russian immigrants who spoke
several European languages in a soft voice. David Lowenthal, Danny
Malovsky and Dave Millman spoke Hebrew with a drawl. Lennie
Sklar, along with Frank Stanczak, Mike Weiss, Terry Verdi and
Harry Weinsaft, were each experts in the various skills needed to run
the ship.

Nat saw Mike Weiss and Abe Siegel were preparing a makeshift
hospital with the help of Abe Lippschitz, who had been a pharmacist
in the war. Particularly impressive was Bill Bernstein, one of the
ship's two mates: the 23-year-old radiated competence and authority.
He welcomed Nat with a 'Good to have you on board.'

After the introduction Bernstein wrote to his mother: 'You asked
me to settle down, go to school. That's all very fine, Mom, but one

doesn't find happiness by continually kidding himself he is happy. Don't you think I would like a nice wife and kids? Of course I would, but I can't do that now. I say this knowing that your thoughts and heart are with me wherever I am and whatever I am doing.'

Bernard Marks had been an officer in the US Merchant Marines. Another veteran of the service was Cyril Weinstein, an 18-stone giant who still walked with a slight limp from polio he had contracted as a child. Born and raised in Brooklyn, he struck up an immediate friendship with Nat when he learned they were near neighbours. Ben Foreman wore with pride on his army uniform the wings of the 82nd Airborne Division; he had dropped into Normandy and fought his way through Europe. He had told Captain Ash he knew nothing about seamanship, but he would learn, just as he had learned to jump from 5,000 feet.

Nat developed a way to remember individuals. Murray Aronoff wore his father's badge from when he had served in the Jewish Brigade. Nat called him the Badgeman, though never to his face; Aronoff was a tough New Yorker with a street-fighting look in his eyes. William 'Big Bill' Millman, with his full beard, had served in the war on the USS *Pittsburgh* and became the cruiser's heavyweight boxing champion. He shared a surname with the other Millman, Dave, who was shorter and sharper in tongue than his namesake and was another cook in Reverend Grauel's galley.

The priest took Nat to meet the ship's radioman, Harold Leidner, who had given up a promising career as a lawyer to join *President Warfield*. The meet-and-greet tour over, Bernstein had told Nat that Danny Malovsky, an 18-year-old newly qualified electrician, would assist him in untangling and replacing the wiring left by the British. Their first task was to get the heat circulating through *President Warfield*. The weather was sub-zero and some of the crew were suffering from frostbite.

Avi Livney had spent weeks trying to track down what seemed an increasingly unlikely story: that a secret Jewish organisation had been formed to create a fleet of ships to rescue Holocaust survivors. Avi was a 19-year-old sailor who had been discharged from the US Navy after the war and, like other young Zionists, he was enraged at the way Britain had refused Holocaust survivors the right to go to Palestine. He regarded that as the re-enactment of his country's founding fathers' struggle in their War of Independence. The thought had made Avi even more determined to join this mysterious fleet, but the organisation appeared to have no headquarters where he could offer his service. He called every Jewish group listed in the telephone book of New York, but each call produced the same denial of any knowledge of the secret organisation. He had tried Zionist youth clubs and called upon rabbis at their synagogues. Everyone was polite and one or two asked him to leave his telephone number in case they heard anything.

But Avi was persistent and finally decided to visit the Jewish Agency offices at 342 Madison Avenue. He didn't get beyond the front desk and was once more told to leave his name and a contact number. He turned away, convinced that if the mysterious organisation existed he would never discover how to contact it.

Avi was heading for the street when Shind entered. Impulsively the young sailor asked Shind if he knew how he could get in touch with Aliyah Bet. Avi recalled Shind saying, 'Who's asking? I told him who I was and why I wanted to know and asked who he was. He replied, "I work for *Eretz Yisrael*." I said I wanted to do the same. He said I should meet him next day in the library of the Jewish Theological Seminary, a place I had never heard of. I thought, "Oh, God, he thinks I want to be a rabbi." When I got to the library Shind introduced himself and the man with him, Captain Ash. For a couple of hours they grilled me about my Navy record, then asked me to wait outside. When they called me back in I was told to take a train to Baltimore. Captain Ash gave me instructions to go to the ship called *President Warfield*.'

Like Nat Nadler, Avi Livney became another member of its crew after being sworn into the Haganah. Each sailor had his own story of why he had signed on. One had worked in a Jewish DP camp in Germany. Another volunteer had signed on after his brother was killed in the last weeks of the war during the battle for Berlin. One was the son of a rabbi; another was on board so he could go to Palestine to work in a collective settlement. Several had no seagoing experience and could not speak Hebrew or Yiddish, only a thick Brooklynese, laced with GI expletives.

There was now urgency about the refitting of *President Warfield*. In London the Labour government was exerting pressure on Latin American governments, threatening to cancel trade agreements if ships continued to sail under their flags and were suspected of being blockade-runners. Already a Colombian diplomat in Bogotá had told the local Aliyah Bet shipping agent that he had been instructed to no longer provide registration papers and visas. A small portion of the $50 million Golda Meyerson had raised at the Thursday luncheon was transferred to the diplomat's bank account in Miami. No more was heard of the threatened withdrawal of the essential paperwork. The visas continued to be provided.

The British Embassy in Washington informed the Honduran ambassador it had instructions from the Foreign Office to cancel Britain's deal to import bananas from Honduras by the United Fruit Company. The firm was owned by Samuel Zemurray, an American Jew who had emigrated from Eastern Europe in the 1890s and became the largest exporter of bananas to Britain.

Ze'ev Shind was in the process of negotiating a deal to buy two of the banana boats for Aliyah Bet. He had flown to New Orleans to see Zemurray at his estate. The two men had talked late into the night. As dawn broke Zemurray had called the president of Honduras and told him he had learned the price of bananas was going to fall. To help him bear the loss he wanted to sell two of his boats as soon as possible so he could continue to pay the current market price as long as the boats sailed under the Honduran flag. Shind had closed the deal for both ships to sail under a foreign registration out of Baltimore.

Nat had been on board a week when Ze'ev Shind arrived with Captain Ash and Teddy Kollek, a veteran of blockade running and close to Ben Gurion and now one of the key members of Haganah's expanding operations in the United States. With them was a tubby, short man who swayed as he walked.

William Scholastica Schlegel, a staunch Roman Catholic from Bavaria, was a member of the powerful Masters, Mates & Pilots union of America. The union was in the middle of a major strike, having failed to come to terms with shipping companies, and its members were not allowed to take a ship to sea until the dispute was settled. Captain Ash had spotted the loophole he needed. As the union's former vice-president, he knew the ban did not apply to anyone offered a job to sail under a foreign flag. *President Warfield* was registered in Honduras. Schlegel could be hired without breaking the strike. Captain Ash had engaged the paunchy, florid-faced ship's master for 'a one-run job to deliver a ship to the western Mediterranean'. No further details were provided or asked for.

With his heavy German accent and a fondness for drink, Schlegel would not have been Captain Ash's first choice. But he was being pressed by Aliyah Bet to sail as soon as possible and Schlegel was available, having been out of work for months.

With Shind were a number of suntanned and muscular young men for whom Teddy Kollek had arranged to have visas to enter the United States. They were members of Palyam, the Haganah's secret navy. One was a slim, thin-faced, fair-haired man who looked even younger than his 22 years. His name was Yitzhak Ahronowitz. Throughout the Haganah's High Command he was known as Ike. The son of ardent Zionists, he had gone to sea as a deckhand on his 16th birthday, a month later becoming a founder member of Palyam. Recognising his potential, the Haganah had paid for Ike to study seamanship and navigation at a maritime college in London. Details of his training, including his tuition fees paid by the Jewish Agency from its Great Russell Street office in London and supported by the Manchester Shipping Company 'to qualify for a Third Mate's ticket' in the British Merchant Navy were passed in 1947 to MI6. His role in Aliyah Bet had become 'a matter of interest' to the Secret Intelligence Service. The documents remain in the MI6 registry to this day. Through his Haganah membership, Ike met Saul Avigur, who controlled Aliyah Bet operations in the Mediterranean. After meeting Ike, Avigur recommended he should be given command of *President Warfield* on her first voyage as a blockade-runner.

Early in 1947, Ike was told he was going to be an extra mate on a British ship bound for New York. Shind had been waiting for him on the dockside and brought him to Baltimore. After Shind asked the crew to assemble in the dining hall, he introduced Ike as their chief mate and Schlegel as the ship's master. Schlegel abruptly stood up and said that as the master, his orders would be final. In complete silence he walked out of the room.

Chapter 11

The Haganah Spy

In January 1947 Ralph Goldman could look with satisfaction at his efforts for Aliyah Bet's fund-raising not only in every Jewish community in the United States but also across the border into Mexico and down through Latin America. Even small congregations in remote areas had raised money to help to buy boats that were being refitted in shipyards between Boston and Baltimore. As each one came off a slipway it bore the name of a pioneer of Zionism: *Josiah Wedgwood, Hochelaga, Henrietta Szold*. In all there were 10 boats at various stages of refurbishment being readied to cross the Atlantic and join the other 40 ships that Goldman's fund-raising had helped buy and make ready for the journey to Palestine. Often aged and derelict, little more than hulks, they were under the command of Saul Avigur, the Haganah's senior officer who ran Aliyah Bet in Europe.

Immigrants still remember those days in the 1920s when he planned the defence of settlements in Palestine; others recalled how Avigur organised the *Velos*, the first pre-war immigrant ship that had landed them on a beach near Tel Aviv. Then, when the war started, he went to Iraq, wearing a British Army uniform, and brought Jews out from Baghdad and to Palestine. In 1942 Avigur had done the same in Bulgaria and Romania. At the end of the war he had moved to Paris, into a cramped bedroom in the Ceramic Hotel in Montmartre, to set up Aliyah Bet across Europe. For Ralph Goldman, the soft-spoken veteran with years of rescuing Jews was the ideal choice to run the operation.

In New York it was not only raising funds to enable Avigur to expand the secret fleet that occupied Goldman. There was a need to make use of the growing number of volunteers who had failed to pass the strict interviews of Ze'ev Shind and Captain Ash. If someone did not have the necessary experience the two men now demanded, he could be used in another way. Goldman set up a new agency called Land and Labor for recruits who had served in the US Army and now wanted to go to Palestine to fight in what he saw as the inevitable conflict with the Arabs.

For those volunteers 'Hatikvah', the Hebrew hymn of hope, became a rallying call:

> If you long to inherit the land of your birth,
> Buckle on the sword and take up the bow
> And go in the footsteps of your fathers.
> With weeping and tearful pleadings
> Zion will not be won.
> With sword and bow – hark ye!
> Jerusalem will be rebuilt!

These words, written by Naftali Hertz Imber, which later became the national anthem of Israel, could be heard in the corridors of the Breslin Hotel in New York's downtown area, where Goldman had set up Land and Labor. He spread the word that any Jewish ex-soldier should go to the hotel. Scores came: infantrymen, tank drivers, mechanics, armourers, anyone who might be useful in the conflict that the Yishuv would soon face.

Each volunteer swore the same Haganah oath of allegiance as the Aliyah Bet sailors who would bring them to Palestine. In the meantime, the soldiers would wait in the hotel until a ship was ready to sail. Each man was warned that any breach of security could also lead to facing a Haganah court martial. No one knew what that entailed, except it sounded fearsome.

Ralph Goldman was certain no one – neither the Haganah staff who controlled the hotel nor the recruits – would break the tight security. Yet one morning he was stunned when a member of his senior staff told him that one of the Haganah staff had been discovered to be a spy, working for the FBI. Only in his 93rd year would Goldman confirm that the man was known as Joe Reuben and had lived in Jersey City. Why he had betrayed his trust and what he had passed to the FBI, or what use the information could have been, were matters that Goldman still felt inappropriate to discuss. All he would say about what became of Reuben was, 'May he rest in peace.'

But there were more highly trained spies working against the Haganah in Europe at the time of Reuben. None was more remarkable than Frederick Vanden Heuvel, a Count of the Holy Roman Empire, who had worked for MI6 for 20 of his 62 years. Ostensibly a Foreign Office diplomat, he was commander of the Secret Intelligence Service in Berne, Switzerland, until 1945, when he was transferred by Stewart Menzies to Italy. His brief was to disrupt the traffic in illegal immigrants to Palestine.

With his bushy side-whiskers, black homburg and a pre-war Rolls-Royce, Count Vanden Heuvel could have been a wealthy doctor in one of the discreet clinics in the Tuscan hills where he had his villa, a palatial home hidden from the road by cypress trees and guarded by a wooden gate opened by one of his servants. There were rumours that the villa's well-stocked larder was filled with choice cuts of deer, wild pig and fish from the local lakes. His two regular visitors usually arrived on Friday afternoon and left on Sunday afternoon.

One was Derek Vershoyle, a former Bomber Command pilot. The other was David Smiley, who, when asked what his war had been like, would invariably reply, 'Oh, pretty good.' He had been a colonel in the Blues – a regiment that had fought with distinction in Europe – until the Count had arrived in Italy and recruited both men into MI6. They had undergone a course in sabotage and became founder members of what Stewart Menzies named the 'Kent Corps Specials'.

Vershoyle and Smiley were given the task of discovering which ports had been chosen by the Haganah to launch their immigrant ships. They had both been sent to the Royal Navy Shallow Waters Diving School on Malta. By the end of the week's course they had learned how to plant a variety of explosives, including mines, on the hulls of various-sized vessels. Each weapon should be fitted with a timer, so the ships would explode in international waters, making rescue more difficult.

In early February 1947, Vershoyle and Smiley drove up from Rome for their regular weekend meeting with Count Vanden Heuvel. He had just returned from Haifa and they were eager to hear what had transpired. The three men enjoyed an affectionate relationship, well beyond the coldly calculating demands of their daily work. In the privacy of the villa the Count was 'Funny Fixer', Vershoyle was 'Bombs Away' and Smiley was 'Cliff Hanger', from his skill at climbing the Alps.

Over dinner the Count revealed that Stewart Menzies, with whom he had met to discuss the latest tensions in Palestine, had said he expected the blockade-runners to contain even more illegal immigrants, who might be well armed. Sir John Cunningham, who had chaired the discussion, said he had already taken measures to deal with any such threats and had introduced Lieutenant Commander Bailey to explain his boarding tactics. The First Sea Lord then read out a copy of a telegram Foreign Secretary Ernest Bevin had sent to the British ambassador in Washington, Sir Oliver Wright: 'Inform the State Department the UK has convincing evidence that the Romanian Government, with the approval of the Soviet authorities and the acquiescence of the French Government, plans to collect a large number of handpicked Communist sympathisers and transport them to Palestine.'

Menzies had explained the 'convincing evidence' had been provided by MI6, who obtained it through Operation Gold, the code name for a joint operation run by GCHQ, the newly formed Government Communications Headquarters in London, and the American National Security Agency, NSA.

Sir John had said that he would order the Palestine Patrol to be strengthened and extend its surveillance beyond Cyprus towards Gibraltar to block any access from the Atlantic. In the meantime the Foreign Secretary would lodge a formal protest with the French government over its increasing support for the illegal immigrants.

On the bridge of HMS *Childers*, Lieutenant Commander Bailey watched the 28 marines undergoing their ship-boarding exercise. Wearing gas masks and protective arm shields, they moved back and forth across the deck under the watchful eye of the ship's gunnery officer, Lieutenant Robert MacPherson, a brusque Scot who had been assigned by Bailey to lead the boarding party into action when the time came.

On Bailey's order, a signal flag was run up and the two other destroyers on either side, HMS *Chieftain* and HMS *Charity*, swung into column formation to confirm their boarding exercise was complete for the day.

On board HMS *Charity* Lieutenant Roger Pearce had been appointed the ship's boarding officer and had picked his own squad. They included a sick-bay attendant – the equivalent to a civilian paramedic – a radioman and an engine-room petty officer who would control the engine room of an immigrant ship when it was brought to Haifa under guard. The remainder of the 15-man squad were seamen and stokers.

Over 400 sailors and marines had by now been trained to ensure there were sufficient crew to maintain a campaign of maritime interception.

A mile away to the port side of the trio of warships, the Bay-class frigate HMS *Cardigan Bay* increased its speed to take up position at the rear of the group. The ship had been launched in December 1944 and had taken part in the liberation of Norway, which had given able-seaman (radar) Geoffrey Barwell his first taste of war. The 22-year-old spent his working day in the ship's radar shack, watching the blips on his screen come and go.

HMS *Cardigan Bay* had come to Haifa when the Palestine Patrol was still a small unit in the Mediterranean Fleet. But since the arrival of Sir John and his decision to use Bailey's boarding tactics, the patrol had become a powerful fighting force, able to call upon 18 cruisers, 20 destroyers, nine frigates and 24 minesweepers to stop the blockade-runners. It gave the Royal Navy the largest fleet in the Mediterranean.

Late in the evening in his book-lined study on Keren Kayemet Street in Tel Aviv, David Ben-Gurion turned to a task that he always found deeply moving. Of all the duties which fell upon him as the country's prime minister in waiting, he regarded this one as the greatest honour. It was to give a Hebrew name to another illegal immigration ship. He had performed the function since the custom was introduced by the Haganah at the end of the Second World War. By March 1947 Ben-Gurion had chosen appropriate names for over 60 ships. There were so many ships, so many names. Sometimes it had taken him hours to settle on one. Other times he would confer with Rabbi Weingarten and draw on his erudition and advice.

On his desk was a single sheet of paper. It had been sent on the headed notepaper of the Weston Trading Company in New York. Written in the Hebrew code Ze'ev Shind used, it said *President Warfield* was almost ready to sail.

Ike Ahronowitz had spent his first hours on board the ship reminding himself that *President Warfield* had crossed the Atlantic in war and survived U-boats, and could make the journey again. The ship was still fast, with a cruising speed of 14 knots, which could be increased to 18 over a short distance, such as the three-mile territorial limit in the waters around Palestine. With her shallow draught, she would be able to sail closer to land than the Royal Navy destroyers. Once near the beach, the passengers could make their own way ashore.

He had spoken personally to every crew member to assess their motivation. Was it purely humanitarian, to help the survivors of the death camps? Was it that old-fashioned patriotism that imbued all Jews? Was it a sense of adventure before settling down to a life ashore, into marriage and raising children? A number had been members of the Zionist Youth Movement and would, Ike decided, be the 'moral backbone of the crew'.

The Palyam sailors Ze'ev Shind had brought on board were the professional sailors, men trained to cope with all weather and emergencies. They had been hand-picked for that reason. Reverend Grauel had impressed Ike. The minister's religious background gave him status. Captain Ash had told Ike that, since coming on board, the minister had shown himself to be prepared to do any job as well as running the galley; well into the night he scrubbed, hammered and painted and had been the first to take an oath to serve the Haganah, swearing his allegiance on the Methodist Bible he always carried.

In those first weeks Ike had seen *President Warfield* fitted with a $600 gyro compass and the radio shack equipped with the latest seagoing technology and updated maps covering the Atlantic and the Mediterranean. The engine had been descaled and the oil tanks filled. While the battleship grey of the hull below the guardrail remained, her superstructure had received an off-white coating which hinted of past days on the Chesapeake. The galley pantries were filled with tinned provisions, including crates of drinking water to supplement the ship's fresh-water tank. There were also three million packs of American cigarettes to sell on the European black market in case funds were needed to pay for emergency repairs on the voyage.

Day by day preparations gathered pace. From his office in Baltimore's Jewish quarter, Dr Herman Seidel, a 60-year-old physician full of charm and energy, had persuaded the city's pharmaceutical companies to donate drugs, dressings and surgical equipment. He had provided an obstetrics kit and had arranged for the crew, a dozen at a time, to come to his surgery to be physically examined and inoculated against tropical diseases. Another Zionist, Moses I. Speert, had used his contacts in Baltimore's business community to provide bedding, hundreds of life jackets, cots for children, tableware and crockery. Finally, a local lumber company had given several trucks of timber with which the crew would build bunks.

Ike's only concern was William Schlegel. The ship's master took little interest in the refurbishment, spending long periods in his cabin, from which he would emerge smelling strongly of alcohol. But Shind had assured Ike that when the time came the master would do his job.

In the last week of February 1947, Shind and Captain Ash had met Schlegel on the bridge and they had agreed *President Warfield* was ready to sail once she received her Lloyd's clearance. To ensure there would be no hitch, Shind had arranged for a former US naval officer, Paul Shulman, to inspect the ship. In 1945, having graduated from the naval academy in Annapolis, he had met David Ben-Gurion and learned about the plight of the immigrants. He resigned from the navy and had gone to Tel Aviv to advise Palyam before returning to Baltimore, where, from time to time, he had visited *President Warfield* to check on her progress. He confirmed not only that Lloyd's would have no problem in passing the ship as seaworthy, but that he would travel with her on the last leg of her journey from France to Palestine.

Another convoy of Jewish Brigade trucks arrived in Sète, bringing the total number of refugees in the area to over 4,000 men, women and children. The majority were Jews from Eastern Europe, but among them were a handful of British Jews who had travelled from England to come and help the immigrants get to Palestine. They included Dr Yossi Cohen, a mild-mannered physician with the quintessential bedside manner, always taking his time to diagnose, but always certain of what he found. He had grown up in one of Glasgow's hard-living areas and, though slow to anger, if aroused he could floor a boy twice his size with one punch. His family had fled to Scotland from Lithuania during one of the pogroms at the turn of the century. He had been raised through the Depression and before the outbreak of war his brother joined the Royal Navy. For a while Yossi had wondered whether he should follow him to sea, but instead he had decided to enter medicine and became, to the delight of his parents, the first doctor in the family. With its docks, Glasgow had been a target for the Luftwaffe, and working in the casualty department of the city's major hospital had given Dr Cohen first-hand experience in trauma medicine and stress-related illnesses.

At home he spoke Hebrew and read the Bible. In many ways he was growing up in the family tradition: a soft-spoken scholar filled with zeal that his life would be devoted to helping people. The plight of the Holocaust survivors fuelled his determination. He *must* go and help them and the place to be was in the South of France; the *Glasgow Herald* was reporting that its ports had become the gateway to Palestine. He withdrew his savings and used some of the money to buy himself a one-way ticket to Paris. Three days later he was in Marseilles. From there it was a bus ride to Sète, where he was told the immigrants were assembling. Arriving in the port, he went to a café crowded with immigrants. The babble of voices was impossible for him to understand and he ruefully realised that his Scottish burr made it even harder for him to communicate as he tried to explain why he was there. Eventually one of the immigrants left and returned with Yossi Harel. They spoke in Hebrew and Harel told Dr Cohen that he could be the ship's doctor on the next voyage to Palestine. In the meantime, he could spend his time treating some of the immigrants in the area.

Rachel Biber had been a *Kindertransport* child who had arrived in London on the eve of the outbreak of war in 1939. She already had a sister in Palestine and her burning hope was to join her. When the London Blitz started she, along with the city's other children, had been evacuated to the country. Rachel went to Northampton, where she became a children's nurse at barely 15 years old. In London the Jewish Agency had placed her name on its list of Polish children who had come to Britain. Saul Avigur regularly checked such files in the hope of finding someone who could be useful to him. His finger had stopped as it ran down the column of names. Later he called it 'instinct' as he sent for the single-page document on Rachel's background. He decided that the pretty-faced girl with rosy cheeks would be more valuable working for Aliyah Bet, with her fluency in Hebrew, than remaining as a child minder. After learning skills as a typist, Rachel eventually became a wireless operator for Haganah. In 1946 she had been sent to Marseilles, where she was taught Morse code. She would become the link with each immigrant boat from Haganah's secret headquarters in the city.

In February 1947, Rachel had followed through her headset the drama of a blockade-runner as it managed to outwit the Palestine Patrol before deliberately running aground on a sandbank off the beach of Haifa, whereupon its passengers had scrambled overboard to wade ashore. Waiting were armed British soldiers, who arrested them. A week later the ship had been pursued by another patrol boat. With 800 immigrants on board, the cutter landed them on a beach south of Tel Aviv. This time waiting lorries drove them off to Jewish settlements while the Mandate troops conducted a fruitless search.

Every time Yehuda Arazi and Ada Sereni spread the word of such successes to the waiting thousands of immigrants around Sète, they were asked the same question: when would their boat come?

In his office at the rear of the British Embassy in Washington, Sir William Stephenson received a call from an MI6 officer using a pay phone on Pier Five at Rutlet Pier Terminal on the Baltimore waterfront. Two days earlier *President Warfield* had been towed from Pier Eight to the more elegant surroundings of the terminal. The officer had established that the following day, Sunday, the ship would receive the leaders of East Coast Jewry whose money had paid for her refit. Next day she would sail for Europe. Stephenson had gone to the embassy's communications room and dictated a message to the duty officer: 'Ship named President Warfield to depart Baltimore noon, February 25. Flying flag of Honduras. No passenger list available. Destination Azores to refuel. Final port given as Marseille, France.'

The cable was addressed to Stewart Menzies, with a copy to Prodome, the telegraphic address of the Foreign Secretary.

Within the ranks of the Labour Party Bevin's stand against what he persisted in calling 'illegal immigration' continued, causing embarrassment to rising stars in the movement like Denis Healey. A strong supporter of the Jewish cause, he saw Bevin's determination to continue the blockade as a threat to America's own foreign policy which could seriously affect its relationship with Britain. In the United States

the Zionist Movement had a huge political influence. But Healey knew
for him or any other Labour politician to try and dissuade Bevin from
maintaining his abrasive attitude to Jews 'was a no-hoper'. The news
that another ship was en route to France to collect yet more Jews would
only have inflamed the Foreign Secretary further.

The departure of *President Warfield* had something of the atmosphere
of the pre-war sailings from Baltimore to Norfolk. Led by Rudolf
Sonneborn, leading Zionists from New York, Boston, Philadelphia
and Baltimore made their way on a Sunday morning to the snow-
covered Pier Five at Rutlet Pier Terminal. All had contributed to the
costs of refurbishing and purchasing the provisions for the voyage.

The boilers had been fired up and the on-board rat population
had virtually disappeared under the tireless work of one of the crew
appointed as rodent catcher; hundreds of trapped carcasses were
dropped into the water.

Together with the entire crew, the guests crowded into the dining
room where once passengers had dined on sumptuous meals as they
cruised the Chesapeake. Now there were only bagels, lox and bottles
of soft drinks. On a table stood one bottle of champagne – only to be
opened at sea when the ship reached the Palestine coast. Ze'ev Shind
presented Ike with a blue-and-white flag, displaying the Magen
David, to be hoisted at that moment.

The tensions between the captain and Schlegel had been noticed
by Reverend Grauel. In an effort to ease the situation, the minister
told the guests of an incident he had witnessed during the invasion of
Europe when a US Army unit was bivouacked outside a Catholic
monastery: 'On the eve of the Jewish Sabbath, your Jewish soldiers
wanted to hold their traditional service. But under your laws there
must be a *minyan* or ten men present. Casualties had left us with only
nine Jews. I pointed to a statue of Christ in the monastery garden
and reminded them that Christ himself was a Jew. The service went
ahead with his blessing. So will this voyage.'

The applause echoed around the room.

*

In the small hours of 26 February 1947, the snowflakes trying to settle on the decks of *President Warfield* were blown away on a blustery wind. By dawn she was heading out into the Atlantic. In the wheelhouse Schlegel reminisced about the war: the sinking of the liner *Athenia*, the loss of the *Royal Oak*, and the U-boats which had once hunted along the course they were now following. At his lookout station, Murray Aronoff started to whistle 'Give Me Five Minutes More'. Ike watched the barometer dropping. As dawn broke, the ship was being pounded by long rolling waves, with deep troughs being whipped by the wind to smash against the hull. Below deck the first of the crew, Ben Foreman and Reuven Margolis, were being seasick.

By full daylight the snow had stopped and the sky had turned an ugly yellow. In the radio shack, Ike listened to the weather reports. The forecast was for storms to rise to a full Force 10 gale sweeping the entire North Atlantic, with winds of 60 miles an hour over a vast area. That evening a US Coast Guard had rescued nine crewmen on board a sinking schooner, *Catherine L. Brown*.

By dawn, part of the wooden guardrails of *President Warfield* – all that stopped a seaman on deck being swept into the sea – were breaking away. Water poured below deck. Chief Engineer John Crabson cracked a rib as he slipped on the engine-room floor. Alarm spread among the crew as they struggled to cope; some were exhausted and lying in their own vomit.

Next morning the full fury of the gale still held *President Warfield* in its grip. Some 200 miles northeast of Bermuda, a US Navy tug was fighting to take in tow the freighter *Georgia*, which had lost its propeller. From ships all over the Atlantic came distress signals; it was the worst storm off the East Coast for more than a decade. On board *President Warfield* it shaped the personalities of the crew. Those who had never been to sea – like Avraham Sygal and Frank Levine – found from somewhere the physical strength to go about their duties. The Palyam sailors were multi-tasking, tending to the seasick and the injured, carrying them to cabins on the hurricane deck, fitting them with life jackets in case the order came to abandon ship.

Ike was determined that would never happen. For him there was no fixed duty, no break to snatch even a brief rest. He was everywhere, using his leadership to ease the crew's ordeal as much as possible. He checked watertight doors and hauled a pump to clear the water from the main deck. In the engine room Roger Rofe and Samuel Schiller responded immediately to his every command from the bridge. In all Ike said and did, he was a tower of strength, holding everything together by sheer determination. His presence was a tremendous reassurance to everyone and he gave of himself unstintingly, even though his hours without sleep continued to mount. He was utterly fatigued, but he knew it was part of the job of command: the reverse side of the respect he had been accorded. The weather would not defeat him. For Bill Bernstein, the mate, it was an object lesson in captaincy.

As the waves crashed against the wheelhouse windows, Schlegel pushed aside the helmsman, Bill Millman, and took the wheel himself. Each time *President Warfield* ploughed into a trough and refused to come around, swinging her stern up to the next oncoming wave – a move which threatened to sink her – Schlegel corrected the threat with brute strength and skilled seamanship. *Three-quarters right wheel. Amidships. Right rudder. Three-quarters right turn.* Slowly he brought the ship under his control. He deliberately allowed her stern to run up on the next comber and her bow, heavy with water, to cut low through the next trough. But he knew he could only maintain this for so long. The gale wailed like a banshee, sending icy spume shattering over the wheelhouse and tons of water crashing against the hull.

At 5.48pm on the second day Ike ordered Harold Leidner, the radioman, to send an SOS giving their position and course. It was picked up by the Coast Guard District Headquarters in Norfolk. From there it was relayed to the Coast Guard cutter *Cherokee*. It was one of 27 mayday signals transmitted that day.

On board *President Warfield* conditions worsened. The number of sick and injured increased. Abe Lippschitz ran out of seasickness tablets. Soon only six men were physically able to handle the ship. The Reverend Grauel believed 'the next events were out of my hands and in those of the Almighty. I found my bunk and fell into a dreamless sleep.'

On 27 February, the tanker *H. C. Sinclair* stood off *President Warfield*, using its bulk to act as a shield against the mountainous seas and raging winds.

On board an argument had broken out on the bridge. Schlegel wanted to head for the safety of Chesapeake Bay. Ike, his mind on his commitment to the Haganah, was reluctant, but he finally admitted there was no alternative. Pounded and battered, with water spilling in below decks, her engine room in immediate danger of flooding, her superstructure threatening to collapse, crewed by a handful of seamen themselves so physically drained they could barely move, *President Warfield* limped back into Chesapeake Bay. Chief Engineer Crabson was taken to hospital and the rest of the crew slowly recovered. Over the coming weeks, the ship was pumped out, her flooded storerooms emptied and replenished, her guardrails repaired and finally the engine pistons tested.

The *New York Times* had run a story under the headline: PALESTINE-BOUND MYSTERY SHIP BATTERED BY SEA IS BACK IN PORT. The report had been planted by Sir William Stephenson as a further move in the propaganda war over the blockade-runners. Stephenson had briefed the newspaper reporter that the British government was increasingly concerned that the Haganah was preparing to send 'a fleet of ships bought by wealthy Jews in the United States'. There was 'credible evidence' – a phrase which had become familiar in Stephenson's lexicon on the subject – that 15,000 illegal immigrants were being readied to sail to Palestine and that their arrival could finally trigger a full-scale war with the Arabs, a conflict which would inevitably involve the United States.

In off-the-record briefings, the British Embassy Press Office in Washington said the French government was providing 'shelter and protection for the immigrants in the South of France'. Increasingly alarmed over developments, Foreign Secretary Ernest Bevin had flown to Paris to meet Georges-Augustin Bidault, then the French Foreign Minister.

The elegant 52-year-old Catholic and Sorbonne graduate had worked for the French Resistance, rising to become president of the Conseil de la Résistance, and his reputation for helping Jews was renowned. While Bidault had joined Bevin in consolidating Europe's response to the Marshall Plan and in efforts to parry the Soviet threat to the West, he had made it bluntly clear to Bevin that his opposition to anti-Semitism was as strong as his fight against Fascism. He had told the Foreign Secretary that he would continue to give all support possible to immigrants wanting to go to Palestine. According to Bevin's secretary, the Foreign Secretary's language on the flight back to London was 'volcanic'.

The tension Reverend Grauel sensed between Captain Ash and Schlegel had increased since the master brought *President Warfield* to her dry-dock berth in Philadelphia, where the repairs were carried out. Schlegel had suddenly insisted he would not submit the ship's papers to the port authorities certifying she was sea-worthy. Without the documents signed off, *President Warfield* could not sail.

The row on the bridge became a shouting match, with Schlegel bellowing that the ship would sink unless further repairs were done and Captain Ash roaring that *President Warfield* had once more been certified by Lloyd's. Ike suggested they should all inspect the ship to see if there were any defects. Schlegel hollered that the whole superstructure needed further bracing. Shind proposed that if Schlegel took the ship to the edge of territorial waters and still found any problems, then *President Warfield* could be brought back to the harbour. Schlegel refused. Suddenly Captain Ash erupted and told Schlegel he was fired. The master screamed that was the best news he had heard because the ship was a floating wreck. He stormed off the bridge and stumbled down the gangplank. Shortly afterwards he was admitted to hospital and would never sail again.

Within hours Captain Ash had hired a new master, Vigo Thompson, who admitted he liked a drink – but only at the end of a voyage. However, after walking through the ship he asked for his total fee upfront. When Ike asked why, Thompson explained it was 'insurance'.

Captain Ash wrote out a cheque for $5,000 for Thompson to take *President Warfield* to Marseilles after refuelling in the Azores. Ash had chosen the port because the Haganah had an agent based there to deal with all its ships that needed refuelling on the journey to Palestine.

That evening John Crabson, still hospitalised, was replaced by a new chief engineer, Frank Stanczak. The following morning, Saturday 29 March, with the pilot on board to guide *President Warfield* down the Delaware River into the Atlantic, Shind received an urgent telegram from the Honduran consul-general in New York: 'I am instructed by his Excellency the Ambassador. He has had strong representations from the British Embassy to cancel your registration papers.'

Shind calculated that the consul-general would need several hours to reach Philadelphia. He telegraphed back that the documents and flag would be available for collection by mid-afternoon. At noon helmsman Bill Millman followed the pilot's orders as *President Warfield* edged out into the Delaware. At the back of the bridge Ike and Vigo Thompson smiled at each other. On the ship's masthead flew the Honduran flag.

In the Admiralty, there was a new communications suite manned around the clock, its naval Wrens linked to Haifa, Cyprus, New York, Washington, DC and the office of Stewart Menzies at 54 Broadway, in the centre of London, from where the Secret Intelligence Service had operated since 1924. There was a map room, its walls covered with charts of the Mediterranean and enlarged images taken from RAF surveillance aircraft of harbours around the coast. In another room were photographs of all the blockade-runners intercepted since 1945, together with details of when and where they had been stopped, the number of immigrants on board and which warship had carried out the arrest. A smaller room was used for conferences, with telephones linked to the Cabinet office in Downing Street and the Foreign Secretary's secretariat.

On 20 March, following the *New York Times* story, the entire question of illegal immigrants was the main item on the Cabinet agenda. Sir John Cunningham had flown in from Haifa for the occasion and told ministers that he had ordered four more warships to be transferred from the naval base in Hong Kong to Haifa. He had also arranged for detention camps in Cyprus to be ready to receive up to 10,000 immigrants once they were caught by the Palestine Patrol. Having explained the new boarding tactics, he added: 'The success of a boarding operation largely depends on the ability of the boarding party in getting over a large number of our men at the first moment of impact, and subsequently on their courage, resourcefulness and good temper in the face of determined and provocative opposition.'

The Attorney General, the government's senior law officer, had next dealt with the legal position of Haganah ships sailing under a flag of convenience: 'It would not be unreasonable to assume the right of self-defence against the possibility of armed men attempting to land in Palestine to attack its legal government or instigate civil war. It is essential to make it clear to all ship's crews sailing under a flag of convenience that HM Government would use the full rigour of the law to discourage ships from carrying illegal immigrants. Captured crews should expect to be brought swiftly to trial and receive a heavy sentence.'

That said, there could still be difficulties. One would be arresting crew members if they were American Jews able to call upon their own country to intervene on their behalf. Another problem could be bringing a crew to trial, as their lawyers could demand the arresting ship's captain to be examined on where at sea the arrest had taken place. In the Attorney General's view, it would be undesirable to reveal such details. It would be better to impound a ship, arrest and place the immigrants in a detention camp and allow the crew to go free.

By the end of March, the Admiralty communication centre had given *President Warfield* its own code name: Operation Mae West. The name of the Hollywood star had been chosen by Stewart Menzies when the Cabinet Office set up the Illegal Immigration Committee, after Bevin returned from Paris following a second meeting with Georges Bidault to try and persuade him to impound *President Warfield* should she arrive in French territorial waters. Bidault said it was impossible to offer any action until the ship arrived – if it ever did.

A furious Bevin returned home to order the committee to take every possible step to stop *President Warfield*. The first move was to inform the British ambassador in Lisbon to persuade the Portuguese government to deny her fuel when she arrived in the Azores.

Chapter 12

Bird Flown Coop

In Sète in the late spring of 1947, Zvi Tiroche knew that soon the first heat of summer would return to the Mediterranean. The slim, tanned youth had a countryman's knowledge of the weather and could read cloud changes as well as any forecaster. Born and raised into a French Zionist family, he had sensed his parents hoped he would one day become a doctor, a respected figure among the surrounding grape growers. But Zvi knew they would never press him on a choice of career; they had raised him to believe he should always make his own decisions.

With the war over for two years and a sense of order steadily returning to that part of France, Zvi had considered several options before going to medical school. But after a year he felt another vocation calling him.

Still in his late teens, like many of his Jewish friends he was determined to play a role in preparing for a future Jewish state. He had discussed the matter around the family dinner table and said he wanted to volunteer to work on one of the farms the Haganah had set up to train French Jews for the new collective settlements in Palestine.

With the agreement of his parents and sufficient pocket money, he had spent a winter ploughing and sowing grain. The farm's manager – a Haganah settler from Galilee – had taken him aside one day and told him he was about to put into practice all he had learned: he would be leaving for Palestine very shortly.

Next day, his clothes in an old kitbag and family photographs in his wallet, Zvi had been given a one-way train ticket to Marseilles by the manager. From there he would board a boat to take him to Palestine.

As they had parted, his manager had assured him that everything had been arranged by Aliyah Bet, an organisation Zvi had read about in his local newspaper. At the synagogue there had been a regular collection for its work. With a final handshake, Zvi had taken the bus to Paris and caught the train south.

There were about 50 young Zionists travelling with him. They had come from DP camps in Germany and spoke no French or English, only Yiddish or Hebrew. By the time they reached Marseilles, Zvi had become their translator. Waiting for them on the station platform was a soldier in a British Army uniform. He announced in Hebrew that he had come to take them to their camp. The others looked at Zvi in dismay. Had they come all this way to end up in another DP camp?

Zvi reassured them. The soldier's uniform was British, but his shoulder flash identified him as a member of the Jewish Brigade. They relaxed and began to sing as they boarded their trucks.

Two hours later they drove through the open gates of the camps. Waiting for them were more soldiers with the same flashes on their khaki uniforms. One of them, his clipped voice used to giving commands, smiled at them. Eliyahu Cohen asked if anyone spoke French. Zvi stepped forward. Cohen said that after a meal the group would help his own soldiers to prepare the camp to receive 1,500 refugees, who would arrive in the next few days. Cohen indicated some of the huts and, while Zvi translated, told them that stored there were fold-up beds, blankets, food and water, which had all been given by the US Army to Aliyah Bet. A member of the astonished group asked why. Cohen had smiled and said, 'That's what friends do.'

Cohen told the group that from now on Zvi would be his liaison officer. Any questions would go through him. The teenager, whose only previous orders had been to guide his oxen team on the Haganah farm, found himself appointed as deputy commander of the camp. No doubt it would make his parents and farm manager proud of him. But, he wondered, would the expected arrival of those immigrants delay his own hopes of catching the boat to Palestine while he remained on camp duty?

The sun was rising above the Pico volcano, the highest in the Azores at over 7,000 feet, when Nat Nadler joined some of the other crew leaning on the deck rails watching Faial Island, the nearest in the Atlantic archipelago, emerging in the morning haze. In a couple of hours *President Warfield* would dock in Horta, the island's harbour. Captain Ash had selected it as the port for refuelling on the eastern route from the United States and comfortably within *President Warfield*'s range. However, Captain Thompson had taken the ship on a slightly southern course which had left the oil tanks almost empty.

For many of the crew there was an exciting reason to reach Horta. Its two brothels were renowned for having the prettiest prostitutes. Contemplating the pleasure ahead, they had listened politely to Reverend Grauel describing another attraction of Azores life: its many religious festivals during which three-hour-long processions moved through streets lined with flowers and crosses made from Japanese cedar trees imported centuries before.

Nat had spent the 2,400-mile journey as the ship's fireman, working in the engine room firing up and checking the ship's boilers. Once or twice the trade winds had freshened – the reason why Captain Thompson had changed course – causing the sea to surge and the ship's superstructure to creak. Several of the crew had looked uneasily at each other and wondered if Schlegel had been right after all when he had said that the old timbers needed further bracing after the earlier Atlantic storm.

As *President Warfield* moored near the end of the long quay which acted as Horta's breakwater, Captain Thompson and Ike watched the portly figure of Ben Saude trotting along the quay. Within minutes they knew why. Saude was Captain Ash's refuelling contact in the Azores and his firm had been told from its London headquarters not to refuel the ship. The order had been reinforced by the local administration. The demand had come from the Foreign Office in London.

Saude suggested *President Warfield* should move to Ponta Delgada and wait there while he tried to resolve matters. As he left the ship, Saude called up to the crew lining the deck rail that the women in the town were as attractive as in Horta and even more plentiful.

At midday on 5 April 1947, *President Warfield* entered Ponta Delgada, the largest port in the Azores. Ike and Captain Thompson had spent most of the short voyage from Horta in the radio shack waiting for news from Ben Saude. None had arrived by the time the ship berthed, so Ike agreed to give the crew shore leave and each sailor received a handful of US dollars. As Nat Nadler recalled: 'A brothel was the only place I could get a beer as we weren't carrying liquor on board. The girls in the brothel were absolutely beautiful, a mixture of Spanish and Caribbean, really gorgeous. The Palyam boys had never seen girls like this.'

Finally a message came from Saude. There was no chance of officially overcoming the ban on refuelling, but he gave them a contact number at Ponta Delgada. It turned out to be in one of the port's brothels and the contact was a Norwegian captain. Vigo Thompson recalled:'Once he heard we were Jews he could not have been more helpful. He showed us how oil could be tapped from the pipeline running from the concrete tanks and linked to our ship's oil line. He refused our money but said we would need American dollars to bribe the guards at the tanks and then we could take what we wanted.'

That night Ike and Thompson went around the brothels collecting the crew. In the early hours of the morning Ike led them back to the oil tanks and paid off the guards. The oil line from *President Warfield* was run over to the outlet hose on a tank. Two hours later the ship's tanks were filled. Nat Nadler was given the order to fire up the boilers and, with the sun once more rising over Pico volcano, *President Warfield* slowly steamed out into the Atlantic, heading north.

An Algerian-class minesweeper of the Mediterranean Fleet lay half a mile beyond the Straits of Gibraltar. To port were the lights of La Línea de la Concepción, to starboard, Punta de Europa. Towering over both was the peak of Gibraltar, bristling with communication masts, through one of which the minesweeper communicated every six hours with Fleet headquarters in Haifa. Each time it had reported there was no sign of *President Warfield*. On the 11th day the mine-sweeper was withdrawn into Gibraltar harbour for victualling.

Meanwhile, 10 miles off the African coast, *President Warfield* lay motionless in the water without a single navigation light showing: every glimmer signalling her presence had been turned off; even smoking on deck was not allowed. At 2am on 23 April, Ike ordered Thompson to start engines and take the ship slowly towards Gibraltar. With only the lights of the Rock and fishing boats off the Spanish coast glimmering, *President Warfield* entered the Mediterranean.

On 3 May 1947, HMS *Childers* made her slow progress across Famagusta Bay in Cyprus and began to head back towards Haifa. Apart from the inshore fishing boats, there was no other vessel to be seen, no blockade-runner coming out of Greece or Turkey. The sea was calm under unbroken cloud. On the bridge Lieutenant Commander Bailey had heard the RAF aircraft pass overhead and guessed the twin-engined Warwick's crew would have little to concern them as they made their reconnaissance sweep westwards towards Malta.

On that morning, as HMS *Childers* headed back to Haifa, the radar screen was blank. In recent weeks it had so often been like that: a box search between Haifa and Cyprus, a sweep outside the territorial waters of Greece and Turkey combing for a suspicious radar blip. But there was nothing, least of all the one ship Bailey had been ordered to search for: *President Warfield*.

Fog enveloped *President Warfield* as she entered the Golfe du Lion, the bay on which lay its destination, Marseilles. The fog was sufficiently dense for Vigo Thompson to open the voice-pipe cover on the bridge and order Chief Engineer Frank Stanczak urgently to reduce speed.

Nat Nadler set the revolutions to minimum and Ike ordered extra lookouts posted on deck. The ship's siren announced its presence every 30 seconds as she moved slowly across the bay. From somewhere in the fog came responding blasts.

Suddenly a lookout in the bows yelled he had spotted a floating object heading towards the boat that looked like a mine. Thompson shouted orders to helmsman Bill Millman, who began to spin the wheel furiously. At the same time Ike snapped open the voice-pipe and called to Stanczak for full power to reverse, while Reverend Grauel ran to the opposite side of the bridge to peer down into the sea. Within moments he shouted that everyone could relax, it wasn't a mine but a box drifting on the water.

Hours later the fog had lifted and *President Warfield* picked her way past the Second World War wrecks that cluttered the approach to Marseilles harbour, as she headed for her berth at the still-unfinished Quai Grulet next to the coal piers. In the port's signal station, the clerk noted *President Warfield*'s time of arrival and telephoned the shipping agent appointed to handle her refuelling.

Shortly after *President Warfield* docked, Reverend Grauel had asked Ike if he could go to Paris to visit Notre-Dame Cathedral and the Louvre Museum. Ike had not hesitated: the clergyman was a respected member of the crew and would be the ideal person to give David Shaltiel, now in charge of Haganah operations in the French capital, a full and accurate report of events since they had left the United States. In turn Shaltiel would be able to update him on the latest moves the British government were making. Reverend Grauel accepted the mission with his usual good humour, saying he had always wanted to be 'God's messenger in a dog collar'.

From the top of the gangway Ike watched Yehuda Arazi and Ada Sereni coming on board with Joe Baharlia, the Haganah shipping agent in the city. Arazi had recruited the ship's chandler on his first visit to Marseilles at the end of the war. Baharlia proved to be a shrewd choice. In a port where crime had long been established as a way of life, Aliyah Bet could well have foundered without him. Behind Baharlia's smile, which never reached his eyes, there was cold

determination to avenge the murder of his entire family in
Auschwitz; it had been fuelled by the way he saw the immigrants
being treated by the British. Nurtured by Arazi, the Hungarian had
become a vital link in the chain which led from fund-raising in the
United States to helping Saul Avigur find ships. When British-owned
oil companies refused to provide fuel for the blockade-runners, Joe
Baharlia found oil on the black market. He knew who to bribe to get
sailing papers and fake ship manifests, which company would supply
food and lifebelts without questions. There was nothing he could not
fix. For Arazi, 'Joe was the smartest operator around the
Mediterranean. Haganah's debt to him was beyond calculation.'

Ike led them to the bridge, where Thompson waited, and Arazi
thanked him and said a ticket had been booked for the captain to
catch the train to Paris and a reservation made to sail from Le Havre
next day to New York. Arazi then briefed Ike. The French government was still resisting increasing pressure from Bevin; the Foreign
Secretary had begun to lobby 15 other European foreign ministers
who were to take part in discussions in Paris on the Marshall Plan.
This European recovery programme grew out of President Harry
Truman's post-war determination that the United States would have
the key role in rebuilding devastated Europe. Congress had voted an
initial $597 million to kick-start the ambitious programme for
economic aid.

Bevin had promised the ministers they could count on Britain's
support for their own demands if they backed the United Kingdom's
position that all immigrants in France 'waiting to go illegally to
Palestine should be transported back to their original countries.
There they could then apply for legal permission to enter. The
Haganah and Aliyah Bet agents must be expelled from France for
their illegal activities.' In his latest visit to Paris, Bevin had bypassed
Bidault and gone directly to the French prime minister, Paul
Ramadier, to press his expulsion demands.

Arazi said it was now more important than ever that *President
Warfield* should move every refugee waiting at Sète to Palestine. Ike
had explained that first there would be a need to fit the ship with

sufficient sleeping accommodation to carry all the immigrants. The wood to construct the bunks had been donated in America, but it had been too risky to build them in Philadelphia, when the ship was not licensed as a passenger vessel. It had also lost its Honduran registration, which had caused a refuelling problem in the Azores. What was needed was a safe place where *President Warfield* could be moored and the bunks installed. The ship could then return to Sète, load the refugees and sail to Palestine.

Ada Sereni agreed that Marseilles was untenable. But she knew a safe harbour: Portovenere in Italy. From there she had operated successfully until she had to close her network and move to Sète. There were workmen in Portovenere who would help the crew to install the bunks. Fired by her enthusiasm, Ike and Baharlia agreed it was as near as possible a perfect solution. Gone from French waters, *President Warfield* would no longer be a temptation for its government to give in to Bevin's demands. But none of them had an inkling that Count Frederick Vanden Heuvel had a villa in Portovenere.

In a back-street café in Sète, mid-afternoon on a summer's day, business was slack and the owner stood watch in the doorway for any suspicious movement. He was a local agent of the Haganah who, during the war, had fought in the French Resistance against the Vichy government. In 1945 he had been recruited by Shmarya Zamaret, one of two men at a table in the back of the café drinking coffee. Zamaret was the local commander of Aliyah Bet. Opposite him sat Yossi Harel, who had become a member of the Rekash, the Hebrew name for the Haganah's arms acquisitions department, which had procured, either by theft or by bribery, substantial amounts of weapons and ammunition to ship to Palestine on boats Zamaret obtained.

Avigur had decided that Yossi should switch from arms running and become a people smuggler. The café meeting was to discuss his role in the biggest operation Aliyah Bet had staged. For Harel: 'I knew it would be dangerous. But I was used to that. I also sensed that if we succeeded the operation would break the back of Britain's opposition to illegal immigration. Sure, the British had the largest navy, air force and the best intelligence. And this would be no ordinary run to Palestine. I was told that our people in New York had decided we had to make a point to show that the State of Israel wasn't just going to be a name the UN would create. We were soon going to be a country ready to challenge anybody who tried to stop its people coming home. The British would fight us. That I knew. But I would do everything to surprise them.'

That afternoon in the café the two men discussed their plans. Between them they pooled the latest information they had obtained. In New York and Washington members of the Sonneborn Institute, founded by Rudolf Sonneborn, had established that in Washington the State Department was pressing for the present British monthly immigration quota to be increased from 1,500 to 4,000.

Zamaret later recalled: 'Yossi was emphatic this should be the minimum number of passengers we should carry. It would give the issue of immigration a worldwide platform from which Bevin would be swept aside in the resulting publicity.'

At the time he told Harel, 'New York wants you to be the ship's commander. You will look after all the passengers.' As he remembered, Harel had one question: 'Who will actually captain the ship?' Zamaret did not hesitate: 'Yitzhak Ahronowitz. Ike is a good man. Saul Avigur approved him.'

Yossi Harel made no comment. His silence was the first hint of the tension which would emerge between Harel and Ike Ahronowitz, who would 'dismissively refer to Yossi by his diaspora name, Hamburger', wrote Linda Grant, who was preparing his biography when Ike died in December 2009.

For the next two days Yossi Harel visited the refugees who were steadily arriving in the mansions and houses around Sète and the camp where Zvi Tiroche was liaison officer. With him he had brought Dr Yossi Cohen to choose the women who would assist him on board *President Warfield* during the voyage.

He told each one they would have to be able to work long hours in the intense and often breezeless heat. Seasickness would be only one ailment they would have to cope with. Many of the passengers would still be suffering from malnutrition after years in concentration camps and could have not only physical but also emotional illnesses. Yossi knew the women Dr Cohen would select had themselves endured a terrible life in the camps; but they must put those experiences to the back of their mind if they were to nurse others. Among them was Helena Levi. Her father had been a doctor and had taught her the basic requirements of nursing. Another was Miriam Bergman. Like Helena, she had the essential qualities of kindness and patience.

Dr Cohen had warned Yossi there would inevitably be dysentery on the ship because conditions would be cramped and toilet facilities limited. Yossi doubted if there were going to be any bedpans. Other refugees could have tuberculosis and some might die before the ship reached Palestine.

On the morning of 4 May, an RAF reconnaissance aircraft had overflown Marseilles harbour and the plane's high-resolution cameras had collected a number of images before flying back to its base in Nicosia, Cyprus. Photographic interpreters had identified *President Warfield* by comparing the aerial images with the close-up photographs taken by the MI6 agent in Baltimore. There was no sign of any activity aboard the ship. The analysts confirmed she was far bigger than any of the other ships previously used as blockade-runners. A Royal Navy intelligence specialist, working with data provided by the Admiralty about her wartime service, decided *President Warfield* could outrun most pursuit under full steam.

In the late afternoon GCHQ in London received the details from Cyprus. They were immediately sent to MI6 headquarters. Stewart Menzies ordered David Smiley and Derek Vershoyle, who were in Paris tracking Haganah activities, to travel to Marseilles. They arrived in the early hours of 5 May. Shortly afterwards the MI6 night duty officer received a message: 'Bird Flown Coop'.

Under cover of darkness *President Warfield* had left the harbour. The harbour signal station had logged its departure at 10.30pm local time. In the column 'Destination' was one word: 'Unknown'.

As Reverend Grauel came out of the Louvre in Paris, a chilly wind blew off the Seine and he was glad of the topcoat Ike had lent him. Linking her arm in his was Shulamit Arlosoroff, the vivacious daughter of Chaim Arlosoroff, who had been a close friend of David Ben-Gurion and the head of the Jewish Agency's political division until he was murdered walking on a Tel Aviv beach by an Arab terrorist. Shulamit had been 18 at the time, and at her father's funeral she had asked David Ben-Gurion to find her a place in the Haganah. A few days later she had been sent to a settlement to be taught transmission skills by a radio operator who had served in the Jewish Brigade. With her fluent French, learned at school, she was posted to Paris to work in Aliyah Bet's communications network across Europe. Arm in arm the couple looked like father and daughter walking along the bank of the Seine.

When Shulamit had met Grauel at the train station, she explained she would be his bodyguard because there was fear on the streets of the city, not this time from Arabs but from Jewish terrorists: Irgun extremists had come to Paris. The first sign of their presence was posters depicting a rifle thrust aloft above the motto 'Only This'. The posters had been stuck on walls outside the British Embassy and British-owned businesses. Less than a year earlier the gang had destroyed a wing of the King David Hotel in Jerusalem, and shocked the world and outraged fellow Jews by hanging two British Army sergeants and booby-trapping their bodies. This had been in retaliation for the hanging of some of their own members by the British.

Not only had the outrage hardened British public opinion against illegal immigration, but, Shulamit told Reverend Grauel, it could also change French support. Its intelligence service had warned David Shaltiel that the first attack by an Irgun gang in Paris could create reprisals against the city's Jewish community. It was as much a priority for Haganah to hunt down the Irgun extremists as it was for MI6.

To reinforce the seriousness of the situation, Shulamit casually opened her handbag. Inside Reverend Grauel saw a pistol. She closed the bag and they walked into Notre-Dame. Waiting in a side chapel was Shaltiel, sitting in a pew at the back. Shulamit sat at the front of the chapel, giving her a view into the main body of the cathedral.

Shaltiel listened without interruption as Reverend Grauel delivered Ike's report. When he had finished, the Haganah man's voice was low and intense: 'The sooner our Jews are moved out of Sète, the better. This morning a letter bomb was delivered to the British Embassy, almost certainly by Irgun. Bevin is due here any day now. A direct attack on him would be enough to stop French support. For us, so, yes, the sooner your ship leaves for Palestine, the better. How many can she really carry?'

Ike had not given Reverend Grauel the number. All he knew was that *President Warfield* had been built to carry 400. Shaltiel's response was decisive: 'We've had fishing boats carry more than that. Tell Ike he will have to get at least 3,000, ideally another 1,000, on board. I've got more than that still waiting in the camps.'

They shook hands and Shaltiel was gone.

In Marseilles, MI6 agents David Smiley and Derek Vershoyle had been busy. They had persuaded the harbour master to levy a fine of 20 million francs for violating sanitary and port regulations on *President Warfield*'s owners, the Weston Trading Company, and had helpfully provided its address at 24 Stone Street, New York, and that of its lawyer, Herman Goldman. Soon the agents were back in the harbour master's office with more information. A ship, *Northland*, which had arrived in Marseilles the day after *President Warfield* left, had been bought by a representative of Weston. Vershoyle handed over a copy of the payment cheque drawn on a Lisbon bank handling the money transfer from Chemical Bank in New York. In return, the harbour master had his own news. He had received a report from his counterpart in Ponta Delgada that *President Warfield*'s mate, Ike Ahronowitz, was suspected of the theft of a substantial quantity of oil and a local shipping agent, Ben Saude, was under investigation.

The documents, together with a sworn affidavit from the harbour master, were transmitted to MI6 in London and sent to William Stephenson in Washington. For the first time, MI6 had an edge in its battle against the blockade-runners.

Ada Sereni stood on the bridge of *President Warfield* as Ike continued to watch helmsman Bill Millman steer her southeast out of French territorial waters towards the Italian Gulf of Genoa. During the voyage Ike had received a radio message from David Shaltiel in Paris, asking if Genoa was a possible harbour from where the Sète refugees could board. Ada had explained that the harbour had not been completely cleared of mines and, besides, there was no local Aliyah Bet organisation after she had disbanded her network. Shaltiel had replied that *President Warfield* should continue to Portovenere.

The ship dropped anchor there mid-afternoon. When her stern faced the picturesque little town and the sheer rock promontory behind, her name was clearly visible. On top of the cliff was the villa from where Gordon Lett had kept watch for blockade-runners. Count Vanden Heuvel had bought the property as a coastal retreat where he could entertain Vatican friends who wanted to escape from the August heat of Rome. Now, on that day in May, he was the first MI6 officer to sight *President Warfield* since she had left Marseilles.

He began to draft a cable to London.

Ada had gone to Rome to see her uncles, Admiral Mario Sereni and Roberto Sereni, the Chief Secretary in the Ministry of Naval Affairs. Over lunch in Roberto's private dining room, Ada was told that the Foreign Office in London was pressing the Italian government to order *President Warfield* out of its waters. If it did not do so, the British government would no longer support Italy's application to join the United Nations. Roberto added that the Foreign Office had argued there were ample grounds to expel *President Warfield*: 'its dubious maritime documents, its improperly registered crew, its limited scope of movement as defined by the ship's licence, its cancelled Honduran registration'.

To Ada's relief, Mario told her that the Italian government would not bow to any pressure that could not be legally upheld. She had driven through the night back to Portovenere to find more good news: the work she had commissioned from local carpenters had started. The first wooden berths were being installed for the immigrants in Sète. But her optimism faded two days later when David Shaltiel radioed from Paris. Both France and Italy were 'dragging their heels under even more threatening pressure from London. In Rome the government has reluctantly agreed to patrol its northern border to stop more refugees from heading to the Mediterranean'.

For Ada the situation became more worrying when, on 1 June 1947, despite objections from Roberto and Mario Sereni, the Italian navy sent a gunboat to drop anchor across *President Warfield*'s bows and detain her until further notice.

While the work of installing bunks continued, Ike and Ada had spent their time on the radio to Paris and Tel Aviv to explore another possible solution: to sail from Italy to Bremen, an American enclave in the British sector in northern Germany which provided the only sea exit from the American zone. But to get to Bremen would require the refugees to cross the British sector. The proposal was put by Ben-Gurion to the State Department and immediately rejected. Washington was not prepared to disrupt its relationship with the United Kingdom.

In the first week of June 1947, Sir John Cunningham had approved plans to deal with the probability that the detention camps in Cyprus would soon be full. He had just returned from a meeting in London of the Joint Intelligence Committee at which Stewart Menzies estimated there were over 35,000 Jews waiting to go to Palestine. Sir William Stephenson had reported that there were 18 ships, many of them in the United States, in various stages of preparation to carry some 20,000 illegal immigrants.

There were also two decommissioned Royal Navy sloops, HMS *Shoreham* and HMS *Lowestoft*, which had been bought by the Haganah through Colonel Bustard's Palestine Maritime League. MI6 had discovered both sloops were to be refitted and used as blockade-runners.

Sir John had asked the Cabinet to approve the restarting of a method known by the League of Nations after the First World War as *refoulement*: the practice of returning immigrants to the country from where their voyage started. The Attorney General agreed it could be possible. Sir John said he had three transport ships available: *Runnymede Park*, *Empire Rival* and *Ocean Vigour*. Each could carry up to 1,500 immigrants. In a letter to the Foreign Office the First Sea Lord noted: 'Although conditions will be basic, past experience has shown that immigrants are frequently unhygienic in their habits. We will also have to take suitable physical measures to guard against attempts to overcome any of our ships.'

The three transports were ordered to proceed to Haifa.

Throughout June work continued with installing bunks on board *President Warfield*. Meanwhile, Ada had used an old Packard limousine she had borrowed from a contact in Portovenere to bring visitors to the ship. The first to arrive was Paul Shulman, the US Navy Academy graduate who had been asked by David Ben-Gurion to advise the Palyam and help *President Warfield* obtain a Lloyd's sea-worthiness certificate. He would remain on board for the journey to Palestine. Yossi Harel had arrived, along with David Shaltiel. He had come from Paris, arriving at nightfall and leaving before dawn after holding meetings in Ike's cabin with Ada and Yossi. Reverend Grauel had returned to the boat and exchanged his clerical garb for fatigues he had bought in a flea market in Paris.

Ada had also collected several Palestinian Jews from Milan who had been discharged from the British Army and remained in Italy. One was Enava Barak. Already a trained radioman, he had been picked by David Shaltiel to be taught Haganah's own Hebrew code, which would link the ship with Tel Aviv once the voyage started. Harold Leidner would handle other communications.

The newcomers also included another American, Arthur Ritzer. The former US Marine had fought across the Pacific and Ze'ev Shind had interviewed him in New York after the war and offered him a job. Like many of the American crew, Ritzer spoke no Hebrew

and was among the first to say that, with *President Warfield* in port for
some time, the Americans expected to spend their off-duty time
ashore as well as having morning and afternoon breaks for coffee.
Within days, the Italian carpenters were demanding the same breaks.
Ike confronted Ritzer and said he would send him home. Yossi
recalled the aggressive marine squared up to Ike: 'You sack me, the
others walk as well. We are all volunteers, so do what you want!'

Ike discussed the issue with Yossi and Ada, and still wanted to send
Ritzer home. Ada pointed out it would be impossible to find replacements given the pressure to get the ship ready for the voyage, so Ike
agreed to give the carpenters the same breaks and allowed the
Americans shore leave. As quickly as it had threatened, the crisis was
over.

To celebrate, Ike, Yossi and Ada took the crew on a walkabout in
the town and Ada astonished them with her knowledge of
Portovenere's history. It had been a naval base for the Roman fleet
and the site of a temple to Jupiter, then more recently home to the
English poets Byron and Shelley. Her discourse drew applause and
that evening she led the singing in a campfire cookout on the beach.
Next morning the crew were back at work before sunrise, unaware
that their every hammer blow was being heard and observed by
Count Vanden Heuvel. At the end of each day he sent a progress
report to London.

Late in the afternoon of 22 June, Ike, Yossi and Ada conducted
their daily inspection of *President Warfield*. The last of the bunks had
been installed in the hold, in what had once been the ship's smoking
room, the gallery deck and the social hall. The elegance from a time
long ago had been replaced by a functional atmosphere: the bunks
were unpainted and only clothes hooks hung on the walls. Each bunk
was the width of two planks and 18 inches separated it from the one
above, the same gap as in the concentration camps. They rose in six-
foot tiers, supported by cross-bracing.

On the bridge, Ike, Yossi and Ada agreed *President Warfield* was
ready to sail. The only obstacle was the Italian navy gunboat
anchored across its bows.

At dawn the next day Ada drove through the dark streets of Portovenere to Rome. She was going to see her Uncle Mario. What transpired at their meeting remains uncertain, but when she arrived back in Portovenere she told Ike and Yossi that next morning the local carpenters should be paid off – each given a bonus, she insisted – and the ship should be discreetly readied for sea, to await the sound of the Packard's horn blowing on the dockside.

On 25 June, Ada was in the office of the harbour captain, a splendid figure in his heavily braided uniform, when an envelope was delivered. She saw the Admiralty crest on the letter ordering the captain immediately to lift the gunboat blockade on *President Warfield*; she saw the signature over the title 'Admiral'. The captain did not recognise the signature, but he knew there were many admirals in Rome and the notepaper was authentic. Nevertheless he decided he would double-check the order. He placed a long-distance call to Rome and was told by the local telephone exchange it could take many hours. Unlike the postal system, the Italian phone system was still struggling to recover from war damage. But the letter was clear. *Immediately to lift the blockade.* He would not wait to make his confirmation call. He typed and signed a note authorising the gunboat to withdraw and instructed his aide to take it to the gunboat's captain. Within 30 minutes the ship had moved across to a berth on the other side of the harbour. An hour later the owner of the Packard drove on to the dockside and honked the horn.

On the bridge of *President Warfield*, Ike and Yossi turned to Ada and smiled as helmsman Bill Millman began to guide the ship out of the harbour.

On the balcony of his villa Count Vanden Heuvel stared in astonishment as *President Warfield* gained speed. What followed remains part of the Count's account in his personnel file in MI6 records:

In the port captain's office his call to Rome had finally come through. He was told no one had authorised the ship to sail. No doubt knowing his own career was certainly over, he appears to have ordered the gunboat to set off in pursuit. But the ship was already hull-down on the horizon. I was told a furious row broke out between the port captain and the skipper of the gunboat who refused to start out in pursuit because he had no written order to do so. Finally when the captain threatened him with arrest, the gunboat set off, smoke billowing from its funnel. But the day was closing and the ship with its running lights turned off had vanished into the night.

Chapter 13

Brief Encounters

Zvi Tiroche had become the person to ask for anything at the camp where Gertruda and Michael were billeted. She saw him as 'a special person, for whom nothing was too much trouble. There wasn't a child he didn't have a cheerful word for an adult he hadn't reassured that soon they would be leaving for Palestine.' His day was filled with dealing with requests for fresh milk for nursing mothers and kosher food for the kitchen and ensuring the laundry was open from early morning to dusk. Nothing escaped his attention: a candle for a child's birthday, the camp rabbi to visit someone who needed spiritual help.

The camp had been a military barracks with showers and baths. Zvi had organised soap and towels and arranged a schedule so everyone could bathe, set up play areas with footballs Ada had provided and arranged races around the camp. Children who had been nervous as they jumped from the tailboards of the trucks that had brought them to the camp – painfully thin children who clung to their mothers – with Zvi's encouragement had started to roam the camp and the sound of their laughter echoed everywhere.

Meanwhile, Zvi made sure that adults were kept occupied. There were vegetables to prepare, meals to cook, clothes to wash and be hung out to dry in the warm sun, beds to be made, floors to be swept, toilets to be cleaned. Miriam Bergman recalled: 'There was no such thing as "woman's work" or "man's work". Everyone did what Zvi wanted done.' Ada had recommended that Zvi should have a job on the voyage and Yossi Harel had immediately agreed.

When a refugee was sick, Dr Cohen was sent for. Saul Avigur had arranged for money for him to buy medicines from the 'war chest' Ike kept locked in his captain's cabin. Occasionally, when the physician needed medicine not stocked by the pharmacy in Sète, he would travel into Marseilles and make his way to the waterfront area, where a ship's chandler shared a building with a pharmaceutical wholesaler. Across the street was a pavement café. What he heard coming from there one day made Dr Cohen stop: 'English voices from men sat at a table, too well dressed for sailors. Young and educated voices. We had been warned by the Haganah that British spies were operating all around the Mediterranean. The way the two men spoke and behaved fitted the image of those spies. They were looking around, checking the ships and the people coming and going from them.'

Dr Cohen went into the pharmaceutical wholesaler and, having bought medicines, he looked out of a window at the café. The two men had gone. Had they been British agents? He knew he would never be certain. But the sooner the ship left for Palestine the happier he would feel.

Saul Avigur knew he had finally arrived in Port-de-Bouc, the second busiest port in the South of France after Marseilles: the air reeked from the cod-drying factories and the pungent smoke emerging from the chimneys of the port's two chemical plants. Close to them were the shipyards – the small, family-run businesses which built the trawlers that for over a century had made Port-de-Bouc a thriving harbour. *President Warfield* had arrived there after its escape from Portovenere.

Some 65 miles from Sète, it was the perfect place to keep the ship safely under the protective eye of the French intelligence service, DST, its director had told Avigur. They shared a dislike of British intelligence – whether its military branch or MI6. It had been the Frenchman who had cemented their relationship when he proposed that Avigur should set up the Haganah's radio transmitter in the director's spacious villa, his home in a Paris suburb, from where Avigur could communicate with the Haganah in Tel Aviv. Attempts by MI6 to intercept the transmissions were thwarted by DST technicians in another part of the villa. When he told his French colleague about the arrival of *President Warfield* in Port-de-Bouc and its purpose, Avigur recalled, the DST chief immediately sent more agents to the Mediterranean. 'Some were posted around each of the camps. Others were in Marseilles and Sète. They never went inside the camps so as not to alarm the immigrants. But the DST also had local police support to stop any British spy and demand his passport. Without that he wouldn't be able to do much, and could even be arrested and sent back to England. The DST could make life difficult for the British.'

Bevin had flown to Paris to see Georges Bidault once more. The Foreign Secretary had a new approach: 'The extreme misery that immigrants must be suffering is caused by the controllers of this infamous traffic, Jews being forced to sell their possessions in the hopeless expectation of buying at extravagant rates their passage to Palestine. France should understand that her indulgence to Jewish unauthorised persons and troublemakers might well cause alarm among the Arabs of French North Africa. I have myself taken steps to make sure that British subjects cause no trouble in areas of French interest. Is it too much to ask the French government to reciprocate in this matter of illegal Jewish traffic?'

If Bevin hoped that Bidault would agree he was disappointed. Bidault spread his arms, the only gesture he made.

Standing with Ike and Yossi Harel on the quayside at Port-de-Bouc, Saul Avigur was struck by the size of *President Warfield*. She was far bigger than he had imagined from photographs. He was no longer in doubt that she could hold the 4,500 refugees Yossi and Ike had allowed for. It would be a tight fit, but the crew could sleep on deck between watches. Yossi had doubled the number of cooks in the galley and the huge cauldrons installed by the US Navy before D-Day would provide sufficient hot food. The shortage of toilets was unavoidable; to plumb in more was impossible in the time. The life rafts which Ada had arranged to be bought in Marseilles had been tied to the rails on the upper decks. The sun room aft of the galley was rigged out as a hospital, complete with an old operating table, theatre trolleys and overhead lights.

Ike had removed all but one of the ladders leading from the boat deck to the promenade deck, to reduce attempts to reach the wheelhouse. Hosepipes had been connected from the engine room to the boat deck, ready to direct steam or oil towards any boarders. The ship's strake, the six-inch-wide band of iron-coated wood around the entire hull, six feet above water level, to protect the ship if she struck a jetty in choppy water, could also stove in the hull of a smaller destroyer coming alongside. Suspended from the hull was barbed wire to stop scrambling ladders being used.

Overall, Avigur decided, Ike had done a good job to prepare for the inevitable clash with the Royal Navy.

In the operations room at naval headquarters in Haifa, Sir John Cunningham told the officers around the conference table that MI6 was satisfied that *President Warfield* would have Irgun terrorists on board. He had therefore decided to use his most experienced captains to deal with the blockade-runner. Lieutenant Commander Bailey would be overall commander on HMS *Childers*. HMS *Charity* would be under the command of Lieutenant Commander D.W. Austin; HMS *Chieftain* would be under Commander G.E. Fardell; Captain R.D. Watson would command HMS *Chequers*; HMS *Cardigan Bay* would be commanded by Captain J.V. Wickin; HMS *Rowena* would be commanded by Captain R.H.C. Wyld; and Commander J.V. Wilkinson would lead HMS *Cheviot*. The First Sea Lord would sail on HMS *Ajax* with Captain S.B. Conway-Ireland on the bridge.

The force would sail for Malta and remain there, ready to intercept *President Warfield* once her course had been confirmed by one of the RAF Warwick reconnaissance aircraft. Commander Bailey then briefed his fellow captains on the problems they could face. Boarding parties would be unable to board *President Warfield* by the usual means from a destroyer's fo'c's'le. He explained: 'However, with the help of sextant angles, I have worked out that she is 320 feet long and each of her decks is above sea level. The poop is 16 feet above water; the promenade deck 32 feet. With our destroyer's fo'c's'le only 19 feet above water level, it means our boarders can only access the lower level of the Jewish ship, its foredeck. We must regard that as the killing area, where they would be trapped while the immigrants and the boat's crew attack them from above.'

Bailey had pointed to the latest reconnaissance photographs taken the day before by an RAF Warwick: 'As you can see, the middle deck and the promenade deck are blocked off with life rafts that will offer protection. Our boarders will have no chance of climbing up to the boat deck as all the ladders, bar one, have been removed. But this deck is the primary objective since it houses the control centre of the ship, its wheelhouse.'

From his briefcase Bailey produced a drawing and placed it beside a photograph of the boat deck: 'This deck is level with the highest point of a destroyer's superstructure. And the ship's bridge is more than six feet inboard of its guard railings. That gap is too big for a boarder to leap when he is carrying his weapons. The only answer is a special boarding platform. Made of wood, it will have guard rails and protective netting. Our boarders can cross over it and reach the wheelhouse.'

Bailey said it would take no more than a few hours for naval carpenters to build a platform for his own ship and for two other destroyers, HMS *Chieftain* and HMS *Charity*. Using the platforms, he planned to put 50 boarders on to *President Warfield*.

By July 1947, 15 refugee camps had been established between Marseilles and Port-de-Bouc. The staging areas were set up in abandoned army camps, empty villas and mansions standing in their own parkland. Some of the camps were derelict houses, others little more than huts. But for the thousands of refugees who had made the arduous journey across Europe, they were places to recuperate and prepare for the voyage to Palestine.

In 1945, a thousand immigrants had set out to make the journey. A year later the dining room in the McAlpine Hotel in New York had resounded with cheers at the Thursday fund-raising luncheon. Over 20,000 refugees had left some of the camps to board boats that donations had enabled Saul Avigur to buy. By that summer several million dollars had been pledged.

In Washington, DC, Leo Bernstein announced at a fund-raising function held by the United Jewish Appeal that their donations had already helped another 40,000 immigrants to prepare to sail for Palestine. Once more Bernstein's audience gave generously in the hope their money would enable passengers on ships to avoid being arrested and taken to the detention camps Ernest Bevin had ordered to be set up on Cyprus.

On another visit to New York, David Ben-Gurion had described life behind the high barbed-wire fences: 'They wait there in awful conditions for their turn to be allowed to trickle into their homeland. No more than fifteen hundred a month. Those camps are outposts of a war we will win. Their gates will finally be left open on the day the State of Israel becomes a reality.'

That promise had echoed among the waiting immigrants in those camps along the Mediterranean coast.

Saul Avigur, his deep-set eyes giving his face the look of a man who led an ascetic life, had within the upper echelons of the Haganah a reputation for incredible courage and for making decisions calmly and rationally. One had been that each camp must have a Jewish commander, someone who would understand the realities of what the job entailed. Avigur had told each man he had selected it would still be hard for every man, woman and child to accept that their years of brutality and degradation were finally over. The only way he could be a successful leader was never to forget that.

Avigur had chosen Noah Klieger to command Camp Kayol, on the road to Sète. French by birth and the son of a distinguished Jewish writer, with aspirations to follow his father as a published author, Noah had become a Zionist in Auschwitz. He was 16 years old when he entered one of its sub-camps and, for the 31 months he remained there, he was convinced every day was his last. He never forgot how many times he saw others taking their last walk to the gas chambers or the gallows or being wheeled on carts from the ovens. But somehow death itself evaded him.

In early 1945 he was among those sent on a death march from Auschwitz; thousands were shot during the weeks he had stumbled through the snow. But once more he survived. Finally, reaching the Harz Mountains in Germany, he was liberated on the eve of his 19th birthday. He headed west to Belgium. It was one of those impulsive decisions that had become part of his life in Auschwitz and had given him a maturity well beyond his years. Noah had become a man who guarded his privacy and chose his words with care.

A week after finally arriving in Brussels, he was strolling down the Avenue Louise, the city's battered but still proud main thoroughfare, when he stopped and stared at two parked British Army trucks. They were no different from any others seen on his long march, except they each had a blue-and-white Magen David stencilled on the door.

Not quite knowing what he should do, Noah was suddenly grabbed by two soldiers in British Army uniforms who had emerged from a café, yelling at him in Hebrew. Breaking free, Noah rolled up his sleeve and pointed at the concentration camp number tattooed on his forearm. The men stepped back.

'They blinked back their tears and began to embrace me, saying they had made a terrible mistake. I was a Jew like them and wasn't going to steal a truck. We went back into the café and over a drink they said they worked for the Jewish Transport Brigade. In no time I was recruited to help collect Jews from a local DP camp. As I spoke French, I was made liaison officer with the Belgian border police officers to get immigrants across the border and down to Marseilles. Soon Avigur had put me in charge of running Camp Kayol.'

Noah had created an area behind the camp's huts. Every morning assembly was at 7.30am, followed by 30 minutes of physical exercise. Afterwards the children were sent to a hut which served as a synagogue for religious instruction by the camp rabbi.

Meanwhile, Noah conducted his own daily routine: inspecting the sleeping accommodation, kitchen, showers and latrines. His years in Auschwitz had shown him the value of cleanliness; so many prisoners had died from failing to follow basic hygiene rules.

Early in July 1947, Noah was summoned to a meeting of the camp commanders in a back-street café in Sète owned by the Haganah local agent. Saul Avigur told them that they were to return to their camps and repeat to the immigrants what he would now say.

An hour later Noah was back in Camp Kayol and addressing the refugees in his usual laconic style. Soon they would be sailing to Palestine. On board the ship with them would be thousands of other immigrants. It would be the largest number ever sent in one ship-ment. They must prepare themselves for the voyage. The discipline they had followed within the camp would continue on board, though life would be far more cramped, so personal hygiene was essential, to reduce the risk of illness. Each adult could bring only one small bag; two children would share a bag. They should expect the Royal Navy to continue its policy of interception. On board ship any orders they were given must be obeyed at once. In the meantime, no one was allowed to leave the camp until they were taken to the port.

For three days Ike and Yossi Harel had been on board *President Warfield*, finalising the embarkation plans for the passengers. All told they would number 4,515.

Immigrants billeted in camps furthest from the port would be brought to the ship first. Priority would be given to women, children and expectant mothers. After that would come the aged and infirm. Each truck would have two physically fit immigrants, who would act as guards in the event of trouble. Yossi Harel recalled: 'None was expected, as the French authorities were on our side. Our concern was the British spies. We knew that Dr Cohen had not imagined their presence. They were everywhere.'

The physician and his nurses would board with the first convoy to check out the on-board hospital. Just 12 hours had been allowed for the entire boarding process.

Meanwhile, Joe Bahalia had driven an oil tanker from Marseilles, carrying enough oil to top up the ship's fuel tanks and last for the estimated seven-day voyage. Yehuda Arazi was in the final process of checking the supplies brought to the quayside from local shops. Avigur had also arranged for a number of Aliyah Bet men to patrol the quayside and turn away anyone who had no business with the ship.

Some of the crew had been given shore leave and a few had abused it, returning drunk having broken the curfew to be back on board by midnight. Ike had severely reprimanded each sailor and confined him to his room. A different problem arose when one of the crew had been discovered smuggling ashore cartons of coffee to sell on the black market. The offence was sufficiently serious for Ike to order the culprit to undergo a Haganah court martial. Yossi Harel remembered: 'It was an open and shut case. The man had been caught red-handed and the guilty verdict called for severe punishment. Aliyah Bet was in a deadly business and we could not tolerate that. After the verdict the man was driven away by Avigur, never to be seen or heard of again.'

On the bridge, the silence of the night had done nothing to lessen the tension between Ike and Yossi. Ike had made no secret of the fact that he thought, though he was the younger man, he had the edge on Yossi when it came to seagoing experience. He was a man of few words. It was not that he didn't repect all that Yossi had done – fighting alongside Orde Wingate, commanding other Aliyah Bet ships, setting up escape routes for Jews in Lebanon, Syria, Iraq, Turkey and Transjordan. The truth was, probably, that both men came from different backgrounds and had very different temperaments. Ike had a steely personality; Yossi was imbued with a natural charm. Perhaps it was as simple as that. Ike was the ship's captain, while Yossi, as ship's commander, was effectively his deputy. In an ideal world they would have got along. On the surface they did; but below their politeness to each other was tension.

Even before he set eyes on the ship, Yossi Harel had asked Ada to drive him from Marseilles railway station to the camps along the Mediterranean that housed the refugees. Between them they held

1,561 men, 1,282 women, 1,017 adolescents and 655 children. They would be the passenger complement of *President Warfield*.

Ada recalled Yossi saying, 'I wanted to be certain they were both mentally and physically ready for the voyage. This would be unlike any other journey they would have taken. None of us could say what would happen. I wanted to make sure our people had prepared them, especially the children.'

Harel's need for that reassurance had deepened after visiting the first camp to which Ada drove him. It was filled with orphans. The only adults he saw were the camp commander, his staff and teenagers looking after the young children. They watched him as he walked among them, their solemn eyes following him, perhaps wondering who this tall, tanned and healthy-looking man was who spoke to them in their own language, Hebrew or Yiddish and sometimes Polish. What could he understand about their years behind barbed wire, spent scavenging for a piece of bread, picking lice off their bodies, praying to a God who had seemed indifferent to their fate? Yossi could understand that beneath their hesitant smiles and polite nods on hearing his promise that their voyage would end in freedom were unspoken questions: What was freedom? How did it work? Was there more than one kind of freedom? How could they enjoy freedom when they had no mother or father to share it with?

Walking around the camp, Yossi had spoken to as many children as he could as they sat in their huts on fold-up beds set out in rows after being shipped from the US Army barracks they came from. He had seen the desperation in their eyes as he tried to reassure them that this time their hopes would not founder and they would reach the land inhabited by their forefathers centuries before. But he knew that, even as he spoke, he could not give them the hope they wanted: that their parents would miraculously be waiting for them when they arrived. No one could promise that.

It was in those moments that he had sensed how empty his words must sound. How many times would they have heard similar promises from well-meaning people who wanted to move them on? The nuns and priests who had sheltered them in monasteries and convents, the workers in the DP camps? How often had those children been put on a train or a truck to carry them on the next stage of their journey to this camp by the sea? For them, its huts must have seemed so far from what they remembered a real home looking like.

It had been Ada who had seen the pain in Yossi's eyes and heard it in his voice as he spoke to them. She remembered the time another man's emotions had had the same effect on her. Her husband, Enzo, had rescued other Jewish children from Iraq shortly before the Nazis executed him.

When she finally drove Yossi from the camp, the Haganah officer was close to tears. He told Ada that if he did nothing else in his life he would not fail those children.

Yossi recognised that there was one issue which urgently needed his undisputed skills and charm: visas for the passengers which would pass scrutiny.

In the past bribery had usually done the trick. Many foreign diplomats had added to their own salaries by illegally providing blank forms, which were imperfectly filled out in the hurry to board an Aliyah Bet ship. Ada Sereni remembered that on more than one occasion she had scribbled them out on a quayside. But while many of the immigration officers who waved aboard refugees often displayed sympathy for them, there was a change in Paris. The French government continued to support the Holocaust survivors' right to go to Palestine, but there was growing concern among its diplomats not only about the deteriorating French–British relationship, but also about hostility in the Arab world to the illegal immigration.

In the past an Aliyah Bet ship had a licence to sail to one country while its passengers carried bogus visas to go to another, but now, Yossi realised, it could be only a matter of time before it became critical to have travel documents that were properly prepared.

The British ambassador in Paris, Duff Cooper, told Bevin, 'There is evidence that incompatibility between visas and their owners are settled by money on the spot by the organisers of this illegal traffic.'

The Foreign Secretary sent a letter to his French counterpart,

Georges Bidault, demanding, 'Illegal groups from the south of France must be stopped from travelling without officially approved visas.'

Yossi knew that to obtain visas for all 4,515 men, women and children was a huge task, more so in the time he had. 'My first step was to visit all the foreign embassies and consulates in Marseilles to see if they could provide travel documents. In the end Colombia did. They wanted five American dollars for each. I said okay. The diplomat asked how many. I told him.'

The official may well have smiled after he had done his mental arithmetic. He was probably about to make more money than he earned in a year. However, he realised that to prepare the documents and then stamp the blank forms in the official places would take the best part of his working day – so, after pocketing the money, he handed over a franking machine and showed Yossi where each form should be stamped, including the photographs of each applicant.

If Yossi was startled he did not show it. How was he going to find sufficient photographers and have the photos developed and printed? Then he remembered. The tourists had returned to Marseilles now the war was over. Along the waterfront and in the town roamed photographers making a living by snapping the visitors. In no time he had rounded them up to take passport photos of the refugees in the camps. He had solved another problem.

But later, after the impressive-looking visas had been distributed and the passengers were on board, Yossi knew he would have a further act to perform. The visas would be collected and burned. 'They had served their purpose. No visa meant no identification for any passengers.'

Yossi saw that as important. Without identification, the passengers could not be sent back to where they had come from if they were caught while the ship was at sea. Yossi was certain that, given the problems France had endured over immigration, it would not allow them to return. Without Colombian visas, the passengers could not be sent to Colombia. Without identification papers, no country would take them. The only place they could go to was Palestine. Or so Yossi hoped.

*

It was still early morning when Ike and Yossi stood on the bridge of *President Warfield*. An hour earlier they had completed the final embarkation logistics. The Jewish Brigade trucks which had brought the refugees to the camp had been parked in a sheltered area by Joe Bahalia in preparation for ferrying the passengers to the ship.

It was going to be another cloudless day, with no breeze to cool the oppressive heat. Beyond, the townspeople were already putting up awnings. But unusually at that hour, there was no sound of traffic. The only vehicle coming along the quayside was Ada's car. She parked and came running up the gangway with Arazi, their faces already flushed by the heat. Each carried cardboard boxes containing the Colombian visas. Now there was a more difficult problem to resolve. The Communist-run transport union had ordered a national strike, which had stopped all traffic movement, including military trucks, across France. The strike was in protest against the way Ernest Bevin had used the Paris meeting of European nations, conveyed to discuss the Marshall Plan, to rail against Jewish immigration.

Yossi said that the governor of the province, Sol Weiss, was a Jew who lived in nearby Montpellier. Ike asked Ada to drive him and Yossi to see Weiss. In the meantime, Arazi was to contact Saul Avigur, explain the situation and ask how the strike could be lifted for long enough to bring the immigrants to the ship so that it could leave.

Two hours later Ike returned with a letter signed by the governor authorising that the strike be lifted between Port-de-Bouc and Sète for 24 hours. Meanwhile, Avigur had deposited one million French francs in the transport union's fighting fund to help the strikers. Yossi Harel spoke for the others on the ship's bridge when he said, 'That's money well spent.'

Ada Sereni would recall how she brought relief workers to the camp holding the orphans to help them prepare for the voyage. She and the other women discovered that under their pillows many of the children had hidden family photographs. Creased and faded from handling were the faces of a mother, a father, a grandparent, older brothers and sisters. Perhaps the last trace of an entire family, perhaps of an entire community. Each photo was carefully wrapped in a piece of clothing before being packed and placed in one of the cardboard boxes Ada had brought from Marseilles.

When the packing was finished and each box bore the name of a child, they were stacked outside the huts to wait for the trucks. The camp commander, a tall young man with a quiet strength whom everyone called Moshe, announced the pick-up would be at sunset. In the meantime, the children were to go to the mess hut for their final meal before leaving. According to Ada, 'For them there had never been a childhood. Their parents had perished. You can't replace a mother's bedtime kiss with the smiles of well-meaning strangers who had risked their own lives by sheltering them. In that camp of orphans, in all the other camps they stayed in, those children must have felt abandoned, unwanted. The more anyone tried to show them that was not true, the less they believed.'

The telephone connection from Paris to the harbour master's office in Port-de-Bouc crackled, making it harder for Yossi Harel and Ike to hear as they each pressed an ear to the phone. The caller was Venia Pomerantz, Aliyah Bet's liaison with the French Ministry of the Interior. The soft-spoken Pomerantz had fed his contacts with the carefully prepared story which Avigur had created. Due to engine problems *President Warfield* would be unable to sail for at least another week. The young liaison officer had been given sufficient technical information to convince his ministry contacts, knowing that given the way they worked the news would quickly spread. In his last call Pomerantz had said that *President Warfield*'s engine failure was nothing other than a brief report in Paris newspapers, but still, as Avigur intended, it would have reached the British Embassy.

Then, in mid-afternoon, a waiter from a café opposite the harbour master's office arrived on the quayside. Yossi met him at the top of the gangway to be told an urgent call had come from Paris. Yossi and Ike ran back to the harbour master's office.

Venia Pomerantz had shattering news. Ernest Bevin had telephoned from London to the French Foreign Minister, Georges

Bidault, with news that MI6 had discovered that the provincial governor had given clearance for the transport strike to be broken long enough for the refugees to board the ship.

Straining to listen to the crackling line, Yossi grabbed a sheet of paper off the harbour master's desk and began to scribble down what Pomerantz was saying. Bevin was demanding that the camps be closed down immediately and the immigrants be sent back to where they had come from in Europe. Meanwhile, Bevin planned to ask US Secretary of State, George Marshall, to order the ship returned to the United States and its crew impounded for breach of maritime law. As the phone line continued to break up, Yossi scribbled for Ike to read over his shoulder: 'Minister has told Venia we must sail at once. Says pressure too great on his government. He says we are on our own now.'

Ike had smiled tightly and, with a polite nod of thanks to the harbour master, they ran back to the ship.

On 9 July 1947, the sun was setting over Port-de-Bouc when Smiley and Vershoyle stood among a waving crowed as *President Warfield* moved away from her mooring and out past the old fort, then headed on a westerly course into the Mediterranean. Her larders had been restocked with boxes of fresh fruit and vegetables, together with large sacks of potatoes stacked outside the galley, and fresh water tanks had been topped up.

Murray Aronoff, his father's Jewish Brigade badge proudly pinned to his shirt, sensed that 'There was an air of expectation, more excitement than tension. Ike had told us we were going to find out why we had come halfway across the world. Soon the ship would be filled with several thousand men, women and children who had one dream, going to *Eretz Yisrael*. Waiting to stop them would be the most powerful navy in the world. It was going to be our job to outsmart their ships.'

Reverend Grauel's cheer had led those which echoed around the ship. As *President Warfield* gathered speed, he assembled his cooks and told them to start preparing cauldrons of soup and jugs of coffee, together with hot drinks for the children, ready for the first refugees when they began to board in the coming hours. Yossi Harel and several deckhands were putting bedding on the bunks. On the bridge, Paul Shulman was one of the lookouts. He had become a liked and respected personality among the crew. The muscular figure of former 82nd Airborne paratrooper Ben Foreman stood watch on the starboard side. Near his foot was a wooden club; several of the crew were similarly armed. For Foreman: 'We weren't looking for a fight. But if there was going to be trouble we needed to look after ourselves. We had all heard stories about how the British could play rough.'

Ada had driven to Sète to alert Yehuda Arazi to start moving the immigrants from the camps. Eliyahu Cohen now had 70 trucks to bring them to Sète.

Yehuda Arazi had arranged with the Sète harbour master where *President Warfield* could anchor among the maze of breakwaters and basins filled with fishing boats and canal barges. Many of the waterways were unable to accommodate a ship the size of *President Warfield* and finally he had settled on a breakwater behind the outer harbour which had steps leading up to a road where the trucks could park.

The Reverend Grauel had started to write his diary: 'We Americans on board were nicknamed the Shu-Shu-Boys by the Palestine Jews of Aliyah Bet. They were forever admonishing the American volunteers on the importance of secrecy and silence. In Yiddish, a person warning another to be silent or secret would put an index finger to his lips and blow on to it with a word, *shu*, which probably came from the Yiddish *sha*.'

Bearing the scars of battle, the *Exodus* docks at Haifa port. Waiting on the dockside are British soldiers to bring passengers ashore. Many were put on board prison ships. In the background is one of the press photographers who turned the story of the *Exodus* into an international scandal.

The fight is over: British soldiers lead away the injured and the destitute and the frightened to a processing station at Haifa port where they would be subjected to a body search before their injuries were examined. Some were treated. Others were taken to one of the prison ships, where they received minimum medical attention.

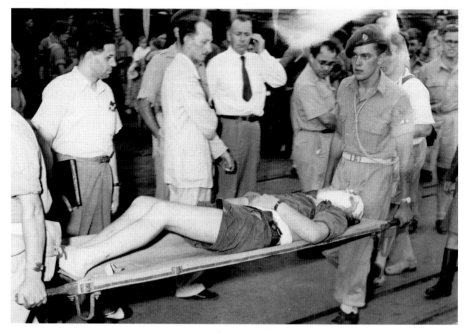

The voices of thousands of passengers singing 'Hatikvah', the Hebrew hymn of hope floated down to the quayside as the first of the wounded was carried off the ship. More than one passenger owed their life to the skill of the ship's doctor, Yossi Cohen. During the relentless sea battle he had bound head injuries, stitched wounds and found time to comfort terrified mothers and children.

The ship's doctor, Yossi Cohen, whose medical advice swayed Ike Ahronowitz to surrender the battered ship to the navy task force. Ike did not want to surrender and insisted he could bring the ship to a landing beach near Tel Aviv. But Dr Cohen, supported by Yossi Harel, argued that further lives would be lost unless medical help was summoned from the navy.

A photo taken by soldier Harold Gardner of Palestinian soldiers, safe on dry land, looking over at the battered hulk of the *Exodus* in dock at Haifa.

Reverend John Stanley Grauel, an ordained methodist minister, gave up his ministry to join the American Christian Committee for Palestine. A passenger on the voyage, he testified at the United Nations and his graphic account, based on his diary, marked a turning point in the UN decision on partition.

Mothers ashore with their children, who gave a poignant meaning to the odyssey of *Exodus*. But even as they were having their papers checked, they were told they were being sent back to Germany. All they would see of the land they had dreamt of for so long was the escorted walk to the prison ships.

The *Ocean Vigour* at port in Haifa. The British Army spokesman told reporters from all over the world that the grey-hulled ship had been converted into a 'comfort ship' for refugees. In reality it provided the harshest conditions of all three prison ships. For breakfast there was only salty tea and maggot-infested biscuits. Supper consisted of potato soup swimming with maggots. Passengers were told to eat the maggots as they were 'protein'.

Britain's Foreign Secretary, Ernest Bevin, had approved the use of three wartime transport ships to bring the *Exodus* passengers back to Germany, fitted out with cages to contain the passengers. Bevin had planned to put them ashore at Port-de-Bouc, the starting point of the voyage, but the French government found itself embattled with Bevin over landing conditions.

Exodus passengers sit in the hold of the British transport ship *Runnymede Park* as the ship arrives in Port-de-Bouc in France. Described by a British Army spokesman in Haifa as a 'hospital ship', it was in fact a prison ship. There was a latrine with six holes to serve the 1,500 people on board. Below decks, the hold became their living room and bedroom. In reality they ate and slept on the steel floor.

All his life Mordechai Rosemont had been a leader; in the Warsaw ghetto uprising, inspiring his fellow Polish Jews to fight the Nazis with bare hands. On board *Exodus* he had created groups to fight the Royal Navy boarding parties. Finally he became the voice of the refugees on the *Runnymede Park*, a prison ship named after the site where Magna Carta was signed.

Life on board the prison ship taking the passengers back to Europe.

As the prison ships sat at anchor in the bay of Marseilles and the refugees refused to disembark, a small boat loaded with food was taken out each day to the ships by members of the Haganah.

French-born Noah Klieger was a resilient camp survivor who was not only useful on board the *Exodus* for translating and organising the passengers, but also became a hero among the passengers for his epic swim after diving off one of the prison ships. Here we see him in 1947 and more recently.

When *Exodus* arrived at Port-de-Bouc the Haganah encouraged newsreel and still cameramen to film the *Exodus* passengers on the three prison ships. The newsreels became the lead stories in cinemas around the world and the photos made the front pages.

The British paratroopers were ordered to deal firmly with male passengers. In their hands they clutch the steel batons they had been ordered to use by their commanding officer at Hamburg.

A demonstration in Italy against illegal immigrant return. The banner pictures Bevin as a Nazi. In cities and towns all over Europe there were similar protests.

Kept behind barbed wire the media still managed to get their story. It made headlines around the world.

Hamburg's wharf was lined with British troops from the Sherwood Foresters battalion who were sent on board the prison ships to drag the refugees out of the holds, across the deck and down the gangway to the quayside. Some were beaten with batons or kicked.

Passengers make their way from the prison ship to one of the trains at Hamburg port to take them to a detention camp. The refugees cried out at the row of watching soldiers that they were being returned to Auschwitz. The troops stared indifferently. The Jews were herded into old wooden rail coaches which rumbled out into the German countryside.

Yosef Reich's graphic account of the battle is unforgettable. He was an eye witness to the shooting by the navy boarders. His account challenged the claim later made by the Royal Navy that it was the sound of Chinese fire crackers they were using to simulate gunfire.

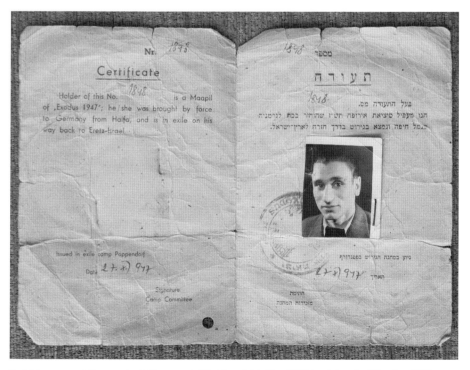

Reich's papers at Poppendorf. They read: 'Holder of this No. 1848 is a Maapil of Exodus 1947; he/she was brought by force to Germany from Haifa, and is in exile on his way back to Eretz-Israel'.

The watchtower at Poppendorf's Displaced Person's Camp stands as a shocking reminder of the grim architecture of the Nazi death camps: the watchful sentry, the dirty ground, the barbed wire, the empty space beyond, known in the death camps as the killing field, where any escapee would be mowed down by a sentry on the watchtower. Here the refugees can stand and wait for release – not death.

Among the refugees were Dov Mills (third from left) and Gerald Landau (far right). Both men were part of a plot to sabotage *Empire Rival*, one of the transport ships. The intention was to force the ship to dock and give the passengers a chance to escape into France. Dov had smuggled ten kilos of dynamite on board the ship. Landau helped to conceal them.

In the Tel Aviv Museum, on Friday 14 May 1948, David Ben-Gurion reads the Proclamation of the State of Israel. Above him is a picture of Theodore Herzl.

On 26 August 1952 a mysterious fire broke out on board *Exodus*. It had been moored off Shemen Beach as part of a plan to turn her into a floating museum. In 1954 an Italian firm tried to salvage her for scrap. To do so they cut her in half. As the bow broke the surface, the wreck suddenly sunk back to the bottom of the sea. There she remains. The only crew member to witness her end was Ike.

Chapter 14

Boarding

Standing on *President Warfield*'s bridge, Ike watched the first convoy begin to discharge its passengers before driving away to collect the next refugees waiting in the camps. Emerging from the trucks were the orphans, Moshe, their camp commander, Dr Cohen and his nurses.

In the gathering darkness the townspeople of Sète moved among them, smiling reassurance and handing out sweets and soft drinks to the children, then guiding them down the steps to the quays. It had been Ada's idea to involve the local people, to let them know how much their help had been appreciated in the past weeks.

On the dockside the orphans had stared in wonder at the ship, its hull towering above them, and at the faces staring down and calling out a welcome in Hebrew as they slowly climbed the gangway, each carrying their box and visa.

Reaching the boat deck, the children handed over the document to Bill Bernstein, the ship's mate. He dropped them into an open bag to be burned later. Standing at the foot of the gangway, Yossi and Ada were relieved that the French gendarme had given only a cursory glance at the documents.

Reverend Grauel recorded in his diary: 'After getting hot drinks ready, I had gone up on deck to watch the boarding. Trucks came and went. There was a mood of joy, pride, tears and some anxiety as they came on board. I could understand the anxiety. This was finally happening. I could see Ike up on the bridge watching everything. He had told me that the voyage was to mount a huge illegal immigration operation that would draw the world's attention.'

While the nurses were escorted down to the bunks reserved for the children, Dr Cohen was directed to where the ship's hospital had been set up by Abe Lippschitz, who had already laid out the medical equipment for inspection. Dr Cohen estimated that, with over 4,000 potential patients, he would never have time to assess their medical condition. But he had noticed several of the women were in the advanced stages of pregnancy and he was glad to see there was an obstetrics kit. He also suspected from swellings on their legs that some passengers had severe diabetes and from their breathing as they climbed the gangway that others had heart problems. Under normal conditions he would have recommended they didn't sail. All he could do was hope he had the right equipment to help them.

The doctor asked for the expectant mothers to be given bunks close to the makeshift hospital. One of the crew pointed out the lifeboats and rafts, explaining that there would be sufficient time to launch them. He added that, in an emergency, sick women and children must have priority when it came to launching the lifeboats.

Fira Neimark had quickly earned the nickname Roll Caller at the camp outside Marseilles. Every day without fail she had counted her brood of 52 children when they woke and before they went to bed. She slept close to the hut door to make sure nobody entered during the night. She told the boys, many little more than children themselves, they were to help her to protect the girls. When it was their turn to leave the camp, she insisted on lifting each child on to the truck and refused to sit beside the driver, saying she must travel with them.

Ada Sereni saw how, arriving on the quayside, Fira once more lined up the children and counted them before leading them to the gangway, clutching a bundle of visas. When the French policeman glanced at them Fira pointed to the children and said, 'All mine.'

The astonished officer shook his head and handed back the documents. Fira smiled graciously at him and shepherded the children up the gangway. She recalled: 'It was like boarding a show boat, a love boat, a boat all the way from America. There I was with my children. Everything seemed so clean and so friendly, waiting to receive us. This was the beginning of our *bon voyage*. I had already been told to explain to the children what they were allowed to do, what not to do and now, where exactly we were going.'

When Yossi, who was standing on deck, suggested the children might have to bunk in different parts of the ship, with the older ones looking after the smaller children, she stared fiercely at him and replied, 'We have come here together and we stay together. When we get to the homeland we will live together in a kibbutz. That was why I was chosen to do what God asked of me.'

By midnight the last of the townspeople who had watched the arrivals had gone home to bed. Only the lighthouse at the end of the Saint-Louis mole, where *President Warfield* was berthed, continued to send out its beam every 30 seconds. So powerful was the light that it pierced the darkness for 14 miles across the Golfe du Lion.

Looking down from the bridge, Ike saw another camp commander descend from the lead truck of his convoy and stride up and down the road, watching the refugees leaving the other trucks, hurrying them along. There was something unsettlingly familiar about the stride. Ike closed his eyes for a moment, reminded of those photos he had seen of other Jews being transported to the gas chambers. He opened his eyes. That would never happen again. Nobody could turn what was to be a mercy mission into anything else. He would see to that.

It was in the early hours, as the first light of dawn began to soften the sky over the sea, when Zvi Tiroche led his camp refugees down from the trucks on the quayside. The lighthouse beam reminded many of them of the concentration camp searchlights and some of the children started crying and clung to the adults. Zvi moved among them, offering reassuring words as they walked slowly towards the gangway.

He understood their tension and fears. How many times had they been herded like this into cattle trucks? For their sake he was determined to be calm, because he knew they wanted him to be the leader who had kept them all together in the camp. He pointed up at the ship and said that was where their new life could start. He spoke with a certainty that calmed and drew smiles. If Zvi promised, then it had to be true.

As he arrived at the foot of the gangway Ada took him aside and introduced him to Yossi, who was gently motioning for the line to move faster. He knew there were more than 2,000 people still to board. The ship's commander informed Zvi that Ada had told him about his linguistic skills and said he wanted him to serve in a similar capacity on board ship.

Zvi's first duty was to select from among the passengers translators who were fluent in the numerous languages spoken on board. As well as the two prime languages, Hebrew and Yiddish, they should be able to speak Polish, Russian, Romanian and German, the languages of the camps. Yossi explained it was essential that his orders be communicated quickly. That would be Zvi's responsibility and he must post on each deck translators who would be constantly available to act as a link to Yossi's broadcasts over the ship's public address system. Zvi was to familiarise himself with the system and ensure his translators accurately passed on Yossi's words. From time to time throughout the day Zvi would use the system to relay information to the passengers about various events on board.

As Michael Stolowitzky and Gertruda arrived on deck and dropped their visas into the bag being held open by a sailor, Mickey squeezed her hand, told her everything would be all right and said that he would look after her. She smiled, reminding herself again how those weeks in the camp had seen a remarkable change in him; with ample food, exercise and sea air he had gained weight and was becoming a strapping boy.

As the first rays of the morning sun rose over the horizon, replacing the lighthouse beam, Gertruda blinked away the tears of happiness as she bent down to kiss Mickey's forehead. 'You're right. There is nothing to worry about. In a few days' time we will be home.'

Stepping out of the truck which had brought him from Camp Kayol, Noah Klieger burst out laughing at the sight of *President*

Warfield. He had never seen such an ugly ship, with its single funnel rising like a dirty factory chimney into the blue sky. He asked himself, 'How could anybody think the ship could carry the 4,500 we had been told about in that briefing in the back-street café?'

He asked the question again when he reached the ship's deck, the sun already hot in his face. Waiting was the first mate, Bill Bernstein, holding a blue-and-white trimmed blazer which he held up against Noah, nodded and then told him to put it on, saying, 'It will do. Now in answer to your question, this old bucket will fit all these people in with the help of people like you.'

He turned and indicated a set of stairs that led to the bridge. Noah was to stop anybody going up there. When he asked why he had to wear the blazer, Bernstein sighed: 'Because it looks good on you, gives you authority.'

Noah nodded and thought, 'This is going to be fun.'

He had hardly taken up position when a slight figure tried to run past him. He wore only a vest and shorts. Noah blocked his path and ordered him away. A shouting match started, the youth in Hebrew and English, Noah in French.

'He was a little fellow so I was not afraid. But he got on my nerves. Suddenly Bernstein ran up and told me to back off. I said no way. I was doing what he had told me to do. Bernstein looked at me and shook his head and said that didn't include attacking the ship's captain.'

Ike looked at Noah, grinned and told Bernstein to sign Noah on as a crew member. But he didn't have to wear the blazer to show his authority. He had just demonstrated that.

Many passengers had formed lines outside the galley to collect bowls of soup, fresh coffee and hot drinks for their children. Their smiles and nods of gratitude brought the kitchen staff close to tears.

Gertruda and Michael had followed Cyril Weinstein down to a tier of bunks in the hold. He apologised for the cramped quarters, but Gertruda smiled and said after the camp it was comfortable. She and Mickey set off to explore the ship, picking their way through the new arrivals being led along the gangways by members of the crew, helping the old and infirm with their bags. Some of Moshe's orphans had already familiarised themselves with the ship and were running around various decks. In the bowels, the engine-room engineers checked the controls. But until the order came from the bridge, there was nothing for Nat Nadler and the others to do.

Throughout the morning trucks continued to rumble through Sète's cobbled streets and refugees boarded the ship, clutching battered suitcases and bags filled with possessions they had carried across Europe. For Reverend Grauel: 'Beneath the dirty, ragged clothes was something so noble, so wonderful on their faces. It was liberation. They were going home.'

Ada counted that 3,000 had made their way up the gangway. People were lining the deck rails and the sounds of children laughing carried down to the quayside. Suddenly they began to turn and point. A plane was flying above them; it slowly banked and once more passed overhead. Ada recognised the markings of an RAF Warwick surveillance aircraft.

On the road, Eliyahu Cohen stepped out from the lead truck and raised four fingers to the bridge: four more convoys, so 24 trucks, which meant 1,500 refugees still to board.

Thursday 10 July was a sultry day in Paris, one that matched Bevin's thunderous mood as the Foreign Secretary entered the Quai d'Orsay to once more confront Georges Bidault. Earlier that day Stewart Menzies had told Bevin that his officers – Smiley and Vershoyle – had observed *President Warfield* loading passengers. The news had been enough to send Bevin Channel-hopping to see Bidault.

Duff Cooper – a seasoned diplomat who more than once during the war had soothed outbursts from his friend Winston Churchill – was waiting at the airport when the Foreign Secretary and his aides arrived. The ambassador thought he had persuaded Bevin to calm down by the time he led him into a Quai d'Orsay conference room. But the two groups across the table had barely sat down before a messenger from the British Embassy arrived and handed the ambassador an envelope. The diplomat read the contents and passed the paper to Bevin. The Foreign Secretary's face, long puce from his liking of whisky, darkened as he rose to his feet.

As one of his aides noted: 'Bevin said *President Warfield* had become a serious affront to His Majesty's Government and that he had just been informed by our consul-general in Marseille the ship was about to sail. One of Bevin's aides handed him a document and he waved it across the table. It was the Lloyd's seaworthiness certificate which clearly stated the ship was excluded from carrying passengers and His Majesty's Government wanted the French government to take immediate steps to remove them.'

In the silence that followed, Bidault pushed back his chair and walked to a phone on a side table and placed a call. When he was connected, he told the police chief in Sète to have all the passengers on *President Warfield* removed.

The last immigrants had boarded *President Warfield* and its decks were packed with people; windows and doors were propped open to circulate air below decks on what was the hottest day of the year. Reverend Grauel sent his kitchen crew around the decks with pails of iced drinking water. Despite the heat there was a cheerful mood among the passengers as they sang and reassured each other that soon they would be on their way. They cheered as two barges moored at the end of the Saint-Louis mole were moved to allow *President Warfield* a clear passage, past the lighthouse and into the Golfe du Lion. There were more cheers as from the engine room came the sound of the first pistons running. All seemed to be ready for departure until Ike and Yossi were called to the radio shack, where radioman Enava Barak had received a coded message from Saul Avigur over the transmitter in the DST director's villa in Paris. Yehuda Arazi and Ada Sereni were summoned and Bill Bernstein was placed on guard at the shack's door.

Ike said Avigur had learned that Bidault had ordered the harbour master to move the ship to a new berth behind a drawbridge, which would then be lowered to effectively block her passage to the sea. The manoeuvre had to be completed by dawn, after which all passengers were to be escorted ashore on to buses to take them back to the camps. French police had been ordered to escort them through striking union members.

Ike said he would call upon the governor at Montpellier, while Yossi and Ada would go and see the harbour master, accompanied by Zvi Tiroche. None of the passengers should be told of the situation, with one exception. Ike wanted Noah Klieger to accompany him. His determination and language skills had impressed the captain and his presence would ensure an accurate translation of the governor's words.

Noah found himself translating at high speed as words flew between the governor, his officials and Ike. Ike warned that unless the boat left it would be a political disaster for France, which had done so much to stand up to the British over its immigration policy. The passengers were now at the mercy of the governor: sick babies, pregnant mothers, the infirm. Ike thought of anything and everything that might gain the governor's sympathy. Their Colombian visas were valid only for a voyage to Palestine. They had no other documents. They would be like their forefathers, wandering Jews. Until they arrived in Palestine the only home they had was the ship. They must be allowed to remain on board and sail there.

Noah had never seen such a masterful performance as Ike passionately argued his case point by point. The governor began to nod and look at his officials. They too nodded in agreement. Finally the governor sat back in his chair and said he would do everything possible to help. Meanwhile, the passengers could remain on board and the ship would not be moved. His secretary typed his decision, which the governor signed and gave to Ike, and then he asked her to place a call to Paris.

Yossi and Ada had met with sympathy from the harbour master – but little else. On his office desk was an order from the Foreign Ministry that the ship must have part of its engine disabled so that it could not sail. In the meantime, arrangements were under way to return the passengers to the camps.

Defeated, Yossi and Ada prepared to leave the office when the telephone on the desk rang. The harbour master picked it up and listened, then began to write rapidly on a pad, glancing at his visitors, nodding and saying, '*Oui, oui.*' Finally he put down the phone and looked at Yossi and Ada in astonishment. 'You have powerful friends. That was the French Minister of Labour, Monsieur Daniel Meir. He has instructed me that you can leave this port by two o'clock tomorrow morning at the latest. If you are not gone by then you will be detained.'

The harbour master stood up and walked to a wall map of the port, pointing to where *President Warfield* was berthed and the route she must take through several docks to reach the sea. For that they would need a pilot, who would require a suitable fee. That would be a matter for the ship's captain to settle. Yossi smiled. He understood the rules of negotiations.

On the island of Malta, Lieutenant Commander Bailey hosted a dinner for Sir John Cunningham on board HMS *Childers*. With the First Sea Lord at one end, the captains of the other destroyers and HMS *Ajax* sat around the wardroom's table, which was glittering with the ship's finest tableware that was usually brought out only to celebrate the King's birthday or Christmas at sea. Like Sir John, the guests were in their formal mess kit. Each captain had been ceremonially piped aboard before Sir John arrived on his gleaming sleek barge and once more the piping-aboard party had snapped to attention. The next day Bailey would lead the task force out of the harbour and begin their patrol towards the French coast.

On board *President Warfield*, the galley had served a meal for all the passengers and ship's crew. By midnight the immigrants had settled in their bunks and the ship was quiet except for the deck patrols and crew assigned by Yossi Harel to walk through the sleeping quarters to make sure there were no problems. From time to time Dr Cohen went to see the pregnant women to make sure none had gone into labour. In the galley, Reverend Grauel and his cooks had started preparations for breakfast. Below, in the engine room, Frank

Stanczak and Nat Nadler remained ready to start the engines once the signal came from the bridge.

In the radio shack Harold Leidner sat before the silent radio while Enava Barak slept on the shack's bunk. By 2.30am there was no sign of the pilot. On the road above the quayside Ada waited for him. Some 30 minutes later he had still not arrived.

Ike and Yossi stood in one corner on the bridge, their voices low; helmsman Bill Millman sensed the tension between them. Yossi insisted that leaving the harbour in the dark would be far more difficult than their arrival in daylight with a pilot had been. Ike was adamant. They could not wait any longer. Earlier he had sent Arazi to the pilot house to give the pilot 10,000 francs and had returned with the man's promise he would be on board well before midnight. That was over three hours ago. Ike repeated they must leave without him.

In the strained silence they both stared out to sea, where the fishing boats were bobbing on their way to the fishing grounds. Millman heard Ike say again, his voice calm, his mind made up, 'Yossi, we've got to go. The entire operation depends on it.'

The other two men on the bridge, Bill Bernstein and Bernard Marks, the second mate, heard the sudden flare of anger in Harel's voice as he told Ike that neither of them was familiar with the port's channels. To sail without a pilot was to endanger the lives of thousands of passengers.

Moments later they heard Arazi shouting from the quayside. He had been standing beside the lighthouse and saw his beam sweeping over a grey-hulled ship out at sea. The warship was moving slowly through the water.

Ike turned from Yossi and spoke by voice-pipe to chief engineer, Frank Stanczak, and told him to start engines.

Bernard Marks, who had his Masters, Mates & Pilots qualification, was to recall that through the voice-pipe came the muffled response that the ship could not move because it was held fast by a cable still tied to a bollard on the quayside: 'I was in my shorts and lowered myself from the guardrail into the black, filthy water and swam to the mole. Moving along the edge of the concrete, I reached the line and the bollard that held it. I tried to fall the cable. It was then when I realised a French gendarme was staring down at me. He suddenly shrugged and pointed. His meaning was clear, why hadn't I simply asked him to throw off the line? So he went and fetched an axe. Strand by strand the cable was cut through. It suddenly parted and dropped under our stern. I ran up the gangway. Immediately on the bridge Ike ordered them to start engines.'

On the quayside, Arazi and Ada guided the crew on deck as the gangway was lowered. *President Warfield* began to move. As Ike recalled: 'The way back to sea was a twisting route, 90 degrees to starboard, then 120 degrees to port. Even with a tug and a pilot it was a nightmare. One moment the bow was dangerously close to the quay on the port side. I called for Millman to give me engines astern. Next it was hard right rudder and full power. She bounced again along the breakwater. Once more she backed up. Then she was moving again.'

Slowly but surely, Ike brought the ship through one dock after another, each set at a different angle, causing the hull to continue banging against the concrete walls. Gertruda and Michael, Fira and her children were among the passengers who were jerked from sleep by the noise.

Zvi Tiroche quickly gathered his interpreters and told them to reassure the passengers. In the galley Reverend Grauel asked his crew to prepare jugs of coffee and distribute them among the crew, who were additional lookouts as the ship continued to manoeuvre its way through the next dock.

Ike had ordered Millman to maintain slow speed as the ship continued to move past the breakwater where Ada and Yehuda were standing. They waved and pointed ahead: the sea could be heard slapping against another breakwater.

Now Ike ordered the engine to be stopped. He knew that before continuing he had to be certain that the hull had suffered no serious damage. Once more Marks jumped into the water. He surfaced to report that there was some minor denting but the ship itself was seaworthy. But when Ike ordered the engine to be restarted, it did not. The piece of cable the policeman had cut free had become entangled in the propeller. In his usual enigmatic way Ike described it as nothing very dramatic. 'Marks freed it. We started sailing towards the entrance of the port.'

Ike guided *President Warfield* past the final dock. Soon it would be dawn and he would be able to see if that warship was still there.

The further Yossi went below deck the more oppressive the air became, a mixture of body odours and engine fumes. But no one complained. He was about to retrace his steps to the bridge when a grinding sound swept through the hull and the noise of the engine shuddered to a stop.

President Warfield had run aground on a sandbank. Helmsman Millman had mistakenly turned to port instead of starboard. On the bridge Ike called down to the engine room for a report. Lookouts peered into the water. The sea was starting to foam around the trapped hull.

Yossi made his way forward again and climbed the ladder to the bridge. The ship had begun to tilt starboard and for a split moment Yossi wondered if she would capsize. A terrible silence settled over *President Warfield*.

Ike sounded unperturbed as he called down his orders to the engine room: 'Start up again. We're going to drive through this bank.'

He turned to Millman and asked if he was ready. The white-faced helmsman nodded and gripped the wheel. The engine started and stopped again.

President Warfield began to move very slowly forward, reversed and waited, then once more went forward. To Nat Nadler in the engine room, 'It was as if we were trying to chisel through concrete. I watched the gauges climbing into the red and I kept thinking it was against the laws of engineering and we would all blow up.'

Fira Neimark had gathered her children together and told them they should remember what Yossi had just said. Over the public address system he had assured everyone that there was no danger.

Noah Klieger had returned to his position to stop any passengers attempting to reach the bridge. From there he could hear the calm voice of Ike calling out instructions. Noah couldn't be certain, but the ship appeared to have moved a little since he had last glanced towards the lighthouse. From below the Reverend Grauel emerged with a tray of steaming mugs of coffee, gave one to Noah and carried the rest up to the bridge. Noah looked again towards the harbour; the ship definitely seemed to have moved a little further away from the shore.

President Warfield continued to inch forward. On the bridge no one spoke except to respond to Ike's orders. Yossi gave a thumbs-up to Ike. The ship was no longer listing.

Dr Cohen noticed the ship was upright when he stood up from examining one of the pregnant women and smiled in relief.

There was a sudden sucking sound from beneath the hull. Ike called down for an increase of engine power. The sucking sound increased as if the sand was reluctant to let go. Then there was a final splurge-like sound and *President Warfield* lurched suddenly forward.

Within an hour of grounding on the sandbank she was free.

In the distance Ada Sereni and Yehuda Arazi were waving goodbye. Ike ordered Millman to steer a course. Ahead lay Palestine.

Reverend Grauel had worked late and his diary entry for 11 July 1947 provides a vivid glimpse into life on board as the ship left Sète: 'We had reached the open sea; it was the first time that a ship of our size had succeeded in leaving that small harbour without a pilot. People began to run all over the deck like madmen, congratulating each other. As for me, I took the time to mumble a small prayer. We were sailing! The spirit of these people was marvellous to witness. The mere thought of reaching their beloved land seemed to make them withstand everything.'

Yosef Reich had a special reason to rejoice. Not only did he have a bunk outside on the top deck of the ship, from where he could enjoy the salty freshness of the air, but, most wonderful of all, his older brother was also on board with his wife. They all had only one thought in mind. They were going home.

*

Shortly after dawn, HMS *Cheviot* was on a southeasterly course some 20 miles off Narbonne at the mouth of the Canal du Midi, the long waterway which ran from the Bay of Biscay across France to the Mediterranean. Its captain, Commander J.V. Wilkinson, a war veteran and holder of the Distinguished Service Cross and the George Medal, had recently taken command of the ship, which was launched in the week the war in Europe ended. He had expected to be sent to the Far East, but had been posted to the Palestine Patrol instead and was not overly pleased.

In the past week HMS *Cheviot* had sailed back and forth outside French territorial waters off Sète. At 6.30am her radar had picked up a large blip moving steadily across the Golfe du Lion. The radar officer went to the map room behind the bridge, where there were up-to-date photographs of the blockade-runner provided by the Admiralty. On the bridge Commander Wilkinson began to scan the sea. At 7am he went to the radio room and told the duty operator to signal HMS *Childers* that *President Warfield* had been sighted.

The sun was up when the first passengers appeared on deck. The sea was calm and empty and the French coast a blur. Over the loudspeakers Yossi made the first of his daily broadcasts. Zvi Tiroche's recruits began to translate.

Mordechai Rosemont, a leader of the Warsaw uprising, understood the need for Yossi's reminder that everyone must show self-discipline and obedience when either he or one of the crew gave an order. Everything had a reason. The huge number of people on board presented problems which could affect the ship's stability if there was a sudden mass movement from one side to the other. Everyone had been given an assigned deck and must remain there. Discipline and organisation were essential.

While Yossi spoke, Zvi moved among the translators, listening to see if his words were being correctly interpreted. Once he was satisfied they were understood, he moved on.

Rosemont had taken up position by a group of youths. He asked them if they had understood the importance of what they had heard.

When they nodded he said that for him coming on board 'was like coming from hell to heaven. I guess we all feel a bit like that, standing here in the sun, breathing in the sea air. But we can only breathe it properly if you understand the spiritual side of this voyage.'

The sun was high by the time the passengers had filled the decks and the crew had rigged awnings and side curtains as protection against the sun. Many of the passengers still looked exhausted from lack of sleep. Several had fallen out of their bunks and spent the night curled up on the floor. No one had complained and several had apologised for disturbing their neighbours.

On the promenade deck Gertruda and Michael found a space near the railings. From below came the muffled roar of the turbines spinning the propeller and smoke billowed from the stack.

Fira Neimark had marshalled her children to wait in line to enter the toilets, then wash their hands and faces ready to go to breakfast.

One of the nurses had brought two of the three pregnant women tea, while behind a screen Dr Cohen was examining the third. When he emerged he said she had started labour and soon he would move her into the hospital.

After making sure that breakfast preparations were under way, Reverend Grauel found a corner in the lee of the promenade deck to make his first entry of the day for 13 July: 'The swell has created severe seasickness, along with heat, food and water problems. There is diarrhea, and sanitary facilities are overloaded. But complaints, overcrowding, difficult circumstances are not the focus for the refugees. They are going home. By now passengers and crew have been welded into one big family. Several said having me on board is an omen of good luck. Yossi told me that to have a minister as an eye witness to the world who was not a Jew was doubly important.'

Even on deck the stench rose from below. For Aviva Porat the smell, the two-plank width of the bunk, the queue to the toilets, standing in line to collect her food, the noise, the constant shaking of the boat: none of that mattered. She was 15 years old and a new life beckoned: soon she would be in Palestine. Behind her would be the year she had spent in the camp at Rosenheim, where thousands of orphaned children had been brought together. Aviva had worked long, hard hours in the camp laundry until that day she had been given her visa and a seat on one of the Jewish Brigade trucks for her journey to Sète. She remembered: 'People who had come on board the ship as strangers became friends. This was a time to exchange stories, to get more and more excited at the thought we were coming closer to our homeland.'

In the radio shack Harold Leidner had managed to pick up news from the BBC short-wave transmission, which Zvi Tiroche had read over the loudspeakers and the translators converted into half a dozen languages. By the end of the day he had also created a single-sheet newspaper for passengers to hand round and had faced his first problem as well. Ultra-Orthodox Jews wanted assurance there would be no cooking on the Sabbath and Zvi had explained why that was not possible, given the number of passengers who would need to eat. Another problem came when the religious Jews asked to be allotted separate places to worship. It had finally taken Yossi to resolve the issue. He asked the group if they had a separate God; they looked at him in astonishment and the issue was not raised again. Yet on the whole the passengers lived happily together and there was little or no friction.

Yossi had assigned some of the passengers duties: toilet cleaning, collecting refuse in bags and tipping them over the side, serving and clearing away after meals. To keep them occupied in between, there were classes in Hebrew for all ages and lectures. Yossi gave a lecture on the geography and history of Palestine and its climate, vegetation and wildlife. Ike gave a talk about the Haganah. Nat Nadler spoke about life in New York. Reverend Grauel gave a discourse on the power of faith. Mothers with older children helped those with babies and one of the staterooms served as a nursery during the day.

Zvi had set up an office on the promenade deck. From there he prepared the daily schedules for using the few bathrooms the ship had, dealing with children who couldn't find their way back to their family and maintaining food supplies. In between he broadcast news of the ship's progress. There was, it seemed to him, never a moment to relax. But he had never felt so exhilarated.

He circulated notices giving the time of community singing or pageants that passengers were putting on. Some of the crew had brought on board musical instruments, which they played after a meal. There was also an art class held on the foredeck where one of the passengers, a teacher everyone called Nathan, encouraged passengers to sketch each other using the paper and pencils he had brought on board. Yossi was asked to judge the best drawing, which was then pinned up.

On the bridge, helmsman Bill Millman held the ship's wheel firmly and lookouts swept the empty horizon. Nothing disturbed the sea but the water rushing past the hull. *President Warfield* was averaging 15 knots and Ike expected to be close to the Palestine coast ahead of schedule.

In the gathering dusk Dr Cohen told Johann Goldman and Freddie Kronenberg to stretcher his patient in labour into the hospital area. Abe Lippschitz was monitoring a man with heart failure. Simone Smeckler, the only trained nurse on board, was halving lemons and handing them to passengers suffering with seasickness.

There was another problem that concerned Dr Cohen: 'No matter how often they were cleaned, the latrines were far from being hygienic. And there were queues all the time, a recipe for disease to spread. There was only a litre of fresh water per person every day. That could create dehydration and all sorts of problems. The stink was awful all the time. Though I had bought whatever medicine I could get in Sète, there was a shortage. If there was an outbreak of anything serious, food poisoning or diarrhoea, it could create a real crisis.'

In the radio shack, Enava Barak suddenly smiled. After hours of tuning he had finally located the Haganah radio frequency to link him to the house on Hayarkon Street on Tel Aviv's seafront. His call was answered by a professor from the Hebrew University of Jerusalem. Since *President Warfield* left Sète, there had still been no response to Ike's question: what name had David Ben-Gurion chosen for the ship? The American crew had proposed *Roosevelt*. Ike and Yossi had reminded them the ship must carry a Hebrew name and had suggested *Ha-Meri ha'Evri*, meaning 'Hebrew Resistance'. Ike had asked Barak to contact Haganah's secret radio and now he had his response: 'Your name will be *Haganah Ship Exodus 1947*.'

Yossi Harel used the loudspeaker system to announce the name. Many immigrants wept openly at its biblical connotation. That evening Ike and Yossi laid out a board on the deck of the bridge and on it Bill Millman painted the ship's new name.

As the days passed, so the longing for the journey to end heightened. Mordechai Rosemont recalled: 'Everyone was with his own fate, thinking the same. Will we succeed? All the rest was bearable: the food, the water rationed, the procedure of standing in line for a time to go to the toilet, the putrid air below deck. We all laughed at this. It was paradise compared to Auschwitz or any other camp. So we were not gloomy but excited. We were going home. People said it all the time. *We are going home.*'

Chapter 15

Dark Side of the Moon

Since sailing from Malta on the morning of 14 July, Lieutenant Commander Bailey had spent his time on HMS *Childers* studying the incoming reports from the other ships he had positioned. HMS *Cardigan Bay* was patrolling off the Egyptian coast in case *President Warfield* planned to enter the shallow water of the Nile Delta, where she could unload her passengers so they could travel overland to Palestine. HMS *Chequers* had been stationed off the Palestine coast south of Tel Aviv. HMS *Ajax*, with Sir John Cunningham on board, was stationed to stop the blockade-runner making a dash for the beaches of northern Palestine. HMS *Charity* would remain on the port side of HMS *Childers*, both with their boarding platform in place. HMS *Cheviot* would remain on station. Once *President Warfield* had been sighted, HMS *Chieftain* would take up position on her stern, ready to block any attempt by passengers or crew to launch life rafts.

Earlier that day Bailey had had breakfast with the First Sea Lord in his day cabin on HMS *Ajax* in Valetta harbour, reviewing the plan. Sir John had ordered the task force to remain out of sight while *President Warfield* was off the European coast. The RAF would maintain aerial surveillance. Nothing should raise suspicion of the impending interception.

The details were in a file including aerial photographs and those taken at Port-de-Bouc by the two MI6 officers, together with Admiralty blueprints of the ship's interior after it had been converted for its role on D-Day. Stewart Menzies had provided reports from his agents in Palestine and across Europe that the ship had become a subject of intense discussion. From New York Stephenson had sent details of fund-raising drives to buy more ships if *President Warfield* broke through the blockade.

Sir John had given Bailey his view of why the Haganah and its political leaders were poised to exploit the voyage. Though Britain had almost 100,000 troops in Palestine, they were trying to block illegal immigration while coping with Jewish terrorism. There was also the global sympathy for the Holocaust survivors and the support of the Truman administration, mobilised by Jewish lobbyists and the world press. Like Bailey's own crew, many of the Mandate's forces were young and working in an atmosphere of constant danger and growing tension. Sir John concluded by saying that *President Warfield* was no ordinary blockade-runner and if its mission was a success it could lead to the Jews getting their state. Bailey was told all those considerations must be kept in his mind when action began.

On board HMS *Charity* Lieutenant Roger Pearce watched his team practise. They stood on the platform, crouching as if ready to jump, weapons at the ready, gas masks covering their faces and sweat running down their cheeks from the boiling sun.

Pearce had told them that the actual boarding would take place at night and to create confusion they would board *President Warfield* three at a time, to give the appearance of an endless rush of a formidable force. Pearce's target would be the ship's wheelhouse. The other boarding team, from HMS *Childers*, would capture the engine room. Pearce had warned his team that they should expect to meet heavy resistance and sustain casualties. They should limit their own response 'to only what is essential'.

Geoff Glover was a sick bay attendant (SBA), equal to a highly qualified paramedic in civilian life. After being trained at the Royal Navy teaching hospital in Portsmouth, he had joined HMS *Formidable*, an aircraft carrier, on its way to the Far East. However, reaching Malta, Glover had been reassigned to the Palestine Patrol, working on its ships as they stopped blockade-runners. His job was to board each boat and offer what medical help was needed. Instead,

'I received abuse and often outright hatred. There was a feeling among the passengers that the Mandate was no longer capable of properly governing and this was reflected in their mounting expectations of the Jews.'

Glover was glad to escape the hostility by going on shore leave to his favourite haunt, Beirut. He returned from there in mid-July to be told that he was to join the boarding parties for *President Warfield* as their SBA. When he learned the number of illegal immigrants the ship was carrying he blinked. He had never had to treat so many potential cases; suddenly he felt apprehensive. He was told that, while he would wear the regular medical uniform of blue trousers and white top, he must replace his spectacles with protective hospital goggles and wear a tin helmet. He should fill his backpack with sufficient equipment to deal with knife wounds, smashed teeth and bullet wounds. He had been told his duties as a medic provided no guarantee he would not be attacked, as some of the ship's crew would be armed. 'Not armed to the teeth, but armed.'

Lawrence Carey was a radar operator on HMS *Ajax*. Shortly before the cruiser set sail from Malta, a powerful water cannon was hoisted on board. The 19-year-old operator was puzzled, since the ship was already equipped with the latest fire-fighting equipment.

Already the presence on board of the First Sea Lord and the coded signals which had come and gone from the radio room to the Admiralty in London had fuelled mounting speculation. The coupling of the water cannon to a hydrant on deck and a test firing of its powerful jet of water over the sea had done nothing to quell the rumour circulating in the seamen's mess hall that they were going to the Pacific. Carey was one of the few on board who knew better. Before leaving Malta the ship's radar officer had briefed his operators that HMS *Ajax* was going to 'strike a powerful blow against illegal immigration by stopping *President Warfield* and impounding its passengers'.

At noon on 17 July, his second day at sea, Carey spotted a blip on his radar screen. It was some 125 miles south of Crete and travelling at an estimated speed of 10.2 knots. The position of *President Warfield* was immediately sent to the First Sea Lord.

Shortly afterwards the radar operator on HMS *Cardigan Bay* confirmed the position. He was coming to the end of the ship's patrol from Haifa along the Palestine coast when his ship had been told to join the task force.

Until the sighting of *President Warfield* there had been nothing to relieve his boredom. Now he noticed that the blip on his radar screen had slowed. Minutes later came a confirmed sighting from HMS *Cheviot*. Shortly afterwards a signal arrived from the First Sea Lord to each captain in the task force: 'Intelligence informs that failure to stop this immigrant ship from landing on Palestine shore will almost certainly lead to very serious disorders in the Tel Aviv area. The risk to your men or damage to your ships must not deflect you from stopping her.'

After breakfast on 17 July, Ike held another of his by now regular meetings at the back of the bridge with Yossi Harel, Frank Stanczak, Dr Cohen and the Reverend Grauel to hear their overnight reports.

The ship's chief engineer said that while the engine room continued to run smoothly, the gauge on the drinking-water tanks indicated that there would soon be a need for rationing and recommended that water should only be available at mealtimes in bottles and handed out in an emergency at other times. Ike agreed. Dr Cohen reported his pregnant passenger had only a few more hours to go before she gave birth. But there had been a growing number of seasickness cases and he wanted an increase in the teams cleaning the latrines. Ike agreed. Reverend Grauel said that several Ultra-Orthodox Jews continued to badger him to prepare food before the Sabbath so there would be no cooking on that day. He had explained to them that the galley did not have sufficient refrigeration facilities to ensure the food did not spoil in the heat. Dr Cohen said the last thing he wanted was an outbreak of food poisoning. Ike asked Yossi to make it clear for the last time that 'Demands like those are off the table.'

Yossi had raised another complaint from several passengers. They felt that the ship was going too slowly and, as there was no sign of the Royal Navy, that it should go faster.

Ike sighed. Before the meeting he had gone to the radio shack to listen to the BBC morning news short-wave broadcast. There was no mention of *President Warfield* or, for once, Palestine. But he was only partly reassured. Instinct told him that British intelligence would not allow the ship to escape so easily, let alone Foreign Secretary Ernest Bevin.

While the others watched, Ike spread out one of the few navigation maps on board and began to point to various areas of the sea. 'Somewhere out there beyond the horizon the Royal Navy will be waiting. They have their radar. We have nothing like that. All we have is our speed.' He then reminded them that even with their unprecedented number of passengers the ship could still achieve a maximum speed of 18 knots. It was possible that the Palestine Patrol had not allowed for that. To encourage them in their ignorance, he had set their speed to 10 knots. Once more Ike swept his hand over the map, a confidence in his quiet voice. *Here was the Egyptian coast. There were the beaches of Palestine. This was where they now were.*

The others began to nod. Ike indicated another point on the map. His finger was close to the edge of Palestine's territorial waters. It was where he would start his dash for the beaches. Even if the Palestine Patrol had by then spotted them, it would be too late to stop the ship.

Stanczak, a devout Catholic Pole, hugged Yossi and said that even in his prayers to the Blessed Virgin Mary he could not have devised a better strategy.

The warmth of high summer had helped the passengers settle. Only Ike's instinct warned him that the blue sky and placid sea could be precursors of trouble. It came late in the morning, when an RAF surveillance plane flew over the horizon. Everyone on deck stared up as the aircraft began to circle, keeping a distance, before suddenly flying directly over the ship. Then, just as suddenly as it had appeared, it banked away and was gone.

Ike knew it was checking their course and speed. He also knew now that any hope the voyage would be peaceful had vanished. From the crowded decks below came murmurs of unease. He grabbed the public address loudspeaker: 'Other planes may come and behind them even ships. But the eyes of the world will be upon our ship. Not even the Royal Navy will dare attack us. So please continue to relax. Everything is under control to bring you all safely home.'

Returning from lunch, Dr Cohen realised he had a medical emergency on his hands and little equipment to deal with it. The obstetrics kit packed back in Baltimore would not be sufficient to cope with the breech birth he now faced. He needed an anaesthetic machine, clamps, forceps and a range of other equipment. The baby was premature and would require a Caesarean section.

Dr Cohen had tried turning the baby, manipulating it through the mother's abdomen, knowing the risk of complications were high. By late afternoon, the mother's breathing had grown more desperate and exhausted between contractions. Dr Cohen continued to encourage her to push. Suddenly the baby emerged in a flow of blood, bottom first and legs flexed at the hip and knees near the ears. The infant was cleaned and wrapped in a towel; the mother died shortly afterwards of a haemorrhage. Dr Cohen went to the bridge to report what had happened.

Ike and Yossi agreed there was no place to store the body until they arrived in Palestine. The only solution was to bury the mother at sea. Yossi explained over the loudspeaker what had happened and asked for a volunteer to nurse the baby until they landed. Helena Levi said she would.

A Polish family came forward to prepare the corpse and cover it in a shroud. In mid-afternoon Ike rang down to the engine room for Frank Stanczak to stop the engines. *President Warfield* began to gently rock in the swell.

Four of the crew – Cyril Weinstein, Roger Rofe, Ben Foreman and Murray Aronoff – carried the shroud, weighted with links of chain, down to the crowded main deck, which was completely silent, like all the other decks. Miriam stood beside Helena, who was cradling the newborn infant in her arms. As the burial party approached the guardrail, Johann Goldman and Bill Bernstein positioned a plank on the rail. The four pallbearers placed the shroud on the plank and Ike and Yossi stood on either side.

The silence was broken by the strong, clear voice of a rabbi beginning to say *Kaddish*. The words were taken up on other decks so that in moments over 4,000 voices murmured the prayer. Ike looked at Yossi and nodded. Both men stepped back a pace. In one smooth movement the pallbearers tilted the plank and the body slid into the sea.

The only sound was the weeping of women trying to comfort the husband of the dead woman. Over the public address system Yossi said, 'When our ancestors left Egypt they buried their dead where they were before continuing on their way to their Promised Land. We shall do the same now.' In the silence that followed, Ike walked back to the bridge and rang down for Frank Stanczak to start the engines.

The funeral cast a shadow over the passengers and some of the more deeply religious wondered if they should sit *shivah*. One or two of the older men produced pairs of small square black boxes, *tefillin* or phylacteries, each box containing parchment inscribed with prayers. They bound them with leather thongs round their head and left arm while they prayed for the mother. After the evening meal, passengers stood on deck and sang traditional Jewish songs and Reverend Grauel walked among them, offering words of consolation.

That night he wrote in his diary: 'I was told by one of the passengers that the mother was not in a condition to travel by sea. But she insisted on going. The pull of *Eretz Yisrael* was too strong to resist.'

On board HMS *Childers*, Lieutenant Commander Bailey and Lieutenant Robert MacPherson, the ship's boarding officer, sat around the wardroom table for dinner. Outside the open portholes a moonless night enhanced the lights from HMS *Charity*, two cable lengths away. The conversation focused on whether sea conditions would allow a safe boarding on *President Warfield*; one slip and a man could drown or be crushed between the destroyer and the blockade-runner. Bailey had stressed to MacPherson that his prime consideration should be that once the attack was launched it must be over quickly so as to allow no time for the ship's crew or passengers to retaliate.

Bailey told him that the role he had been asked to perform was 'nevertheless painful and filled with unacceptable implications'.

The First Sea Lord reminded him that *President Warfield* could not be fired on. One shot might sink the ship or cause heavy casualties. The result would be worldwide condemnation and very probably legal proceedings, which would have unprecedented results for all those involved.

Bailey was interrupted by a message from the radar room. *President Warfield* had been sighted 15 miles to the south of HMS *Childers*.

Bailey led his officers to the plot room to prepare a new course and to signal the task force to tell them what was going to happen. On the table were images from the morning's surveillance by the RAF plane.

After the evening meal, Ike left the bridge after instructing Millman to maintain his course and speed while he continued his captain's rounds. He knew his presence would reassure the passengers and lift their spirits after the funeral. It would also give him an opportunity to check the ship's preparations.

Ike's first visit was to the hospital. The area was more crowded than the last time. There were passengers being seasick, children crying, old men groaning, women who still managed a smile. Ike could only admire the way Dr Cohen and his nurses coped with the steady flow of patients. He had a word for them all before he moved on down into the ship.

While the day had passed without another aircraft overflying or sight of another ship, Ike knew that the hours of darkness would be the dangerous time, and he had posted extra lookouts on the bridge and the decks. He had already walked around the decks to make sure that the ship was properly darkened, with no chink of light betraying their presence, and that the lifeboats and life rafts were prepared for launching (each raft was equipped with paddles, a keg of water and a watertight tin of provisions). Ike checked nothing had been removed since the last inspection.

He had given instructions against unnecessary noise on deck after dark. He knew this would irritate those passengers who liked to stay on deck and enjoy the night air after their meal. But following the morning's aerial reconnaissance flight, they should give their pursuers as little help as possible; voices always carried further at night and he suspected the Palestine Patrol would have the latest listening devices.

Below, Ike met the patrolling seamen in the gangways. He knew all of them by name: the American volunteers and the young men of the Haganah's naval unit, the Palyam. He liked the way they hid their own tension behind polite smiles and an assurance there were no problems. On his stop at the galley he reminded Reverend Grauel to make sure all the crew on duty had regular mugs of coffee. Nothing was omitted from the checklist in Ike's mind.

Yossi had already selected several passengers to lead groups of young and physically fit volunteers. They included Noah Klieger, Zvi Tiroche and Mordechai Rosemont – men he had decided would stay calm under attack and show the kind of leadership that would inspire confidence in the others. Each had been asked to select his own group from the passengers to form the ship's defence force.

None of the groups would be armed with guns – there were none on board – but they would have heaps of potatoes to throw, together with tins of food, and hosepipes attached to steam and oil outlets from the engine room to spray the boarders. For Ike, 'If nothing else their fighting spirit would make it all that much harder to capture the ship.'

If that happened, Ike knew that he and key members of his crew could expect rough handling from the boarders. The crews of other blockade-runners had suffered similar treatment.

By nightfall Ike was back on the bridge, where he had left Yossi in command. Completely dark apart from its navigation lights, *President Warfield* moved through the sea. Red-eyed from lack of sleep, Ike finally went to his cabin to rest.

Yossi told Millman to increase their speed to 16 knots. The ship began to roll slowly in the swell and the engine began to pound a little louder. Mist drifted over the water. From a deck came the voice of Mordechai Rosemont telling his 120 youngsters that he wanted them to place sacks of potatoes and tinned food close to the hosepipes. Noah Klieger and Zvi Tiroche were conducting similar deployments on other decks.

Standing beside Millman, Bill Bernstein, the first mate, sipped his coffee and continued to explain why he had abandoned his career as a lecturer at Annapolis Naval Academy and volunteered to join Aliyah Bet and go back to sea. Millman recalled later how Bernstein had grinned and said he had to do so because he needed more action after the Second World War. Then he startled the helmsman by adding that he felt he was going to see it that night and would die happy. Millman had told Bernstein, 'You are nuts! Drink some more coffee!'

On board HMS *Charity* Lieutenant Roger Pearce stood with his boarding party in the lee of the bridge, staring out to sea. In the distance the bow wave of HMS *Childers* ruffled the water. About half a mile ahead was the wake of *President Warfield*, no more than a vague shape in the darkness. Either side of where he stood, Pearce saw the two sailors standing behind powerful searchlights, the 21-inch lens forward and the 10-inch aft.

Above Pearce, protruding from the bridge, was the boarding platform. He had told the team they could remain at ease for a while but should make sure their protective equipment was in place: a long baton, a reinforced leather box to protect their genitalia, an elbow protector and a tin helmet fitted with a thick cloth to protect against a blow to the back of the neck. They should use their rifles and sub-machine guns and tear-gas grenades once on board only to ward off attacks. He had a revolver and would give the order if they had to fire. He reminded them that a large number of the passengers would be women and children and though they would undoubtedly resist, as immigrants on previous blockade-runners had done, tear gas should be sufficient to stop them. To simulate gunfire boarders would use the Chinese jumping firecrackers they had been given. Lieutenant Pearce concluded that he expected the capture of *President Warfield* to be a swift affair.

*

On his last visit to Dr Cohen in his hospital that night the Reverend Grauel had learned that the supply of lemons to treat the growing number of seasickness cases was running low. He brought the teenagers to the galley and gave them each a cup of coffee. Their story would finally be told by Yoram Kaniuk, the distinguished biographer of Yossi Harel. But there was a romance on the ship which has remained untold until now.

In those first days at sea Reverend Grauel had taken Fira and her children under his wing, making sure they had enough to drink, that they had a good place on deck to listen to the nightly concerts given by musicians among the passengers and crew, or see the folk dancers spinning across the deck. By day Reverend Grauel had stood beside Fira as she proudly watched her children, joining in the singing or sitting on the deck learning Hebrew. He would often find time to be with Fira, teaching her English. For the teenager, 'He was just wonderful. Always ready to help. He brought the children water. He didn't leave me for one minute. I felt comfortable with him.'

Fira was not only young, but attractive. With her smile and the way she walked, she caught the eye of more than one of the young men on board. She was polite to all of them but she made it clear the children were her life. The men would try and sit near her at mealtimes, telling her of their plans once they reached Palestine, and she would smile and listen while they brought food for the children to the table.

To Reverend Grauel it was 'kind of first-date flirting . . . all innocent and going nowhere'.

Then one day she became aware of Efraim. 'Suddenly he was standing there. He was beautiful and tall with red hair. He had everything a girl could want. I knew then he had found me and I him. It was love at first sight. Me in my dress and he in his three-piece suit. The children knew right away that something was happening. Everything was beautiful. We just looked at each other. There was no need to say anything. We just knew this was love.'

*

For two hours *President Warfield*, now bearing the name *Haganah Ship Exodus 1947* on a board hung over the side, forged steadily ahead in all-enveloping darkness. It was a few minutes before midnight. Suddenly the ship was bathed in powerful blinding white lights, which began to play slowly back and forth from bow to stern.

To starboard, the magnified voice of Lieutenant Commander Bailey demanded to know, 'What is your course, *President Warfield*?'

Woken by the lights and now terrified by the cold disembodied voice, passengers screamed and wept as they climbed to the decks. Dazzled by the lights, they then stumbled back below.

Ike returned to the bridge, shielding his eyes with one hand. Once more the clipped English voice insisted, 'Captain, will you tell me, what is your course?'

Ike grabbed the loudspeaker: 'This is the captain of *Haganah Ship Exodus 1947*.'

On board HMS *Childers*, Lieutenant Commander Bailey gave his first order: 'Captain, you will now alter your course and follow behind me.'

Ike did not hesitate: 'We will stay on our course.'

Both searchlights switched off and the warships vanished into the night as swiftly as they had appeared.

Ike held the loudspeaker and delivered his orders calmly. Passengers who had specific orders to defend the ship should remain or go to their posts. Everyone else must return or remain below deck in their bunks to better cope with the seasickness, as he had just ordered an increase in speed that would get them much faster to Palestine. From below deck came the first sound of cheering.

For Dr Cohen: 'Ike had once more shown brilliant leadership in calming the passengers. But having failed to scare us, the navy would be back. I sensed there would now be a battle.' While his volunteers would be helpful, he would really depend on pharmacist Abe Lippschitz and Simone Smeckler. Between them, they would be responsible for triage, separating the slightly injured from those who had more severe wounds. How many there would be he could only guess. Would he have sufficient surgical equipment, medicines and bandages?

In the radio shack Enava Barak had completed his transmissions to the seafront house in Tel Aviv, detailing what had happened. A voice in his headphones said that Kol Yisrael, the Voice of Israel, was now broadcasting on 45 metres long-wave and asking if there was a passenger on board able to describe to the world in fluent English what had happened.

Harold Leidner returned with Reverend Grauel and sat him before a microphone. In his powerful preacher's voice, the Methodist minister announced: 'This is Reverend John Grauel, a member of the American Christian Committee for Palestine, broadcasting to you from the *Haganah Ship Exodus 1947*. We are heading for Palestine. We have recently buried at sea an expectant mother, but her baby is alive and well. All of those on board this ship only wish to enter their homeland and are peace-loving people. But we have already been threatened by British warships and we can expect even worse. We ask all of you listening to support and pray for us. Stay tuned to this wavelength as I bring you further reports.'

He sat before the microphone scribbling furiously in his diary, which he now carried everywhere with him.

'On the upper deck a group of boys and girls stand, between the ages of about 13 and 16, their chins thrust forward defiantly, one fist clenched, the other holding a potato. They are prepared to defend themselves with the only weapons they have. I was born and nurtured with the precious milk of freedom. These youngsters are momentarily bathed in the aura of Concord and Lexington and all the words I have ever read about the birth of America and her fight for freedom. I now know that aboard this ship I am watching the birth of a nation.'

He switched on the microphone and continued to speak.

On the promenade deck Aviva Porat sat beside a pile of tins, her weapons, and stared out to sea, filled with a sense of adventure and mounting excitement that Mordechai Rosemont had included her as a member of his battle group. She knew she would not let him down; she could throw as well as any boy.

Down in the hold where Gertruda and Michael waited in their bunks, along with hundreds of others, the sound of the sea was louder as *Exodus* increased speed. In the engine room Nat Nadler had been told that if an attack was launched, he should go to the main deck and use one of the oil pipes to make its surface slippery, while other crewmen were to direct jets of steam on to the boarders.

HMS *Cheviot's* searchlights had given Lieutenant Pearce his first close look at *President Warfield*. Her size, superstructure and hull covered in wire indicated the problems his boarders would face. The jump from the platform even in a slight swell would be tricky; he estimated it would be a 15-foot drop to the ship's deck. Though they had trained for that, it could result in injury. He had also glimpsed something even more worrying: on the decks figures crouched beside what looked like piles of what could be some sort of ammunition.

The cool-headed young officer had seen enough to realise, 'This could be a far tougher job than I had anticipated.'

Zvi Tiroche had finally managed to snatch a cat-nap after another long day spent organising the passengers. When the searchlights illuminated the ship he stumbled out of his small office and went to his young volunteers. He told them to have their potatoes and tins ready to hand to throw if boarders arrived.

Further along the deck Noah Klieger was organising his group to lay out hosepipes in the way he had seen firemen do. Each hose was linked to either an oil tank or a steam vent in the engine room. It was now 1am on 18 July 1947.

On board HMS *Ajax*, Lawrence Carey watched the blips on his screen showing the task force cruising to the south of the blip of *Exodus*.

On the bridge, Sir John Cunningham had ordered the radio room to try and contact her. The cruiser's navigation officer had calculated that the weather conditions could delay the blockade-runner and leave her short of food and water. The ship's radio officer would radio that *Exodus* could have supplies on the understanding that she made no further attempt to enter Palestine waters. HMS *Ajax* would send a team over to bring across the supplies. For Carey: 'Once on board the sailors could take over the ship and bring it to Cyprus.'

The radio officer called *Exodus*. There was no response. Sir John ordered the next move.

During the night Yossi made another round of the ship, while Ike maintained his course, making sure 'I still had a couple of knots in hand.' He had asked a number of American volunteers who had signed on in Baltimore to string barbed wire around the bridge. He was convinced that any attack would focus on the control centre of the ship. During the brief moments the two warships had swept past he had glimpsed the platforms built out from their bridges. He was still trying to figure out how they would be used when Dr Cohen arrived with the news he had just delivered another baby, a boy.

Out of the night HMS *Ajax* bore down on *Exodus*. A voice in German filled the darkness: 'You are suspected of going to Palestine with illegal immigrants. If you enter Palestine territorial waters, we will have to board and arrest you. Please do not resist. We have superior forces here and in Palestine. If it becomes necessary to board you, we will use force.'

The message had been drafted by Sir John Cunningham.

Ike switched on the bridge microphone and replied, 'Speak English! We are not the *Graf Spee*!'

As the cruiser disappeared into the night, Ike and Yossi Harel gave a stiff-arm salute of the Royal Navy and Ike said, 'That's three warships so far. How many more do they have?'

In the Haganah seafront house in Tel Aviv, Moshe Bar-Gilad had ordered Reverend Grauel's broadcast to be turned into Hebrew handbills. Within hours, youths had started to post them all over the city, while other members of the organisation drove to do the same in Jerusalem and Haifa. The handbills called for Jews to resist any attempt to stop *Exodus* landing its passengers. People should close their shops, restaurants and factories not only to protest against the Mandate, but to rally the whole world to support the ship.

In High Commissioner Sir Alan Cunningham's residence on the Hill of the Council of Evil in Jerusalem, the night duty officer in the mansion's communications room was telephoned by his counterpart at Navy Headquarters in Haifa and told that *Exodus* was making all speed towards Palestine. The duty officer dialled Sir Alan's bedroom extension and was instructed to inform General Sir Gordon McMillan, commander of British troops in Palestine. Soon the first tanks and troop carriers would be heard rumbling through the streets of Haifa.

In his home on Keren Kayemet Street in Tel Aviv, David Ben-Gurion sat in his pyjamas beside a wireless in his study, the dial set for the next broadcast on the Kol Yisrael wavelength.

Chaim Weizmann had been awakened by a phone call at his home in Rehovot to tell him that *Exodus* had 'broken through the blockade'.

He turned to Vera to discuss what would be the best move he could make. Although Weizmann had continued to try and persuade his contacts in England and Europe that their governments must understand the foundation of the State of Israel required a solution to the immigration problem, the response had been lukewarm. Would *Exodus* change matters? He began to call his contacts across the world.

It was, Vera reminded him, 'the night of the dark side of the moon'.

In the early hours on 18 July, Ike ordered an increase in speed to 18 knots, driving *Exodus*'s four-cylinder reciprocating engine to maximum output. The log recorder, which kept track of her mileage, showed the ship was now 17 miles from the Egyptian coast.

Soon Bill Millman would execute Ike's order to turn north to the landing beach. Ike knew that, with her flat bottom, *Exodus* could not be followed by any warship over that last half-mile, because the water would be too shallow. While driving the ship ashore would effectively wreck her, it was a small price to pay for bringing home some 4,500 immigrants.

In the past hour Ike and Yossi had conducted yet another tour of the ship to check its defences and reassure those who manned them they were sufficient to keep at bay any attempt to board. In the galley, Reverend Grauel's cooks had boiled water to pour over boarders and Frank Stanczak had distributed spare engine spanners and hammers to arm deckhands. Dr Cohen had discharged all his patients and ordered his team to prepare to cope with the new ones.

On board HMS *Childers*, Lieutenant Commander Bailey stood on the destroyer's bridge, watching the boarding party on the platform a few feet away. It was even harder to see their faces through the gas masks. Each man in his white jersey was armed with a sub-machine gun, a carbine, a steel-tipped truncheon or a fireman's axe. Several also carried tear-gas grenades or Chinese firecrackers. Two of the marines had battering rams. Each man wore a steel helmet. In addition, Lieutenant MacPherson had a Very pistol tucked in his waist belt with which to signal. Beside him stood a radioman with his transmitter/receiver pack on his back.

On HMS *Charity* Lieutenant Pearce lined up his men to stand on the platform.

Chapter 16

The Attack

Throughout the night coded signals in Hebrew had passed between *Exodus*'s radio shack and Haganah's headquarters. To further confuse the task-force radio operators – none of whom could speak the language – Saul Avigur (code-named Ben Yehudah) had given Ike and Yossi a copy each of the code book he had devised before they left Sète. France was Neter; *Exodus* was Ha-Kli; Tel Aviv was Zelig; Palestine was Artzi. Ike was Arnon and Yossi was Ammon. Cyprus was identified as Rice. Finally any message to or from Ami came from David Ben-Gurion.

Each signal was decoded by Enava Barak and brought by him to the bridge. The first had been a request from Matityabu – a code-name for Moshe Bar-Gilad – to inform him of the estimated time of arrival off Bat-Yam, the designated landing beach south of Tel Aviv. Ike had responded he hoped to reach the area before dawn.

Back came the immediate order: 'If unsuccessful make for Zelig as discussed.'

At a meeting in Sète, Yehuda Arazi, code-named Hofshi, and Ada Sereni, Ur, had unfolded a back-up plan for *Exodus* to sail some six miles off-shore in shallow water towards Tel Aviv. With the town in sight, the ship would make a dash for the beach close to Nordau Street, where the Haganah would have waiting a large force of fighters, supported by the population, to engage Mandate troops in any attempt to stop the immigrants coming ashore. Meanwhile, fighters who had gone to Bat-Yam would be taken by bus to reinforce those at Nordau Street. By then the lifeboats and rafts would have been readied to carry the passengers and, once the ship had run aground, strong swimmers among the crew would jump overboard and, carrying ropes, swim ashore and begin pulling the lifeboats and rafts on to the beach. Buses would be waiting to take them to the settlements. The operation would be repeated until all the immigrants were off the ship.

There was an element of daring-do about the plan which appealed to Yossi, reminding him of his times working with Orde Wingate. But Ike was more cautious. The Nordau Street beach was smaller and it would not be possible to spirit away some 4,500 refugees from Tel Aviv before Mandate forces blocked all the exit roads. Sensing Ike's hesitation, Arazi had stressed the plan was only a back-up.

Shortly after HMS *Childers* and HMS *Cheviot* had made their first pass on *Exodus* came a new message from Bar-Gilad: 'Propose you directly make for Zelig.'

Yossi had come to accept Ike's concern that the arrival of HMS *Ajax* had reduced any hope of bursting through the blockade and making a dash for the alternative landing beach at Tel Aviv. Not only was it smaller, but they would arrive there around mid-morning and while daylight would help the passengers to disembark, it would also mean that every move *Exodus* made could be observed from the shore by British troops. Going to Bat-Yam was still a better option.

Their deliberations were interrupted by further orders from the Haganah: 'We are preparing a beachhead at Zelig. In the meantime ensure Ha-Kli is fully secured against attack by enemy forces.'

The joint reply from Yossi and Ike was short: 'Have made all preparations.'

Their pique and tiredness showed behind the words of what Yossi later called 'the growing disagreement between the ship and the people on land'.

Another message arrived and set out what was required in the next broadcast the Reverend Grauel would make. He was to transmit before sunrise and make clear in his opening words that *Exodus* was still afloat. He would follow by describing the following: 'The suffering of the passengers and their desperate wish to go to Palestine, a protest at Britain's closed-door policy, a call for United Nations intervention over the attacks on the ship, a call for global solidarity in support of *Exodus* and a declaration that immigration would continue'.

The orders had been sent by Ami. David Ben-Gurion had publicly joined the battle to save *Exodus*.

After thanking them for the message, Ike sent yet another one. In 15 minutes he would turn *Exodus* towards the Egyptian coast and enter the shipping lanes in and out of the port of Alexandria. He knew the immediate problem for their pursuers would be how to intercept the ship in busy international waters without creating a worldwide outcry. While in France, Ada had shown Ike hostile newspaper reports she had helped to organise about the methods the Royal Navy had used to stop other blockade-runners and Moshe Bar-Gilad had reported that Reverend Grauel's first broadcast had already attracted growing publicity, with reporters arriving to cover the story.

Once within the shipping lanes Ike would set a new course to take him along the coast towards Egypt's border with Palestine. The shallow water would force the destroyers to reduce their speed while, with her flat bottom, *Exodus* could maintain full speed.

Ike planned to make a run past Gaza to Bat-Yam, the landing beach, leaving the task force desperately trying to pick its way through the shallows. It was a daring plan and one that Bar-Gilad and the other Haganah commanders agreed Ike could execute.

In the radar room on board HMS *Cardigan Bay*, Barwell sat transfixed before his screen. A cone of light had locked on to *Exodus*, holding the blockade-runner in its glare, the way searchlights had settled on a Luftwaffe bomber over London in the war. From out of the night, HMS *Childers* and HMS *Charity* had emerged once more and were steering in parallel only a few yards away on each side of *Exodus*, their officers studying her from the destroyers' bridges.

Across the sea came the shrieking of *Exodus*'s whistle. The relentless light and piercing sound combined to create a terror of its own.

*

Once more Reverend Grauel painted a powerful picture of the scene in his broadcast: 'The night has turned to day under the searchlights from the destroyers. A fleet of destroyers seem to be running abreast of us as if they plan to converge on us. During the night someone has secured to our single smoke stack a mammoth poster. On it is a picture of a woman holding a baby in her arms, a small child at her side. An inscription reads: "England, this is your enemy."'

Had the energetic broadcaster been dazzled by the searchlights and imagined he saw the poster? Certainly it was an image which could only have had a powerful effect on his radio listeners. Yet none of the passengers or crew recalled seeing the poster on the smoke stack. Certainly no one has ever admitted to placing it there. Did it blow away after Reverend Grauel saw it?

The proximity of the HMS *Childers* and the blinding light rooted everyone on *Exodus*. Ike stood at a port window, Yossi at one on the opposite side of the bridge. Bill Millman gripped the wheel even tighter, his mouth working but no words coming. The ship's mate, Bill Bernstein, kept his hand on the whistle, its deafening howl drowning his cursing.

Zvi Tiroche, Noah Klieger and Mordechai Rosemont were shouting out to their groups to prepare for an attack as they handed out potatoes from sacks and tins of food that Nat Nadler had brought up from the engine room.

Over the public address system came the resounding music of Elgar's 'Pomp and Circumstance March'. It had been Ike's idea to broadcast the record one of the passengers played during mealtimes on his gramophone.

Dr Cohen had taken his triage team, Abe Lippschitz and Simone Smeckler, out on to the deck ready to treat any casualties. In the hold, having assured Michael there was no need to be frightened, Gertruda went from one bunk to another offering reassurance. For Michael: 'She was a symbol of calm and civility. She understood fear.'

On the bridge the two dumbfounded lookouts were staring into the night, where, in the destroyers' lights, they could make out white-jumpered figures standing on the platforms above HMS *Childers* and HMS *Charity*. Swaying with the movement of the sea, in their gas masks and helmets, clutching their weapons, they looked like aliens who had fallen from the sky.

Abruptly the cone of light from the destroyer's searchlight went out. Ike waved for Millman to stop the whistle. As if linked by an invisible cord, HMS *Childers* and HMS *Charity* moved on either side of *Exodus* through the pitch black of the night. Ike called down the engine room voice-pipe: 'Reverse!'

Lieutenant Pearce's instructor had told him to spring outwards from the platform to make sure he was clear of any obstructions, the way a paratrooper did when exiting an aircraft door. The instructor had added that a parachutist usually had hundreds of feet to fall before hitting the ground, more than enough time to prepare his landing position: feet slightly apart, legs and body relaxed.

Pearce knew it had been calculated that from the platform to the landing point on the *Exodus*'s top deck would be 15 feet. Depending on the rise and fall of the waves, he would have at most two seconds to prepare to land.

On the HMS *Childers*'s last run past *Exodus* he had spotted the carly rafts, flat, wooden life rafts, attached to the deck guardrails. Beside them were some nets on the deck. Rafts and nets could be used to repel boarders. Pearce recalled: 'I couldn't really see very much. And from where I stood the sea swell added to the problem. All I could think of was to get control of the wheelhouse as soon as we landed on board the other ship.'

From the bridge came Bailey's command for Pearce to stand by to jump. The young officer braced himself. Standing in the dark, there was no way to judge the exact distance. All he could sense was that *Exodus* was moving backwards. He looked quickly at the men on either side of him. *It was now or never.* He breathed in and jumped.

*

The powerful sound of HMS *Childers* only yards away from the radio room had brought Reverend Grauel running out on deck to go to where he had left Fira and the children settling down for the night.

'They were not there. At that moment the destroyer nudged our ship midships and then pulled away. I ran up to the hurricane deck. I just hoped they had gone up there like they had done regularly, before going to sleep. There they were, the kids huddled around Fira, standing in the middle of the deck. Fira just looked at me in relief, saying to the children it was going to be okay. She was a heck of a fine lady. When Efraim arrived her happiness was complete.'

Reverend Grauel said one more time that everything was going to be all right, then headed for the opposite side of the ship, from where shouting was coming.

On the bridge of HMS *Childers*, Lieutenant Commander Bailey had watched Lieutenant Pearce jump. A moment later 'one of the lookouts shouted, "The Lieutenant has landed on one of the carlys! Looks like he is in the water!" I ran to take a look and shouted for a searchlight to be switched on. The lookout shouted that Pearce was safe and up on the deck. But there was a hell of a fight going on there.'

When Pearce landed on one of the rafts he somehow managed to avoid sliding into the sea. A fusillade of tins and potatoes greeted him. He waited in a cabin for the rest of his team to arrive. 'There was a terrific noise going on outside. I sensed the ship was zigzagging, making it even harder for the rest of my boarding team to land safely. I got back out on deck to join up with them so we could advance on the wheelhouse. But out on the deck the opposition had strengthened.'

When Pearce came out of the cabin he heard the thud of boots hitting the deck as the other boarders landed. A can flew past his helmet. Teenager Aviva Porat picked up another tin and threw it, shouting, 'Down with the British Empire!'

Further along the deck Mordechai Rosemont moved among his group, calmly telling them only to throw their potatoes or tins when they were certain of hitting a target.

Suddenly *Exodus* rocked from side to side after it was rammed by

HMS *Childers*, the sound of steel striking hull resounding throughout the ship.

Nat Nadler grabbed his hosepipe and continued to aim a jet of steam at the regrouping boarders. Two of them fell, but Lieutenant Pearce motioned them to their feet and led them towards their first target, the wheelhouse.

Standing in the radio room of HMS *Childers*, Lieutenant Commander Bailey ordered the radioman to alert the task force that *Exodus* was heading for the Egyptian coast. He ordered HMS *Ajax* to block her passage and the other destroyers to close up on her and try to force her to stop. HMS *Charity* was to return to its position alongside *Exodus* and launch a further boarding party to support a second team that would be launched from HMS *Chequers*.

In that night of sudden terror memories began to be sown. Passengers like Yosef Reich, who had gone to sleep believing that when he next saw daylight he would be that much closer to Palestine, had awakened 'to the sound of shooting. People started to cry and panic. We thought we were going to die.'

From his vantage point on the top deck, Dr Cohen realised that if the battle continued much longer his small medical team could be swamped. 'I knew that some of the wounded would probably have to be treated where they fell. The more serious needed to be carried by their friends or the crew to the hospital. But luckily the fight was going in phases. The boarders could only push forward under the continuous fusillade of tins and potatoes. The sounds of shots continued and I realised that we faced being overwhelmed.'

The sound of gunfire that Dr Cohen and other passengers heard was caused by the Chinese firecrackers that Pearce had ordered his boarders to light and toss into the superstructure.

Zvi Tiroche decided that the most effective forms of resistance at his disposal were the cans of fruit and jets of steam some of the crew were directing. 'It was a sight you don't forget. Not ever.'

The indefatigable Reverend Grauel, having once more checked that Fira and the children and others were safe, made his way back to the radio shack to translate the order that Ben-Gurion had earlier sent. Around him the sound of fighting had intensified. 'The boarders were throwing tear-gas grenades and the acrid stench filled my lungs and brought tears to my eyes.' Reaching the shack, he noted that the wall clock showed an hour had passed since the attack had started.

The crew would also have their lasting memories of that first hour of action. For Nat Nadler it was the loudspeakers of HMS *Childers*. 'A voice kept saying "Give up. You don't have a chance." We responded by playing Elgar's "March of Pomp and Circumstance" over our PA system.'

The towering figure of helmsman Bill Millman recalled shouting, 'Come on, you Limeys. We are ready for you.'

Deckhand Dov Mills would later write: 'My memory is of the repeated ramming. I felt as if we were going to be split open. And all the time the British were throwing smoke bombs and tear-gas bombs. The commotion, smoke and stench were overpowering.'

Pearce's 15 boarders found themselves fighting foot by foot to gain control of the upper deck and reach the wheelhouse. From below came the cries of terror. In his official report to the Admiralty Pearce would recall: 'The bombardment of tins proved too heavy so we entered a cabin on the port side. I got separated and I found myself alone in a cabin with tins, potatoes and bottles coming through the window. The remainder of my boarding party entered a cabin aft, full of women and children. An American shouted my men had five seconds in which to come on deck, threatening to kill them if they did not obey him.'

The boarders fought their way out of the cabin and back on deck. Their advance on the wheelhouse continued.

Lieutenant Pearce realised that *Exodus* had changed course and increased speed and was now heading southeast. He had briefly wondered if that was the reason why the fighting on deck had intensified, to drive him and his boarders overboard before they reached whatever was the ship's new destination. But there was still some way to go to reach the wheelhouse and for his team to cut their way through its protective barbed wire; only then could he stop the ship's course. The top deck itself was slippery with oil pouring from one of the hosepipes, while the fusillade of potatoes and tins continued.

Pearce ordered his men to release yet more Chinese firecrackers to simulate gunfire. But one of the defenders had doused them with a steam hose. What shocked Pearce was how young some of the attackers were. 'Little more than kids, hurling anything they had to hand. There were young women as well, hurling abuse as they threw.'

In the glare of her searchlight, the lieutenant saw that HMS *Charity* was once more sailing alongside and more boarders were jumping from her platform.

Beyond, in the gathering dawn, HMS *Ajax* surged ahead to block *Exodus*'s progress and the rest of the task force was closing up to stop any attempt by her to switch course. Pearce knew that effectively the ship was surrounded and that any captain concerned about his passengers would 'recognise the game was up'.

But *Exodus* surged on and the fighting grew fiercer.

Having broadcast the decoded message from Ben-Gurion, Reverend Grauel continued: '*Exodus* has been rammed by destroyers of the British Navy. They are still here. Other warships are all around us, trying to crush us into surrender. Only the skills of our captain and crew have stopped them from sinking us.'

Another loud shudder of metal striking metal came as HMS *Childers* once more rammed *Exodus*. The terrified screams of women and children increased.

On the upper deck seaman Frank Levine used a hosepipe to douse another salvo of Chinese firecrackers. Beside him Aviva Porat threw another potato at Pearce's men. It was brushed aside by an arm shield. Beside Aviva a more powerful arm drew back and, with unerring aim, sent a sailor staggering. Gertruda had scored her first hit in the battle with a tin. As potatoes and tins continued to rain down on the boarders, some of them slipped, victims of the oil Nat Nadler and others had used to coat the deck. Back on their feet, the boarders continued to advance.

From his vantage point, Dr Cohen saw a defender fall, a man

struck by a baton. The boarders stepped over him, using their weapons to club and push their way towards the wheelhouse. Dr Cohen and his nurses rushed to bring the passenger to the hospital; he was bleeding profusely from a head wound which required stitching. From below came the sound of splintering wood as one of the boarders smashed open a door leading into the super-structure. Above was the wheelhouse. Lieutenant Pearce led the way into the ship.

On the bridge, Ike had studied the deployment of the task force. HMS *Ajax* was positioned so that any attempt to pass the cruiser would almost certainly result in *Exodus* being rammed. But he had spotted a possibility. The other destroyers had left large gaps between while they were manoeuvring.

Ike ordered the strapping Millman to resume the ship's original course and called down to the engine room over the voice-pipe: 'Give me absolute full speed.'

The steering wheel began to spin in the helmsman's powerful hands as *Exodus* created an arc in the water. Like a fox shaking off its pursuers, the blockade-runner sped away from HMS *Charity*, swept past HMS *Ajax* and moved into a gap between two more destroyers. Only HMS *Childers* managed to continue in pursuit. The sheer skill and speed of the manoeuvre astonished Lieutenant Commander Bailey.

Knowing he had only minutes to stop *Exodus* escaping, he raised the loudspeaker to his mouth. 'Captain of *Warfield*. You will now cease all resistance, stop your engine and prepare to be towed into Haifa. You are now in the territorial waters of Palestine.'

Ike's pent-up fury exploded: 'You are a liar! We are in interna-tional waters. You are committing an act of piracy for which Britain will have to answer before the United Nations.'

Bailey ordered his destroyers to ram *Exodus* once more. In that same moment, hoisted by Yossi, a blue-and-white flag bearing the Star of David rose up the mast as the ship shuddered again under the impact of the ramming. It was followed by the haunting sound of voices singing the 'Hatikvah'. Joining in, Yosef Reich felt, 'There was nothing else we could do. The British were shooting and we were singing.'

By the time HMS *Charity* had once more regained its position alongside *Exodus* and the other destroyers were closing up, shepherded by HMS *Ajax*, Bailey had ordered HMS *Childers* to ram *Exodus* twice more. Seamen on the destroyer hurled smoke bombs and tear-gas grenades across the narrow gap of water into the blockade-runner.

On board the upper deck Nat Nadler handed out more weapons to the defenders as supplies of potatoes and tins dwindled, replacing them with rescue flares he had taken from the lifeboats and rafts. He showed the defenders how to light them, then count to three, before hurling them at the boarders. A trail of sparks would explode against their gas masks. Roars of pain followed the impact of the flares and the eye-smarting fumes from the gas grenades and smoke bombs as the deck became obscured by a choking yellowish fog. Through it staggered the defenders pursued by the boarders. And as the battle for control raged, the shouts of Zvi Tiroche, Mordechai Rosemont and Noah Klieger could be heard, rallying their groups and ordering those who were injured to get medical aid.

The smoke had drifted into the hospital and Dr Cohen had ordered his nurses to wear face masks as they went about their work. 'Many of the casualties were head wounds, some of them pretty bad. When they had been sewn and bandaged, they were laid in a row on the deck and one of them started to sing softly and others joined in.'

The fighting grew more savage. A crewman, Arthur Ritzer, snatched a carbine from a boarder and pulled its trigger. The mechanism jammed. Ritzer used the gun to club the sailor. Aviva and Gertruda continued to throw tins. One smashed the eyepiece of a boarder's gas mask. Bottles, oars from the lifeboats and buckets of boiling water were used in running battles.

From behind the bridge Lieutenant MacPherson and his team from HMS *Childers* fought to gain control. Bill Bernstein and half a dozen crew equipped with crowbars and fire axes had been placed there by Ike to stop any attempt to capture it.

It was not until shortly before 4am that Lieutenant Pearce and his men finally reached the wheelhouse. It had been a battle all the way, through air thick with smoke and a continuous hail of missiles, mostly from women passengers, some middle-aged, who hurled bottles, cups, plates and cutlery while spitting and shouting abuse. The boarders had fended off the attacks as best they could in the narrow gangway. But the further they advanced the harder they found it to obey Pearce's order to keep retaliation to a minimum against the passengers, as even spittle spattered against their gas masks and children tried to trip them up. For Pearce: 'Frankly we had not expected such resistance. It was like going through a gauntlet of hatred.'

Bill Millman, his muscles glistening with sweat from his spell at the helm, had gone in search of Nat Nadler. It would be the first time that the two friends had joined forces since the battle had started. Both shared a passion for boxing. With an honourable discharge after the war, he had volunteered to join the Haganah and sail on an Aliyah Bet ship. Captain Ash had chosen him for *Exodus*. He had only one thing in common with his namesake Dave Millman, who had joined the crew shortly before Bill. Both had full beards.

Nadler and Millman had stood side by side at the burial at sea of the young mother, another moment which had imprinted itself on the young electrician's mind: 'As the body slipped into the ocean I had held the flag on her shroud to stop it from falling into the ocean. As I carried the flag up to the bridge tears ran down my face.'

Now, as he stood with Millman on the top deck, their mood was one of determination. Rushing on deck were two boarders. 'Bill didn't hesitate. He grabbed one by the throat and crotch and moved to throw him over the side. The other guy took out his revolver, a .38 Webley, and the guy Bill was holding shouts, "Shoot him! Shoot him." He shot Bill in his jaw. The bullet went into his chin, then into his shoulder. Then I was clubbed in the eye.'

Both men were carried to the hospital, where Dr Cohen tended them. While he stitched up Millman, the helmsman had turned to Nadler and yelled, 'We really showed them, Nadler, didn't we? I said,

"Yeah, look at you, you big schmuck!" His whole head was bandaged. The doctor had also done a good job on mine. But I couldn't just lie there while I could hear the fighting going on. I shouted, "The British still don't have control of the ship." So I am off to help stop them.'

Nat Nadler staggered from the hospital to join the fighting once more.

Smashing open the wheelhouse door, the boarders braced themselves for an even more violent assault and stopped in astonishment. While the fighting raged in and around the bridge, the wheelhouse was empty and brightly lit by one of the searchlights on HMS *Charity*.

Pearce went to the port-side window. Below on the deck hand-to-hand fighting continued, while only yards away, level with the wheelhouse, was the bridge of HMS *Childers*, its helmsman at the wheel. The lieutenant turned to the unmanned steering wheel of *Exodus*. While the ship continued to surge through the water, the experienced navigator knew why. The enunciator, the mechanism which linked the wheel to the engine room and rudder, had been disconnected. Pearce knew the ship was being controlled from an emergency steering wheel, positioned most likely at the stern above the rudder. To steer from there required skilled seamanship.

Leaving the other boarders to defend the wheelhouse, the lieutenant took two of his men with him to locate the emergency wheel, which would be the only way he could gain control over *Exodus*.

Daniel Feinstein had been the last passenger to board *Exodus* at Sète. He had been told by Bill Bernstein, the first mate, that he would have to sleep on the deck with the crew, as all the bunks were taken. He was given a space on the promenade deck. It was no hardship for the child orphan from the ghetto, who had collected bodies in a concentration camp for burial and survived a winter-long trek to a DP camp, where he was inspired by Ben-Gurion's words to go to Palestine. The 15-year-old was a worldly-wise and wiry youth with an easy smile and fearless gaze. In many ways Daniel resembled Ike and he had caught the captain's attention. The pair had bonded after Daniel, pointing at Ike's cap, asked if he was the son of the captain.

Ike grinned and replied, 'I am the captain.' Since then, when Ike did his daily rounds, he had always singled out Daniel for a chat. He was like an elder brother.

Daniel had been on the promenade deck, near the stern, when Lieutenant Pearce and his men boarded. From then on Daniel had been in the thick of the battle. Tears running down his face from gas grenades, his body hit with steel-tipped batons, he had fought back. More than once he fell to the deck under the force of the ship being rammed. Each time he was back on his feet, waiting for a new target to come within range, when Ike came running past. He motioned for Daniel to follow and posted him on the stern deck, telling him to shout out when a destroyer was approaching on another ramming run. Then the captain stood behind the emergency steering wheel and began to guide *Exodus* forward.

The battle for control of the bridge continued. Bill Bernstein grabbed a fire extinguisher and began to spray the boarders with foam. Suddenly the mate collapsed, his skull split open with a truncheon, its spike embedded in his head before a sailor ripped it out, sending blood gushing over the deck.

Murray Aronoff, a burly New Yorker, seized the boarder's carbine and fired; the shot lodged in the roof. The deckhand grabbed the barrel and used its butt as a club, forcing several of the boarders to withdraw. Meanwhile, Millman and Yossi had carried Bernstein into Ike's cabin and laid him on the captain's bunk. Yossi told Millman to stay with Bernstein and ran to find Dr Cohen.

Below deck, Sol Lester, a small US army-trained commando, had picked up a tear-gas canister and rammed it into the gas mask of a boarder, smashing its visor, leaving him screaming that he couldn't see. Lester took the man's axe and went in search of another target. Near the hospital, Yossi grabbed a boarder by the seat of his overalls and threw him to the deck, ripping off his gas mask before running on to reach Dr Cohen. The physician explained: 'Yossi, we've got all kinds of wounds, gunshot wounds and deep cuts from axes. Truncheon blows have opened a man's cheekbones and smashed a woman's hand. We need blood for transfusion. We need everything.

All I have are some very gutsy nurses, trying to do the impossible.'

When Yossi told him what had happened to Bernstein, Dr Cohen grabbed a tray of instruments, then ran with Yossi to Ike's cabin and stood at the bedside. Millman and Yossi instinctively drew back, silent and watchful, while Dr Cohen checked for vital signs. He had lost count down the years of how many times he had done those checks, so that he could decide how long he would have custody over the dying. Bernstein's pupils were dulled. Part of his brain had trickled out on his scalp. Nothing could save the mate.

Dr Cohen recalled: 'I could not be certain what weapon had been used. But it had broken his skull completely open. His death was not from a gunshot wound but a hatchet blow.' Beyond the silent cabin the sound of fighting was even louder. Dr Cohen gently closed Bernstein's eyes and turned to Yossi and Millman: 'He's gone.'

The doctor drew up the sheet and covered the helmsman's face. He turned and hurried from the cabin. Yossi and Millman followed, back into the world where they could help. Bill Bernstein had fulfilled his premonition that he would die before dawn.

Nat Nadler had rejoined the fighting, leading a group of Mordechai Rosemont's teenagers in their defence of the hurricane deck. It was filled with mothers and children who had emerged from below deck and were being pushed by a boarder up against the rails. For Nat: 'The fighting was no quarter given. I grabbed the sailor by his helmet strap to try and choke him and eventually got him off the deck. I could see the fear in his eyes when I ripped off his gas mask. He had probably never been in a fight like this. He was just a kid, maybe 17, 18 at the most. But we were desperate to protect our women and children.'

In the gathering daylight the battle raged throughout *Exodus*. The balustrade on what had once been the elegant staircase in the main salon was wrenched off by Sol Lester, using the axe he had snatched from the boarder. He chopped the wood into club-sized lengths and distributed them among the passengers. As he would recall: 'We fought the boarders with anything we could lay our hands on – cans of corned beef, signal rockets we took from the life rafts, nuts and bolts from the engine room, anything we could get our hands on.'

Yossi had given Gerald Landau, a passenger, a task once he had come on board at Sète, assigning him to keep a friendly eye on a group of younger children. Many were barely in their teens, orphans who needed his skills to keep them occupied. His years working on a Haganah training farm in the English countryside of Kent had taught Gerald to mix good humour with patience and discipline.

When the battle started they had been forbidden by Yossi to take part in the fighting. But Gerald had found them a role to play when he set up on the ship's sundeck a distribution point for a stockpile of potatoes and tins of food. The boys were told to carry the ammunition down to the top deck, where one of the group leaders would be waiting to send them straight back up to the sundeck. Instead, some of the boys and girls had joined in the throwing, hiding behind the life rafts to do so.

The fair-haired Zvi Yakubovich had survived Buchenwald and had become a popular figure on board, with his devil-may-care attitude and his crystal-clear singing voice which had always encouraged the others to join in. As the fighting increased Gerald ordered the children not to go down the deck. But in the darkness Zvi had slipped away to see his new friend, Daniel Feinstein. Unwilling to leave the rest of the group unguarded, Gerald could do no more than wait for Zvi to return, when he would reprimand him.

Zvi Yakubovich remained sheltered behind a life raft, waiting for the moment when he could run the few yards across the deck and get back to the sundeck. Beside him was Mordechai Baumstein, a 23-year-old who had befriended Zvi. Further back at the stern, Zvi could see the crouched figure of Daniel Feinstein. It was still dark in the lee of the battered ship's superstructure. From within came the sound of shouting, but out on deck the fighting had all but stopped.

Zvi stood up and began to move. Close behind followed Mordechai. Suddenly there was a burst of gunfire and Zvi and Mordechai fell, mortally wounded. The boarder had disappeared.

Running out of the superstructure came one of Dr Cohen's nurses. She knelt beside each body and shouted for help. The identity of the sailor who had shot Zvi and Mordechai would never be discovered.

Daniel Feinstein recalled he was in the stern when he saw the killing: 'I saw the British kill the boy. I was maybe no more than five metres from Zvi. A nurse was looking after him, shouting, "He's alive." Then she stopped and cried, "No, he is not. He is dead. We cannot give him first aid." People, passengers, were calling out for the shooting to stop. But for Zvi it was too late. I don't know why he was shot. He wasn't armed. He was just there and he was shot.'

Lieutenant Pearce and his two boarders had been forced to move slowly as they made their way towards the stern, from where, he was certain, *Exodus* was now being steered.

Below, the stench in the gangways was overpowering and the dim lighting made it hard to see ahead. Shadowy figures, mostly elderly men, women and children, screamed and spat at Pearce and his men before retreating back into their quarters. Every time the ship was rammed the thunderous crash was louder than on deck and created further fear and panic around Pearce. There were shouts for the boarders to be taken prisoners. Recognising the danger, the lieutenant raised his baton and ordered passengers out of the way, his voice calm but firm. The last thing he wanted was a repetition of the fight to reach the wheelhouse.

The further Pearce and his men advanced towards the stern, cabin doors suddenly opened and either a passenger or a crewman appeared and threw potatoes and tin cans before slamming shut the door. At other times crew members appeared in the gangway, wielding navy batons that Pearce guessed they must have taken from other boarding teams. When he drew his revolver it was enough to force the crewmen to retreat. But the attacks soon resumed and the lieutenant and his men found themselves forced to take shelter in a cabin. It was filled with tins, sacks of potatoes and bottles. From the gangway an American voice ordered them to come out. Pearce demanded to know who was speaking.

'I am a minister of the cloth. You are safe.'

Revolver in hand, Pearce opened the door. Facing him was Reverend Grauel. He told the lieutenant he would be escorted to his own cabin, where he and the two boarders would be safe. Not knowing whether to believe him or not, Pearce and his men followed Grauel back down the corridor.

Waiting in his cabin were two crewmen. Each bore a concentration camp number on his arm and held a steel pole in his hand. The minister explained to them they were to guard 'our prisoners but under no circumstances must they come to any harm'.

Reverend Grauel would recall: 'The officer didn't look afraid. He looked at my American flag badge on my sleeve. I told him I was a news correspondent. He nodded and said that maybe when this was over they could all go to America.'

From the deck above came the sound of gunfire. Pearce knew this time he was not listening to Chinese firecrackers but to a rifle.

Helmsman Cyril Weinstein, who took turns steering with Bill Millman, had made his way down to Ike at the stern wheel. The captain, stripped to his vest, his face stained with sweat and grime, had only his physical strength and incredible determination to help him. The wheel's magnetic compass had ceased to function and his own hand-held compass offered limited guidance for him to remain on course. Weinstein was using his own brute strength to turn the wheel and keep *Exodus* surging towards Palestine, while Ike had gone forward to see what was happening.

During the night the destroyers had taken turns to come racing across the water to try and ram *Exodus*. Almost every time, Weinstein managed to spin the wheel to escape. In the engine room chief engineer Frank Stanczak, though a devout Catholic Pole, was cursing fluently in Hebrew as he tried to coax even more speed from his boilers.

In the growing daylight Bernard Marks, the second mate, and Yossi Harel made their way to Dr Cohen's hospital, walking through the promenade-deck housing, which had been split open, leaving timber bulkheads shredded as if they had gone through a gigantic sawmill. The cedar dance floor had been torn up to be used by some of the crew for weapons. Doors had been ripped off, windows were shattered and entire sections of walls sagged. Through a gaping hole in the superstructure, they could see the task force. For Marks, they were 'like wolves circling for a kill'.

Yossi and Bernard could only stand and watch as Dr Cohen skilfully performed his work, knowing there was nothing they could do, marvelling at what was being achieved. Everyone seemed to need immediate attention in the crowded deck space. The doctor had placed in one corner the more seriously wounded, the most exhausted, those in fear of death and those in so much pain they cried out to die. The wounded included several of the boarders.

One boarder had been scalded by a hosepipe, which had burned his hands and part of his face when the steam penetrated his gas mask. For Abe Lippschitz: 'He looked like he had been fried and roasted. His eyelashes and eyebrows had gone and his eyes were filled with terrible pain.' The pharmacist had squeezed some ointment over the burns, knowing that no matter how gentle he was he could not stop the man's agony.

Dr Cohen beckoned to Yossi and Bernard and explained the sailor needed to be in a hospital burns unit. 'I told them there were six other people seriously wounded who would not survive unless they also got full medical help. My prime and only concern was saving my patients. I said we must ask the British for help.'

Yossi said he would go and find Ike and discuss the matter. He knew that the savage manner of Bill Bernstein's death and the shooting of Zvi Yakubovich and Mordechai Baumstein had stunned a number of the American crew. More than one had told Yossi they had not expected such killings.

On his way to find Ike, Yossi had stopped at the radio shack to order Enava Barak to contact the Haganah in Tel Aviv, only to be told that radio contact with Tel Aviv had been interrupted shortly after the battle had started. Yossi told the radioman to keep trying to send the message that the constant ramming had damaged not only the hull but also the upper deck along with the superstructure. In

Yossi's view: 'While the British had yet to gain control of the ship, it would now only be a matter of time. So many of our people had been beaten and bruised and choked by smoke and tear gas. Dr Cohen's judgement on the critical condition of the injured convinced me we had to get help – even if that meant surrendering.'

By daylight Lieutenant MacPherson, the senior naval officer on *Exodus*, had three more boarding parties ready to go into action, a total of a further 60 well-trained sailors. They were led by Lieutenant Gill (HMS *Childers*), Lieutenant R.B.W. Bundle (HMS *Cheviot*) and Lieutenant K.P. Swallow (HMS *Chequers*). While the others had leapt from the platforms, Swallow and his team had managed to scramble aboard when their destroyer had slammed into the side of *Exodus*.

The teams made a concerted rush to the bridge, where MacPherson had set up his command post. He ordered the newcomers to overpower the crew and passengers below deck. Within minutes they had recovered Lieutenant Pearce and his two boarders and freed them to rejoin the fight.

Gasping from smoke, Lieutenant Swallow sent one of his men back to the bridge to report that more boarders were needed. The request was transmitted by Lieutenant MacPherson's radioman to HMS *Childers*.

Three of the boarders had already had their life jackets snatched, and two had had their overalls doused with oily waste, though an attempt to ignite it failed. From a cabin a woman had hurled a bag filled with faeces at a boarder.

On the promenade deck, Reverend Grauel and Gerald Landau crouched beside a bucket and doused pieces of cloth in cold coffee to swab the inflamed eyes of a growing number of children affected by tear gas. When supplies of cloth ran low, a woman ripped up pieces of her underslip.

Meanwhile, Ike had reached the radio shack to find that its transmitter was back on air. After he had learned about Yossi's message, Ike ordered Enava Barak to send the Haganah a message in his name: 'We continue to resist.'

For Ike: 'Only a seaman in a situation like we were could know the meaning of that. In Yossi's mind *Exodus* would sink before she reached the shore. I knew she wouldn't. Everyone on board was fighting for the ultimate right to exist. So, people got injured and killed. That is what happens when you seek independence. I absolutely believed my passengers wanted me to go on and bring them to that beach near Tel Aviv.'

Those words symbolised Ike's own passionate belief that resistance held an important part in the life of every Jew. As he made his way to the hospital to check on the number of casualties, he assumed that his crew and passengers shared his view that surrender was unthinkable.

Chapter 17

Floating Concentration Camps

Within the Haganah leadership in Tel Aviv a different plan had already taken shape: they intended to use the battle on board *Exodus* as a political lever.

The United Nations Special Committee on Palestine (UNSCOP) had arrived in the country, its 11 members charged with recommending a solution to the Palestine problem. While there were three Muslim, or partly Muslim, states on the committee – Iran, India and Yugoslavia – there were no Arab or Great Power members. David Ben-Gurion feared that the Muslim members, along with two former members of the British Empire, Canada and Australia, would continue to support London and oppose raising the number of immigrants. Then unexpectedly the Soviet Union, whose policy had been pro-Arab but remained firmly anti-British, had suddenly declared its support for the Jews. Its Foreign Minister, Andrei Gromyko, told the United Nations: 'We must not forget their exceptional and indescribable sorrow and suffering during the Holocaust and the pain the survivors faced as displaced persons wanting to get home since then. They are at least entitled to that.'

Moscow's support for Jewish self-determination was seen by David Ben-Gurion and the Haganah leadership as an opening to influence UNSCOP and began to plan accordingly. Three key members of the Jewish Agency's Political Department were attached to the committee as 'guides': Aubrey (Abba) Eban, David Horowitz and the Spanish-speaking Moshe Tov.

Palestinian Arab leaders had greeted the arrival of UNSCOP with a one-day strike and its leaders, led by the Mufti of Jerusalem, refused to answer questions. Paul Mohn, the deputy chairman of the committee, observed: 'In Beersheba Arab teachers continued with their lessons when we entered classrooms and the pupils were ordered not to look at us. In Ramla we were greeted only by children who cursed us. No adult leaders would see us.'

By contrast, the Jewish Agency warmly greeted UNSCOP, often with flowers and cheering crowds. At meals each committee member was carefully placed next to a settler who spoke his language. In a meeting Ben-Gurion set out a persuasive case for creating a Jewish state from the whole of Palestine, but even agreed to discuss partition, in which part of the country would become a Jewish state while the remainder could be united with Jordan, adding, 'Separating the Jews and Arabs will lead to fertile cooperation between the two nations.'

After the meeting one of the Haganah men who followed the committee everywhere reported that a delegate had said, 'What asses those Arabs are. This country is so beautiful and, if given to the Jews, it could be developed and turned into a new Europe.'

The attack on *Exodus* had immediately been seen by Ben-Gurion as offering a political lever that could clinch UNSCOP's growing support for a Jewish state. Certainly, the closer *Exodus* came to Palestine, the greater would become the determination of the task force to capture it and the more aggressive its tactics. The British government would find it increasingly hard to claim that its actions were within the law. This would provide further news copy for the growing number of reporters arriving in Palestine to cover the story. Within UNSCOP the feeling grew that even if *Exodus* was forced to surrender, it would symbolise the sheer brutality of Bevin's policies. Ben-Gurion was not the only strategist in Tel Aviv who realised that Ernest Bevin would be forced into a corner by his own obsession to keep immigration under his control.

From the bridge of HMS *Childers*, Lieutenant Commander Bailey followed the battle. Four hours after it had started the fighting continued unabated. He caught glimpses of figures falling to the deck and struggling to their feet, but he could not be certain if they were boarders, immigrants or members of the *Exodus* crew. The only certainty was that the intensity of the battle meant the objectives he had given to Pearce and MacPherson had not yet been fulfilled.

Exodus's erratic course reminded Bailey of the zigzagging pattern of wartime convoys trying to avoid U-boats. He marvelled at the desperate attempt to shake off pursuit. After the blockade-runner had completed another evasive pattern, Bailey ordered a further ramming attack. Three times he had ordered one since the boarding team had landed Pearce's team on the upper deck. He had glimpsed the lieutenant leading his team up towards the bridge area. But since then there had been no further sighting of the officer. Shortly afterwards Bailey had spotted a man holding a hosepipe on the upper deck spraying what looked like oil, which he thought might explain why people had fallen in the darkness. But there was no way of telling when the searchlights were switched off before a ramming run. The attacks alternated between his own destroyer and HMS *Charity* on the port side.

Ramming under the prevailing conditions – the darkness, a choppy sea and the bursts of dazzling searchlights – made it difficult to judge the right angle of approach and speed. There was also the fusillade of tin cans to cope with every time HMS *Childers* came within range.

On board *Exodus*, Enava Barak and Harold Leidner took it in turns in the radio shack to note down the incoming coded messages from Tel Aviv, translate them and run with them to the bridge. One was the text of a message the Haganah High Command wanted them to send to Emil Sandstrom, the head of UNSCOP. It was to be transmitted word for word in open text. The sender explained that it would have more impact if it appeared to come directly from *Exodus* and was sent in the name of its captain.

It read: 'Dear Sir, we implore you to arrange to take the testimony of 4,500 refugees and our suffering at the efforts we are making to reach the safety of our homeland. Witness for yourself the cold-heartedness of the British as they try to expel us from the shores of our homeland in order to incarcerate us behind barbed wire in concentration camps which cannot but remind us all the time of those concentration camps we were interred in during the days of the Nazis in Europe.'

Ike was surprised by the text but agreed to send the message in his name. Yossi said nothing and took the response to the radio shack. Minutes later came a second coded message from the Haganah. *Exodus* was to set course for the beach at Kiryat Chaim, north of Haifa. Ike was even more surprised. The proposed landing site was close to where the Palestine Patrol was based. From beyond the locked door of the radio shack the sounds of fighting grew louder.

Before yet another ramming attack the searchlights had given Bailey and his bridge officer a clear view of the stiff opposition the boarders were facing around the *Exodus*'s wheelhouse. On its deck some of the migrants were also using a familiar technique: men hiding behind women, exploiting the standing Palestine Patrol order that unless it was absolutely essential no woman or child must be manhandled.

As the battle continued Bailey had another problem to consider. Having placed HMS *Childers* and HMS *Chequers* on either side of *Exodus*, hoping to reduce the area *Exodus* had for its zigzag steering tactics, he had increased the possibility that the continuous ramming would result in *Exodus* suddenly turning to ram one of the destroyers. Given the damage the two destroyers had already done to the blockade-runner's hull, *Exodus* might well attempt such a manoeuvre. Bailey's experience of dealing with other such ships had shown that Jews who had survived the concentration camps were willing to resist any opposition to travel to Palestine. The reports from Lieutenant MacPherson had begun to describe how storming parties were being driven back, how a baton charge had scattered under a hail of tin cans and shards of broken window glass were being used as weapons to slash at boarders:

03.34. Scale of fighting heavier. Immigrants using 12-foot iron scaffolding poles, crowbars, hosepipes, coshes, sticks. More boarders injured.

04.00. Distress flares (American) produced fierce flames and smoke. Mostly thrown by youths on upper deck.

04.10. Second *Childers* storming party arrives to help defend wheelhouse citadel. One badly injured and six boarders with lesser injuries.

04.15. Fighting so heavy boarding party forced to join first team in cabin. Immigrants attempting to smash through deck head.

04.18. *Childers* boarding platform so severely damaged unable to be further used.

05.02. Three boarders (Petty Officers Fyann, Green and Moreton) overpowered and their guns taken. Moreton badly injured and semi-conscious.

05.15. Lieutenants Stein, Pearce and Swallow led boarding party to capture Engine Room, Boiler Room and Steering Compartment. Doors of the Engine Room and Boiler Room are made of steel and firmly locked. The Steering Room is totally protected by barbed wire. Boarders have no alternative but to make their way back to the wheelhouse.

05.20. Boarders forced to take shelter in cabin full of immigrant women and children. Petty Officer Harris attempts to dress severe head wounds of small girl.

06.00. Lieutenant MacPherson, two petty officers and nine boarders successfully drove off further attempt to retake wheelhouse.

At 6.15am the radioman transmitted Lieutenant MacPherson's report that on the upper deck resistance was fading. However,

Bailey's relief was short-lived when a further update revealed that the fighting continued below deck.

From there came the sound of splintering wood as bunks were turned into weapons. Fumes from tear-gas grenades and smoke bombs drifted upwards after being thrown down into the bowels of the ship, followed by the panic-stricken screams for the fighting to stop.

Zvi Tiroche had led his group of teenagers down below and told them to help anyone who needed assistance. Among them were women in various stages of pregnancy. Others were nursing babies who had been born during the night. Stripped to their underwear, they cuddled and suckled their newborn. Zvi had not heard one complaint about the stench and the thunderous sounds of another ramming.

Around the mothers exhausted men, women and children slept. Others lay in their bunks but joined in the singing. Noah Klieger had found a bottle of water to encourage the cantor to continue to sing, his deep voice reaching to the bunks furthest from where he stood, hands clasped, sweat running down his face.

In another part of the ship Mordechai Rosemont held his group in thrall with one story after another; usually rumbustious teenagers sat in respectful silence, absorbing every word. Stripped to his waist, he revealed his whole life with his words.

With no more tins left to throw, Gertruda had returned from the upper deck to join Michael in the hold. She had saved for him one last tin of fruit from among those she had been hurling at the boarders and now she sat stroking his hair as he sipped the pineapple juice. For Michael it was the best drink he had swallowed in hours. 'She told me about the fight up top. How she had stood eye to eye and thrown and thrown. When I looked at all the others around us I thought how lucky I was. I had Gertruda. There was nobody like her on the boat.'

She hugged him, like mother and son, and Michael felt secure just being close to her. Nearby a woman had cried out that a white flag should be raised. But no one was ready to provide a white cloth.

A gentle voice called out, 'No one surrenders now we are so close to home.'

The question of surrender would become a topic of discussion in Dr Cohen's hospital after Ike arrived there from the steering wheel at the stern. He found himself stepping around wounded patients, many with head and facial injuries, more than he had expected, and their condition shocked him. Reverend Grauel, who had brought water from the galley for the wounded, saw that Ike was close to tears.

This was his first command and there were those in the Haganah who had expressed reservations about putting the slim, elfin-faced man in charge of such an important mission. But Saul Avigur had persuaded them that though Ike was only 22 years old he was the right choice. Ike had already demonstrated his skill when manoeuvring *Exodus* out of Sète harbour and during the voyage. His handling of the ship had only once been challenged. When he had ordered an increase in speed and Yossi had asked if it was really necessary to add to the passengers' seasickness, Reverend Grauel remembered how 'Ike had snapped and asked what did the passengers want? Coping with their sickness or ending up behind wire in a British concentration camp?'

Now, kneeling beside each patient, Ike expressed his concern at what they were suffering and promised they would soon be landing and in hospital. However, reaching the two injured boarders, he glanced at them and moved on. As Reverend Grauel recorded: 'What could Ike say? The wounded sailors were the result of what the British had done. You can't thank them for that. But I could see in Ike's face his concern that some of our injured could be close to death.'

In one corner lay the bodies of Zvi Yakubovich and Mordechai Baumstein, their faces covered with pieces of cloth. There had been no time to move them to Ike's cabin, where Bill Bernstein lay. Reverend Grauel wondered how many more would die among the hundred injured that lay on the deck or were propped against bulkheads, blood seeping through their bandages. To him the nurses 'were heroic beyond description. Their faces were spattered with blood and sweat.

Whatever was going on outside the hospital they reassured the wounded there was nothing to worry about. Their calm courage was a huge help. And there is only one word for Dr Cohen. Magnificent.'

Out on the deck, away from where the less seriously injured lay, Ike noticed Dr Cohen and Yossi in deep conversation and joined them. The physician asked the captain for his impression of what he had seen. Ike said that some of the cases looked very bad. Dr Cohen explained that five were so severely injured that they were unlikely to live another day unless they received blood transfusions – and he had no plasma or suitable equipment. The only place such things would be available was on the British ships.

Yossi interjected that almost certainly they would provide medical assistance if *Exodus* surrendered. Once more the three men stood in silence, considering the situation, then Dr Cohen said, 'From the medical standpoint surrender would be acceptable. Their ships will also have good doctors who could assist.'

Yossi gathered himself and when he spoke his voice had a new authority. Just as Ike had command of the ship, he was in charge of the safety and well-being of the passengers. From what he had heard and seen, surrender was no longer up for discussion – it was now a matter of urgency.

Ike's voice took on a sudden hardness. Why should they trust the British to honour any conditions of surrender? Their continuous ramming of the ship had terrorised the passengers. They had already murdered Bill Bernstein and two passengers. Meanwhile, *Exodus* was coming closer to its destination.

Yossi could not quite conceal his own anger. 'We will never reach there! There's been so much damage done already by their ramming that we could sink before that!'

Their raised voices fell silent as they stared at each other. Dr Cohen calmly intervened to say that only the lives of his patients mattered to him and if surrender was the best way to achieve that, so be it. Having made his position clear, he took a step back, leaving Ike and Yossi to continue to confront each other.

Ike gathered himself, his voice once more measured. He too

regarded it as his priority to save those patients. But in a few hours the ship would be closer to their landing beach. Then all the medical help they needed would be available. He could send a message to Tel Aviv to arrange that. Yossi asked Dr Cohen whether that would be too late. The doctor said it was a strong possibility. Perhaps someone should go to the British commander on board and inform him that the ship was ready to surrender in return for guarantees of urgent medical help.

Having distributed bottles of water, Reverend Grauel came out of the hospital to join the group. He agreed that surrender was the only option.

It was Ike who now broke the silence by reminding them that he had signed on as captain for a voyage to show that the British blockade could be broken. Such a triumph would resound around the world and mobilise public opinion in support of the right of all Jews to go to Palestine. To surrender now would undermine all the planning which had brought them so close to the landing beach.

Once more the silence stretched out between Ike and Yossi.

Yossi Reich was among the passengers who overheard the confrontation: 'Harel was not a sailor and he did not know anything about how ships are constructed. He was a man who was sent by the leadership and all kinds of people for whom we did have so much regard.'

A more moderate view came from Reverend Grauel: 'It was paramount that the ship reached shore as quickly as possible. I heard Yossi say that Ben-Gurion wanted people not bodies brought to Palestine. Water had begun to pour in through holes in the superstructure. We had the choice of asking for a ceasefire and surrendering, or continuing the struggle and reaching shore with the dead and wounded. Yossi's concern, along with Dr Cohen's and my own, made us decide in favour of a ceasefire.'

Standing on the deck outside the hospital, Ike was left out in the cold and, when the time came for him and Yossi to go into hiding, the captaincy would be handed over to Bernard Marks, who had already been made first mate to replace the dead Bill Bernstein. In

his own mind Ike 'was sure Yossi had already made his decision to
surrender before we spoke. I don't want to say any more. If he had
been a seaman he would not have pressed for that decision. He
thought the ship would sink under all the attacks. That did not
happen and would not happen. Yossi was a political figure. We all
cared about our passengers. But they would have wanted me to sail
on. I also had no doubt that I would have landed them all.'

Ike had sent for Marks and told him *Exodus* was going to surrender
and he was to become captain. The 24-year-old former US
Merchant Marine was a competent and respected officer who
scarcely looked his age.

Controversy continues to surround the surrender of *Exodus*. Neither
Ike nor Yossi, right up to the latter's death in 2009, would discuss
the subject that had affected their relationship for years. Clearly, they
were both brave, dedicated men, born leaders. Ike, the ship's captain
and a highly skilled and experienced sailor, always felt that he could
have landed the ship. Yossi, his commander and, at 29, a veteran of
the Haganah, was likely to have been more attuned to the intricate
political chessboard whose players were in London and elsewhere,
more likely to have been privy to the thinking in Tel Aviv and to
have had the broader picture in mind. For each of them, it was an
agonising decision.

Certainly, the whole episode has led to a considerable amount of
speculation, including the claim by Stewart Menzies that the decision
to surrender was part of a well-orchestrated Haganah plot. The MI6
chief's well-known dislike of Jews led him to write a report in
September 1947 in which he asserted that the entire voyage had been
designed to embarrass Britain and hasten the formation of the State
of Israel. All the evidence suggests the Menzies report was no more
than an attempt to exploit *Exodus* for Britain's own use, as well as to
justify the attack on the ship.

From the bridge of HMS *Ajax*, Sir John Cunningham and the cruiser's
captain and senior officers, together with Surgeon Lieutenant

Commander Gaskell, the ship's doctor, studied *Exodus* in the morning light. No one could recall such damage to a blockade-runner. The rubbing strake around the hull hung loose in places, exposing the deep dent to the hull plates from the ramming. A large portion of the superstructure had also been smashed. Gaskell's main concern was to get aboard *Exodus* and begin to deal with what could be a serious medical emergency. Lieutenant Commander Bailey had radioed that the latest number of casualties on *Exodus* were 'well over 150'.

Reverend Grauel made his way along the passage in search of a senior naval officer to whom he could offer the ship's surrender. Suddenly a cabin door flew open and Murray Aronoff emerged, his eyes blazing with fury and clutching an axe in his hand. He screamed at Grauel, 'They are killing women and children! That's what they are doing! Killing them! So I am going to kill them, Rev!'

Down the corridor came three boarders, guns levelled. Reverend Grauel grabbed Aronoff's axe and handed it to one of the boarders: 'I explained that Aronoff was plainly upset at all that had been happening. I pointed to my armband with the American flag I'd sewn on, explaining I was a US citizen and a reporter for a religious newspaper and I wanted them to take me to their commander so that I could discuss surrender with him. They just looked at me hard for a moment then said I was to follow them.'

Minutes later Reverend Grauel stood face to face with Lieutenant MacPherson in the wheelhouse. From the deck below came the renewed shouting of Aronoff: 'The sons of bitches are shooting women and children! Babies are being drowned in the bilges! They are worse than the Nazis! They *are* the Nazis!'

Reverend Grauel firmly ordered Aronoff to be quiet. On the hurricane deck the fighting had resumed. The burly New Yorker fell silent. For a moment the naval lieutenant and the minister looked at each other. The sound of fighting had increased.

Reverend Grauel shouted, 'Stop! All of you, stop now!' Then he turned back to Lieutenant MacPherson and asked if he would give the same order to his boarders. The fighting stopped. Beyond, the task force circled, its decks lined with armed sailors. Lieutenant

MacPherson asked for the ship's captain to be brought to the wheelhouse.

Shortly afterwards Marks reached the wheelhouse and confirmed that he was the captain and would take the ship to Haifa. MacPherson said he would arrange for additional medical help. Marks rang up 'stop' on the engine-room telegraph. *Exodus* began to wallow in the water, surrounded by her captors.

In his destroyer's log, Lieutenant Commander Bailey noted the surrender had been accepted at 8am.

Over the loudspeaker system the new captain announced that the fighting had ended and shortly the navy would be sending a medical team on board.

Dr Cohen and Lieutenant MacPherson were waiting when the first team, led by Surgeon Lieutenant D.C.S. Bett, came on board from HMS *Chequers*. Shortly afterwards he was joined by Surgeon Lieutenant Commander Gaskell. As well as Gaskell and his three sick-bay attendants, including Geoff Glover, Bailey sent over another SBA. There were eight experienced doctors and nurses ready to help Dr Cohen as he led them to the hospital.

It was the team's first close look at the damage and, for Bett, it was 'a shock. There were huge holes in the superstructure and you could see men and women standing inside staring at us. The decks were littered with spent flares and smoke bombs.'

With the group were boarders ready to deal with any renewed fighting, but only shouts of anger from below caused the medical team to glance around uneasily. Dr Cohen explained it was simply fear that had provoked the reaction. Reaching the hospital, the navy doctors and nurses split up and moved from patient to patient, while Dr Cohen and his own staff explained their injuries.

The doctors held a brief meeting and agreed that the three boarders – two fracture cases and a burns injury among the by now 160 injured – would be treated by Bett. The more serious casualties would be dealt with by either Dr Cohen or the two navy doctors. Dr Cohen's nurses and the SBAs would treat the others. The two fatalities – Zvi Yakubovich and Mordechai Baumstein – would be carried by crewmen to join Bill Bernstein in the temporary morgue Ike's cabin had become. Gaskell explained to Dr Cohen that neither he nor Bett could perform surgery for severe head wounds as they had no specialist equipment with them, or on board the ships. Neurosurgery could be carried out only when they reached Haifa. Dr Cohen agreed.

By then steering control had been restored, once Marks had ordered Cyril Weinstein to come forward from the stern wheel and take over the steering from the wheelhouse. *Exodus* began to move slowly forward in the morning sea after Surgeon Lieutenant Commander Gaskell ordered its speed reduced to enable the medical team to work more easily.

In the meantime, Geoff Glover had been ordered to search for more wounded. Blinking in the gloom, the bespectacled young SBA picked his way further down into the ship. Sensing that the boarder at his elbow – assigned to be his escort – was nervous, he told the man to remove his gas mask and not use his cosh to intimidate any-one. Panic or confrontation was the last thing Glover wanted in the confined space below deck. Time and again he smiled at passengers, assuring them the fighting was over and he was only there to help.

It was only when he entered the superstructure and began his descent that the distinctive smell struck him. Anyone who joined the navy had to get used to the mix of engine oil, food and, for those who worked in the sick bay, chloroform and antiseptic, along with the body odour from scores of seamen sleeping in hammocks. But this was as if a cesspool had been emptied and was seeping up the steps, a sickening, eye-smarting stench that threatened to make him and his escort vomit.

Everywhere there was evidence of the battle: pieces of wood from broken bunks and empty bottles. Cabin doors had been ripped from their hinges and, when Glover opened those which were closed, he was confronted mostly by women and children who stared at him sullenly.

While the boarder watched, Glover rummaged in his backpack

and began to treat bruises and minor cuts with ointments and bandages. He had seen newsreel footage of prisoners released from Nazi concentration camps, but the people he looked at below deck were different. Two years after the end of the war, etched into their faces was all the pain of losing their family, their parents, everything. There was an empty look about so many of them, as if they had tried and failed to recall once-familiar faces, a look that aged them as if they had also tried to expunge other memories that one day, perhaps soon, would die with them. He realised he didn't know very much about the history of these people. Perhaps it was being expressed in the singing he had heard coming from somewhere else in the ship.

As Glover descended deeper into the ship he came across a group of children squatting round an elderly woman. She pointed to a number tattooed on her arm, standing out on her pale skin, explaining in halting English that she and the children had all been in Buchenwald. She motioned for Glover to leave; it had become a familiar gesture when he offered treatment. The medic wondered if their reaction was a legacy of the camps, where to ask for anything could lead to a beating, or even worse. Elsewhere, those who allowed him to help smiled gratefully and more than once cried as he tried to ease their pain.

Distributing his medicine and tablets, Glover saw that in places the gangways were smeared with faeces and the smell made him gag. More than once he sensed the anger his presence provoked, even when he patiently explained that he only wanted to help.

Freddie Kronenberg had been sent below by Dr Cohen to see if Glover and his escort needed help. Freddie recalled: 'God knows what they were expected to do down there. Checking them all would take hours. There were enough passengers who could need attention to fill a large hospital.'

Freddie stayed with Glover, acting as a translator. Finally, his backpack empty, the SBA made his way up on deck, breathing in the fresh air and wondering how much longer all those below would remain in such fetid conditions.

*

Immediately after his successful mediation Reverend Grauel had gone to the radio shack and sat before his microphone. In his sweat-stained shirt, with his crucifix glistening against his suntanned chest, his long blond hair plastered to his forehead and his blue eyes, he had the look of a medieval figure. His voice contained a combination of excitement and lucidity: 'This is John Stanley Grauel broadcasting live for the last time on the Voice of Israel from the *Haganah Ship Exodus*. Today we have survived attack by the might of the Royal Navy. On our deck are the dead, the dying and the wounded. But the rest of our 4,500 immigrants have survived to reach *Eretz Yisrael*. Though we have been compelled to sail to Haifa, we are coming home in triumph. Out of defeat has come victory.'

In the hospital, Surgeon Lieutenant Commander Gaskell and Surgeon Lieutenant Bett wrote a short case note and pinned it on each patient they treated. Many of them were teenagers who had, in Bett's words, 'Come off very much the worse yet were quite aggressive. But once they were treated and told we were going to Haifa they calmed down.' Seeing how low the medical supplies had become, Gaskell asked MacPherson to radio HMS *Ajax* to send over more.

By early afternoon Reverend Grauel and his galley staff had prepared what he called 'a makeshift meal of the last of the potatoes, together with the rest of the tins. We had enough water as one of the destroyers had sent over supplies.'

Ike had removed his captain's cap – it would never be found again – and, dressed in blue denims and vest, he walked among the crew and passengers, speaking to them quietly. To the watchful boarders he looked like another teenager. Sometimes he would glance up towards the battered wheelhouse. Outside the radio shack stood a boarder, rifle in hand. Ike nodded to him and moved on. Enava Barak and Harold Leidner were no longer there.

In the wheelhouse Lieutenants Pearce and MacPherson stood behind Cyril Weinstein at the helm. They could see in the distance the shimmering outline of the coast of Palestine.

*

Since early morning in Haifa, Tel Aviv, Netanya, in all the towns
and settlements of the Yishuv, everything appeared to have closed
down: shops, factories and offices had not opened their shutters.
Their occupants had started converging on the port of Haifa after the
radio announced that *Exodus* would arrive there before sunset on
their Sabbath day. Also heading for the harbour were print and
newsreel cameramen who had been briefed by the Haganah High
Command.

On the outskirts of Haifa tanks, half-tracks and trucks filled with
troops emerged from the barracks and began to seal off the port area.

Inside a Mandate staff car, Major Philip Cardozo, wearing the red
beret and rank ensign of the British 6th Airborne Division in Palestine,
nodded approval. In his early forties, he controlled his emerging
paunch by daily army callisthenics, determined to be as fit as his
young paratroopers. However, despite his exercising he had
developed a double chin, fleshy lips and chubby jowls, giving him the
appearance of an overfed child. In a jacket pocket was his Order of
the Day. It had been signed by Sir Gordon MacMillan, the
commander-in-chief of British forces in Palestine. In the past two
years the pinched-faced general had signed a similar order 47 times.
Each one was to deport illegal immigrants arrested off the coast of
Palestine.

Major Cardozo anticipated that by sunset on this Friday, 18
July, his carefully prepared plan would have seen the number of
deportations increase by the arrival of *Exodus*. Nothing would
stand in his way. Expulsion was part of his own family's history, for
the Cardozos had been expelled from Spain during the
Inquisition. In Holland they had been persecuted for being
Catholics and had finally settled in England. In the war he had
served in the Eighth Army before being posted to the Mandate.
But there was no mistaking his personality: he was as unbending
as the major's baton he twirled as he walked down the line of
paratroopers standing at ease in the intense summer heat along
the harbour waterfront.

Every so often he would pause to remind a paratrooper that when the time came he should smile. It was important to get the immigrants off *Exodus* with no resistance.

By the time he reached his office, a small cabin at the end of the harbour, Major Cardozo could see that the details in his Order of the Day were reaching completion. The pen where the press were to be held was already filling, its occupants contained behind a steel fence.

The three navy transport ships – *Runnymede Park*, *Empire Rival* and *Ocean Vigour* – were moored at the quayside. Further along the quay was a fenced-off empty space where rows of chairs had been set out and a notice announced UNSCOP. Out on the water, all the fishing boats had been moved to the far side of the harbour. Further back on the quayside stood a line of military ambulances.

By early afternoon a platform was trundled into place to face the reporters and cameramen. Standing on it, gripping its handrail, Major Cardozo smiled a welcome. Ruth Gruber, on assignment for the New York *Herald Tribune*, noted: 'He looked like a man who knew that this was a big show, maybe the biggest peacetime circus he would ever participate in, and that destiny had chosen him to be the ringside barker.'

He told them that shortly *Exodus* would arrive, but anyone attempting to talk to the refugees would be removed from the port immediately. Reporters scribbled furiously as he dispensed information. *Her registered name was* President Warfield . . . *had served under the British flag on D-Day. Now she flew the Haganah flag . . . They had crammed almost 5,000 on a ship designed to hold 400 . . . They ignored a request to stop resisting . . . Their radio here in Tel Aviv has claimed they had three dead and many wounded . . . We have no independent confirmation of that.*

Questions rained down from behind the fence.

The *Daily Mail* reporter asked what would happen to the passengers when they arrived. The *New York Times* reporter wanted to know if that was why the three ships were there. The reporter from Reuters asked if they were going to be taken to Cyprus. The *Daily Express* reporter wanted to know if the Lease-Lend ships the United States had sent to help Britain during the Second World War were being used as prison ships. *L'Humanité*'s reporter asked if Major

Cardozo would comment on the suggestion that the ships were 'no more than floating concentration camps'.

Barely able to control his anger, Major Cardozo stepped off the platform and marched back to his office, twirling his baton furiously.

Chapter 18

The Return

At 3.30 that afternoon, 18 July, a Palestine Police launch came alongside *Exodus* and a uniformed superintendent climbed a rope ladder up to the deck before making his way to the crowded bridge. He then turned to Lieutenant MacPherson and asked him to identify the captain. The naval officer pointed to Bernard Marks. The policeman produced a notebook and asked for Marks's papers. He handed over his American passport. After noting down the number and returning it, he formally arrested Marks for 'breaching international maritime law by entering Palestine territorial waters for illegal purposes'.

The captain calmly explained that *Exodus* had been boarded in international waters and that he had been forced to bring his ship into Haifa. That, he reminded the superintendent, was an act of piracy under maritime law. As an American citizen, he intended to report the matter to his government.

The police officer shrugged, then demanded that Cyril Weinstein produce his papers and provide evidence that he was a qualified helmsman. The New Yorker flexed his massive shoulders. Marks's glance warned him not to start a fight. Weinstein handed over his American passport. The police officer noted down its number and demanded to know how many of the crew were American. Marks replied that they all were. The superintendent stared at him and said they would all be deported when they reached Haifa. In the meantime, Marks was to ensure that no attempt was made to delay that.

Geoff Glover was helping to prepare the wounded for disembarkation, rebandaging their injuries and connecting fresh plasma bottles. There were now 198 casualties, including several more boarders struck in the final minutes of the battle but suffering only minor injuries. The more serious cases had been placed close to the rails so that they would be the first to be carried ashore. Glover had himself been hit with a piece of wood as he had emerged on deck from below. Trying to ward off the blow, he had been cut on his wrist and mouth. He had quickly treated himself and joined the nursing team.

On the deck below, boarders were picking through debris, collecting what Glover called 'trophies . . . anything to remind them of the day they went on board *Exodus*. One had picked up an alarm clock and another had acquired a Netherlands flag. Tins of food and potatoes were bagged, ready to be taken back to their destroyers. They would make a welcome addition to our rations.'

Throughout the afternoon passengers emerged from below, clutching their belongings as they came on deck and watched Mount Carmel becoming clearer through the heat haze. They joined in the singing of 'Hatikvah'. The tremulous voices of the 646 children on board brought tears to the eyes of many of the adults.

Michael Stolowitzky would recall that several of the girls had managed to keep clean the dresses that the Jewish Agency relief workers had given them before boarding the ship. The garments carried the labels of stores in New York, Washington and Baltimore, paid for by fund-raising events.

Gertruda had never lost her readiness to help, often leavening it with a touch of humour. Before the battle had started, she lay in the darkness in what little space was allotted to her and Michael and sang, knowing that in doing so she provided support to young men like Herbert Adler, who had watched his crippled mother being dragged from her wheelchair in Vienna and forced by an SS officer to scrub a street; Taube Biber, who was only a child when he hid in a coal cellar in Frankfurt as other members of his family were taken outside their home by an SS officer and shot dead one by one until his pistol ran out of bullets; and John Fink, who had been ordered to carry out from the brothel for camp guards in Buchenwald the bodies of young Jewish women who had been shot after being diagnosed by the SS camp doctor as having venereal disease, one of them his sister.

On deck stood Aviva Porat, who had been one of Mordechai Rosemont's group and had stood beside Gertruda hurling tins until there were no more to hurl. The teenager said that it had all been worthwhile for her as she watched the slopes of Mount Carmel drawing even closer, greener than she had ever imagined.

Rosemont stood beside her, white shirt open to the waist, black trousers rolled up, his long black hair ruffled by the wind, his eyes staring at the approaching coast. He had become a hero on board when people learned that he had been a leader of the Warsaw Uprising and, when it failed, had led a group to safety in the Polish woods, where he had become head of a partisan group, waging ruthless attacks on the Germans. He had recounted his experiences in a matter-of-fact voice which made them sound even more heroic.

Among the passengers on deck were the American crew, planning to join the passengers when they went ashore. They chewed bubble gum or smoked, talking quietly among themselves, young men trying to control their emotions: men like Eli Khan, David Starek and Avi Livney, who had been lookouts, spending hours sweeping the horizon with their binoculars. Some spoke Hebrew with soft accents which seemed far from home. David Williams had the crisp voice of Boston. All agreed that when the time came they would attend the funeral of Bill Bernstein, the ship's first mate, whose death had badly shaken them. They remembered how, after a hard day's work building bunks in Portovenere, Bernstein had staged an impromptu concert on deck, blackening his face and using a deck mop to hide his red hair as he sang in a passable imitation of Al Jolson.

The boarders stood facing inwards, backs to the deck rails, staring silently at the singing passengers. Among them was the man who had shot Bernstein.

With the Jewish Sabbath just starting, Cyril Weinstein slowly steered *Exodus* towards the breakwater at Haifa port. HMS *Childers* was slightly ahead. The rest of the task force was spread out behind the steamer, matching her speed and keeping her boxed in. As *Exodus* moved across the harbour towards the waterfront of Haifa, with the slopes of Mount Carmel visible beyond, thousands of voices could be heard joining in the singing of the haunting and timeless 'Hatikvah', which was to become the National Anthem of the State of Israel.

A Reuters correspondent confined with all the other journalists in their enclosure jotted in his notebook: 'The battered steamer was flying the flag of Zion and as she turned into the harbour we could see her name: *Haganah Ship Exodus 1947*. It was a magnetic moment.' Others watching *Exodus* approach, moving past one crane after another, raised their arms as if in salute.

On the quayside the paratroopers adjusted their steel helmets and formed a line, guns at the ready, in front of the empty space where *Exodus* would berth.

In their own enclosure the 11 summer-suited members of UNSCOP sat in their chairs, heads shielded by parasols against the sun, cooling themselves with fans Major Cardozo had handed out, together with the mimeographed single sheet of paper that identified *Runnymede Park*, *Empire Rival* and *Ocean Vigour* as 'comfortable troop ships. *Ocean* is a hospital ship and equipped with beds and toilets and milk for mothers and children.'

There was no mention of when or to where the ships would depart, Major Cardozo confining himself to 'soon'.

The veteran reporter Ruth Gruber made another note: 'Major Cardozo grins for the camera. He knows this is a historic day. Destiny has chosen him to strut upon the stage. He does not walk; he dances on the pier.'

Sir Alan Cunningham, the High Commissioner, had made it clear that 'Having three deportation ships waiting, full of illegal immigrants, in Haifa port was nothing less than a time bomb. They must depart as soon as possible.'

Since March, before Exodus had left France, the Irgun terrorist gang had already killed more than 20 British soldiers and sabotaged the Haifa oil refinery. The arrival of *Exodus* could only further inflame a tense situation. The High Commissioner wanted the passengers deported as fast as possible, before the members of UNSCOP were caught up in the arrival they had reluctantly been allowed to witness.

The committee was coming to the end of its five-week visit to Palestine and the Mandate authorities had taken care to provide only the minimum information on the fate of the immigrants. The order to do so had come to Sir Alan Cunningham from Foreign Secretary Ernest Bevin before he flew to Paris to take part in further discussions on the Marshall Plan. While in Paris, he told the French Foreign Minister, Georges Bidault, 'This was by far the most difficult and dangerous boarding so far and we cannot consider a repeat operation. Two of our destroyers have been damaged and one of them, HMS *Cheviot*, will be out of commission for three or four months.'

It was against this background that *Exodus* moved slowly towards her berth.

In the wheelhouse the Palestine Police superintendent and Lieutenant MacPherson stood behind Bernard Marks as a harbour tug nudged *Exodus* towards the space on the quayside a couple of hundred yards away from where smoke had started to rise from the funnels of the transports. The singing had stopped and passengers were looking uneasily from the ships to the quay, from where they could hear the harsh sounds of military commands sending troops trotting to form lines in front of the transports. On the transports' decks other soldiers were erecting huge cages; some pointed at *Exodus* and scratched themselves and beat their chests like monkeys.

Soldiers were forming a semicircle towards which *Exodus* was slowly moving. The ambulances moved closer, their back doors open, and on the quay was a pile of stretchers.

On board *Exodus* the passengers facing towards the dockside saw the look of disbelief on the faces of the smartly dressed men arrayed in their own compound. In the ship's prow Reverend Grauel motioned for the UNSCOP members to come on board. They began to move towards the compound exit where Major Cardozo stood, smiling and twirling his baton.

He explained that, reluctantly, he could not allow the committee to go on board *Exodus*, for reasons they could see for themselves through the gaping holes he claimed the immigrants had created in the super-structure: ruined bedding, broken pieces of furniture and the first sniff of overflowing toilets they had broken. Because of the risks to their health from disease, the passengers must first be medically examined. Then, after a meal and a rest, Major Cardozo would see if they were willing to meet the committee. In the meantime, he suggested they should return to Jerusalem, where he would contact them when he had further news.

Watching the committee being driven out through the port gates, Major Cardozo walked over to study the faces staring down at him from *Exodus*, baton twirling. Suddenly a potato whistled past him, splattering on the ground. He shook his head and walked away.

On the bridge the pilot rang down to stop engines and *Exodus* drifted the last few feet to a halt against the quayside.

Frank Stanczak and Nat Nadler arrived in the wheelhouse with the chief engineer, who was carrying a bunch of keys. As he started to hand them over to Bernard Marks, Lieutenant MacPherson took them. As Nadler moved to grab them, a boarder stepped forward and threatened him with a club. Stanczak swore under his breath in Hebrew. Lieutenant MacPherson smiled at Marks and removed one of the keys from the bunch, then handed it to the captain as 'a souvenir'. The moment of tension was over.

Over the ship's public address loudspeaker Lieutenant MacPherson announced that disembarkation was to commence shortly. All crew members holding American passports were to remain on board until the last immigrant had come ashore after the injured had been brought off. Any resistance would be dealt with firmly. Zvi Tiroche and his translators repeated the instructions in various languages.

Zvi realised that any attempt to jump overboard – as he had heard some of the younger passengers discussing – was now out of the question. Police launches had formed a cordon on the harbour side and after MacPherson's announcement they had started to drop explosive charges in the water.

Zvi was part of another, and more daring, plan he had played an important part in formulating. After the decision to surrender, Ike had told him that the dozen Palyam crew members were to remain hidden on board the ship. They would be smuggled off when the time came and sent to serve on other blockade-runners already being prepared in the United States. Zvi would remain with them and could later join the Palyam as it continued to expand.

In the meantime, his responsibility would be to find hiding places for the crew members. Zvi had spent his time moving through the bilges and had come across a large, empty water ballast tank. In the hurry to leave Baltimore, removing it had been overlooked. He saw immediately how it could serve his needs.

First he had ordered all the passengers near the bilges to pack their belongings and go up to the deck. When the area was cleared, he collected the Palyam crew and told them to bring ropes, spades and a hand drill down to the bilges. There they dug out the sand out of the bilges and used the ropes to pull the tank across to fill the hole. The excavated sand was packed around the base or scattered in the other bilges. Under Zvi's supervision, one of the crew drilled air holes in the sides of the tank. Another seaman was sent to a storeroom and returned with a large canvas cover. Draped over the top of the tank, it hid the air vents so that from the outside the tank looked to be part of the ship. This would be their hiding place. Zvi warned them that the air intake would be limited and inside there would be no room to stand. They could bring only a few bottles of water with them and some food. He estimated they could remain in the tank for up to 12 hours after they had docked. Meanwhile, they should return on deck and go about their normal duties.

The time to enter the tank had come with Lieutenant MacPherson's announcement. One by one, Zvi and the Palyam crew casually made their way down to the bilges.

The silence was broken with the recitation of *Kaddish* as first Bernstein's body, then those of Mordechai Baumstein and Zvi

Yakubovich were carried off the ship and placed in an ambulance. Reverend Grauel had made the sign of the cross over each body and, as they were carried down, fingered the rosary Bernstein had asked him to keep the night before the first mate's prediction he would die before sunrise. Reverend Grauel planned to send the rosary to Bernstein's family in San Francisco.

In the hospital Surgeon Lieutenant Commander Gaskell had arranged the order in which the wounded would be taken off. On the quayside the injured boarders were immediately loaded on an ambulance and driven to the military hospital on Mount Carmel. Then it was back to the ship for Geoff Glover to continue helping to bring the rest of the wounded down. But unlike the injured boarders, the immigrants had their bandages removed by one of the army doctors to check whether their wounds warranted hospital admission. The majority were sent to the transport *Ocean Vigour*, the ship Major Cardozo had claimed was a hospital ship.

By late afternoon the last of the wounded were still being brought off the ship. Major Cardozo came on board and told Lieutenant MacPherson to allow Dr Cohen and his nurses to help bring the injured on to the quayside to speed up disembarkation.

It was the first time Dr Cohen had seen the full extent of the damage and he wondered how *Exodus* had managed to stay afloat so long. Water was seeping through cracks in the hull and life rafts dangled over the side. Everywhere the superstructure was ripped open. The sight confirmed to the young doctor that he must accept Yossi's offer to remain in Palestine, where his services would be invaluable. When they were still in Port-de-Bouc the idea had not been uppermost in his mind, but the savage attack on *Exodus* and the resulting casualties now made him determined to stay.

The number of injured passengers he was helping to manoeuvre down the gangway included 43 pregnant women he had told Major Cardozo should be sent to the nearest maternity hospital. Smiling reassurance, the officer had said there was no need to do that; *Ocean Vigour* had all the facilities needed to deliver infants. Before Dr Cohen could enquire further, the major was gone, stick twirling, to determine who should go in an ambulance to hospital and who should be directed past a line of paratroopers to climb the gangway of one of the three transports.

Dr Cohen realised that the ships were for one purpose. Between them they would carry the immigrants from Haifa. He tried to find out where they would be going, but his questions were ignored. He watched a pregnant woman being slowly helped up the gangway on to *Ocean Vigour* by her husband, while nearby a smiling Major Cardozo shouted for everyone to move faster.

Having seen the last of his patients being herded on board the transport, Dr Cohen returned to *Exodus* in search of Yossi and told him he would like to accept his offer to stay in Palestine. Yossi led him to a cupboard at the end of the aft deck and told Dr Cohen to lock himself in. The Haganah would do the rest.

The Palestine Police superintendent escorted Bernard Marks and Cyril Weinstein off the bridge. In their place Lieutenant Pearce and other leaders of the boarding parties arrived and gave Lieutenant MacPherson their reports. These would eventually go to Sir John Cunningham and then to the Admiralty. Subsequently there would be no formal inquiry into the attack.

The boarding parties led by their officers tramped down the gangway to where launches waited to take them back to their destroyers. The responsibility for *Exodus* was now in the hands of the British Army and the Palestine Police.

While the superintendent brought Marks and Weinstein to the dockside, the remainder of the American sailors who had signed on at Baltimore were being brought ashore by more policemen. Among them was Nat Nadler, the Brooklyn electrician, whose head wound had started to bleed; Miriam Bergman had rebandaged it. Two of the deckhands, Lennie Sklar and Lou Selove, had helped the wounded Bill Millman, who had shared helmsman duties with Weinstein until, defending the wheelhouse, one of the boarders had clubbed him. Pinned to his vest was a card: 'Patient requires urgent hospitalisation'.

The note bore the name of Surgeon Lieutenant Bett.

On the quayside there was a brief discussion between Major Cardozo and an army doctor. The major wanted Millman put on board the *Ocean Vigour*. The doctor insisted he should be admitted to Haifa Military Hospital. He won the discussion and the helmsman was loaded into an ambulance. Major Cardozo drew himself to his full height and walked off to prepare his last task: supervising the transfer of over 4,000 immigrants out of Haifa by sunset. He had assured Sir Gordon, now General, MacMillan it would be done.

Two police vans brought the American crew to the port police station. They were fingerprinted, photographed and body-searched before being charged with entering the country illegally. As they had no visas, they would be held in Haifa jail until arrangements could be made to deport them.

Reverend Grauel was told that as he had a valid visa, acquired on his visit to Paris, and because of his religious status, he would be held, at his expense, in the Savoy Hotel. It was where Orde Wingate had also stayed on his first night in Haifa. Reverend Grauel recalled that when he reminded the police officer of the fact, the officer replied he hoped this would be his last night in Palestine. Reverend Grauel had smiled. He had other matters to attend to.

There was a romance between teenagers Aliza and Yosef that had caught the imagination of the passengers and, in their last hours below deck, their sleeping area had been concealed behind clothes draped on a line to give them privacy. In the morning, when they had come up on deck, the couple received small gifts and were clapped as they walked through the crowd like any other newlyweds.

All day they had stood on deck looking towards land as they sipped from their small bottles of water and shared their plans to make their life together somewhere beyond the towering mass of Mount Carmel. There were others doing the same, but perhaps none with the poignancy of Aliza and Yosef. Among them were parents who yearned for their own children, gone forever in the charnel houses of the concentration camps. For them Aliza and Yosef had become family. The sun was low in the sky when the couple were invited to lead the passengers when the order came to leave the ship.

At the foot of the gangway a soldier stood behind a table stacked with three piles of paper bearing the stencilled names *Ocean Vigour*, *Runnymede Park* and *Empire Rival*. He selected two sheets and handed one each to Aliza and Yosef: *Runnymede Park*. These were their boarding passes.

As they moved forward, another couple were handed their passes. Major Cardozo's loudhailer began to order: 'Passengers must hand over all bottles, knives, pens, scissors and razors when arriving at the search table.' Further along the quay were more long tables behind which stood paratroopers. Behind them were Arab porters.

The contents of Aliza's and Yosef's small bags were tipped out and rummaged through. Yosef's set of paint brushes and sketchbook were set aside; Aliza's small hand mirror was thrown to the ground and stamped under a boot. When Yosef began to protest, Aliza restrained him. Their other belongings were stuffed back and their bags were given a sticker marked with the letter 'C'. The paratrooper explained it stood for Cyprus. One of the porters stepped forward and took the bags to start a pile behind the tables.

As Aliza and Yosef walked towards *Runnymede Park* the long line at the search tables stretched all the way back to the gangway and up to those still waiting to descend from the deck of *Exodus*.

Reaching the deck of *Runnymede Park*, the couple saw that inside a wire-framed cage were some of the wounded passengers from *Exodus*, not speaking, lying on the deck, prisoners once again. A policeman with the neatly trimmed black moustache favoured by the Palestine Police opened a door in the cage and motioned the young couple inside. Aliza struggled not to cry and Yosef put his arms around her. Then the young lovers were escorted from the cage down below into a hold whose walls were made of metal.

A group of Hungarian teenagers they had heard laughing as they climbed the gangway burst into tears. In the distance the loudspeaker of Major Cardozo continued to repeat his instructions.

*

The romance between Fira and Efraim had also developed. They explored their past lives and the more they did so, the closer they became, taking turns to listen attentively as they described their family histories. According to Reverend Grauel: 'In the language of the time they were born for each other, sweethearts.'

Efraim was 29, the only survivor of a family of 10, and had been conscripted into the Red Army. The war over, he returned to Poland, making his way to Cracow. It was the time when the men from Aliyah Bet arrived in the city, looking for young Jews they could send to Palestine to work as kibbutzniks.

Efraim knew he had an aunt and a brother who had gone to America when he was still a small child, but he didn't know how to begin to find them. Going to Palestine could be a starting point. Besides, it was the only opening he could see for himself. He had 'no money, no relatives, nothing'.

Efraim's journey from Poland had taken almost a year before he had walked up the gangway to board *Exodus*. 'I had no romantic thoughts in my mind, then I saw this young lady with all those children. I just thought she was the most beautiful lady on the ship. There were plenty of other women on board, but no one as beautiful.'

And so began their love story. Efraim had never thought of marrying anybody. He was impecunious and very much doubted if he had any immediate prospect of earning enough to keep a wife, let alone a family. He had been told that working on a kibbutz was hardly the road to wealth. 'But when I saw Fira I told myself this is the time, now or never. That she is going to be my wife.'

Before the battle he had walked with her and the children around the decks, sat with Fira at meals and helped her with the children. He was like any husband devoted to his family. When the battle had started Ephraim was there, a protective arm ready to defend the woman and children he loved with a passion he had never before felt. More than one of the American crew members told Efraim he was the luckiest man on board.

Efraim and Fira did not know – how could they? – that their plans for the future – to settle on a kibbutz and raise their children – would be cruelly threatened from the moment they boarded *Runnymede Park*.

As the three transports left Haifa in the late evening, the reporters who had remained penned up all day erupted. Their story had sailed away before their eyes. They had not been allowed to interview any of the passengers. With the ships disappearing from sight, Major Cardozo returned with a bundle of press releases. As they scanned the document, several reporters shook their heads in disbelief and Maurice Pearlman, a Reuters correspondent, demanded, 'Is this why we have been cooped up all day, while this piece of fiction was being concocted?'

The mimeographed document read:

In order to remove any doubts which may have been raised by inaccurate broadcasts from the illegal immigrant ship *President Warfield*, the following facts are recorded: The *President Warfield* arrived in Palestine waters early on the 18th of July, carrying approximately 5,000 Jewish illegals. In order to avoid being boarded, she took violent evasive action which in the ensuing boarding operation resulted in damage to herself as well as to ships of the Royal Navy. Her sides had been planked up and barbed wire had been strung fore and aft. The boarding party met strong resistance backed up by tear gas, fire-works, smoke bombs, steam jets and various missiles. She also dropped life rafts from a height on to the decks of the naval vessels.

One single shot and one burst of machine-gun fire were used by one of the naval ships against an immigrant who was threatening to decapitate one of the boarding party with an axe and another who was about to use a rifle. The shot and burst missed, but frightened the men who dropped their weapons. No other fire was used by naval personnel. Some fifty Navy personnel in all were used in the boarding party.

The *President Warfield* entered Haifa Port under her own

steam on the evening of the 18th. Two illegal immigrants were found to have died from fractured skulls and a third has since died in the hospital from the same cause. Twenty-seven others were admitted to Haifa Hospital: some of these persons, though not all, were suffering from injuries received when the *President Warfield* was boarded. Three naval ratings were injured and admitted to hospital.

A battery of questions came from the reporters. Could they interview the injured? Where had the immigrants now been taken? Could they see the damage to the navy ships? Why had they not been allowed to inspect *Exodus*? Could the boarders be interviewed?

Major Cardozo ignored every question. Finally Pearlman traduced him, promising Cardozo would be held responsible for a public relations disaster. The major shrugged.

Before driving away, he ordered buses to collect and drive the frustrated journalists out of the port. Nobody was to enter until the morning cleaning crew arrived. The major had ordered that instead of the usual Arab cleaners a Jewish company should be hired to have *Exodus* sanitised.

The majority of reporters were headquartered at the Savoy Hotel. This time the story did not disappear under their noses but was waiting for them in the bar. Standing there, nursing a whisky, was Reverend Grauel. They recognised his voice: his broadcasts from *Exodus* had already provided front-page stories. Here was the eye-witness they had given up hope of finding. He did not disappoint them. His detailed account of events from the moment the battle started was later described in major newspapers as: 'A stunning in-dictment', 'A public disaster for the British government', 'Behaviour not expected of the founder of democracy'.

Within hours letters poured into the White House and the State Department, demanding the US administration protest to London. Ralph Goldman and the Jewish Agency in New York organised demonstrations along the East Coast which quickly spread throughout North America. From their Jerusalem hotel, UNSCOP members revealed how they had been refused access to the passengers. In London the embattled Foreign and Colonial Office in Whitehall found its switchboard jammed with protest phone calls.

Ernest Bevin, supported by Prime Minister Clement Attlee, desperately tried to stem the growing tide of anger, arranging for the American crew to be immediately deported with all charges against them dropped. It did nothing to calm matters.

One by one, members of the Haganah High Command slipped through the shadows into the building at 44 Hayarkon Street in Tel Aviv. Since dawn they had been in Haifa, monitoring developments in the port. At dusk, once the last of the immigrants were on board the transport ships, they had returned to Tel Aviv for a meeting with David Ben-Gurion. He knew that the fate of the *Exodus* immigrants could have a vital effect on the political discussions taking place in the United Nations General Assembly on the future of Palestine.

Throughout the day he had been busy mobilising his contacts in the United States. In London Chaim Weizmann, having held no official position in the Zionist Movement since December 1946, tried and failed to meet Bevin. It was an approach Ben-Gurion did not welcome.

In his hiding place behind the engine room, Ike sat on the cold steel floor, head resting against the hull on a pillow he had taken from one of the bunks on the aft deck. At sea the engine room would have been a place of shouted orders, the vibration of the engine at its normal cruising speed and the regular ring of the bridge telegraph with some change of course. Now there was only silence.

He suspected that later, when he was off the ship, he would be questioned about his tactics and decisions. He knew the ship's logbook would confirm that *Exodus* had been unlawfully attacked in international waters, a crime on the high sea. He knew that the deaths of Bill Bernstein, his closest friend on board, and the two passengers were nothing less than murder. But he suspected that their deaths would never be brought before a court. Saul Avigur had once told him there was only one law, the one the victors made.

For that reason he had wrapped the log in an oilcloth and buried it in bilge sand, close to where Zvi Tiroche had chosen to hide the Palyam crew. When the time came Ike planned to retrieve the packet.

Pressing his ear against the hull, he could hear English voices, paratroopers standing guard over *Exodus* on the quay. Ike wondered what there was to protect. The ship had been trashed, from the smashed side doors leading to the bridge wings and the 11 shattered windows in the circular pilothouse, all the way down below the decks. A less well-built ship could have sunk under such a hammering.

The first light of dawn brought the sound of two trucks coming to a stop on the quay where *Exodus* was moored. There was a brief exchange with the paratroopers, followed by men in blue overalls and rubber-soled boots running up the gangway with their buckets, brushes and spraying equipment. Some carried two pails and brushes. Others had refuse bags. They were the employees of the Haifa firm ordered by Major Cardozo to clean and fumigate *Exodus*. Reaching the upper deck, they began to sing Hebrew songs as they moved down through the ship.

Ike was the first to hear them. 'I smiled. There was nothing else for me to do. Just smile and wait.'

Coming closer to his hiding place was the sound of soft, rapid knocking, then there was a pause before the footsteps resumed, coming closer still, until there was a knock on his door. A voice called out, 'Solel Bone.'

Ike repeated the words and opened the door. Standing there was a cleaner. Ike identified himself and the cleaner stripped off his overall. Underneath was another identical blue garment. The cleaner gave the first one to Ike and told him to put it on. Then he handed him a refuse bag and face mask and told him to start gathering up rubbish. When his bag was full he was to take it down to the trucks, still wearing his face mask, and wait in a vehicle. One by one, the rest of the hidden men, dressed in overalls and carrying cleaning equipment, came down the gangways. The paratroopers ignored them.

When a voice called out outside his hiding place, Zvi Tiroche put into action another plan the Haganah had devised to get the Palyam crew off the ship. Zvi recalled: 'The British limited each passenger's baggage to one item each. The rest would be stacked on deck or on the quayside and collected for distribution later.' The passengers were told that Solel Bone, one of the largest Jewish companies in Haifa, with a service contract for the port, would collect the baggage.

On deck, Zvi joined company employees carrying the luggage down the gangway. Hoisting an extra-large bag, he staggered down to the quay, dumped the bag in the back of a waiting truck and jumped in beside the driver. 'I was driven to Bat Galim, a Haifa suburb, and I was hidden by a family. I had a bath and shave and after a week I was sent to a Palmach training unit. I was in the navy.'

Within an hour the Haganah plan to extricate Ike, Yossi, Dr Cohen, Zvi Tiroche and the Palyam crew was complete. As the sun began to rise, the last of the trucks drove out of the port, its driver leading the singing of 'Hatikvah'. Seated beside Yossi, Ike opened his refuse bag and pulled out the ship's logbook that he had retrieved from the bilges. The two men shook hands as they continued to sing.

On Sunday 20 July, an estimated 15,000 mourners gathered at Martyrs' Row in Haifa Cemetery to bury Bill Bernstein, Mordechai Baumstein and Zvi Yakubovich. The pallbearers included some of the American crew who had been released from jail. Bernstein's body was wrapped in the American flag, the other two in simple white shrouds. Reverend Grauel stood at the edge of Bernstein's grave holding the rosary beads the first mate had given him. Somewhere in the crowd were Ike and Yossi and members of the Haganah High Command.

Chapter 19

The Gates to Hell

On board HMS *Cardigan Bay* radar operator Geoffrey Barwell could see the three Ministry of Transport ships, *Runnymede Park, Ocean Vigour* and *Empire Rival* – slow-moving blips in the centre of the convoy. Leading it was HMS *Ajax*, accompanied by HMS *Province*, a minesweeper, and, bringing up the rear, HMS *Cardigan Bay*.

On deck were 60 paratroopers from the 6th Airborne Division, stripped to the waist, their red berets pulled low over their faces to protect against the morning sun. They would not be needed until the transports docked and the paratroopers would be ferried across to them to ensure that disembarkation went smoothly, as had the embarkation at Haifa. The soldiers, like the immigrants, believed their destination was Cyprus.

For the paratroopers, bringing refugees to the island from captured blockade-runners had become a familiar exercise in the past year, since Sir Alan Cunningham, the Palestine High Commissioner, had said there was no more room in the Mandate detention camps.

Barwell knew that escorting the immigrants to the Cyprus camps was, as one paratrooper described, a journey to the gates to hell. Both detention camps looked little different from the Nazi concentration camps with their watchtowers, double rows of towering barbed wire, tin-roofed huts which made them unbearable to sleep in at night during summer and ice cold to touch in the frost of winter. There was no plumbing and rancid-tasting water was brought once a day in army water tanks. There was often little more than a tin mug for each refugee.

In the past year 25,000 Jews had been imprisoned in the camps. Every month 750 immigrants, along with an equal number held in DP camps in Europe, received Mandate entry permits for Palestine, the quota that Bevin insisted upon. The Foreign Secretary had approved the order of departure to be based on 'first in a camp, first out'.

More than once a healthy immigrant had given up his permit to allow a sick inmate to leave, while he waited his turn to be released. The camp commanders called it a 'fair and balanced method'.

However, Barwell suspected that the blips on his screen were not heading for Famagusta port, the usual disembarkation point for the camps. During the night the radio traffic from HMS *Ajax* had ordered the convoy to reduce its speed to five knots, barely a crawl through the calm sea. No reason was given and on board HMS *Cardigan Bay* it added to the speculation that new orders were coming and that the mess-deck gossip had been right in its claim that their destination was Tripoli, with a view to off-loading the refugees for a camp in the Libyan Desert. Watching the blips maintain their course due west, Barwell shrugged off any idea they were bound for North Africa.

The convoy had stopped when *Runnymede Park* asked HMS *Ajax* to send over a doctor to deal with a medical emergency. Shortly afterwards came a report that a passenger on *Ocean Vigour* had jumped overboard and had been picked up by HMS *Providence*. He claimed he wanted to talk to a relative on *Empire Rival*, but after being given a hot drink he was returned to his own transport.

In the early hours of 21 July, the tone of the messages from HMS *Ajax* became more urgent. HMS *Welfare* and HMS *Skipjack*, both minesweepers, would be joining the convoy off Malta. From Valetta harbour, HMS *Troutbridge* would come to replace HMS *Ajax*.

The rumour spread through HMS *Cardigan Bay* that *Exodus* immigrants were being taken back to France. During the night the frigate's radio had picked up news reports that Bevin said he intended to implement *refoulement*, the policy of returning immigrants to their port of embarkation.

Britain's Foreign Secretary failed to understand the enormity of the Pandora's box he had opened with his decision. His misreading of the situation began with the telegram Sir John Cunningham, the First Sea Lord, had sent him immediately after he had come ashore in Haifa: 'It is most undesirable that any mention is made that this vessel was boarded outside territorial waters.'

Bevin chose to ignore this while he pondered his next move to press the French government to bring ashore the immigrants at Port-de-Bouc. In the United States his hope of keeping secret the details of the attack on *Exodus* had been shattered by Reverend Grauel's revelations. The *New York Times* had published details of where and when *Exodus* had been seized and Bernstein murdered. Within hours the Jewish Agency in New York had organised a 22,000-strong gathering in Madison Square, where the call was made for the officers of the Royal Navy task force to be charged with the murder of the first mate and piracy on the high seas.

In Paris Britain's ambassador, Duff Cooper, had warned Bevin of what would happen if *refoulement* was implemented: 'Forcible removal from British ships is likely to provide lurid anti-British propaganda, to which French public opinion may well be receptive in view of German persecution of the Jews under occupation. The man in the street is totally ignorant of Palestine problems and sees only in these illegal immigrants survivors of a persecuted race seeking refuge in their national home.'

Bevin sent an astonishing response to Duff Cooper: 'Guards in ships have been instructed to use whatever force may be required in order to deliver the immigrants into French hands. This action is being taken on the strength of a verbal understanding reached between M. Bidault and myself.'

The telegram was followed an hour later by a second one: 'We shall have to decide soon whether the convoy is to proceed to France or return to Cyprus. But the French should not be given any indication at this stage that we are contemplating the latter possibility in any circumstances.'

Meanwhile, at a meeting in Paris the French Council of Ministers

laid out its conditions for France to accept the *Exodus* passengers.
They could disembark at Port-de-Bouc, provided they agreed they
were under no pressure to do so by the British government. They
would be fed and given accommodation, along with the right to live
in France as long as they wished, but they could also make
arrangements to go anywhere else in the world. However, it was
emphasised that the offer only applied if no measures were taken to
force them off the transports.

The proposal had been seen by Duff Cooper as a reasonable
solution to an escalating crisis. But after the ambassador had conveyed
it, the Foreign Secretary's office had resounded once more with Bevin's
fury. What the French did with the immigrants was up to them. But
under no circumstances must its government help in any way to return
them to Palestine. Duff Cooper was also instructed to inform Georges
Bidault that Britain reserved its right to remove the immigrants from
the transports by all force needed if they refused to disembark.

The ambassador's response was the calm judgement of a seasoned
diplomat: 'The forcible carrying ashore of 4,500 people of all ages
and both sexes will not only be a very severe strain on the endurance
of those charged with the task, but will also afford a most unedifying
spectacle, of which full advantage will doubtless be taken by
journalists and photographers.'

In Duff Cooper's view, not only would the French police and its
army refuse to cooperate in any enforced disembarkation by the
British soldiers on the transports, but such actions by the British
would only further exacerbate mounting tension in the French
media.

The Foreign Secretary's reply was the response of a man gripped
in continued fury: 'If the transports are to leave France with some of
their passengers on board we would have to land them in Cyprus.
There is no alternative destination. To carry these illegal immigrants
to Cyprus after all that we have endured would certainly expose us
to ridicule and amount to acknowledging defeat.'

Ridicule was not something Ernest Bevin could tolerate any more
than defeat.

In his diary that evening Duff Cooper had written the words of Madame de Pompadour: '*Après nous le déluge.*' It was not long in coming.

When Mordechai Rosemont came on board *Runnymede Park* in Haifa he had observed three things: the cages, the low spirits of his fellow passengers and the lack of leadership among them. There was nothing he could do about the cages, but the other qualities he would provide.

The battle-seasoned guerrilla leader who had fought the Germans in the forests of Poland decided that he must 'take the initiative to become the leader. The people were confused and frightened. No one appointed me. But they wanted answers and I was going to get them.'

First he needed to conduct his own inspection of the ship. Immigrants were crammed into its holds, a thousand in one, 500 in the other one. There were no bunks or bedding of any kind; they would have to sleep as best they could on the steel floor. The only light and ventilation came from the cages overhead. By the time air reached the bottom of the holds it was noxious. The toilet facilities were on deck and consisted of two wash basins with only cold water and a row of communal lavatories, each divided by a shoulder-height partition. Pieces of old newspapers hung on hooks and a trough flushed waste into the sea.

For Yosef Reich: 'Conditions were like a prison. We were on deck in a fenced area, like a cage. The soldiers would open the fence gate to bring food. They were always swearing at us. Every morning they sprayed us with cold water and shouted, "Wakey, wakey, rise and shine".'

There were no beds, so Fira and Efraim, like the other refugees, slept on the steel floor of the hold. Fira didn't mind: 'It brought us both together. With the children around us, it was very cramped and we slept with our legs up under us because there wasn't room to spread out. But being close to Efraim, everything was beautiful.'

One of the army guards on board was Harold Gardner. He

patrolled outside the high metal fences – what the passengers called cages – and had been told they were to stop anyone jumping overboard. 'The cages also gave us better control over them. The fences were about 12 foot high with a gate. If someone was sick and needed to go down to the hospital in the stern two of us were detailed to take him or her there. We were both armed so no one tried anything.'

Mordechai was a pragmatist. There was no way the sanitary facilities could be improved, but he would set up a system where people would form two lines: one for women and children, another for men. It was far from ideal, but offered some privacy between the sexes.

The situation for cooking was one he could resolve. On *Exodus* there had been a constant call by the more religious Jews for a separate kosher kitchen. The sea battle had put an end to the request after Ike had told Yossi it was not an important issue. But Mordechai felt otherwise. Deported from Palestine and the prospect of enjoying their own kosher meals, he was determined they would have what was possible.

Discipline was also going to be important. Walking through the ship, Mordechai sensed the anger simmering inside his fellow Jews. It was there in the way they glared at the armed soldiers; in the way some of the women turned their backs on them and spat on the floor; in the way men cursed the troops in Hebrew or Yiddish, or in one of their own languages. Mordechai also saw how jumpy some of the guards were, their fingers close to their triggers. He made a point of always smiling politely as he passed them. But he knew that a potentially explosive situation must be defused.

Many of the passengers were the teenagers he had formed into the groups that had fought beside him on the upper deck of *Exodus*. He didn't need them doing so on board the transport, but they could help with the distribution of food and water and make the lives of the other Jews more bearable. For this he would need authority. Mordechai had singled out the ship's commander in charge of the soldiers.

Colonel Martin Gregson was the quintessential British Army officer. Tall and suntanned, his cap square on his head, the pips burnished on his short-sleeved shirt and his khaki shorts spotless, Gregson arranged to meet Mordechai in his office behind the bridge. Their opening conversation set the tone of their relationship. Mordechai recalled asking, 'Tell me, mister, what is happening? His answer was, "I am sorry, I don't know where we are heading. I have a closed envelope and at some point I will be told to open it. The minute I know where we are going I will tell you."'

Mordechai decided here was a man he could do business with and explained what he wanted. He would guarantee to maintain order among the immigrants and act as Gregson's liaison, relaying his orders and referring requests from the refugees. To reduce tension the troops should be instructed to be more relaxed and friendly. To a man used to having his demands accepted, Mordechai said the passengers would require their own kitchen, separate from the one which served the crew and soldiers. It would provide the kosher food they longed for; there were a number of cooks among the immigrants who could produce it and the ship's galley had sufficient utensils to meet religious requirements. For convenience's sake, the kitchen could be set up on deck and Mordechai would organise mealtimes. On those occasions, soldiers would withdraw from the area. Mordechai explained that it was part of the privacy the immigrants wanted.

Colonel Gregson nodded, saying he understood Jewish customs. But Mordechai had more to ask of him. 'I told him I wanted an imaginative trench between his soldiers and the passengers. We wouldn't step on his ground and he and his men wouldn't step on ours. There would be nurseries for children and synagogues for religious people. No soldier was allowed in the sleeping area. Passengers who became ill were to be taken at once to the sick bay and given the same treatment as any soldier or sailor on board.'

Colonel Gregson took a deep breath, smiled and said it was a good example of the prisoners running a jail. Mordechai had put him in a difficult position. The Foreign Office had insisted that the Jews must not be given any encouragement that Britain would be soft towards them.

The men looked at each other for a long moment, then Gregson reminded Mordechai the ship was named after the site where Magna Carta had been signed. He would do all he could to deliver the requests.

After this, the colonel met regularly with Mordechai to discuss matters. That morning, while the other passengers breakfasted on food from the kosher kitchen, Gregson told Rosemont that the convoy was heading for Port-de-Bouc, where the immigrants would be encouraged to land by the French government.

Since early morning on 28 July, a steady flow of vehicles had arrived in the once-sleepy port from where *Exodus* had sailed. Port-de-Bouc had now taken on the appearance of a boom town. Bistros and cafés had opened at dawn to cater for the arrivals. British and American reporters, some of whom had travelled from Haifa, had been joined by correspondents from Paris and Marseilles, along with newsreel cameramen. They had filled in time waiting for the convoy to arrive by interviewing people in the town about *Exodus*. Some of the journalists for the international press had rented the few telephones available on a daily basis.

One of the cafés, Le Provençal, had a bold chalked notice on its only pavement table: 'Reserved'. The table had been rented by Count Frederick Vanden Heuvel and its other two occupants were Derek Vershoyle, the new commander of the MI6 station in Paris, and David Smiley, the Secret Intelligence Service spy along the Mediterranean coast. They sipped their coffees and slouched low in their chairs; the count had his fedora hat pulled rakishly over one eye, carefully noting the number of every car.

From time to time either Smiley or Vershoyle strolled past another bistro, Le Commerce, to see who was newly arrived among the French civil servants from Paris. There were over a dozen of them, in sombre suits and with open briefcases from which they exchanged documents, including copies of communications between the growing number of ministries and other organisations involved in the arrival of the convoy.

There were bulky dossiers of correspondence between the Foreign Office in London and the Quai d'Orsay and other government offices in Paris. They included the Ministry of Transport and Public Works and the General Public Health, represented by its inspector general, the handsome Dr Jean Gayla. Beside him sat the intense cigar-smoking director of the Assistance Publique de Marseille. The prefect of Port-de-Bouc, a silver-haired elderly official, sat silent and watchful, overawed by the presence of such authority.

On a separate table sat Marcel Pages and André Blumel. Pages was the deputy director of the Ministry of Interior, an Aliyah Bet sympathiser and a close friend of Saul Avigur. André Blumel represented the office of Prime Minister Paul Ramadier. Seated between them was Hannan Sonneborn, recruited from the Aliyah Bet office in Paris. A fluent linguist, he had been appointed as the group's official translator. Beside him sat a senior officer from DST, the French intelligence service. He had not asked to be introduced and everybody understood why.

The café telephone at the end of the bar was manned by a clerk from the Ministry of the Interior who acted as note taker for all incoming calls. Since dawn he had been busy writing down the latest demands from the Foreign Office in London, continuing to amend the French offer to admit the immigrants.

Bevin had insisted that the French offer should exclude assurances that: 'The French government will not force them to disembark . . . It will give refuge to all who disembark voluntarily . . . Only the French authorities will control the disembarkation . . . There must be no further discussion about returning them to Palestine . . .'

The group around the oval table had shrugged aside the demands. Blumel and Pages had both pointed out that Bevin was behaving in an outrageous way when he demanded that their planned visit to the immigrants on the transports when they arrived should not take place.

The Port-de-Bouc chief of police seated beside the prefect spoke for the first time: 'We know these people from *Exodus*. They are not our enemies. I intend to treat them with respect when they come ashore as we did before. They are good people.'

He sat back in his chair, staring at the men around the two tables until they began to nod. Then he tipped his peaked hat and smiled.

Overnight a van load of gendarmes had arrived from Marseilles to police the port area. The road leading to the harbour had been blocked off and vehicles arriving in the town had their numbers noted and passports inspected.

The exception was Saul Avigur's car. Avigur was the Haganah chief in Paris and was later to be a founder member of the Israeli intelligence service, Mossad. After showing his pass, signed by the Marseilles police commander, he was waved through to the waterfront. Sitting beside him was Yehuda Arazi. In the back seat were Ada Sereni and Rachel Biber. She was a graduate of the Haganah secret wireless training school in Marseilles who had been selected for a special task. With her fluent French, confidence and charm, she was going to pose as a nurse – a skill in which she had received basic training – and go on board the largest of the three transports, *Runnymede Park*. Her documents would show she was a member of a public health team from Marseilles, conducting the usual checks on all immigrants. In her nurse's bag Rachel would also carry a small radio transmitter which would be tuned to a receiver ashore. She had equipped other blockade-runners before with radios, but this was the first time she would plant one on an armed British ship. Her room in the waterfront hotel would face out across the harbour to provide the best reception to and from *Runnymede Park*.

Saul Avigur had rented all the hotel rooms on behalf of the French relief agency Entra'aide Français, a strong supporter of Aliyah Bet. As well as Rachel and Avigur's two other passengers in the car, some of the rooms would be occupied by members of the American Jewish Joint Distribution Committee, who were on their way from Marseilles to the port and would work with Ada to supply kosher food to the thousand observant Jews on the transports. Yehuda Arazi would liaise with the DST officer and together they would go with the official French government delegation to visit the transports when they arrived. Meanwhile, they would continue their surveillance of the three MI6 officers.

Waiting for Avigur outside the hotel were the rest of the Haganah team. They had brought around the coast from Marseilles motor launches that had been rented and refuelled by Joe Baharlia, the energetic chief of the Haganah in the city, who had also selected their young crews. Before leaving Marseilles, the launches had each been equipped with powerful loudhailers. They were now moored at the pier outside the hotel, their skippers sitting around the tables out front. There were a dozen of them and Avigur saw that Baharlia had, as usual, chosen well.

The youths wore shorts or swimming trunks, the girls cotton dresses and skirts. Each had a Star of David around his or her neck. For Avigur there was a reminder of his own past in their enthusiasm and determination. Some came from England, while others had travelled from the United States, sent by their parents to help. As volunteers they received no salary, only expenses. Before they left Marseilles Baharlia had given them a pile of empty tin cans with cork tops and explained what they were for. They were to use the loudhailers to tell the passengers on the transports to fill the tins with letters and toss them back down into the launches so they could be posted.

Standing with the youngsters was a massive figure in flowing black robes, a rope belt girding his bulging stomach, wearing a wide-brimmed hat and with his bare feet encased in sandals. In one leathery-skinned hand he held a satchel.

Yehuda Arazi had dubbed the priest Abbé Tuck – after Robin Hood's Friar Tuck – when he became the Haganah's first recruit in Vichy France and his home a staging post for Jews as they fled from northern Europe to reach the underground network Ada ran.

The Abbé had come to Port-de-Bouc to see how he could help the immigrants when they arrived on the transports. His contacts still included a secretary in the British consul's office in Marseilles. Like him, she was a committed Zionist supporter. Down the years, after he had heard her confession and dispensed his penance, she would pass on something she had overheard and hoped was of interest to the Abbé.

That morning she had told him that the consul had received a telephone call from London telling him that the British government was facing a growing dilemma over the immigrants. From his satchel the Abbé produced a sheet of paper on which he had jotted what the secretary had said. The consul had told his caller from the Foreign Office that the French government now believed the immigrants would not accept its offer to enter France but only wanted to return to Palestine.

Saul Avigur realised this was a dramatic development. Only a few hours before he had learned that the Haganah's trusted contact in London – Sidney Silverman, a Labour Member of Parliament – had discovered from his own French Embassy source that the Paris government would be prepared to encourage the immigrants to go to Colombia, using the travel documents that country's consul-general in Marseilles would issue. France would refuel and resupply the transports for the voyage at no cost to Colombia.

In Tel Aviv the Jewish Agency was discussing the idea. But as quickly as it surfaced it had been dismissed by the Colombian Foreign Office in Bogotá, which made it clear that its government would not accept the immigrants because the visas were forgeries. The British ambassador in Colombia also sent a telegram to the Foreign Office: 'Unless the consul-general, who is a retired army general, is out of his mind, or completely corrupt, it looks as if a forgery on a grand scale has been attempted.'

While any plan to send the passengers to begin a new life in Colombia – one that Bevin may well have supported – was dead, nevertheless Avigur recognised it could be exploited. Throughout the afternoon he sent and received coded messages from the Haganah High Command in Tel Aviv. Ben-Gurion agreed that everything must be done to keep the immigrants on board the transports until they were allowed to return to Palestine. It was a bold and daring proposal, but Avigur believed it could work. The French government would not allow the refugees to be bundled off the ships, especially in full sight of the world's assembled media. In the meantime, the Jewish Agency would continue to mobilise its own powerful contacts in the United States to force Bevin to allow the right of return.

Bored with the monotony of patrolling outside the wire fence of the cage, Harold Gardner had developed contacts with some of the refugees inside the wire and he began to listen to their stories of life in the camps: of the death marches in temperatures well below zero; of walking with almost no clothes to keep out the icy cold; of the dysentery and frostbite which had dogged every footstep; of how they had learned to bow their heads when the snow fell and shuffle to reduce the impact of the wind.

He didn't tell them that he had served in Palestine before coming on board and that, despite the acts of terrorism the Irgun and Stern Gangs had committed, it had not affected his attitude towards those inside the cage.

Gerald Landau had once more woken with the first light of dawn seeping down into the cold steel floor of the hold on *Empire Rival*. Around him over a thousand people lay huddled together, exhausted by another night without proper sleep. They included the teenagers he had protected on *Exodus* and he had continued to protect them when they came on board the transport. Since they had left Haifa Gerald had organised their lives, encouraging them to sing and read the few books that had not been taken from them. Though he could read neither Hebrew nor Yiddish, the officer in charge of the para-troopers on the *Empire Rival* had banned the books and ordered them to be burned in the ship's boiler. The children of the Bible had spent their first night on board mourning their loss.

That morning the daylight would be accompanied by the tramp of army boots and English voices laughing as they peered down into the hold. For many, recalled Gerald, most degrading of all was being stared at like animals. Soon the sun would be high in the sky, its furnace heat causing fresh sweat to run down already perspiring bodies. There were men stripped to their underclothes, while mothers with little milk in their sagging, unwashed breasts cried when they could not suckle their newborn babies. Gerald wondered how many cases that day would bring what he called 'incarceration fatigue.' The first to suffer were pregnant women and the mothers of infants who had no option but to breast feed their babies before everyone else in the hold and the paratroopers staring down.'

Gerald imagined the same conditions prevailed on the other two transports until he heard one paratrooper on the *Empire Rival* say it was the worst prison ship he had served on. Staring up at the cage wire, listening to the stirring around him of the people awakening, Gerald realised the transport's engine was silent. In its place was the sound of a motor launch and a woman's voice calling out through a loudspeaker. In Hebrew came the words of Ada Sereni: 'Hello, passengers. You are now in Port-de-Bouc. We have come to welcome you on behalf of the Jewish Agency. You are asked to remain on board whatever the British order or threaten you. We want to bring you home to Eretz Yisrael.'

From the hold, rising like an anthem of renewed hope, came the words of 'Hatikvah', the voices of Fira and Efraim soaring skywards as they stood holding hands.

Looking even dirtier in the dazzling morning sun, the three transports lay at anchor at the edge of the three-mile limit, with *Runnymede Park* positioned between *Ocean Vigour* and *Empire Rival*. Each ship was separated by a few hundred yards of water and further out rode the Royal Navy escorts. Between them and the transports patrolled French police boats, constantly in touch with their shore base to report any activity. All that was visible on the escorts was some of their crew sunbathing or fishing from the decks of HMS *Cardigan Bay*.

From one of the launches ferried from Marseilles, Ada had delivered the same message through her loudspeaker to each transport and taken her first photographs of their cages. The gendarme who had accompanied her had pointed to them and shook his head in disgust. From behind the wire were glimpses of half-naked people, shouting and waving for them to come closer.

Ada's launch had disappeared behind the harbour's grey stone breakwater when Mordechai Rosemont discussed with Colonel Gregson the implication of her message that no immigrant was to leave their ship. The officer was bewildered: would they not be better off on shore? Mordechai had asked if he could address the passengers.

Standing on steps mid-deck, he waited until every man, woman and child had gathered. His piercing eyes swept over them, settling on a face, sometimes nodding, other times remaining impassive before moving on, waiting for total silence. When it came he waited a little longer, the action of a man who knew he commanded respect. When he finally spoke his voice carried to the furthest listener, the chopping hand motions emphasising its powerful tone.

Mordechai began by saying that what some of them had heard from the woman with the loudhailer was true. He stopped and repeated the word: *True*. He waited for the rustle of whispers to end. Then he continued in his slow, measured voice: 'It is true because it comes not only from the Jewish Agency but no doubt from David Ben-Gurion. I can tell you that more than anyone else he wants us off these transports. But for his plan to work we must do what is requested. No one is getting off, either here or anywhere else. We leave only when we get to our homeland. No doubt, there are people out there who are working for nothing else but to bring us home. They will go on doing so. I trust them. You should do the same. Do not leave the ship.'

A roar of applause greeted the words.

On the quayside at Port-de-Bouc, members of the American Jewish Joint Distribution Committee had arrived with trucks of kosher food and clothes and the latest news from America, where the State Department had said it would not support any use of force in French waters against the refugees and had indicated that there would be diplomatic repercussions against Britain if any such action took place. Meanwhile, the Haganah media campaign had led to newspapers across the United States claiming the baggage of the *Exodus* passengers had been stolen from Haifa harbour by Arab workers. Another rumour soon found its way into print. Food intended for the refugees on the transports had been eaten by the troops. In the anger over the deportation, these reports found a willing readership. In the Foreign Secretary's office the stories further fuelled Bevin's fury.

When the French government submitted a list of the names of its delegation to visit the transports – a legal formality, as they would be stepping on to sovereign British soil – Bevin had once more erupted, this time over the name of André Blumel. Stewart Menzies had already told Bevin that Blumel was the head of all Zionist organisations in France. It was not true, but in the prevailing atmosphere truth had become a casualty in Bevin's world.

Bevin told Duff Cooper that to allow Blumel on board any of the transports would be to encourage the immigrants to continue to defy Britain by refusing to land. Georges Bidault had reluctantly agreed with the ambassador's polite request to remove Blumel's name from the list.

Ocean Vigour was the transport moored closest to the breakwater and became an immediate focus of attention for all the boats coming from and going to the quayside. One carried a French medical team of doctors and nurses, led by a short, smiling physician. After boarding the ship, he began to assess the level of help needed and set to work.

Doctors and nurses were assigned to examine the children and check on pregnant women. Miriam Bergman took the lead doctor to where Nat Nadler lay in the ship's sick bay. Since leaving Haifa the young electrician's leg had started to swell and fester. After a quick examination, the doctor ordered Nat to be immediately transferred to hospital. Two gendarmes carried him down to a launch; that afternoon he underwent surgery to save his leg. He would eventually be repatriated to New York by the US Consulate in Marseilles and, with Reverend Grauel, later became a much sought-after speaker at Jewish functions.

Meanwhile, the number of boats circling *Ocean Vigour* had increased, bringing food from members of the Joint. With them were reporters and photographers, who brushed aside attempts by the soldiers to stop them. Within an hour they had collected witness testimony and pictures that showed the transport was very different from the reassuring assertion by Major Cardozo that it was a fully equipped hospital ship.

On deck immigrants were stuffing messages for posting into the tin cans the young Haganah volunteers had thrown on board and which were now being tossed back.

That same afternoon Rachel had come on board *Runnymede Park* with another health inspection team from Marseilles. They had been brought out to the transport in a launch laden with fresh food in large baskets by a curly-haired young man who looked like a farm worker. In reality he was a Palmach operative, as well as a member of DELPHI, the Haganah intelligence service. Code-named Marshalik, he had been told to mingle among the immigrants. Once Rachel had handed Marshalik the radio, he would begin to transmit and receive bulletins for Mordechai Rosemont to keep the immigrants informed.

In keeping with his cover, Marshalik had been winched on board in one of the baskets and carried the produce to the kosher kitchen, all the time observing his surroundings: the rope stretched across the aft deck and the bored-looking soldiers watching the hundreds of immigrants behind the rope. Picking up another basket, Marshalik walked to the kitchen behind the rope, moved into the crowd and disappeared among them. Only then did he speak.

'*Ich bin von der Haganah in Eretz Yisrael.*' I am from the Haganah in the Land of Israel. As well as Marshalik's radio skills there was another reason Palmach had sent him. He was an explosives expert.

When the French government's delegation later came on board *Runnymede Park*, its members knew they had the full support of the American government for the immigrants to be allowed to return to Palestine. The latest newspaper reports had changed matters. Voices in Washington that had before hesitated now supported the idea. They included Secretary of State George Marshall and Henry Morgenthau Jr, the former Secretary of the Treasury. The reports had been reinforced by UNSCOP: its members had made plain their shock at what they had witnessed on the quayside at Haifa.

Golda Meyerson had once more gone to New York and her voice held her packed audiences spellbound as she described what was happening to the *Exodus* immigrants. Beside her on the platform was the tall red-haired figure of Ze'ev Shind, who in many ways symbolised what Aliyah Bet represented.

As the delegation climbed the gangway up to the deck of *Runnymede Park* a Haganah motor boat chugged between the transports, repeatedly broadcasting the message that no one was to leave the ships. Mordechai Rosemont briefed the visitors. He told them the refugees were determined to continue demanding to be returned to Palestine. His words impressed the delegation.

However, what they saw when he took them on a tour of the ship shocked them. Entering one of the holds, they came across a woman sitting on the floor with her newborn baby, blood smeared all around her. Ruth Gruber of the New York *Herald Tribune* wrote: 'The baby was wrapped in a piece of the woman's dirty dress. She was crying. One of the French officials touched her shoulder and asked if she wanted to go to hospital. He could arrange that at once. She shook her head. "I am crying because I'm afraid they're going to force me off the ship. I won't leave. Don't let them make me."'

With her words echoing in their ears and the constantly repeated message over the motor boat's loudspeaker that no immigrant was to leave, the delegation returned to Port-de-Bouc, having assured Mordechai Rosemont they would do everything to help.

That evening *Runnymede Park* received another visitor. The man was young, dressed in the white uniform of a hospital nursing assistant, and he carried a medical bag. He explained to the guard at the top of the gangway that he had to deliver urgently required medicine that one of the doctors in the delegation had sent for a pregnant woman. The soldier motioned him on board. The orderly walked along the deck to where he had been briefed Marshalik would be waiting. At this hour the deck was empty; all the immigrants had gone to the kosher kitchen to have their supper. The orderly handed over his bag and Marshalik hurried away, returning a few minutes later. In that time the medicines had been delivered to treat the new mother in the hold. The rest of the bag's contents had been hidden in the bilges. They were sealed sticks of dynamite.

A little later a launch brought out Rachel on another visit to the transport. Still dressed in her nurse's uniform, she had already become a familiar sight on the ship. She went to the toilet block where Marshalik was waiting and removed the sealed timers she had hidden inside her bra. When the time came they would prime the dynamite sticks to explode.

British Navy intelligence officers in Haifa claimed that the Palmach was responsible for thwarting Palestine Patrol attempts to capture blockade-runners. It had its own command structure and many of its members had served in the Jewish Brigade or had received training from Jews who had operated in the SOE alongside British saboteurs.

In August 1946, the Palmach's role had changed from teaching blockade-runner crews evasive tactics at sea, for that month the Mandate announced it would deport all immigrants caught to Cyprus. As a result, the Palmach decided to set off small explosive charges to stop transports leaving Haifa. While accepting that some action was necessary, both the Haganah High Command and the Jewish Agency were less than enthusiastic about the attacks. They were seen as counterproductive and a risk to immigrants if the charges were exploded when they were on board.

In late August 1946, Marshalik, who had recently joined the Palmach, planted a bomb on board the deportation transport *Empire Haywood* in Haifa harbour. It caused an explosion in the bilges and the departure of the ship was delayed by a few days. The Palmach decided that larger bombs were required.

The arrival of the three transports in Port-de-Bouc offered a new proving ground. Marshalik was told that an explosion must be triggered only when *Runnymede Park* had disembarked its passengers. The Haganah High Command had not been informed of the Palmach's plan to sabotage the transport.

In the wake of Israel's independence, MI6 opened its first station in 1951, when it appointed David Balfour – who had spent the war disguised as a Greek Orthodox monk in Athens – as station chief. He quickly established a cordial relationship with the newly formed Mossad and one day its first director, Reuven Shiloah, showed him a report that HMS *Ajax* had been the target to be sabotaged in July 1947. The report had been signed by Menachem Begin, then the leader of the Stern Gang. The attack on HMS *Ajax* had been entrusted to the Palyam to show 'that British Intelligence was neither omniscient nor infallible'. The cruiser was hurriedly moved from her berth in Haifa to the British naval base in Malta.

To this day the report remains in the MI6 Registry.

Chapter 20

The Last Place to Send Them

Day after day in Port-de-Bouc the three transporters rode listlessly under the sun on a glassy sea. It was too hot for the immigrants to stand on deck at noon, and even hotter below in the holds. On *Runnymede Park* Colonel Gregson had agreed with Mordechai Rosemont that the ship's fire hoses could be used to cool those on deck or to spray the holds; in minutes the water evaporated. Off-duty paratroopers dived off the deck to swim, then climbed back up the gangway and plunged once more into the water. In the streets of Port-de-Bouc the locals told the reporters that no one could remember such a heatwave since the summer war had started.

On board ship, Mike Pevvetz continued to rise at dawn to find a place for his heavily pregnant young bride, Pessia, to shelter from the blistering sun. Whenever he could, their close friend Mordechai Rosemont would come and visit them, reminding the couple what he had said as he stood between them, holding their hands, as the coast of Haifa faded, leaving only the towering peak of Mount Carmel visible: 'We will return to you, Mount Carmel. We promise.'

Every morning they had been at sea, Mike had placed his coat at one of the few shady spots on deck for Pessia to sit on and regularly fetched her water to drink. When her baby moved, he would place his hand on her stomach, smile and say proudly, 'Not long now, my darling, before we are parents.'

Over the ship's loudspeakers songs blared from the radio and, despite the heat, teenagers and children danced to the tunes. One was Aviva Porat, her deep tan and sun-bleached hair giving her elfin face a hauntingly beautiful look. Like Mordechai Rosemont, she had become a focus for the other youngsters and they followed her everywhere around the deck, vying to sit with her at table. Aviva recalled: 'If people hadn't known this was a prison ship they would have thought it was a holiday cruise.'

As well as dancing, she displayed some of the skills her mother had taught her at home in their kitchen, preparing the fresh food which had come on board, cutting it into enticing shapes and displaying cheese and biscuits on paper doilies. She would wait until the evening meal was over and the other youngsters were sitting around her before handing out these treats. Later, when the sun had set and the air was cooler, the dancing would start again: 'We danced with the soldiers and some of the songs they sang were very much against Bevin for what he had done to us. I am not good at singing but I'd sing songs in Hebrew. The soldiers tried to keep time with the words and if they didn't understand they still clapped.'

But beyond this enchanting world, new and more sinister developments were taking place.

In Port-de-Bouc the first rumour had reached Saul Avigur from Sidney Silverman in London. The Foreign Secretary had told Attlee's Cabinet that the immigrants should be deported to Kenya, West Africa or another outpost of the Empire. On no account should they be returned to an already overcrowded Palestine, which would further inflame the situation with the Arabs. In the meantime, they would be held for a time in the British zone of Germany. It was the first time the possibility had found its way into newspapers.

The reporters had waited for a story to reward their patience and now they had one. Just as Reverend Grauel's revelations had created headlines, so did the rumoured return to Germany. 'Will England Throw Our Immigrants Back into Germany?' asked *Ha-aretz*. '*Exodus* Immigrants Being Returned to German Camps' reported *Davar*. Hundreds of similar stories thundered off the presses.

David Ben-Gurion recognised that this was a cynical attempt to persuade the immigrants to leave the transports and accept the French government's offer of residence. However, in London a Foreign Office spokesman fuelled the story of the return to Germany, saying, 'The immigrants are as close to Palestine as they are ever going to get.'

The next day the spokesman said that the heat was increasing the possibility of an epidemic breaking out on the ships and the French government 'has an obligation for the sake of public health to remove the immigrants from a situation which is threatening to themselves, the ships' crews and anyone who comes in contact with them. It is a situation which the illegal immigrants have created by refusing to come ashore.'

The medical authorities in Port-de-Bouc said there was no evidence of any threat of an infectious outbreak. But the damage had been done. For the first time the population of the town urged that the transports and their human cargoes should leave and go anywhere, even Germany.

Eagerness to keep the story alive had sent reporters to look for evidence to support the spokesman's claim that an epidemic was about to descend on the town. Outside the temporary office of the relief agency Entra'aide Français they found a man lying on a mattress and, squatting beside him, a white-coated figure who said he was a doctor. He announced that the man was an immigrant whom he had brought ashore from *Ocean Vigour*, added that he was waiting to take him to a Marseilles hospital and insisted that patient confidentiality forbade him to discuss his patient. The man refused to give his name. Before further questions could be asked, the pair had been driven away in an ambulance. The Reuters correspondent was certain he had seen the doctor working in the British Consulate in Marseilles.

Another headline came from Dr Jean Gayla, the inspector general of General Public Health. He said that four cases of measles had been diagnosed on *Empire Rival*, but it was definitely not an epidemic. However, as a precaution he had ordered all the children on the transports to be vaccinated. 'We expect 50 births in the next two

weeks. The babies will be British citizens if born on the ships.'
Another story was born.

Edward Ashcroft, the florid British deputy consul in Marseilles,
had joined the other diplomats in town to read out a statement that
he insisted had just been given to him by a Polish immigrant on *Ocean
Vigour*. The reporters listened in disbelief as Ashcroft read: 'Quote.
The immigrants on this ship have no hostility for the British people
or the British government. Above all we have no hostility towards
the soldiers or the crew of the ship. They have treated us with
humanity. We will not disembark but we will not in any way offend
against the good relations which exist between us all. We put our
trust in the democratic feeling of the British government. We do not
believe that while we are under British control anything serious will
happen to us. Full stop. End quote.'

Some of the reporters laughed in disbelief and asked if they could
interview the Polish immigrant. Ashcroft shook his head. One
journalist wondered if Ashcroft had graduated from the same school
of media manipulation as Major Cardozo in Haifa.

The deputy consul walked away.

Pressure to remove the immigrants from Port-de-Bouc came from
an unexpected quarter. On 20 August the Immigration Committee
of Attlee's government was informed by the Admiralty that the three
transports were well overdue back in Haifa and should discharge
their duties as soon as possible. Attached to the request was a memo
from Stewart Menzies, which revealed that five blockade-runners
were about to leave the United States for France to pick up a further
15,000 illegal immigrants and take them to Palestine. The entire
Palestine Patrol, including the ships moored for the past weeks off
Port-de-Bouc, would be urgently required to intercept the
immigrants. Meanwhile, the captains of the anchored transports
reported that their crews were showing increasing impatience,
especially those who were overdue leave.

Count Vanden Heuvel and his two agents, Derek Vershoyle and
David Smiley, talked to the seamen and paratroopers when they

came ashore to enjoy the limited facilities of the port. Some of the sailors were civilians who had signed short-term contracts that had expired two days before, on 18 August. They were now threatening to leave the ships and return home. The transports could not sail without them and to bring replacements from England would take weeks to organise. Seamen who had survived five years of war at sea were increasingly unwilling to return to active service after demobilisation. Menzies had formed the opinion that many of those on the transports were 'from the scrapings of the barrel'.

The MI6 chief had identified a further problem. Palestine had no space for holding the *Exodus* immigrants or the expected 15,000 on the blockade-runners from the United States. They should all be shipped to the British zone.

The Foreign Office had sought the opinion of Harold Beeley, its most experienced adviser on political and diplomatic tangles involving the Middle East. He had echoed Menzies's conclusion, with one suggestion: the announcement of deportation to Germany should be delayed until the last possible moment, giving the Jewish Agency no time to challenge the decision. Beeley proposed that the announcement should be made at 11am on 22 August, with departure at 6pm that afternoon. Bevin agreed.

In London there had been discussions over the original instructions from Bevin that the ships must leave at 11pm on 23 August. In Paris, Duff Cooper received a telephone call from the Chief Rabbi of Marseilles, protesting that the departure would fall on the Jewish Sabbath. For once Bevin had agreed to change his mind. Beeley's timing was approved by the Foreign Secretary.

The decision was taken without any discussion with Clement Attlee. In contrast to Bevin, Attlee's political style matched his physique: short, unprepossessing statements, his manner that of a country lawyer rather than a national leader. From the outset, the Prime Minister had made it clear that immigration was Bevin's brief. In turn the Foreign Secretary counted on the support of Arthur Creech-Jones, the Colonial Secretary, who wrote to Bevin on the morning of the departure of the transports to Hamburg, 'What feeling of distress attends to these people is entirely their own responsibility.'

Deputy consul Edward Ashcroft, his white linen suit standing out against the rust-stained hull, led a team of British diplomats up the gangway to the deck of *Runnymede Park*. Waiting for them were Colonel Gregson and Mordechai Rosemont. A platform had been set up from where Donald Mallet, the press secretary from the British Embassy in Paris, would address the immigrants. Soldiers lined the rails. On the platform was a large blackboard where the translator, Hannan Sonneborn, had taken up his position. Ashcroft had with him two assistants from his office who were to distribute copies of the message, written in French, Hebrew and German, after he had read it out and Sonneborn wrote the words on the blackboard.

The deputy consul's voice was emotionless: 'To the passengers of the *Runnymede Park*, *Empire Rival*, *Ocean Vigour*. This announcement is made to you on behalf of the British government. Those of you who do not begin to disembark at Port-de-Bouc before 18.00 hours, August 22, will be taken by sea to Hamburg.'

Ashcroft led the team back down the gangway to the waiting launch. It was only then that Mordechai Rosemont spoke with a passion which echoed across the deck: 'Our war is the war of a nation fighting for its existence and its right to survive, and not to return to the hell from which we came.'

Unable to understand his Hebrew, the soldiers shifted uneasily. For many of the immigrants the speech was worthy of Elazar Ben Ya'ir, leader of the Jewish forces on Masada who took their own lives rather than submit to the Romans.

When the news spread across the Jewish Diaspora, the feeling grew that to return the survivors of the Holocaust to Germany was an unimaginable outrage.

At 6pm, the appointed hour of departure, it seemed that every little boat in the harbour was accompanying the three transports as they slowly moved past the breakwater crowded with waving townspeople.

Waiting outside the three-mile limit were the Palestine Patrol escorts. Aboard the launches were the young men and women of the Haganah, reporters and newsreel cameramen.

Suddenly an astonishing sight could be seen from *Runnymede Park*. Suspended over a cage was a blue sheet and painted on it was a Union Jack. To its right, painted inside a white circle, was a Nazi swastika coloured from blood collected from women at the birth of their babies. The flag brought tears, then the singing of 'Hatikvah'.

Marshalik moved among the passengers, relaying the news Rachel had transmitted on the secret radio: Jewish leaders in several countries had called for a day of religious fasting and prayer for the immigrants to show solidarity. It was only then that some of the passengers began to wonder if they had been wise not to disembark rather than be sailing now into an uncertain future.

Still hidden in *Runnymede Park*'s bilges were the sticks of dynamite and their timing devices.

As the convoy sailed into the night, the Jewish Agency continued to try and contact Jews across the Diaspora, urging them to send telegrams to the foreign ministers of their own countries and, in particular, to Bevin. Royal Mail vans had delivered many thousands of envelopes to the Foreign Office in Whitehall throughout the day. Officials could not remember such a deluge in the history of the postal service; by the time the ships left Port-de-Bouc there were over 15 sack loads waiting to be read, telegraphed from all over the world.

Some were short. Typical was this one from Sydney, Australia: 'God asks you to let these people go home.' Others consisted of hundreds of words asking the same question: how could Britain, which had fought a war for freedom against the country where six million Jews were murdered, now send the survivors, in the words of one telegram, 'to the land of the death camps, whose smoke still hangs like a pall over everyone'? Several messages said the deportation would lead to all-out war in Palestine, as the Arabs would see the act as a signal of support for launching a bloodbath against the Jewish population.

David Ben-Gurion authorised the Jewish Agency to send a

telegram to all UN member states, including the Muslim states Afghanistan, India, Turkey and Iran, asking them to stop 'a crime against humanity by a superpower against a helpless group of people whose only wish is to secure their freedom and basic human rights'.

It appeared that this intense pressure might succeed when Léon Blum, the former prime minister of France, telephoned Duff Cooper with the proposal that if the British government promised that the *Exodus* immigrants would eventually be allowed to go to Palestine, the Jewish Agency would now persuade them to disembark under no threat of force. Cooper had asked if Blum could quantify 'eventually': was it three or four years? Blum replied, 'More likely three or four months.'

Cooper put the proposal to Bevin. It was rejected. The last-minute attempt to stop the immigrants going to Germany had fallen on deaf ears. So did the telegrams. They continued to arrive in London. Among the most poignant came one from Vera Weizmann, who wrote: 'As a woman and mother of two sons who fought in the last war in the British army and the RAF for freedom, justice and equal rights for all human beings . . . I believe the *Exodus* people truly want to flee from places of their tortured memories . . . to survive among their own people . . . They have nowhere else to go and if life cannot offer them this refuge then life itself loses its meaning.'

No one knows if her plea was ever seen by Bevin or merely joined the growing piles of telegrams destined to go unanswered.

In a villa overlooking Lake Geneva, David Ben-Gurion studied an advance copy of the UNSCOP report, due to be published on 30 August. It unanimously recommended the termination of the Mandate at the earliest possible date and the granting of independence to Palestine by a majority. The report also proposed partition. There would be an enclave under international control that would consist of Jerusalem and Bethlehem. The Jewish and Arab states would operate as one economic entity. In the first two years a monthly total of 150,000 Jews would be allowed into the Jewish designated area. Under partition there would initially be 500,000

Jews in one area and 416,000 Arabs in the other, along with some 90,000 Bedouins who were not to be counted as permanent residents. The Jerusalem–Bethlehem enclave would have a total population of 200,000, equally divided between the Arabs and Jews. UNSCOP called the arrangement 'the most realistic and practical solution'.

Ben-Gurion saw the proposal as 'the beginning . . . indeed, more than the beginning of our salvation'. As news came that the ships had reached Gibraltar, he told his visitors, Saul Avigur and Daniel Levin, who ran the Jewish Agency in the British zone in Germany, that he disagreed with them when they said there was a need for 'extreme action being taken to disrupt the disembarkation at Hamburg'.

Ben-Gurion added that while he understood the temptation to strike back against the way the *Exodus* immigrants had been treated, there should be no sabotage. It would wreck the carefully prepared plans that had been put in place that were to be voted on in the coming United Nations General Assembly Resolution for Partition on 29 November 1947, when he was confident that the State of Israel would become a reality. To destroy that by blowing a hole in the hold of *Runnymede Park* was unthinkable. He asked both men to give him their undertaking that this would not happen.

On board *Runnymede Park* Pessia Pevvetz whispered in her husband's ear that her contractions were coming more quickly. Instinctively he put his ear to her stomach, listened and smiled, then said that the baby was awake. She laughed and said only she could tell that.

The heat of the sun had gone where they sat on deck, side by side, watching Gibraltar come closer. An hour before, the Rock had been no more than a distant outline; now it towered over the skyline as the transport slowly moved into its anchorage. The rattle of the anchor dropping accompanied another contraction and Mike again pressed his ear against his wife's stomach, then said that the baby was coming. She nodded as he stood up and went in search of Mordechai Rosemont. In moments they were back, this time with Colonel Gregson. He smiled and asked Mike and Mordechai to

bring Pessia to his cabin while he went in search of one of the
immigrants who was a midwife.

Dusk was shrouding the Rock when the baby was delivered.
Draped in one of the colonel's towels, the little girl was named
Hannah. Colonel Gregson pressed a coin into Hannah's hand: 'I
believe this will bring you to the land of your dreams.'

Pessia tears were not only for having a healthy baby but also for
the kindness of Colonel Gregson.

For two days the immigrants emerged from their holds to watch
supplies being hoisted aboard. Some of the women lifted up their
babies to show the stevedores and in return received an orange or
some other fruit until an army officer stopped them, shouting it was
forbidden. To Gertruda he sounded like a keeper at the zoo in
Vilnius where she used to take Michael to see the animals.

For Noah Klieger, an officer had reminded him of how different his
welcome had been when he jumped overboard on the way to Port-de-
Bouc. Noah was a member of the three-man passenger committee on
Empire Rival. With him in the deck cage were some 700 refugees and
there were a further 800 in the hold. Noah knew that, like him, they
were survivors of the Holocaust. For them all, the transport 'was a real
prison ship with barbed wire and units of the 6th Airborne Division
guarding us. The conditions were disgusting. Poor food and little water.'

Once the committee had been formed, they were told by the ship's
captain the ships were heading back to France. At their first meeting
the trio had decided: 'None of us on board would disembark in
France. We were prepared to die unless we were brought back to
Palestine. But we had to make sure those on board the other two ships
knew of our decision and would join us. The only way to do that was
to swim to one of the ships so that we could at least let half of those
from *Exodus* know of our decision. Hopefully they would join us.'

Noah knew he was probably the best swimmer on board and had
volunteered to try and reach the nearest transport, *Ocean Vigour*. He
estimated it was a quarter of a mile away on the port side. 'Getting
out of the cage was the easy part. As a committee member I had
freedom to move around the ship. Once out, I ran to the guard rails

and fell backwards into the sea. It was a far bigger drop than I thought, around 90 feet. I went under like a stone and it seemed a while before I surfaced again.'

He began swimming towards the *Ocean Vigour*. He could make out people on the deck waving and shouting. Noah floated on his back, waiting for the transport to lower a boat and come to pick him up, but when he resumed swimming the ship had gone.

'I was alone in the middle of the Mediterranean, speaking to myself in a very loud voice, calling myself an idiot. "First why did you say you were a swimmer, bragging to the girls that you were such a good swimmer? Now you are going to die, not even 21 years old, die like a dog." Nobody was going to remember me. No one would know I had ever existed.'

Exhausted, he wondered how long he could survive. He was sure that he would drown and told himself that he just wanted 'to get this over with', but 'then I heard a siren. And then I touched something. It was a wooden platform.'

A Royal Navy minesweeper, the J354, had spotted him. He was hauled on board and taken to the captain on the bridge.

'He asked what I had been trying to do. I said I had just fallen overboard. Of course he didn't believe me. Why would anyone? People just don't fall overboard from a transport. But all he said was I had been in the sea for 54 minutes. I said that was a long time. He agreed that it was a long time. Had I been on some sort of secret mission? I said of course not. He kept asking the same question. I kept giving the same answer: I fell overboard. Finally he gave up.'

Noah was allowed to have a shower and dinner in the officers' wardroom. The ship's intelligence officer questioned him once more to try to find out why he had jumped, convinced his actions must be part of a special mission. The more Noah denied the truth, the more he was grilled as he enjoyed his meal. Finally, Noah was returned to *Empire Rival*, where he received a hero's welcome.

The ship's daily log recorded that he had been barred from the cage and two soldiers were detailed to guard him.

*

On the second day in Gibraltar a stevedore came on board *Runnymede Park* whistling a traditional Jewish folk song. It was the signal Marshalik had been told to expect. The stevedore was employed by the Haganah. He had received a coded message to tell the explosives expert to abandon the plan to use the dynamite. Some time later he dumped the explosives overboard.

Acting on a tip-off, Naval Intelligence on the Rock arranged for Commander Lionel 'Buster' Crabb, the service's explosives expert on locating limpet mines placed by Jewish terrorists in navy ports around the Mediterranean, to scour the sea. He found no dynamite. In his report to Ted Davis, MI6's naval liaison officer, Crabb wrote that 'the dynamite either quickly deteriorated or sank to the sea bed. Almost certainly being of poor quality it would do no harm.'

On the last morning in Gibraltar, each transporter broadcast the same message. Any immigrant wishing to disembark could be returned to France. Behind the offer was a week of secret moves. The Truman administration had stepped up its demand for Britain to abandon the voyage to Hamburg after the Jewish Agency in New York continued to inflame public opinion. There was a closed-door meeting in its headquarters to discuss whether to urge the immigrants to start a hunger strike; the idea was abandoned when medical opinion said it was essential to preserve their health. There was renewed anger when, having recovered some of the baggage stolen at Haifa port, the Mandate insisted it would only be sent to Germany after the immigrants had disembarked in Hamburg. People like Yosef Reich, Fira and Efraim Memakov had only the clothes they wore.

The *Exodus* immigrants had become pawns in the political world. In Munich, part of the American zone, streets were filled with thousands of protesters marching under the banner of the Central Committee of Liberated Jews to demand the refugees must not go to 'The Bastard Zone'. In London MI5 went on full alert after an informer claimed that the Stern Gang were planning to fire-bomb the city. US Secretary of State George Marshall expressed his own concern about the state of the DP camps in the British zone. Telegrams continued to pour into not only the Foreign Office in London but also the White House and the US State Department.

In Zurich, having stopped the planned sabotage, Ben-Gurion had told a Jewish Agency executive meeting that the fate of the *Exodus* immigrants showed the need for a powerful Jewish defence force because 'it is on this that our future depends. It is in accordance with this issue that we must determine all our Zionist strategy.'

Consequently Ben-Gurion did not welcome the intervention by Chaim Weizmann, who offered to mediate between Britain and France over the immigrants. Ben-Gurion saw Weizmann's efforts as opening 'a Pandora's box in which lurked arguments, when what was vital to have was a controlled and restrained situation'.

Ben-Gurion had assumed that since Weizmann was no longer president of the World Zionist Organisation he would not involve himself in any matter that impinged on Ben-Gurion's decision-making authority. But despite the fact he still felt that Churchill had betrayed him, Weizmann believed that any solution to the problem of the immigrants could only come through a 'calm and considered approach from which the UNSCOP report could be implemented'. With that in mind, he had approached Bevin.

Ben-Gurion's furious reaction was reflected in a letter to the Jewish Agency executive, expressing his anger at Weizmann involving himself 'in any kind of political activity either in England or America'. The fiery chairman of the executive's once-close friendship with Weizmann was in jeopardy. With barely two months to go before the United Nations met to vote on partition, Ben-Gurion could not afford to take such personal matters into account.

As the transports prepared to sail from Gibraltar on 30 August, Bevin sent a telegram to the Danish government proposing that their country should accept the immigrants. The reply came by return. Denmark saw no point in admitting them to any European country after they had already refused to disembark at Port-de-Bouc.

At mid-morning the transports sailed through the Straits of Gibraltar into the North Atlantic and the first autumn squalls.

Meanwhile, in Hamburg preparations to receive the hapless immigrants were well under way.

As the Rock of Gibraltar faded into the swell and waves began to slap even harder against the hull, Colonel Gregson felt a great gloom settle over *Runnymede Park* and sensed it would be reflected on the other transports. He watched from the bridge as Mordechai Rosemont went around the decks, trying to reassure the more agitated passengers. Some were shouting and others were crying, while a number prayed aloud. In the babble of sound came the chant: 'We must not go back to Germany.'

As if in defiance of the desperate cry, the convoy picked up speed and Miriam Bergman and Helena Levi found themselves dealing with their first case of seasickness in the sick bay at the stern. Trying to work on a ship that had begun to roll was difficult: bottles fell from dispensary cupboards and surgical bowls clattered on the floor. The veteran sick-bay attendant who ran the surgery cheerfully told them that the further north they went, the worse conditions could become. They should have been with him on the Atlantic convoys, he said. No matter how many trips you made, you always threw up eventually, usually at mealtimes. They did their best not to feel queasy as he slurped from a bowl of food in between helping them to deal with the growing number of seasickness cases.

Colonel Gregson had decided to allow Pessia and Mike Pevvetz to remain in his cabin with their baby daughter, Pessia. With the departure of Dr Cohen, Mordechai had found a Polish doctor among the immigrants and he had recommended that the family should rest as much as possible. Colonel Gregson found a berth in the ship's officer's quarters and visited the family at least once a day. Their smiling gratitude had been compensation for giving up his quarters. But on his last visit Pessia was no longer proudly showing him little Hannah, but instead kept asking what would happen to the baby once they reached Germany. He told her there was no cause to fear; those days were over. She still looked pensive when he left.

Gerald Landau realised the stop at Gibraltar had not improved conditions on *Empire Rival*. Breakfast was salty-tasting tea and a packet of biscuits which often had maggots when he bit into them. Dinner was usually a potato-based soup, with maggots floating in the bowl. One of the guards had shouted at the immigrants, 'If you are hungry you eat it all, maggots, the lot. Anyway, they're good for you. Full of protein!'

The furnace heat of the Mediterranean, which had turned the cold steel of the hold into an oven, steadily gave way to the chill air of the North Atlantic. The hold took on the feeling of a giant chill-box as rainwater dripped down its steel walls. For three days the sound of coughing had increasingly echoed around the hold and, rather than lie on the damp floor, people tried to sleep standing up, wedged against each other. In the morning the guards lowered buckets and mops to wipe up the condensation. When the immigrants were allowed on deck and could dry their clothes in the sea breeze and such sun as darted in and out of the clouds, they joined hands and sang the words of their folk songs.

One day merged into another, a day further out into the Atlantic, a day nearer Hamburg. The grey sea was empty and only the occasional seagulls reminded Gerald of land. At dawn the three new escorts would once more take on solid shapes. HMS *Burghead Bay* stood guard over *Runnymede Park*, HMS *Tremadoc Bay* over *Ocean Vigour* and HMS *Finisterre* over *Empire Rival*. The sleek destroyer and the two frigates had been waiting off Gibraltar, having sailed from Portsmouth.

The escorts had been sent to replace the Palestine Patrol, which would remain in the Mediterranean, ready to confront the blockade-runners from the United States with their expected 15,000 immigrants.

Every morning since leaving the Rock, Gerald had made his way up to the deck and seen the escorts exactly where they were the previous night, keeping pace with the transports. They were like guard dogs. Sometimes when he looked towards the bridge of *Empire Rival* he saw its captain, a Merchant Navy cap hiding his grey hair, a mug of tea in his hand. The few times Gerald had seen him down on the deck, there was a look of professional inhumanity about him, a lack of feeling which went with his job.

On board HMS *Finisterre*, Commander D.F. Chilton had been briefed to anticipate at Hamburg 'a certain amount of trouble, particularly with the world press and public wanting to watch'.

There was an unwritten law on all the transports. If an immigrant wished to keep his or her background to themselves that must be respected. To have survived was sufficient proof that every man, woman and child had lived through and coped with their ordeal in their own way; each had endured a portion of the Holocaust terror. So, Gerald Landau decided, it was with Dov Mills. 'He did things quietly and everybody trusted him, even the British.'

Gerald was cleaning up the galley for next morning's breakfast, when Dov appeared. 'His shirt was bulging and he said he had some sticks of dynamite and he wanted me to help hide them. I thought he was kidding until he opened his shirt. It was dynamite, all right!'

From that moment Gerald became an accomplice in the plot. The dynamite had been hidden in the garden of a Palyam safe house near Port-de-Bouc and smuggled on board shortly before *Empire Rival* sailed. Dov explained to Gerald that when the transport finally disembarked its passengers in Hamburg, the plan was that the dynamite would be exploded to punch a huge hole in the hull below sea level, making the ship useless for further journeys.

Gerald remembered: 'There was about 10 kilos of dynamite. Dov said it had to be hidden for the moment. I said that wasn't a problem. There was a space around the girders that supported the deck. But when I showed him and he began to stack the dynamite there, people became very nervous. I told them there was nothing to fear. Nothing could happen until the detonators were connected and the clock-timer set. But there was still the matter of getting the explosives down the bilges. Dov had become pally with one of the ship's stokers, a Canadian who hated what the ship was being used for. He gave Dov a crowbar to break through the trapdoor down into the bilge area. My job was to keep guard on deck, so I organised an impromptu concert with all the youngsters singing their heads off.'

Shortly afterwards, Dov appeared back on deck, nodding to

Gerald. Everything was in place. All that had to be done was to connect the detonator and set the timer clock.

There would be claims that Dov had been chosen by Nissan Livyathan, the Palyam commander in the South of France; that he had been a member of the Aliyah Palek group, experts in preparing documents for Yehuda Arazi's agents; or had worked for Brichah, another of Haganah's secret units.

Down the years, the story of Dov's dynamite would become a patchwork of conflicting recollections and press reports. A more accurate and overall account can be found in the archives of Mossad, Israel's secret intelligence service, and those of MI6. Among those who have studied the 'explosive file' is Meir Amit, the former director-general of Mossad. He called the file 'absolutely fascinating'. The judgement is shared by several senior MI6 officers who had access to the file.

A number of indisputable facts emerge. With regard to the decision to sabotage British ships involved in the war on illegal immigration, in the words of Nissan Livyathan at a meeting on 7 December 1947: 'Sabotage is commensurate with resistance. There is a permanent order to sabotage all deportation ships. But the explosion has to take place only after the passengers have disembarked.'

Other documents include reports on how dynamite came into the hands of the Palyam. Several were written by Munya Mardor, a member of the Haganah from 1934 to 1948, who became the director-general of the Israel Weapons Research and Development Authority. They describe 'unorthodox weapons for underwater warfare. One we called the umbrella mine, which could be assembled at sea.'

Another document outlined the role of Solel Bone, the Jewish port contractors who had smuggled Zvi Tiroche and the other Palyam sailors off *Exodus*. A Solel Bone company director, identified by Mardor only as 'Ron', told a meeting with the Haganah High Command in June 1947, 'We are able to provide men who are on good terms with the Mandate port guards and at the same time daring and cold-blooded. The explosives we want would be deposited by their men in our port office.'

Yet another document described arms depots for the Haganah. A particular need was for dynamite, smuggled into Palestine by TAS, a company the Haganah had set up.

The files of MI6 on Palestine contain the mimeographed pages of a report by Count Frederick Vanden Heuvel, dated 11 July 1947. It deals with an agent, identified as 'P', whom the intelligence officer had sent to Port-de-Bouc, where he had obtained a pass to visit the *Empire Rival* as part of his cover. Vanden Heuvel had approved a plan for 'P' to smuggle on board dynamite to enhance his credibility within the Haganah group in the port.

If MI6 had connived in planting the explosives on *Empire Rival*, it would give credence to the claim made about the blockade-runner *Pan Crescent*. It had been undergoing repairs in Venice in the spring of 1947 when it was rocked by an underwater explosion. This was attributed initially by the Haganah to an Arab terrorist group, but after further investigation it was concluded that the damage was caused 'by a British-made explosion'.

As the *Empire Rival* entered the Bay of Biscay on 5 September 1947, Dov decided that his dynamite would be detonated two hours after the passengers came ashore in Hamburg.

Chapter 21

Homeward Bound

By the morning of 7 September, the extensive preparations in Hamburg to receive the immigrants had been completed under the command of Major-General W.H.A. Bishop, the deputy chief of staff of the British Army of the Rhine (BAOR). A railway route from the dockside to the detention camps at Emden and Poppendorf, near the British and Soviet zones, had been selected and the line had been checked and placed under guard against a rescue attempt.

Ever since Hamburg had been designated as the final port of call there had been demonstrations in the city, leading to clashes between the British Army and pro-Jewish militants. Bishop had established his office in the port's operations building overlooking the harbour. On a large map three flags, each bearing the name of a transport, marked the berths where they would dock after they had entered the Kiel Canal.

Though he had a large staff of junior officers and WAAF secretaries at his disposal, Bishop preferred to write his orders in old-fashioned longhand before they were typed and distributed. Each document was headed 'Operation Oasis'. What had started as a single file – 'Warfield/Exodus/ immigrants' – had grown to fill a metal filing cabinet: files on the detention camps; their cooking, sleeping, sanitation, medical and educational facilities; the intelligence officers assigned to interview people; a liaison team marked 'Jewish Contacts'; the names and language skills of interpreters. A separate file, marked 'FO', contained copies of messages from the

Foreign Office. Then there was a bulky file of English-language press cuttings about the various stages of 'Operation Oasis'.

The number of telephone calls he had received from the world's press led Bishop to believe that the file would continue to expand. The thought was a nagging concern. The War Office had sent a senior press officer to handle the media but this had done little to reassure Bishop. Publicity of any kind was anathema to the middle-aged officer. He wondered whether he should deploy some of the soldiers from the battalion of the Sherwood Foresters he had summoned to guard the port and keep the reporters at bay.

From his office window Bishop could see that the fog which had reduced visibility on the Elbe River, from where the transports would come later that day, was lifting. Since morning the entire dock area had been filling with ambulance trucks and steel-helmeted troops. Behind them waited the trains. Further back were the canvas-covered fences to block the view for the assembled reporters and photographers. Bishop had sent for the Foresters because a year ago the regiment had served in Palestine. He wanted men who understood how to handle the Jews.

As the German coastline emerged through the drizzle, Mordechai Rosemont stood on the crowded deck of *Runnymede Park* and delivered what many of his listeners would call his most moving speech. In a voice that held his audience spellbound, he took them on a journey through the centuries, when time and again their ancestors had come close to annihilation. As they listened to every word, people surreptitiously wiped tears from their eyes.

Mordechai paused, gathering himself for his peroration. There were still hard times ahead, he said. Their captors would not take kindly to having failed to get them to obey their orders in France. No doubt now they would try to force them to their will. To resist would attract violence. We have suffered enough.

Tears flowed more freely now as the transports began to sail up the river, close to the shores, past places with familiar names to many on board: Brunsbüttel, Glückstadt and Wischhafen.

Mordechai's voice rose to a thunderous climax: 'Two years after the end of the Holocaust its survivors have been caged in a British prison ship on the high seas only for wanting to live in the land of our fathers. It waits for our coming. Soon we will go.'

The applause resounded around the deck and an accordionist led the audience in the 'Hatikvah'.

Harold Gardner and the other guards on *Runnymede Park* had been told by Colonel Gregson that when the ship docked they would be replaced by a detachment of the Grenadier Guards. 'They were going to turn out in full ceremonial dress: red jackets and busbies, shining boots and perfectly creased trousers. They would look eight feet tall and I thought it would look pretty incredible, like changing the guards at Buckingham Palace.'

The decision to deploy the imposing-looking Guards had been taken by Major-General Bishop as a warning to the refugees not to start any trouble.

Behind the canvas-covered fences around the port area demonstrators from the notorious Bergen-Belsen concentration camp, which the British authorities had turned into a DP camp, had arrived in their hundreds, bearing banners with slogans such as 'End the Bevin Terror in Palestine', '*Exodus* in Hamburg: A Mark of Cain for England' and 'Together with *Exodus* to Struggle for a Free Aliyah'.

During the night the three transports had anchored in the mouth of the Elbe before moving slowly upriver in the early hours of Monday. The decision to do this had been made by Major-General Bishop in the belief that by then the protests would have ended and disembarkation could go ahead without any disruption. He had also decided to cancel the presence of the Grenadier Guards.

Aviva Porat had spent the night sitting with the younger children in the hold of *Runnymede Park*. To keep out the drizzle, the soldiers had rigged a canvas awning across the top of the cage, but soon the body heat of the passengers made it uncomfortable and Colonel Gregson ordered the covering rolled back. The teenager had pointed out to the children the few stars visible through the cloud breaks; she sensed their fear as the younger ones huddled closer to her. She felt the same: out there in the gathering dawn was Germany. How would its people respond to Jews now? To keep her own fears at bay, she helped the children to make sure they had all collected the items that had been distributed at Port-de-Bouc by the relief agencies: under-wear, sweaters, dresses, shoes and socks. Germany, she reminded them, would be cold at this time of the year.

Dawn was breaking when they went up for the last breakfast on board from the kosher kitchen Mordechai Rosemont had organised. On the river the first of the ferryboats were bringing people to work. They stared at the transports but did not respond to the children's waves.

Watching the scene, Aviva was troubled. The ferries were full of defeated Germans who were able to live in their own land and go about their daily lives, while she and all the others on the transports were being returned to the land of their people's murderers. She led the children back down to the hold; it was better to stay there than continue to witness the scenes on the water which could trigger such painful thoughts.

In Hamburg, the Sherwood Foresters had once more taken up position on the quay. Frogmen had searched under the pilings for explosives. None had been found.

Ocean Vigour was the first to dock. On the quay an officer used a loudspeaker to instruct the immigrants to disembark peacefully. A few voices shouted down they would not. The officer repeated his order. The soldiers raised their clubs and held their tear-gas grenades ready as they moved closer to the transport. Peering over the top of the canvas-covered fences were the reporters and newsreel cameramen Major-General Bishop had hoped to keep away; instead they had brought stepladders to give them views of the first refugees coming slowly down the gangway to the dock before disappearing into the cloth-covered wire corridor which led to the waiting trains.

Two-thirds of the 1,406 passengers disembarked without resisting. The remainder started a sit-down protest on deck. The officer with the loudspeaker ordered them to stop. His demand was ignored. He blew a whistle. Soldiers ran up the gangway and dragged the immigrants bodily to the train. When the quay was clear, a truck arrived. Stencilled on its side was 'Bomb Disposal Squad'. Its men boarded *Ocean Vigour*. An hour later they emerged and reported to the officer that there was no sign of any explosives.

Shortly afterwards, *Empire Rival* docked. The same procedure was repeated – only this time its 1,420 passengers left without protest. Among them was Gerald Landau. Once more the bomb squad began to search. Suddenly one came rushing down the gangway, yelling for the area to be cleared. The sticks of dynamite in the bilges had been found. When the area was cleared, the bomb squad brought down the explosives. Ruth Gruber, one of the hundreds of reporters watching the scene, later reported that all but one of the explosives were detonated 'in Hamburg's deserted Barrack Square'.

The remaining stick of dynamite and its detonator were displayed at a BAOR-organised press conference which Major-General Bishop chaired with unconcealed satisfaction. He had been inundated with protests about the way the media had been stopped from having contact with the immigrants. 'You will see now why we had to take steps to protect your lives. Among them were terrorists ready to take more British lives.'

David Ben-Gurion was infuriated by the plan to dynamite the transport. Not only was it a breach of his authority, but it came at a crucial time in the partition vote. He had assigned every member of the Jewish Agency's Political Department to lobby the delegates at the General Assembly of the UN. He had gone to bed one night with the reassurance that the 22 members of the Latin American block, the largest voting group, would be won over, but was awoken from an uneasy sleep with news that the Vatican remained opposed to Jewish statehood. The Soviets still refused to indicate how they would vote; South Africa, New Zealand and Australia had indicated they would support statehood but thought it would be helpful if Israel would agree to the Negev being given Arabic sovereignty, UNSCOP having earmarked the Negev for the Jews.

The explosives had played into the hands of the Arab media. From Damascus to Cairo, newspapers asked how their countries could live cheek by jowl with a nation that had planned such an outrageous act of terrorism. It was seen as further proof that Alexander Cadogan, the UK's representative to the United Nations, had been right when he said, 'The UNSCOP plan is so manifestly unjust to the Arabs that it is difficult to see how we could reconcile it with our conscience.'

To have to deal now with the attempted bombing on *Empire Rival* was a problem the fiery Ben-Gurion could do without.

Runnymede Park had been delayed in berthing until mid-morning on the Monday after the bomb incident. The Sherwood Foresters waited on the dockside while the bomb squad rushed down to the bilges.

The decision to conduct an immediate search was based on Colonel Gregson's estimate of the severity of the threat. Normal procedure would have seen the evacuation of the immigrants, their guards and the entire crew first. But to do that would have required considerable planning if the bomb had been set to explode with the immigrants still on board. For Gregson that was highly unlikely. The Palmach and even the Stern Gang would not have wished to kill their own people. Again, if there was a bomb, it would have been hidden in the bilges, in which case it would probably have caused only minimal damage, as evidenced by the dynamite uncovered on *Empire Rival*. Better have the search over and done with.

The squad returned empty-handed and left. Shortly afterwards, the soldiers who had accompanied the transport to Haifa departed, several of them calling down their farewells to the 1,485 refugees in the holds before tramping down the gangway and marching off. Then came the silence.

The waiting, the uncertainty about what was going to happen, continued to increase the tension. A group of elderly people, the sick, pregnant women and nursing mothers had been stationed by the companionway which led from the hold to the deck. It would be their escape route if trouble erupted. All eyes were on Mordechai Rosemont. He had already passed around the word that the delay in disembarking, the presence of the bomb squad and the unexpected departure of the soldiers who had befriended them indicated that trouble was brewing.

He had already made a strategic decision. After his speech the previous day, he had been told that a number of the immigrants still wanted to resist going ashore and planned to stage a passive strike and remain on board until they were assured they would be able to go to Palestine. While Mordechai recognised the violence they could face, he also admired their determination.

There were two sets of steel steps bolted to the hold's walls. The younger immigrants liked to use these at mealtimes to climb up to the deck – it gave them some much-needed exercise. During the night Mordechai told them to remove one set of steps: 'I ordered the second set of steps to be left intact so that the British could not say people couldn't leave the ship because there were no stairs. When he discovered what had happened the captain had threatened to shoot anyone who made a move to remove the second steps. I said he could shoot me.'

Once more Mordechai had negotiated with Colonel Gregson. Provided there was a guarantee the sick, the elderly, pregnant women, nursing mothers and small children were free to go ashore, the second set of steps would remain intact. However, the dismantled steps would provide excellent weapons, along with the bolts that had secured them. He estimated there were an overwhelming number ready to fight. And so they waited in the lengthening silence.

Suddenly an amplified voice boomed down into the hold. Those assembled by the companionway were to come on deck. Anyone else wishing to disembark should follow and would be peacefully escorted from the ship. Miriam and Helena began to lead their group up to the deck. No one else followed. Freddie Kronenberg and Johann Goldman returned to their places among immigrants ready to resist any attempt to dislodge them. Some held pieces of the ladder.

The silence lengthened. Suddenly the loudspeaker burst into life again, announcing they had one minute to leave the hold. Aviva Porat joined in the cat-calls. Then, from up on deck, came footsteps and orders shouted in English. Steps could be heard pounding down the companionway. Mordechai had positioned himself beneath the still-intact ladder, ready to grab the first of the Foresters climbing down. 'I had positioned myself there for a good reason. Somebody had stuck up a poster which showed British soldiers fighting the Nazis. I was planning to point it out to the soldiers. Instead I was hit in the face with a club, dripping blood everywhere.'

As the Foresters rushed down the ladder and the companionway, weapons swinging, the entire hold rose to their feet and a full-scale hand-to-hand fight began. Soldiers lay about them with their clubs; immigrants hurled anything they could lay their hands on. Aviva would remember how she 'bit and scratched, kicked and pulled the helmets of the soldiers down over their eyes and kicked them in the groin'. Other passengers grabbed soldiers off the ladder and punched them or grabbed their batons and struck out at any Forester who came with range.

Despite his bloodstained face, Mordechai directed the defence of his people. He estimated there were now at least a hundred well-armed troops fighting their way into the hull. 'They were hitting everyone. People who had said they wanted no part in the fight were still bludgeoned. Now everybody was involved, using everything they could lay a hand on . . . bottles, tins, everything. It was like a rerun of the fight on *Exodus*.'

A woman who had been standing near Johann screamed she couldn't see and fell to the floor. She was dragged aside by two soldiers. One of the immigrants was charging with a piece of the ladder, hitting soldiers right and left, screaming like a maddened bull, shouting, 'No quarter given or taken!'

Resistance grew. As the soldiers started to grab individuals and carry them by their arms and legs up the companionway, they were hauled back into the hold. Women retreated into its corners and linked arms to create a solid mass of bodies, their backs against the steel walls, using their feet to kick out at any soldiers who tried to grab them.

A whistle blew twice on deck, the signal for the troops to form a phalanx, rather like a Roman legion, in the centre of the hold. From the deck a powerful jet of freezing water from a hose doused the women. Another whistle blew. The torrent of water stopped and the soldiers once more charged, slipping on the floor as they again grabbed immigrants, trying to haul them up to the deck.

Aviva fought on while, crouching behind her, the children shivered from the water and cried in terror. A soldier tried to grab a boy and Aviva bit his hand. He yelped and looked for an easier target than this fiery-eyed teenager.

Slowly but inevitably, the soldiers gained control and a growing number of immigrants, each held by an arm and leg, arrived on deck, wriggling and twisting as they tried to break free. But the threat from a club stopped them.

Finally, four hours after the battle began, the hold was empty and the last of the immigrants were led to the waiting train. Its windows were covered with barbed wire and armed troops stood at the end of each carriage.

It was getting dark when the train arrived in Poppendorf, near Lübeck. A total of 29 *Runnymede Park* immigrants had been left behind in a Hamburg military hospital to be treated for injuries sustained in the fight. Mordechai Rosemont had been taken to a military police station, questioned by an intelligence officer and, after being cleaned up, received a visit from Colonel Gregson. There was a polite exchange of words in which Mordechai thanked his visitor for all he had done on the voyage and said he hoped that one day they would meet under different circumstances. Gregson said he hoped so too.

For Yosef Reich the train brought back memories of his own journey to Buchenwald: 'The same being crammed together like sardines. The same stench, not just human waste, but fear. For all of us a train like this with barbed wire on the windows had meant a journey which could end in death. In a corner a young couple with a baby were taking turns to warm water in a bottle under their arms to give the infant a drink.'

Some of the passengers stared stoically at the pretty countryside: small villages with steep-roofed houses and people working in the fields, gathering the last of the harvest. The farmers stopped to stare as the train rattled past. Yosef wondered how many trains had passed this way taking Jews to the camps.

For Aviva the journey across northern Germany triggered the simmering anger of weeks of crushed hopes that had climaxed on board the train. Since breakfast none of them had received anything to eat or drink. 'Passengers had become berserk, sabotaging everything they could lay their hands on until the armed soldiers had cocked their weapons. It was raining and I felt the sky is weeping for us.'

Arriving at Poppendorf, they found themselves in a camp that had been hastily arranged to accommodate them and that again evoked memories of concentration camps: the corrugated-iron roofs on huts which, on that first evening, were already cold from the wind blowing off the Baltic Sea. For those who were billeted in tents, conditions were even bleaker. There was no heating and the canvas had holes in it. Each immigrant was given a metal camp bed, a mattress made from potato sacks stuffed with straw, and one thin blanket. Huts built for 60 people now held double that number. The camp, which had until recently housed 2,000 German prisoners of war, now held the immigrants from *Runnymede Park* and *Empire Rival*.

Freddie Kronenberg, once the gatekeeper at Auschwitz, had seen the wire fences and the patrolling troops. But unlike the concentration camp, 'they were not threatening. One or two even nodded and pointed to a large tent. Inside a hot meal had been prepared. I knew then that things would not be too bad.'

Passengers from *Ocean Vigour* were at Am Stau, a camp a mile away. After the bomb incident it had been decided to send them there at MI6's request; the Secret Intelligence Service suspected the transport had on board members of the Palyam, who could be more easily interrogated if they were kept in a separate compound.

Next morning Mike Pevvetz and his wife, Pessia, cradling Hannah, joined the line waiting to be officially registered. Soldiers had set up tables outside the dining tent, where the couple had eaten breakfast and had been given a bottle of warm milk for Hannah. During the meal there had been unanimous agreement that no one should reveal his or her personal identity. It was the start of what Mike called 'our policy of non-cooperation until we received absolute guarantees we would go to Palestine'.

When he came to stand before a table he was asked his name. 'I am Churchill. Winston Churchill. The soldier raised his eyebrows. How had I come to the *Exodus*? I told him I was kidnapped and brought to the transport.'

The nonplussed soldier had stared at Pessia and asked who she was. 'Mrs Churchill, of course. And the baby is our little Churchill daughter.'

He waved the family aside and motioned for the next person to step forward. He gave his name as Neville Chamberlain. Another claimed kinship with the Attlee family, someone else said he was related to Stalin and another to Truman. So it went on, with each name followed by Palestine as the place of birth and current address as *Exodus 1947*.

By midday the registration was abandoned.

A few days after the camps opened, Mordechai Rosemont arrived. The British authorities had failed to find a charge to hold him. He told the assembled crowd at Poppendorf: 'We, the people of *Exodus 1947*, have endured so much suffering that we feel like we are all one big family. We must now work together as a team as we prepare to go to our real home.'

He quickly brought together the various Jewish relief organisations to provide food, soap, religious and school books, ritual items for the coming high holidays, newspapers in Hebrew and Yiddish, warm winter clothes and new shoes. Shoemakers among the refugees were provided with cobbler's hammers and lasts to fit 2,700 heels and 1,700 soles for worn-out footwear; 4,500 toothbrushes and an equal number of tubes of toothpaste were distributed. The majority of the supplies came from stockpiles in the American zone.

Mordechai was determined that all the supplies should be equally divided; he wanted no distinction regarding the previous wealth or position held by an *Exodus* immigrant. Here they were all on a par.

The Foreign Office officials sent to Lübeck to organise the return of the immigrants to France – a move quickly rejected by them – became increasingly alarmed at the growing authority of Mordechai Rosemont. Having already identified him as the prime source of the campaign not to disembark at Port-de-Bouc, which in turn had led to bruising publicity over Operation Oasis, Bevin ordered that there must be no repetition of events. But in Mordechai he had met a wily opponent.

Mordechai told members of the committees he had set up at Poppendorf and Am Stau to organise the daily affairs of the camps that they must 'be polite to the British but also always firm and you must show them we are not afraid. Until we can return to Palestine we must show we regard them as our jailors and oppressors.'

On 26 September 1947, Walter Eytan, the head of the Political Department, strolled down to David Ben-Gurion's office at the end of the corridor in the Jewish Agency building in Jerusalem. He knocked on the door and walked in, one of the two allowed unrestricted access to the chairman. The other was Eytan's deputy, Golda Meyerson.

His face sallow and strained from long days of work, Eytan slumped into an armchair opposite Ben-Gurion's desk. At the end of each day, the chairman would be waiting for Eytan's latest report. As usual he delivered it in his precise voice: 'My latest reading indicates there are now 23 votes for partition and 13 against. The non-deciders remain just that – undecided.'

Ben-Gurion grunted. Those committed to support partition were still short of the two-thirds majority needed at the meeting of the UN General Assembly on 29 November. Eytan expressed his concern that some Jewish Agency officials in New York were not pulling in the votes they needed and were 'motivated by a hunt for *kavod*, glory, personal ambition and prestige'.

That said, Eytan conceded, others he had placed in New York were beyond criticism: Eliyahu Sasson, the Aleppo-born Arabist in the Political Department, had established invaluable contacts with the Syrians, Yemenis and Iraqis, even though they had yet to confirm whether their nations would support partition. Moshe Tov was coaxing, as only he could, the Colombians, Ecuadorians and Mexicans to place their nations' support behind the motion. Russian-born Elyahu Epstein was satisfied the Soviets would commit, but less certain of Luxembourg, Ethiopia and Liberia. Eytan said there was still time to win them over.

Once more Ben-Gurion grunted. Time was not an option. Every hour of every day counted. He wanted a worldwide two-pronged campaign to nail down the undecided. He reminded Walter Eytan: 'To be a nation answerable for its own destiny is a precious ideal, and the Jewish people have abided by that ideal with messianic longing. We have come this far by surviving endless efforts and grim sacrifices. We must never forget that our state cannot simply be set up by declaration. It is created from the foundation of hard work.'

Eytan smiled. Ben-Gurion at his biblical best was a powerful force. The Agency's political mastermind walked back to his office re-energised to resume his search for votes.

Another pressing problem Ben-Gurion knew he must resolve was the future of the *Exodus* immigrants. No one could challenge his commitment to them; in every speech he had made that plain. But if the United Nations vote went as he hoped, all-out conflict with the Arabs would follow as surely as the sun rose over Mount Carmel. The Haganah could no longer be an underground guerrilla force but would have to be a full-scale army, one based on the British Army, whose military discipline he had admired in Europe.

Ben-Gurion accepted that on paper the Haganah could call upon some 60,000 people, but many had only received basic training and there were fewer than 16,000 armed and ready to fight the Arabs. However, there were 28,000 immigrants in the Cyprus camps who were of military age. Should Aliyah Bet not focus on bringing them first to Palestine? Or should he continue to support the view that the priority must be to complete the *Exodus* operation? Certainly it would be an unprecedented triumph. On his last visit to the United States, in the high-rise apartment of Rudolf Sonneborn in New York, that view had been expressed again. In many ways he understood: *Exodus* had become a Zionist flagship.

Yet there was also another factor. For over 4,000 immigrants suddenly to arrive at one time now would have a serious economic effect. The elderly, the sick and the young would all require medical help and others would need proper training in military tactics if they were to be of any real use in defending the country.

Since the start of the *Exodus* operation there had been crucial political changes with the visit of the UNSCOP committee, the endless debates at the United Nations, the decision that Britain was ready to give up the Mandate and, finally, the vote of the General Assembly at the end of November.

Every Jewish man, woman and able child would be needed to defend their people. On his visit to the settlements he would usually end a speech with the reminder: 'You don't become a farmer in a day. Or learn how to make a road or put up a telegraph pole.' Recently he had added another required skill. How many of his listeners could handle a gun?

That evening, after Walter Eytan left, David Ben-Gurion again sat behind his desk, which was piled high with books and papers, and pondered a question. How many of the *Exodus* immigrants would need weapons training? He re-read a letter he had received earlier from the Haganah High Command: 'Like you we are certain that we will soon face a war and we should expect our fallen to be in four-figure numbers. It is most urgent that the suitability of all future immigrants takes that into account.'

How to resolve the matter went to the very heart of illegal immigration. Should all the *Exodus* immigrants be admitted at once? Or should they be allowed entry on a decision taken about their suitability to defend the country? Doctors and nurses must be given priority. Linguists would also have a favoured position, provided they spoke Hebrew or Yiddish and could quickly be trained in Arabic.

Yehoshua Levy, the treasurer of the Jewish Agency, had summarised the dilemma posed by the *Exodus* immigrants: 'While security of the people takes priority over all else, we would be committing a wrong towards the people of *Exodus*, who could rightly be called soldiers, if they are admitted by a selection process.'

The Arabs had enormous reserves of men and money, and no shortage of arms; they used anyone who could handle a gun or drive a vehicle. The Jews must do the same. David Ben-Gurion finally made his decision in the small hours of the morning of 27 September. The *Exodus* immigrants must be brought in as soon as possible after the partition vote.

In the last two months they had gained worldwide support and huge sums of money had been donated to buy more ships to bring other immigrants to Palestine. To do anything that would be construed as delaying the return of the *Exodus* passengers to their homeland would be seen throughout the Diaspora as a gigantic error of judgement. As he sat in his office David Ben-Gurion felt more at peace than he had for some time.

The onset of winter and the overall living conditions there had made Poppendorf and Am Stau unsuitable. The provision of extra blankets had been no compensation for the absence of any heating facilities and heavy rain had turned the ground between the huts into pools of mud. There had been regular overflows in the toilet blocks. Some of the two-storey wooden bunk beds had collapsed from rot. At night rats emerged from holes in the floorboards. The Foreign Office officials in Lübeck had told reporters it was difficult to get German workers to go to the camps and carry out the necessary repairs but that 'other matters are under discussion'.

On 20 October 1947, after a spate of stories about conditions in both camps, Major-General Bishop met with Foreign Office officials in Lübeck and agreed it would be best to transfer the *Exodus* immigrants to two other camps, Emden in East Frisia, and Sengwarden, north of Wilhelmshaven. The proposal was put to Mordechai Rosemont, who issued a statement to the ever-present journalists: 'Nothing will deter us from going to Palestine. Which jail we go to is up to the British. However, as they have shown no threat to transfer us forcibly we will accept the move. But we wish to make clear that our immediate departure to Palestine remains a burning issue and, until that happens, we are still their prisoners and they are our jailers and oppressors.'

For the reporters it was another story which reinforced the status of the *Exodus* immigrants. The fund-raising across the Diaspora, which had eased off in recent weeks, flared back into life. All along the East Coast money poured into events organised by the Jewish Agency to buy clothes and gifts for the immigrants. Jews in Britain, France and Spain sent parcels to addresses that had been published in the press for Jewish New Year. In Palestine the Jewish National Fund asked people to donate saplings which would be planted and registered in the fund's 'Golden Book'.

On 2 November, the transfer of the *Exodus* immigrants began. In an attempt to win over the reporters, a few had been allowed to travel on the trains taking them to their new camps. The newspaper accounts of conditions on board conjured up memories of the Nazi cattle trucks. The new camps at Emden and Sengwarden were similarly described, with vivid accounts of filthy sanitation conditions, huts filled with rotting rubbish and broken windows. This time local German workers were quickly recruited to clean and repair the camps. The gates and the guards were removed. For the first time the *Exodus* immigrants were free to move around as they pleased.

For Fira and Efraim it was a time to talk of marriage. He would remember: 'We talked about the music and the dances. The children would be there. I would find my brother and aunt in America. We talked and talked and still talked. We were just so happy.'

On 26 November 1947 Saul Avigur, Yehuda Arazi and Ada Sereni arrived in the camp in Emden, having driven through the American zone. They had come not only to inspect both the camps but also to plan how the *Exodus* immigrants could be brought to Palestine. It would involve the kind of journey across Europe they had already made to board the *Exodus*. Then the trucks of the Jewish Brigade had been there to help; now they were no longer available and the British most certainly would not assist. At Emden they were met by Moshe Sneh, from the Paris office of Aliyah Bet. He said that the immigrants in both camps had been promised they were 'at the head of the immigration-to-Palestine queue. It is essential to honour that promise because of the pessimistic mood of the majority in the camps. They feel they have been deserted.'

Avigur explained that was why they had come. Mordechai Rosemont had already sent a telegram to Ben-Gurion, giving a grim account of conditions in both camps. Later that day, Avigur went to each camp and addressed the immigrants and reassured them they had not been forgotten: 'You will be wrong to feel you have won all the battles and will lose the war. You are wanted for the greatest war of all that is coming, the war to defend our country.'

Strategically, he said, nothing could happen until after the United Nations vote. In the meantime his two companions – Arazi and Ada – would search for the boats that would finally take them to Palestine.

The 300 delegates of the fledgling United Nations took their seats in a converted skating rink on a cloudy afternoon on Saturday 29 November 1947 in Flushing Meadow, New York. They had come to vote on the future of Palestine. Meanwhile, 6,000 miles away in Jerusalem, it was midnight. Within the city's ancient walls everyone with a wireless was glued to their set, listening to the news from New York over the Palestine Broadcasting System. Those who did not have a wireless gathered round the sets in their neighbours' homes.

In a small stone house in one of the city's new Jewish quarters, Golda Meyerson had invited friends to hear the broadcast. Her home was simply furnished and the dominant feature in the crowded kitchen was the Phillips radio on a shelf between books in Russian and Hebrew, plus a few in English dealing with laws under which the Mandate was operated. The kitchen was her salon and office, where two generations of Zionists had come to seek her advice on business deals, the purchase of a piece of land, her interpretation of a Mandate law. In between they ate her freshly baked cakes and accepted another cup of coffee from the pot she kept brewing on the stove. On that November night the wireless volume was turned up so that those in downstairs rooms or standing in the street outside could hear through the open front door and windows. From time to time Golda would give her thoughts on the broadcast.

By late afternoon in Flushing Meadow the last of the delegates were settling in their seats inside the hall. Among them was Emir Faisal ibn Abdul al-Aziz of Saudi Arabia in his magnificent black and gold *abaya*, who sat in the middle of the Arab delegation.

Since he had led his delegation to their seats, the Emir had sat silent and watchful, his hawk-eyed face staring ahead at the podium. He now knew that the years of secret negotiations with Britain he had encouraged as part of its grand strategy in the region for the Arabs had produced only empty promises – for he had discovered that Britain had also been holding secret meetings with the Jewish Agency under the chairmanship of Sir Alan Cunningham, the Mandate High Commissioner. Among the proposals discussed was that in return for Britain voting in favour of a State of Israel, the Jews would allow British troops to remain in Palestine to defend its own well-established interests in the region.

But now, as the delegates filed in, neither the Jews nor the Arabs knew how the United Kingdom would vote. Their delegation was led by Sir Alexander Cadogan. Surrounded by Foreign Office civil servants, he sat silent, his face impassive, the quintessential diplomat in his custom-made Savile Row suit.

Shortly after 5pm the General Assembly president, Osvaldo Aranha, a slightly built Brazilian, his forehead shining with perspiration from the newsreel camera lights, stepped up to the podium and rapped once with his gavel to announce that the time had come to vote on the partition of Palestine.

An aide stood beside him and held out a tray. On it were 56 slips of folded paper, each bearing the name of a nation represented in the hall. Aranha picked out one and read it. For a moment he stared at the delegates, then he announced, 'Guatemala.' The ambassador of

Guatemala stood and announced his country had voted in favour of partition.

On the other side of the world, in the wire room of the Palestine Broadcasting System, pieces of paper were ripped from the tele-printers and a copy-boy ran across a courtyard to the studio of the Hebrew service. A second messenger went to the adjoining Arab-language studio. Translators turned the copy into Hebrew and Arabic for the waiting broadcasters.

Chaim Weizmann knew that no other decision in the short life of the United Nations had produced such passion over the fate of a slice of land on the eastern rim of the Mediterranean. Like Golda Meyerson, like every adult Jew, Weizmann had followed the weeks of nego-tiations which would soon culminate as delegates finally voted on the proposal to cut the holy land of Moses, Jesus and Mohammed the Prophet into two separate states, one Jewish, one Arab. Most controversially, the United Nations had already rejected the right of either state to have sovereignty over Jerusalem, the city where the political, religious and economic life of Palestine had for centuries been based.

Without Jerusalem as their capital, the Jewish people felt they would have a nation without a soul. For them, the city had not only spiritual but also strategic meaning. In 1947 two out of every three inhabitants were Jews, almost a fifth of the entire Jewish population in Palestine. To lose control over Jerusalem meant vital routes to the Mediterranean and the Judean hills would no longer be in Jewish hands. However, the Vatican had told its papal nuncios – its diplomats – throughout Latin America and Catholic Ireland and Poland to make it clear to the Jewish leaders that in return for the Holy See's support, Jerusalem must be internationalised. Without that guarantee the powerful Catholic vote would not support partition. The Jewish Agency had finally agreed, and Guatemala became the first country within the Catholic fiefdom to vote in favour. Now, on that November evening, it remained to be seen whether the other Catholic countries would vote the same way.

In Jerusalem, the moment voting began Golda Meyerson, cigarette between her lips, started to write down in a notebook each decision on one of three pages headed 'Partition', 'Against' and 'Abstentions'. Below Guatemala she wrote in turn 'Australia', 'Nicaragua', 'Costa Rica' and 'United States'. For the first time she smiled. It looked as if the Vatican would keep its promise. On the 'Against' page Golda wrote 'Cuba', 'India', 'Iraq' and 'Iran'. She shrugged; she had not expected otherwise. Over the wireless the Hebrew broadcaster continued to read out the wire service copy from New York in the same calm voice he used to broadcast stock market prices: 'Fifteen votes have now been counted. There are 41 more to be counted.'

Golda Meyerson brought the first cheer of the night in the kitchen when she said the vote for partition was ahead.

In the radio station the teleprinter chattered out the names of each ambassador as he was called to announce his country's vote: Brazil – in favour, Ecuador – in favour, Luxembourg – in favour, New Zealand – in favour, South Africa – in favour.

Next door, in the Arab-language studio, the announcer proclaimed that Egypt, Greece and Lebanon had voted against. In favour: Sweden, Uruguay, France and Denmark.

Golda wrote steadily in her notebook. Norway, Peru, Canada, Iceland and the Dominican Republic had all voted in favour.

In the Hebrew-language studio the broadcaster was almost shouting into his microphone: Belgium, Bolivia and Paraguay had voted for partition; only Syria, Yemen, Pakistan, Saudi Arabia and Turkey had opposed.

Golda's notebook was filling more rapidly: Venezuela, the Soviet Union, Ukrainian SSR, Poland, Czechoslovakia, Netherlands, Haiti, Liberia, the Philippines and Byelorussian SSR had all cast votes in favour.

The teleprinter in the wire room delivered a spate of abstentions: Argentina, Chile, the Republic of China, Colombia, El Salvador, Ethiopia, Honduras, Mexico, Yugoslavia and the United Kingdom.

There was a pause, then over the wireless came the suddenly

emotional voice of the Hebrew broadcaster: 'Panama. We have succeeded!'

Amid the thunderous cheering in her kitchen Golda continued writing down the names.

Still trying to control himself, the announcer confirmed: 'The General Assembly of the United Nations, by a vote of 33 in favour, 13 against, 10 abstentions, one absent, has voted for partition.'

His words were lost in an even louder rousing cheer in the kitchen. Golda motioned for silence. The broadcaster was shouting: '. . . we will become a fully fledged State of Israel from the stroke of midnight on 14 May 1948. That is six months . . .'

The rest of what he was saying was lost in the new roar of voices now joined by the jubilant cries rising across the city.

Golda picked up the blue-and-white flag bearing the Magen David from the kitchen table beside the wireless. Until now it had been neatly folded. Unfolding it, her voice little more than a whisper, she murmured, 'At last we are a free people.'

All around them, throughout Jerusalem, in the streets and cafés of Tel Aviv and Haifa, in settlements in the country, the same words were repeated: '*Mazel tov!* Good luck!'

On the day after the vote, a wave of Arab attacks left seven Jews dead and scores more wounded. Shooting, stoning and rioting continued apace in the following days. The consulates of Poland and Sweden, both of whose governments had voted for partition, were attacked. Bombs were thrown into Jewish cafés, Molotov cocktails were hurled at Jewish shops, a synagogue was set on fire.

In Jerusalem Ben-Gurion knew that before the Magen David flag could be raised across the world to announce the arrival of a new nation there was much to do: embassies and diplomatic missions to open, ambassadors to be appointed, military commanders to be confirmed, borders to be protected and preparations made for the war he was now certain would come. He had sensed its looming presence in the silence from the Arab quarter of the city. In its souks they were preparing.

As he sat in the back of his chauffeur-driven car, Ben-Gurion knew he would soon be engulfed in a battle for the very life of a nation still only a name. It was all the more important, he told himself, that he should make this journey to the Histadrut Medical Centre in the western suburbs of Jerusalem. As he stepped out of the car into the darkened building, the two armed men in the lobby came to attention. They were the bodyguards of the Haganah's city commander, Israel Amir. One of the guards led him to an office at the back of the building that served as the organisation's headquarters. Waiting there with Amir was Yossi Harel. All three were friends and had met in this building many times; the clinic had been chosen by Amir as cover from both British and Arabic surveillance. Usually the three men would sit over coffee and sometimes play cards while discussing political matters. Tonight there was no time for such pleasantries. Ben-Gurion turned to Yossi and told him it was time to bring home not only all the *Exodus* immigrants but all the remaining Jews in DP camps in Germany. He wanted them back before the State of Israel became a fully fledged nation.

Epilogue

By the day of the partition vote two ships, *Pan Crescent* and *Pan York*, had already been registered with Lloyd's of London under the Panamanian flag. The money to buy them had been raised by Leo Bernstein and Ralph Goodman, whose fund-raising had bought *Exodus*. Both ships were listed as being owned by the F&B Shipping Company of 24 Stone Street, New York City. In the past week the company had registered 12 smaller ships with Lloyd's, all flying under the Panamanian flag. F&B was the former Weston Trading Company, the owner of *Exodus*, and had the same directors, supporters of Aliyah Bet.

Like *Exodus*, *Pan Crescent* and *Pan York* had mixed crews of American-born Jewish volunteers and experienced members of the Palyam, including the dozen who had been smuggled off *Exodus*. Along with Yossi, Ike, Dr Cohen and Zvi Tiroche, they had all been hidden in Haganah safe houses while its High Command convened a court of inquiry to investigate what had happened on *Exodus*. Ike and the Palyam crew had testified that the ship had been surrendered too hastily. Yossi and Dr Cohen were adamant that the medical situation on board had left no alternative but to call for urgent help. Yossi's view had been upheld. But no criticism was levelled at Ike's captaincy. On the contrary, he was highly complimented for all he had done, including saving the ship's log.

Between them, *Pan Crescent* and *Pan York* were capable of carrying 16,000 immigrants. F&B had assured the Panama government that it was engaged in no such traffic. The guarantee was accepted and the two ships had sailed to Europe, *Pan York* to wait in Marseilles for further orders from the Haganah, *Pan Crescent* to undergo further outfitting in Venice. Both ships had been told to remain at their berths until after the outcome of the United Nations vote. By then *Pan Crescent* was undergoing repairs to the hull after being damaged by a limpet mine. The Haganah accused MI6 of planting it. Britain denied it.

The sharp-eyed Ruth Gruber was among the first reporters to notice that the immigrants from both Emden and Sengwarden had left to join one of the trains heading south to the Bulgarian port of Burgas. Their one-way tickets had been paid for by the Jewish Agency.

Yossi Harel arrived there on 2 December, to supervise the loading of *Pan York*, which had initially sailed from Marseilles with a mixed commercial cargo the ever-innovative Joe Baharlia had provided. Nevertheless, on a tip from MI6, the Palestine Patrol had set off in pursuit. Barred by the Montreux Convention from entering the Dardanelles – all warships required special clearance – the naval ships could not conduct a stop-and-search operation.

In London, Foreign Secretary Bevin continued to reel under the media attacks over the deportation of the *Exodus* immigrants to Germany. The government had been divided, leaving many members of its Cabinet filled with grave misgivings. Denis Healey, the international secretary of the Labour Party, called the deportation 'a terrible, terrible mistake'.

Lieutenant John Donaldson, who had sent a detachment of the 6th Airborne Division to escort the three transports, later said his paratroopers never returned to their units in Palestine because 'the ordeal had such an emotional impact that a near mutiny erupted among them. The British Army decided not to file any charges and closed the matter quietly, in order to prevent a political uproar.'

On 12 December 1947, *Pan Crescent* arrived in Burgas. It had been renamed *Ingathering of Exiles* and *Pan York* was now *Independence*. As well as some of the *Exodus* immigrants, the two ships took on board refugees from DP camps in Europe before Yossi Harel led his flotilla out of the port.

Throughout the winter and spring of 1948 there would be other voyages by the blockade-runners. Both Yossi and Ike played a role in bringing them in. Meanwhile, the Palestine Patrol continued with little success to try and intercept the increasing flow of immigrants.

On 14 May 1948, at his usual hour of 7am, Sir Alan Cunningham's batman entered the bedroom of the High Commissioner's official residence overlooking the walled Old City of Jerusalem. The mansion on the Hill of the Council of Evil had remained the official residence of the High Commissioner since it had first been occupied by General Sir Edmund Allenby 30 years, five months and five days before. The batman carefully draped over a clothes stand Cunningham's uniform of a general in His Majesty's Royal Artillery.

The High Commissioner was a slim, moustached man with probing eyes. Any trace of the Dublin accent he was born with had long been replaced by a clipped English public school voice – nurtured at Cheltenham College and the Royal Military Academy – and honed by almost half a century of military service. Those years had earned him campaign medals: a Military Cross and the Distinguished Service Cross in the First World War in the trenches at Ypres. He had commanded the newly formed Eighth Army in the Libyan Desert before General Montgomery took over; there had been campaigns in Ethiopia and Kenya. In a velvet-lined box were his highest honours: the Knight Grand Cross of the Order of St Michael and St George and Knight Commander of the Order of the Bath. These he wore only on special occasions. This day would be one, for by nightfall he would have brought to an end Britain's rule over Palestine.

The batman left the bedroom and returned with the breakfast he prepared every morning: half a grapefruit, poached eggs, tea and toast with a side order of sausages and bacon. Holding the tray, he stood by the brass bedpost and murmured his regular greeting.

While Sir Alan ate, his batman performed another ritual. In the corner of the bedroom was a record player, with a small stack of long-playing records of classical music beside it: Beethoven, Bach, Vivaldi.

The batman selected one, placed it on the turntable, waited a moment for the music to start and then left.

After breakfast Sir Alan wrote in his daily private diary that he felt 'an overwhelming sadness. So much effort expended. So many lives lost to such little purpose. Thirty years and we have achieved nearly nothing.'

He knew he would leave Palestine in the eyes of many a hated figure. Just as he knew there were powerful forces in place on that May day to defend the Jews against attack: the Haganah. The Arabs had the backing of their allies in Syria and Egypt, from where armaments had come to support the fight against the Jews. There was every reason for Sir Alan to feel he had achieved very little. Dressed in his uniform, he stood at the bedroom window. The sun was already high in the sky, gleaming on the church spires of the Old City and beyond the Judean hills. At the foot of the residence flag-pole, a bugler of the Highland Light Infantry began to play as the Union Jack was lowered for the last time.

The Arab gardeners, who had tended the grounds he had so loved during his three years in Palestine, had not shown up for work; he knew it was another sign British rule was at last over. He had lost count of the times he had walked down the gravel paths and paused at the flowerbeds to ponder the fate of a condemned Irgun prisoner or tried to put from his mind the photographs of British bodies killed by an Irgun bomb. He stared for a moment longer at the lavender beds, the climbing roses and the heathers he had arranged to have transplanted from the Scottish heaths. Now he wondered whether they would be dug up by whoever occupied the residence next.

A number of the *Exodus* immigrants watched that May afternoon when the British finally paraded out of Palestine, the rhythmical tramp of boots echoing through the Street of the Jews, the route along which all the other occupiers had left the city: Babylonians, Assyrians, Romans, Persians, Arabs, Crusaders and Turks. The soldiers, rifles on shoulders, eyes unwavering, ignored the hostile faces while they marched to the skirl of bagpipes for the last time through the narrow street.

Behind the marching column came a four-ton Daimler, built for King George VI's tours through the streets of blitzed London during the Second World War. It had been sent to Palestine on the order of Prime Minister Clement Attlee. With the car came an instruction to Sir Alan from No. 10 Downing Street: 'Your departure must lack nothing.'

All morning a soldier had buffed and polished the Daimler until it reflected the faces in the crowd watching the Union Jack flutter from its bonnet as it moved through the city for the last time. In the back of the car, imperious-faced Sir Gordon MacMillan, commander-in-chief of British Forces in Palestine, sat beside an equally grim-looking Sir Alan Cunningham. Beside the driver was a plump British major, the buttons on his dress uniform burnished, the epaulettes on his shoulders displaying the tabards of the Suffolk Regiment.

The car halted opposite the entrance to a cobbled alley. The major alighted from the Daimler. In one hand he held a bar of rusted iron almost a foot long. He strode to a massive arched door, used the bar to rap on its heavy wooden frame, stepped back and waited. The door swung open to reveal an elderly man dressed in the severe black of his calling. Mordechai Weingarten was the oldest and most revered of all the rabbis in the City of David.

His position had brought him into regular contact with Sir Alan and his Mandate administration. The rabbi had also developed a good relationship with the Arab sheikhs who lived in the Old City and who, like him, were venerated by their own people. But the sight of the major standing on his doorstep, the waiting column of soldiers and the brooding silence of the crowd filled Rabbi Weingarten with unease. What last-minute surprise would the British spring?

Those close enough watched as he looked cautiously from the major to the Daimler, then at the iron bar hanging from the hand of the officer as he spoke: 'On behalf of His Majesty King George and all who serve him, I ask you to accept this key to the Zion Gate.'

From a window overlooking the scene, David Ben-Gurion saw the Daimler pass out of sight through the Zion Gate.

Even before Sir Alan Cunningham's Daimler, guarded by

armoured cars and trucks filled with soldiers, had reached Haifa to board a Royal Navy cruiser, HMS *Euryalus*, to begin the journey to Britain, Ben-Gurion had hurried to the Tel Aviv Museum to chair the first meeting of the National Council, representing all the Jews of the Yishuv. His voice filled with pride as he read to them the Declaration of Independence which established the Jewish state, to be known in future as Medinath Yisrael. He was formally appointed as the country's prime minister and Moshe Sharett, who had had led the Palestine Delegation at the United Nations, was made named foreign minister. Fittingly, Dr Chaim Weizmann, who had played such a vital part in the bringing all their dreams to fruition, was appointed Israel's first president. In a letter to Weizmann formally offering him the presidency, Ben-Gurion had written: 'I doubt whether the Presidency is vital to Dr Weizmann, but the Presidency of Dr Weizmann is a moral necessity for the State of Israel.' At this great moment in Israel's history, its two great leaders had put their differences behind them.

On 17 June 1948, Yossi Harel brought out the last shipload of *Exodus* immigrants from the Emden camp and ordered that a message be sent to the pink-stucco-fronted house on Tel Aviv's waterfront: 'We have removed the last of the Exodus people from Amos [Germany]. With the exception of a few sick people, no one remains. We have fulfilled our promise to bring the *Exodus* people home. Inform anyone involved.'

Postscript

1951

The mayor of Haifa announced that *Exodus* would become a floating museum, symbolising the struggle of Jews to claim their homeland. The plan was postponed and never revived.

1952

On 26 August *Exodus* caught fire at its mooring. The harbour fire boats were unable to stop her burning to the waterline. The cause of the blaze was never discovered. The ship was towed to Haifa's Shemen Beach. In no time she had sunk to its sandy bottom, leaving only her top deck visible.

1954

An Italian firm tried to salvage the *Exodus* for scrap. To ensure that she would rise she was cut in half. As the bow began to emerge above water, it suddenly sank, never to be seen again. No further salvage operation was attempted. The only crew member to witness her end was Ike.

Sources

As well as the transcripts provided by Jill Samuels of her interviews over many years with those involved with the *Exodus*, including British officers, politicians and survivors, I have been shown official records, memoranda and a wide range of published and unpublished material by other people. Their contributions have filled the gaps in human memory. Professor Aviva Halamish, a distinguished historian in the Department of Jewish History at Tel Aviv University who has undertaken detailed research on the subject of illegal immigration of Jews into Palestine, has succinctly described the problem of historical research: 'Most accounts were recorded when *Exodus* had already become a symbol and even a myth, and there was a tendency to combine facts on the one hand with commentary, analysis, evaluation, polemic and even wishful thinking on the other. Another weakness lay in the use of archival sources. For the first 30 years following the affair, writers were aided only by documents available from the Jewish side only. But even books written after British documents became available contained ingrained errors, which require amendment and revision in order to present things in as accurate a way as possible.'

Those words have been my guide. They made it easier to examine the different versions given by those who were on board *Exodus* and who inevitably over the years repositioned their own role in events that hold enormous importance in the history of the State of Israel.

There were also other difficulties – not least unravelling the role of the Palestine Patrol of the Royal Navy and MI6, the Secret Intelligence Service. The help of those who served in both services is acknowledged here. Governed by Britain's Official Secrets Act as to what they could confirm, what they did provide proved to be most valuable.

Three others deserve mention: Yoram Kaniuk, Ruth Gruber and David C. Holly. Yoram Kaniuk's biography of Yossi Harel, while contradicting much of what has been written before, sets him in context. Ruth Gruber, now in her 98th year, was one of many reporters who covered the final stages of the voyage of *Exodus*. David C. Holly served as a naval officer in the Second World War and later the Korean War. His knowledge of the steamboats on the Chesapeake was unequalled right to his death in February 1999. Their contributions were invaluable and, along with a number of organisations, deserve special thanks.

Individuals (including passengers on *Exodus*)

Jan Henrik Fahlbusch
Aljons Filek
Benjamin Gruska
Sarah Haake
Shlomo Hammer
Felix Hurlin
Korohy Kofflet
Paul Kononow
Lars Krobitsch
Ursula Litzmann
Tamas Mayrona
Otto Nagyrona
Gunther Scharberg
Melach Schubert
Zeev Schulbert
Klaus Schwammen
Horst Siebecke
Istvan Szeisen

Organisations and Archives Consulted

American Jewish Historical Society Virtual Library
American Jewish Joint Distribution Committee, New York
Archive, *Allgemeine Jüdische Wochenzeitung* (for DP camps)
Archive, City of Lübeck, Germany (for Poppendorf and Am Stau)
Archive, Port Authorities, Hamburg (for Operation Oasis)
British Embassy, Washington, DC
Central Zionist Archives, Israel
Churchill College, Archive Library, Cambridge, UK
Government Press Office, Jerusalem
Imperial War Museum, London
Jerusalem Post Archives
Liddle Hart Centre for Military Archives, Kings College, London
Middle East Archives, St Antony's College, Oxford
National Archives, Washington, DC
National Records (formerly Public Records Office), Kew, Surrey
Naval Historical Branch, Ministry of Defence, Portsmouth (for Palestine Patrol)
Netherlands Institute for War Documentation, Amsterdam
Palestine Post Archives, Jerusalem
Records of the Port Authority of Haifa
Records of the Port-de-Bouc Administration
Records of the port of Sète Administration
Service History of Royal Navy Warships in World War Two, London
South West Maritime History Society, UK (for HMS *Childers*)
State Archives, State of Israel, Jerusalem
Steamboat Historical Society of America, Baltimore
United States Holocaust Memorial Museum, Washington, DC
US Maritime Commission, Washington, DC
Weizmann Archives, Israel
Yad Vashem Holocaust Memorial Museum, Jerusalem

Public Record Office Files
Admiralty Records 1935–47

ADM – 14671 Recruitment of Palestinians

ADM – 18521 M09777 Future of Admiralty Establishments and Naval Requirements in Levant, EM, Red Sea and Suez Canal Areas after the War

ADM – 18542 M010248 CinC Med – Peacetime Policy of the Med Fleet

ADM – 18560 Naval Command in the Mediterranean

ADM – 18584 FOLEM RoP Aug 45

ADM – 19358 FOLEM 169/00184/8 date 30 Jan 46 – RONDINE

ADM – 19377 M688 FOLEM RoP Oct 45

ADM – 19401 M0974 FOLEM RoP Dec 45

ADM – 19402 M983 D3 RoP Nov 45

ADM – 19422 M1115 15th CS RoP Dec 45

ADM – 19433 M01180 15th CS RoP Feb 46

ADM – 19501 M1761 Sale of HDMLS to Palestine

ADM – 19508 M1826 15th CS RoP Jan 46

ADM – 19518 M01991 AGIOS IOANNIS

ADM – 19532 Interceptions May–Aug 46

ADM – 19559 MO2401 CinC Med RoP Jan–Mar 46

ADM – 19560 MO2403 Med Stn RoPs Jun 46

ADM – 19563 MO2419 Med Cmd RoP Mar 46

ADM – 19566 MO2425 Med Stn RoP Jan 46

ADM – 19567 MO2426 Med Stn RoP Apr 46

ADM – 19582 MO2603 GOFFE

ADM – 19615 CinC Med RoP Aug–Sept 46

ADM – 19856 Summary of Jewish Immigration into Palestine by Sea

ADM – 20671 CinC Med Flt RoP Feb 47

ADM – 20677 CinC Med No 2288 Med 47/001415/6/16 date 30 Aug 47

ADM – 20684 Return of Illegal Immigrants to France

ADM – 20685 *President Warfield*

ADM – 20730 RoP RAD Med Apr 47

ADM – 20777 Behaviour on Passage

ADM – 20778 HofC Statement

ADM – 20789 Palestine Illegal Immigration Policy post *Warfield*

ADM – 20917 Note to PM pre *Warfield*

ADM – 21106 Maritime International Law: Diversion and Detention of Vessels on the High Seas

ADM – 21108 VIVARA

ADM – 1705 Palestine Immigration

ADM – 1706 Immigration into Palestine

ADM – 1711–1714 Action against Jewish Organisations

ADM – 1720–1721 Ditto

ADM – 1793–1801 Palestine Immigration

ADM – 1802–1804 Measures Taken to Counteract Illegal Immigration

ADM – 1812–1813 Illegal Immigration

ADM – 2367–2369 Palestine Immigration

ADM – 2371–2383 Measures Taken to Counteract Illegal Immigration

ADM – 2384–2389 Illegal Immigration

ADM – 2393 Illegal Immigration

ADM – 2396–2402 Illegal Immigration

ADM – 2404 Illegal Immigration

ADM – 61802 Palestine – Immigration

Colonial Office Records 1945–8

CO – 23 96

CO – 24 282

CO – 26 96

CO – 65 5

CO – 65 7

CO – 65 8

CO – 65 10

CO – 66 15

CO – 66 56

CO – 67 4

CO – 93 15
CO – 128 2
CO – 129 2
CO – 129 9
CO – 537 1710
CO – 537 1726
CO – 537 2290
CO – 733 429
CO – 733 430
CO – 733 439
CO – 733 445
CO – 733 455
CO – 733 457
CO – 733 461

Cabinet Office Records 1945–7
COR – 24 27
COR – 24 279
COR – 24 282
COR – 733 457

War Office Records 1940–47
WO – 32 10260
WO – 169 1945
WO – 169 19744
WO – 169 22956

Selection of News Reports 1945–61
'An Old Ship's Big Moment', *Washington Post*, 17 July 1967
'Baltimore Ship Reported off Palestine with Refugees', Baltimore *Sun*, 18 July 1947
'Ban Hits Refugee Ship', *New York Times*, 10 August 1947
'Bay Vessel Enters Maritime Hall of Fame: SS President Warfield Inducted at US Merchant Marine Academy', Cambridge, Maryland, *Daily Banner*, 4 June 1987
Bower, Alex, 'Wonderful Warfield', *Army Transportation Journal*, July 1945

Boylan, W.P., 'Affidavit – Loss of the Yorktown', *Sea Breezes*, May 1946, pp.299–301

'British Assailed on Refugee Threat', *New York Times*, 22 August 1947

'British Bring Ex-Bay Liner into Haifa after Long Fight', Baltimore *Sun*, 19 July 1947

'British Fight Terrorists in Jerusalem: Holy Land Disorders Follow Deportation of Warfield's Passengers', Baltimore *Sun*, 21 July 1947

Brown, Alexander C., 'Exodus 1947: An Interim Report on the Career of the Steamer President Warfield', *American Neptune*, April 1948, pp.127–31

Burgess, Robert H., 'Fightin' Steamboats', *Shipyard Bulletin*, Newport News, May 1946

'Chesapeake Boat Now on Seine River Run', Baltimore *Sun*, 18 June 1945

'Convoy Maniac', *Log Line*, Winter 1948 (Vol.3, No.4), pp.22–4

'Day by Day' (article on the Chesapeake Bay), *Baltimore News-Post*, 25 May 1940

'Exodus Head Calls Battle a Mistake', *New York Times*, 11 September 1947

'Exodus Is Home Again', Norfolk *Virginian-Pilot*, 18 November 1947

'Exodus Refugees Get an Ultimatum', *New York Times*, 22 August 1947

'Exodus Zionists May Face Charge', *New York Times*, 30 August 1947

'Ferry to Palestine – Twentieth Century Exodus', Norfolk *Virginian-Pilot*, 17 April 1960

'Former Favorite Bay Steamers Battled Nazi Wolf Packs in World War II', *Daily Press*, Newport News, 25 September 1960

'French Bar Using Force on Refugees', *New York Times*, 31 July 1947

Hardy, A.C., 'More Reminiscences of the Honeymoon Fleet', *Sea Breezes*, December 1946, pp.402–5

Hess, Jean B., 'Last of Their Kind', *Sea Breezes*, July 1961

Hulen, Bertram D., 'Futile US Appeal on Exodus Bared', *New York Times*, 11 August 1947

'It Began in Baltimore Twenty Years Ago', Baltimore *News-American*, 15 January 1967

Item on the wartime history of *President Warfield*, 'Steamboat Bill of Facts', *Journal of the Steamboat Historical Society of America*, No.17, Flushing, New York, August 1945

'Last Convoy Ships Back from Europe: Sailors Swarm Ashore at Norfolk after Seeing Service in Invasion of France', *New York Times*, 26 July 1945

'Model to Honor "Exodus" Ship', Baltimore *Sun*, 13 July 1967

'Ocean Odyssey: "Skimming Dishes" Atlantic Battle with U-boat Pack', *Shipping World*, 13 June 1945, pp.663–5

'Odyssey of Frustration Began Five Years Ago with Ship Leaving Here', *Daily Press*, Newport News, 24 February 1952

'Old Bay Line Gets Up Steam', Baltimore *Evening Sun*, 19 February 1940

'On the "Exodus 1947"', *Jewish Frontier*, May 1957, and 'The Return Voyage', June 1957

'Palestine-Bound Mystery Ship', *New York Times*, 6 March 1947

'Refugees Being Returned to France', *New York Times*, 21 July 1947

Ritzer, Stanley (as told to Peter Michelmore), 'I Ran the Blockade to Palestine: The True Story of the Exodus', *Argosy*, February 1960, Vol.350, No.2, pp.19–21 and 78–80

'Terrorist Tension Reaches New High as Refugees Sent to France', *New York Times*, 22 July 1947

'The Three Lives of the Old Bay Line's President Warfield: Bay Boat, Warship, Then the Famous Exodus – But the End Has Come', Baltimore *Sun*, 9 February 1964

'They called it the "Honeymoon Fleet" Convoy', *Sea Breezes*, May 1946

Timewell, H.C., 'Exodus 1947 Takes on Her Cargo', *American Neptune*, Vol.9, No.4, October 1949, pp.300–301

Untitled article on S. Davies Warfield, *Baltimore News-Post*, 1 March 1941

'USS Warfield Back Home from War', Baltimore *Sun*, 26 July 1945

'Violence Threatens Development of Palestine', *New York Times*, 3 August 1947

'Warfield Repairs Almost Done', Baltimore *Evening Sun*, 21 March 1947

'Warfield Seen under Scrutiny: Ex-Bay Liner Said to Carry Jews in Mediterranean', Baltimore *Sun*, 14 July 1947

'Whistle's History Loud and Clear', Hagerstown, Maryland, *Herald Mail*, 22 May1994

'Willie Harris, Bay Boat Waiter to Notables, Dies. A Son of Bay Line Veteran, His Rolling-R Dinner Call Became Famous', Baltimore *Evening Sun*, 15 September 1942

'Zionist Abduction of Jews Alleged', *New York Times*, 6 September 1947

'Zionists Denounce Seizure of Vessel', *New York Times*, 25 July 1947

Select Bibliography

Antonius, George, *The Arab Awakening: The Story of the Arab National Movement* (London, Hamish Hamilton, 1938; New York, G.P. Putnam's Sons, 1946)

Attlee, Clement Richard, *As It Happened* (London, William Heinemann, 1954)

Avriel, Ehud, *Open the Gates: A Personal Story of 'Illegal' Immigration to Israel* (New York, Atheneum, 1975)

Barbour, Nevill, *Nisi Dominus: A Survey of the Palestine Controversy* (London, Harrap, 1946)

Bauer, Yehuda, *From Diplomacy to Resistance: A History of Jewish Palestine 1939-45* (Philadelphia, Jewish Publication Society of America, 1970)

Begin, Menachem, *The Revolt: Story of the Irgun* (New York, Henry Schumann, 1951)

Bell, J. Bowyer, *Terror Out of Zion: Irgun Zvai Leumi, LEHI and the Palestine Underground, 1929-1949* (New York, St Martin's Press, 1977)

Ben-Gurion, David, *Rebirth and Destiny of Israel* (New York, Philosophical Library, 1954)

Bentwich, Norman and Helen, *Mandate Memories 1917–1948* (London, Hogarth Press, 1965; New York, Schocken Books, 1965)

Birkenhead, F.W.F.S., 2nd Earl of, *Halifax: The Life of Lord Halifax* (London, Hamish Hamilton, 1965)

Blum, John Morton, *From the Morgenthau Diaries* (Boston, Houghton Mifflin Company, 1959)

Churchill, Winston, *The Second World War*, 6 vols (London, Cassell, 1948–53)

Cohen, Gavriel, *Churchill and Palestine 1939–1942* (Jerusalem, Yad Izhak Ben-Zvi Publications, 1976)

Cohen, Geula, *Woman of Violence: Memoirs of a Young Terrorist 1943–1948*

(London, Rupert Hart-Davis, 1966)

Cohen, Michael J., *Palestine: Retreat from the Mandate* (London, Elek, 1978)

Crossman, Richard, *Palestine Mission: A Personal Record* (London, Hamish Hamilton, 1947; New York, Harper & Brothers, 1947)

Crum, Bartley C., *Behind the Silken Curtain: A Personal Account of Anglo-American Diplomacy in Palestine and the Middle East* (New York, Simon and Schuster, 1947)

Dalton, Hugh, *High Tide and After: Memoirs 1945–1960* (London, Frederick Muller, 1962)

Dekel, Efraim, *Shai: The Exploits of Hagana Intelligence* (London and New York, Thomas Yoseloff, 1959)

Documents on German Foreign Policy 1918–1945, Series D, Vol.V: Poland, the Balkans, Latin America, The Smaller Powers, June 1937–Mar 1939 (London, Her Majesty's Stationery Office, 1953)

Documents on German Foreign Policy 1918–1945, Series D, Vol.VI: The Last Months of Peace March–August 1939 (London, Her Majesty's Stationery Office, 1956)

Documents on German Foreign Policy 1918–1945, Series D, Vol.XII: The War Years Feb 1–June 22, 1941 (London, Her Majesty's Stationery Office, 1962)

Documents on German Foreign Policy 1918–1945, Series D, Vol.XIII: The War Years June 23, 1941–Dec 11, 1941 (London, Her Majesty's Stationery Office, 1964)

Drummond, Ian, *Imperial Economic Policy 1917–1939, Studies in Expansion and Protection* (London, Allen and Unwin, 1974)

Foot, Hugh, *A Start in Freedom* (London, Hodder and Stoughton, 1964)

Gilbert, Martin, *Auschwitz and the Allies* (London, Hamlyn paperback edn, 1983)

Gilbert, Martin, *Churchill: A Life* (London, Heinemann, 1991)

Gilbert, Martin, *Exile and Return: The Emergence of Jewish Statehood* (London, Weidenfeld and Nicolson, 1978)

Gilbert, Martin, *Winston Spencer Churchill*, Vol.VII: *The Road to Victory, 1941–1945* (London, Heinemann, 1986)

Gilbert, Martin, *Winston Spencer Churchill*, Vol.VIII: *Never Despair, 1945–1965* (London, Heinemann, 1988)

Gitling, Jan, *Conquest of Acre Prison* (Tel Aviv, Hadar, 1962)

Gruber, Ruth, *Destination Palestine* (New York, Current Books, 1948)

Gruber, Ruth, *Exodus 1947: The Ship That Launched a Nation* (New York, Union Square Press, 1999)

Habas, Bracha, *The Gate Breakers* (New York, Theodor Herzl Foundation, 1963)

Halamish, Aviva, *The Exodus Affair: Holocaust Survivors and the Struggle for Palestine* (London, Valentine Mitchell, 1999)

Hart, Kitty, *Return to Auschwitz* (London, Sidgwick & Jackson, 1981)

Hirst, David, *The Gun and the Olive Branch: The Roots of Violence in the Middle East* (London, Faber and Faber, 1977)

Hirszowicz, Lukasz, *The Third Reich and the Arab East* (London, Routledge and Kegan Paul, 1966)

Hochstein, Joseph M., and Greenfield, Murray S., *The Jews' Secret Fleet* (New York, Gefen Publishing House, 1999)

Holly, David C., *Exodus 1947* (Annapolis, Maryland, Naval Institute Press, 1995)

Jefferies, Charles, *The Colonial Police* (London, Max Parrish, 1952)

Joseph, Bernard, *British Rule in Palestine: A Timely Study by the Military Governor of Jewish Jerusalem* (Washington, DC, Public Affairs Press, 1948)

Joseph, Bernard, *The Faithful City: The Siege of Jerusalem, 1948* (London, Hogarth Press, 1962)

Kaniuk, Yoram, *Commander of the Exodus* (New York, Grove Press, 1999)

Lamb, Richard, *Churchill's Cold War: The Politics of Personal Diplomacy* (New Haven, Conn., and London, Yale University Press, 2002)

Liebreich, Fritz, *Britain's Naval and Political Reaction to the Illegal Immigration of Jews to Palestine 1945–48* (London, Routledge, 2005)

Mardor, Munya M., *Haganah* (New York, New American Library, 1957)

Marrus, Michael, *The Holocaust in History* (London, Penguin Books, 1989)

Morris, Benny, *1948: The First Arab-Israeli War* (Lonon and New Haven, Yale University Press, 2008)

Ponting, Clive, *Churchill* (London, Sinclair-Stevenson, 1994)

Stewart, Ninian, *The Royal Navy and the Palestine Patrol* (London, Frank Cass, 2002)

Index